PSYCHOTHERAPIES WITH CHILDREN AND ADOLESCENTS:

ADAPTING THE PSYCHODYNAMIC PROCESS

PSYCHOTHERAPIES WITH CHILDREN AND ADOLESCENTS:

ADAPTING THE PSYCHODYNAMIC PROCESS

EDITED BY

John D. O'Brien, M.D.
Daniel J. Pilowsky, M.D.
Owen W. Lewis, M.D.

𝒜

JASON ARONSON INC.
Northvale, New Jersey
London

Note: The authors have worked to ensure that all information in this book concerning drug dosages, schedules, and routes of administration is accurate as of the time of publication and consistent with standards set by the U.S. Food and Drug Administration and the general medical community. As medical research and practice advance, however, therapeutic standards may change. For this reason and because human and mechanical errors sometimes occur, we recommend that readers follow the advice of a physician who is directly involved in their care or the care of a member of their family.

First softcover edition 2000

Copyright © 1992 by American Psychiatric Press, Inc.
Reprinted by arrangement with American Psychiatric Press.

Library of Congress Cataloging-in-Publication Data

Psychotherapies with children and adolescents : adapting the psychodynamic process / edited by John O'Brien, Daniel J. Pilowsky, and Owen W. Lewis.
    p. cm.
Originally published: Washington, DC : American Psychiatric Press, © 1992.
Includes bibliographical references and index.
ISBN 0-7657-0253-3 (pbk.)
    1. Psychodynamic psychotherapy for children. 2. Psychodynamic psychotherapy for teenagers. I. O'Brien, John D., 1939– II. Pilowsky, Daniel, 1951– III. Lewis, Owen W., 1951–

RJ505.P92 P78 1999
618.92'8914 – dc21
    99-057474

Printed in the United States of America on acid-free paper. For information and catalog write to Jason Aronson Inc., 230 Livingston Street, Northvale, NJ 07647-1726, or visit our website: www.aronson.com

TABLE OF CONTENTS

SECTION I:
THE PSYCHOTHERAPEUTIC PROCESS WITH CHILDREN

SECTION II:
THE PSYCHOTHERAPEUTIC PROCESS WITH ADOLESCENTS

SECTION III:
THE PSYCHOTHERAPEUTIC PROCESS WITH BOTH CHILDREN AND ADOLESCENTS IN SPECIAL CIRCUMSTANCES

SECTION IV:
THE PSYCHOTHERAPEUTIC PROCESS IN SPECIAL CIRCUMSTANCES

CONTRIBUTORS

Jill Bellinson, Ph.D.
Private Practice of Clinical Psychology and Psychoanalysis, New York, New York; Supervisor of Psychotherapy, Clinical Psychology Doctoral Training Program, City University of New York

Hector R. Bird, M.D.
Professor of Clinical Psychiatry, Division of Child and Adolescent Psychiatry, Columbia University, College of Physicians and Surgeons, New York, New York; Supervising Analyst, William Alanson White Institute for Psychoanalysis, New York, New York

Richard S. Briggs, Ph.D.
Director, Connecticut Psychoanalytic Psychotherapy Center, Norwalk, Connecticut; Supervisor of Psychotherapy, William Alanson White Institute for Psychoanalysis, New York, New York

Judith Brisman, Ph.D.
Director and Co-Founder, Bulimia Treatment Associates, New York, New York; Graduate, William Alanson White Institute for Psychoanalysis, New York, New York

Margaret Crastnopol, Ph.D.
Faculty and Supervisor of Psychotherapy, William Alanson White Institute for Psychoanalysis, New York, New York; Faculty and Supervisor, National Institute for the Psychotherapies, New York, New York

William N. Davis, Ph.D.
Clinical Supervisor, Center for Study of Anorexia and Bulimia, New York, New York; Private Practice of Clinical Psychology and Psychoanalysis, New York, New York, and Swarthmore, Pennsylvania

Richard Gardner, M.D.
Clinical Professor of Psychiatry, Division of Child and Adolescent Psychiatry, Columbia University, College of Physicians and Surgeons, New York, New York; Graduate, William Alanson White Institute for Psychoanalysis, New York, New York

Constance Katz, Ph.D.
Supervising Analyst, William Alanson White Institute for Psychoanalysis, New York, New York; Faculty and Supervisor of Psychology, John Jay College of Criminal Justice, New York, New York

Owen W. Lewis, M.D.
Assistant Clinical Professor of Psychiatry, Division of Child and Adolescent Psychiatry, Columbia University, College of Physicians and Surgeons, New York, New York; Graduate, William Alanson White Institute for Psychoanalysis, New York, New York

John D. O'Brien, M.D.
Associate Professor of Psychiatry, Mount Sinai School of Medicine, New York, New York; Director of Child and Adolescent Psychiatry, Elmhurst Hospital Center, Elmhurst, New York; Training and Supervising Analyst, William Alanson White Institute for Psychoanalysis, New York, New York

Daniel J. Pilowsky, M.D.
Lecturer in Psychiatry, Columbia University College of Physicians and Surgeons, New York, New York; Attending Psychiatrist, Columbia Presbyterian Medical Center, New York, New York

Robin Shafran, Ph.D.
Supervisor óf Psychotherapy, William Alanson White Institute for Psychoanalysis, New York, New York; Associate Clinical Professor, Derner Institute of Advanced Psychological Studies, Adelphi University, Garden City, New York

Leonard Israel Siegel, M.D., F.A.P.A., F.R.A.N.Z.L.P.
Director, Redbank House, Westmead Hospital (Australia); Graduate, William Alanson White Institute for Psychoanalysis, New York, New York

Paul Trad, M.D.
Assistant Professor of Psychiatry and Director of the Child and Adolescent Psychiatry Outpatient Department (Westchester Division), Cornell University Medical Center, New York, New York

Joseph Youngerman, M.D.
Associate Clinical Professor of Psychiatry, Albert Einstein College of Medicine, New York, New York; Supervising Analyst, William Alanson White Institute for Psychoanalysis, New York, New York

Stephen Zaslow, M.D.
Director Emeritus, Long Island Institute of Psychoanalysis, East Meadow, New York; Supervisor of Psychotherapy, William Alanson White Institute for Psychoanalysis, New York, New York

INTRODUCTION

John D. O'Brien, M.D.

The knowledge base of the fields of child psychopathology and child development has expanded greatly over the course of this century. Accompanying this expansion has been a proliferation of therapies aimed at specific entities and symptoms. Psychodynamically oriented psychotherapy addresses the child's overall development—sense of self and self-esteem—as well as the specific (symptomatic) problems. The principles, however, of psychodynamically oriented child psychotherapy were first formulated by Anna Freud (1) and Melanie Klein (2) at a time when most treatable psychopathology was viewed exclusively as a product of internal psychological conflict.

It is the aim of this book to demonstrate how the techniques of psychodynamically oriented psychotherapy can be modified to meet the therapeutic needs of children with specific diagnoses and/or particular circumstances. These modifications may include adjustments of traditional aspects of child and adolescent psychotherapy such as encouragement or discouragement of transference, or an emphasis on the real relationship. In other situations, these modifications may involve an incorporation of other therapeutic modalities such as behavioral, cognitive, family therapies, and so on. Not only will a general technical approach be offered but the use of various strategies at different stages of treatment will also be addressed.

This book will not attempt to cover every psychiatric entity but it will put forth a range of circumstances for which adaptation of classical technique is necessary. For example, William N. Davis, in discussing the treatment of adolescents with anorexia nervosa (Chapter 10), points out clearly that the relatively neutral, passive psychotherapist who conducts treatment by means of inquiry, exploration and interpretation will be ineffective. Initially, most anorexic patients do not wish to inquire or explore because they have an interest in remaining ignorant. The therapist must be active and at times authoritative. The therapist actively assumes the role of expert. In my discussion of the treatment of children with attention-deficit hyperactivity disorder (ADHD; Chapter 6), I advocate that the therapist take a didactic stance during the necessarily long opening phase of treatment. The therapist emphasizes doing rather than talking or interpreting, and actively encourages successes in the session to be transferred to "outside" life. Judith Brisman's treatment of bulimia (Chapter 9) begins with a behavioral contract. Her treatment is a well titrated mixture of behavioral and psychoanalytic techniques.

This book is dedicated to a thorough discussion of technical alterations such as those briefly mentioned above that meet the very special circumstances confronting child and adolescent clinicians daily. These modifications make psychotherapy more useful than a psychotherapy prescribed by a globally codified theoretical system. Each chapter deals with specific interventions designed to fit particular circumstances facing child and adolescent patients today.

Before a discussion of the general theory of psychoanalytic psychotherapy with children and adolescents occurs, it is important to briefly consider the historical unfolding of child and adolescent psychotherapy. (A more comprehensive history can be found in *The Process of Child Therapy* by the Group for the Advancement of Psychiatry [GAP Report 111] [20].) This approach enables us to see the evolution, sometimes over centuries, of thought and consequent interventions that we sometimes view as new and innovative.

THE HISTORY OF CHILD
AND ADOLESCENT THERAPY

Throughout history both the theories and the methods of child and adolescent therapy reflect the changing social attitudes and beliefs of each era, specifically, the beliefs about children and the practices of child rearing. In antiquity, Hippocrates (ca 460–ca 377 BC) declared that insanity was a disease of the brain, but that idea was lost for centuries. Galen (129–199 AD) believed that human endowment was set at birth and that children displayed strongly individual characteristics that could be modified only within limits by training and education. These ideas of Galen are in concert with what was then contemporary thought but, after his death, were soon disregarded.

With Christianity, disease was often considered a punishment for sin. In the Middle Ages, children after seven years of age mixed socially with adults and were not treated specially. The concept of original sin led to a view that children were evil, which justified corporal punishment. However, once parents accepted the church's teaching that children had souls, infanticide was markedly curtailed. The extremely high rate of infant and child mortality that continued until the 20th century contributed to a lack of attachment between parent and child. This lack of attachment led to a lack of special status for children.

During the Renaissance, there was greater empathy for children, whose status was basically recognized as unique and separate from adults. In the 16th century, Comenius (1592–1670) wrote a book on infancy that was a guide to rearing children from conception to age seven. The concepts of individual differences and normative stages are apparent in his thinking. Comenius believed that children were given good habits by perpetual example, wise instruction, daily exercise, and gently regulated discipline. Play, importantly, was recognized as a means of learning and mastery; bad habits were to be nipped in the bud by rebuke, shame and, as a last resort, the rod. Locke (1632–1704) introduced the concept of *tabula rasa*, in which the child was considered to be a blank slate and the environment and the experiences of the child wrote on the slate. He also believed that play would reveal the predominant passions and the prevailing inclinations of the child. Locke's major intervention was reasoning with the child according to the child's capacity and apprehension. He had this to say regarding interventions with a child: "Would you have him open his heart to you and ask your advice? You must begin to do so with him first and by your carriage beget that confidence. Advise as an experienced friend and mingle nothing of command or authority" (3). Rousseau (1712–1778) focused on the innate goodness of children, whose natural development would flower if it was not contaminated by society or pedagogy. He also believed in dealing with childhood fears by giving children tasks to do in the hope that their desire for approval or another emotion would prove greater than the fear.

In 1801, Itard reported on his work with Victor, the famous wild boy of Aveyron. Itard basically believed that he failed with Victor because Victor had not been able to attain speech, but others looked at Victor and found that he had markedly improved. Itard felt that Victor had been deprived and isolated from society. Many, of course, would wonder if Victor had been retarded or possibly autistic. However, if one looks carefully at Itard's work, one sees the forerunner of modern behavioral modification techniques.

Darwin (1809–1882) had a major impact on the thinking about children. His concept of evolutionary phases prefigured current epigenetic concepts of development. Moreover, his thinking about the interrelationship between the individual and the environment is central to the biopsychosocial model of psychiatry.

Coue (1857–1926) discussed a particular kind of intervention which he called "induced autosuggestion," something akin to "Every day in every way I am getting better and better." His ideas focused not only on getting rid of bad conditions, but on cultivating the opposite right ones. This method succeeded by avoiding conflict and implanting positive thoughts.

In the 20th century, the first works of note dealing with children and adolescents were Sigmund Freud's *Little Hans* and *Dora*. It is important to remember that Little Hans was not treated directly by Freud (1856–1939). The first therapist to use play as a therapy was Hermine Hug Hellmuth in 1921. I must also mention Alfred Adler, who applied his particular theory in the schools and with teachers. This is the first known example of agency consultation and community child psychiatry.

Anna Freud (1) and Melanie Klein (2) adapted various kinds of techniques for children. Klein believed that the nature of the play of children was essentially similar to the free association that occurs in adults. She made in-depth interpretations of the play to the child. She believed that the superego developed in infancy and the Oedipus complex occurred before the fourth or fifth year. During treatment, she had little contact with parents or teachers, because she believed the relationship between the child and the analyst was an exclusive one.

Anna Freud did not make interpretations quickly but felt the child needed to be introduced to treatment. The therapist intervened, at times, in the outside world of the child and educated the patient. Interpretations were made judiciously and sparingly. The therapist contacted the parents and teachers regularly to not only get data but give guidance. Although they disagreed on technique, they both worked specifically with children in long-term individual psychotherapy and provided the paradigms for modern psychoanalytic psychotherapy with children.

In the United States, David Levy (4) introduced structured play therapy wherein the therapist would set up a play situation that deliberately replicated an area of real-life conflict for the youngster. Understanding and mastery were emphasized in this treatment. Frederick Allen (5) emphasized the curative aspects of the emotional rapport between patient and therapist in an atmosphere of great acceptance. He focused on the here and now, and quietly insisted on the child's exercising his or her freedom of action and choice. In the ensuing years, there have been many articles and books dealing with psychotherapy with children and adolescents (6–18). Unfortunately, in this introduction I can only mention a few of them.

In 1909, William Healy began working with juvenile delinquents. He established the concept of physician, psychologist, and social worker functioning as a team. He encouraged psychological and dynamic thinking in the assessment and treatment of children. He focused on the individual child through detailed case study and firsthand observation much in the way Adolph Meyer did with adults. Healy's work prepared the way for the Child Guidance Movement.

Round-the-clock treatment facilities first became available after the Civil War. These were refuges for orphans and immigrants. Children's Village in 1855 was one of the first to be built to house homeless children. The first psychiatric hospital facilities were started at Bellevue and at King's Park State Hospital in the 1920s and 1930s. Psychopharmacology was introduced in the 1940s, followed by family therapy in the 1950s.

This abbreviated history reminds us that many contemporary therapeutic strategies have roots far in our past. However, only within the past 20 years has child psychiatry moved from a one-treatment discipline—that of individual psychotherapy—to one that uses multiple therapies. Individual psychotherapy is still the predominant mode of treatment for children and adolescents in the United States (19). Individual psychotherapy is a broad term. Various forms of individual psychotherapy were used to treat psychosis, neurosis, delinquency, habit disorders, and learning disabilities. Only recently has there been an attempt to match diagnosis and treatment. We now are fortunate to have a wide variety of therapeutic interventions. One thing remains constant, however: "the healer believes in himself and his method, and the patient must have faith and hope in him" (20, p. 1).

It is important to recognize that dynamic individual psychotherapy was for many years the only treatment available and, therefore, was used in all conditions. With such wide usage, it came under attack for being irrelevant, ineffective, and possibly damaging. Now that we have other treatments, we must look closely at psychotherapy, and in fact, at all dynamic interventions to see the efficacy of each of them. As shown in this book, psychotherapy must be modified so that it can be adapted to a wide variety of situations.

DIFFERENCES BETWEEN CHILD AND ADULT TREATMENT

There are marked differences between adult and child and adolescent psychotherapy. Adult therapy generally consists of a two group, the therapist and the patient. This is not the case in child or adolescent work—parents are continuously involved. The parental involvement falls along a continuum. Parents may be seen separately once a month, or once a week. Family sessions where child and parents are seen together can also be used with varying frequencies. In adult treatment, the therapist relies on the patient telling what is happening. Often the child either does not tell for various reasons or is unable to tell.

Thus, parents are seen to gather information, to monitor progress, to give them some idea of what is going on in treatment, to prepare them for changes that may arise during and from the treatment experience, and to alter their behavior in relationship to the child. Therapists routinely call the school to obtain information about what is happening with their patients, and in many instances give advice at the request of the school about how to handle certain situations. Therefore, child and adolescent therapists commonly deal with the many institutions that affect the child or adolescent patient. Imagine if the adult therapist called his patient's boss! The child is seen in a social context with all the forces that impinge on him or her as sources of data and potential interactions with the therapist.

Much of what goes on in adult therapy transpires on a verbal level. This is not always the case with children. Play, involving board games such as chess or creative activities such as drawing, is a cornerstone of child and adolescent treatment. Activities play a much greater role in the treatment of children than of adults.

The use of language poses a difficulty for child treatment. One must use language appropriate to the developmental level of the child. Frequently, children misunderstand what is said to them and what the therapist thinks he or she is saying to them may be hardly what the children understand.

Generally the adult comes to treatment on a voluntary basis driven by personal discomfort about his or her state. This is often not true for children. They are usually brought to treatment and the symptoms often are not troublesome for the children themselves; on the contrary, they may derive pleasure from them. The children will externalize and tend to see change as necessary for others and not for themselves. The adult patient sees the therapist as an expert from whom he or she will benefit. This is frequently not true for children. Children will often see the doctor as a source of pain or discomfort or at least as someone who takes them away from television, friends, or school work; the therapist, at least initially, is someone to be wary of. The therapist is frequently felt to be an ally or agent of the parent(s). Thus, the normal positive regard and transference that frequently accompany the initial phase of adult treatment is often not there with children and adolescents. In child and adolescent psychotherapy, the therapist needs to participate more actively and to work harder to gain patients' trust and to interest them in the work at hand.

INDICATIONS FOR DYNAMIC PSYCHOTHERAPY

According to Shapiro and Esman (21), psychoanalytically-oriented psychotherapy seems to be most useful for nonpsychotic children whose symptoms are not severe enough to prevent them from continuing their lives in the community. It also is best for individuals who are significantly discomforted by their disorders and who have some tolerance for introspection. Psychotherapy is helpful for children who have habitual problems in living, children who are temporary victims of social milieu change, such as divorce, which impedes their developmental progress, children with low self-esteem and excessive self-consciousness, children who have problems with peers and their own self-evaluation secondary to or concomitant with problems in learning. Psychotherapy is also advantageous for conduct disordered children who have primary dynamic conflicts, for children who feel chronically low in spirit or are worried about new situations and consequently withdraw from social contact or from the new situations, and finally, as an adjunct to drug and social milieu treatment.

Although it is not the focus of this book, the integration of psychodynamic therapies with other therapies such as pharmacotherapy, family therapy, and so on is a major task for contemporary psychiatry. Judith Brisman in her chapter deals with the integration of behavioral treatment with psychodynamic therapy. Also, Richard A. Gardner in his chapter on separation anxiety (Chapter 1) discusses parental therapy as an essential part of the treatment of the separation disorder in the child.

FUNDAMENTAL THEORY OF PSYCHODYNAMIC TREATMENT

Psychodynamic therapy is one of the most widely used therapeutic approaches for children and adolescents within the broad armamentarium of a contemporary child psychotherapist. This kind of therapy draws on the psychoanalytic model for a theory of how change occurs. According to Shapiro and Esman (21), such treatment is characterized by at least four fundamental tenets:

1. *The centrality of the concept of unconscious mental functioning.* This requires the recognition that symbolic behaviors are not necessarily the simple results of stimulus response complexes. Instead they are viewed as compromise representations of internalized basic human needs that appear as disguised wishes related to early mental organizations. These derivatives of infantile dependence or Oedipal constellations emerge in disguised forms, because they are met by counterwishes that pertain to the demands of reality. These conflicts become internalized and repetitive and seek expression repeatedly throughout life, especially when events precipitate a resurgence of repressed wishes. This recurrent emergence occurs because of the layering of experience of successive developmental states and memories of past pleasure. These motivated constellations give rise to symptoms and behavior patterns that are meaningful when analyzed into their more basic elements; that is, symptoms have significance as representations of past relations recast in the form of present wishes or affectively charged conflicts. They are repeated inappropriately anachronistically at varying points in the life cycle, creating a sense of disturbance, anxiety, lack of well-being, and repetitive maladaptive interpersonal relations.
2. *The notion that conflicts are internalized, leading to repetitive, motivated symptoms that are behaviorally available to observation.*
3. *The view that symptoms have meaning and significance both to the individual and to his or her adaptation to the environment.*
4. *Finally, the critical role of the concept of transference as a means for understanding and interpreting the patient-therapist interaction in terms of past experience with parents and other significant persons.* Transference refers to attitudes and behaviors enacted in the therapy, wherein the child uses the therapist as a foil for attitudes and feelings that more appropriately belong to the past and to relations with significant adults from the early rearing process. Tyson and Tyson (22) have distinguished an aspect of transfer-

ence that they call transference of current relationships, wherein current conflicts, wishes, or reactions to parents are displaced into the treatment. Such enactments of old interactions, or new enactments of old unconscious conflicts, are recognized in the therapy and confronted in order to bring the patient to awareness that what is happening has a somewhat irrational tinge. This may, in turn, help illuminate maladaptive behaviors in extratherapeutic life.

To these four I would add one more. *Children conceive of the therapist as a real object in their lives, one who offers a viewpoint different from others and, above all, one who allows the testing of new ideas and new ways of feeling and behaving in a supporting and supportive environment.* Thus, therapy allows the children to experience and experiment.

All forms of therapy for children attempt to influence the youngster to make changes in three areas: cognitive, emotional and behavioral. The dynamic insight therapist is concerned primarily with the cognitive-emotional sphere and expects that behavior will change as a consequence of changes in these. According to the Group for the Advancement of Psychiatry (20), the three ingredients are influenced in a series of delineated stages or phases that overlap and vary enormously in emphasis and time spent in them depending upon the particular techniques. The phases may be conceptualized in the following way:

1. Establishment of the working relationship;
2. Analysis of the problem and its cause;
3. Explanation of the problem;
4. Establishing and implementing the formula for change; and
5. Termination.

As I mentioned before, the first stage is usually more prolonged than in adult treatment, because the child may need time to believe that the therapist is a person who is important to the child, who can be helpful, and who is a person who knows more about the problems than the child or the child's parents, or who at least knows more about what the problem is and can come up with a solution. Once the child attains this, he or she can have hope—hope for help from the therapist. This first stage of relationship development and the emotional investment attached to it are of utmost importance for work with youngsters. Corrective emotional experience is used here to mean an experience that permits growth through new identifications and that allows for a developmental replay of missed opportunities with parents and parent-like figures. During this phase, the issue of empathy is crucial. Empathy has been described as the process by which the therapist resonates with the child's attitudes and behaviors. Cognitive understanding is probably the beginning of empathy, but the process, if it is to go beyond that, arouses within the patient and the therapist an awareness of childhood. It becomes a cognitive and affective identification—which allows the therapist to move in and out of the youngster's inner world. In psychodynamic therapy, empathy is essential not only to promote access to fantasy life, but also to concealed affects so that they can become available for exploration and understanding. It points the way to further movement slightly beyond the patient's own awareness.

During the second phase (i.e., problem analysis), the symptoms or behaviors to be influenced are selected. The work shifts to a more cognitive level of goal selection. Problem analysis always relates to the life experience of the patient and involves some self-revelation regarding present functioning and past behavior. The examination of the youngster's life experiences can be broad and unstructured or narrowly focused according to the conceptual framework of the therapist and the patient's problems. It is often a search for cause; many feel that the effectiveness of the treatment to follow is ultimately related to the degree to which the child patient participates in the process of inquiry. It is probable that the durability of success increases when the youngster actively chooses the conceptual framework or viewpoint of the therapist rather than passively submitting to it.

The third phase, explanation of the problem may, also, last a variable span of time and can be emphasized or not. In many cases, the explanation must be extended to the child's family to prepare the way for all the behavior toward and from the child. Explanation can be indirect, that is, through the use of play material or stories, and/or direct, through focused discussion. For the child to be willing to learn about him- or herself and to undergo change, he or she must feel that the therapist's formulation is one that the child can adopt and that makes sense. For this reason, this phase is felt to be an educative experience and has strong affective or emotional substance to hold it together. During this phase there is an attempt to split off the symptoms so that the youngster can look at them separate from him- or herself. Within this phase is also the corrective emotional experience—that sense of newness with a different person incorporated into the youngster's life, along with a reworking of behavior and coping patterns based on this fresh new look.

Insight is considered by some to be crucial to this phase. It is an acceptance and incorporation of the explanation of the cause of the problem. It can be experienced as self-understanding and can be arrived at directly, symbolically, or through utilizing the therapist's insight, which the patient accepts as his or her own. Classical psychotherapists feel change follows insight. Others, however, (for example, see my chapter on ADHD) feel that insight in some situations follows change. Still others feel that there is a reciprocal relationship in which insight increases the possibility of change and change brings about new insights. This is a spiral propelled by both insight and change.

The fourth phase is establishing and implementing the formula for change. The last ingredient is to follow the "prescription." The patient is told that his or her improvement depends upon doing or saying or trying certain things or holding certain thoughts or feelings. Behavioral components begin to replace the cognitive and emotional ones that received emphasis in the earlier work. Knowledge is put into practice. Usually the formulas and interactions evoke a strong emotional response, which must be managed if it is to produce behaviors that are more adaptive and durable than the previous patterns. Actual experience seems to overshadow the therapist's "school" or theoretical conceptualization in this stage, as well as the child's style of living before the treatment began. The solutions or new attitudes and behaviors are tried and fed back from new experiences, compared and contrasted to the old maladaptive attitudes and behaviors. Usually there is a need for explanation and instruction to the family and other persons in the child's life at this stage. Here the therapist participates and mediates as a helper between the child and the child's milieu. Sometimes the therapist makes it clear that the process of change is largely in the hands of those who surround the child and that they must carry the main burdens of the treatment.

The final phase is termination, which depends greatly on the child's and the family's acceptance of a mutually satisfactory balance of mastery over certain problems with adjustment to or acceptance of others. There is an attempt to consolidate those changes in behavior that represent progressive gains in the functioning of the personality of the child. This phase is reached when adjustment is so improved that healthy change can continue independent of the therapist's direct presence.

The stages are artificially separated for teaching purposes. In actuality they overlap and vary considerably in length and emphasis according to the patient's issues and the therapist's orientation. They can and should form a process.

GOALS OF PSYCHOTHERAPY

Rutter (23) outlined four goals of psychotherapy:

1. *Symptom reduction.* This is not only an appropriate but a necessary prime goal of treatment. We no longer hold that goals have no place in treatment; goals of both child and parent must kept in mind. In psychoanalytic theory, symptom reduction is a necessary but not sufficient goal of treatment.
2. *The promotion of normal development.* This not only applies to children with developmental delays but to any child with a psychiatric disorder. Because children are developing organisms, fostering normal growth becomes an important issue. However, another reason to be concerned with the promotion of healthy growth is the fact that some forms of psychiatric

disturbance in childhood are associated with adult outcomes of personality disorders.

3. *The fostering of autonomy and self-reliance* is another purpose of psycho-therapy. Helping children gain skills needed to deal with future problems without psychiatric disorder occurring and without further professional help is an aim.

4. Settling for change in the therapeutic setting is not enough. *Change in real life settings, such as at home or at school, needs to be a fundamental aim of the treatment.*

The changing and developing child and his or her problems provide difficult new challenges to parents. Parents need to be prepared for changes and the challenges that accompany them. They must gain improved coping skills lest they be forever dependent on professional help. For treatment to be effective, change that occurs in the child must be accompanied by change in the child's parents. Also, direct treatment of the child, whether dynamic or otherwise, is conducted with substantial efforts at environmental modification. A major form of treatment may be changing the environment. A child's behavior must be viewed in a social context and treatment may have as its focus the social system—school or family. Both individual and social elements in functioning must be taken into consideration when treatment planning occurs. One good example of this is that improvements in one environment, such as the treatment setting, may lead to detrimental effects in other settings, such as the home.

OUTCOME STUDIES

Research on purely psychological treatment of children and adolescents lags well behind that with adults. There are some recent results of adult research regarding psychological treatment. It has been clearly shown in the adult literature that psychotherapy can be effective even on a short-term outpatient basis with diagnosed antisocial patients in a methadone program, provided that they have a current diagnosis of a depressive disorder (24). It has also been shown, generally, that for depression, combined psychotherapy with psychopharmacology is more effective than either alone and more effective than placebo (25), and, finally, that psychotherapy with depression is as effective as pharmacotherapy (26).

When we look at empirical findings on the overall efficacy of psychological therapies in the treatment of child psychiatric disorders, we find that there are few well-controlled comparisons of different forms of treatment effects. Some psychological therapies can and do influence children's maladaptive behaviors in beneficial ways. It has been shown that supportive therapy or counseling is less effective than the bell and pad in the treatment of nocturnal enuresis (27).

However, even this is more complex. Family difficulties are associated with an increased relapse rate among those who became dry using the alarm. The meaning of these differences remains uncertain but it is apparent that there are sizable individual variations in response to any treatment. As Shaffer succinctly states (28), "Well planned and executed research . . . should be able to answer the question of for whom and for what problem does what type of psycho-therapy work" (p. 559).

Psychotherapy outcome research with children and adolescents is very difficult to do. A control group is necessary because children may show higher spontaneous remission rates than adults. A researcher needs to make sure that the remission rate results from the intervention and not from some other variable, such as development. The effects of age and IQ, also, need to be looked at in any outcome study. How parents are involved in any treatment process is another important variable. The outcome in child and adolescent treatment is probably more dependent on circumstances (i.e., social milieu) than outcome in adult treatment. Although outcome research in psychotherapy is very complex, it must be done so researchers and therapists alike can be aware of the effects of their interventions. Modifications of technique to fit varied circumstances such as divorce or foster care are suggested in this book. It is our hope that such modifications will improve outcomes.

I have tried in this introduction to discuss globally child and adolescent psychoanalytically-oriented psychotherapy. Although fundamental tenets, stages, and goals of psychoanalytic psychotherapy may generally be the same for work with children and adolescents, there are marked differences in the application of these concepts to work with children and adolescents who have certain diagnoses and who are in special circumstances. The authors of the following chapters will discuss particular techniques that have been adapted by experienced clinicians. These techniques have been found to be successful in dealing with special circumstances involving children and adolescents.

REFERENCES

1. Freud A: The Psychoanalytic Treatment of Children. London, Imago Publishing, 1946
2. Klein M: The Psychoanalysis of Children. London, Hogarth Press, 1932
3. Locke J: Some thoughts concerning education, in English Philosophers of the Seventeenth and Eighteenth Centuries. Edited by Elliot CW. New York, Collier, 1910, pp 10–22
4. Levy D: Release therapy in young children. Psychiatry 1:387–390, 1938
5. Allen F: Psychotherapy With Children. New York, Norton, 1942
6. Adams P: A Primer of Child Psychotherapy. Boston, MA, Little, Brown, 1979
7. Axline V: Play Therapy. New York, Ballantine Books, 1947

8. Bornstein B: The analysis of a phobic child. Psychoanal Study Child 3–4:181–226, 1949

9. Carek D: Individual therapies: individual psychodynamically oriented therapy, in Basic Handbook of Child Psychiatry, Vol 3. Edited by Noshpitz J, Harrison S. New York, Basic Books, 1979, pp 35–57

10. Ekstein R: Individual therapies: psychoanalysis, in Basic Handbook of Child Psychiatry, Vol 3. Edited by Noshpitz J, Harrison S. New York, Basic Books, 1979, pp 21–35

11. Erickson E: Childhood and Society. New York, WW Norton, 1950

12. Fraiberg S: A therapeutic approach to reactive ego disturbances in children in placement. Am J Orthopsychiatry 32:18–31, 1962

13. Ginott H: Between Parent and Child. New York, Macmillan, 1965

14. Harrison S, Carek D: Guide to Psychotherapy. Boston, MA, Little, Brown, 1966

15. Marans S: Psychoanalytic psychotherapy with children: current research trends and challenges. J Am Acad Child Adolesc Psychiatry 28:669–674, 1989

16. Schowalter J: Psychodynamics and medication. J Am Acad Child Adolesc Psychiatry 28:681–684, 1989

17. Shapiro T: The psychodynamic formulation in child and adolescent psychiatry. J Am Acad Child Adolesc Psychiatry 28:675–680, 1989

18. Sholevar G, Burland J, Frank J, et al: Psychoanalytic treatment of children and adolescents. J Am Acad Child Adolesc Psychiatry 28:685–690, 1989

19. Silver L, Silver B: Clinical practice of child psychiatry. J Am Acad Child Psychiatry 22:573–579, 1983

20. Group for the Advancement of Psychiatry: The Process of Child Therapy (GAP Report 111). New York, Brunner/Mazel, 1982

21. Shapiro T, Esman A: Psychotherapy with children and adolescents. Psychiatr Clin North Am 4:909–921, 1985

22. Tyson R, Tyson P: The concept of transference in child psychoanalysis. J Am Acad Child Adolesc Psychiatry 25:30–39, 1986

23. Rutter M: Psychological therapies in child psychiatry: issues and prospects, in Childhood Psychotherapy and Development. Edited by Guze S, Earls F, Barret J. New York, Raven, 1983, pp 236–249

24. Woody G, McLellan A, Luborsky L, et al: Sociopathy and psychotherapy outcome. Arch Gen Psychiatry 42:1081–1086, 1985

25. Conte H, Plutchik R, Wild K, et al: Combined psychotherapy and pharmacology for depression. Arch Gen Psychiatry 43:471–479, 1986

26. Weissman M, Klerman G, Prusoff B, et al: Depressed outpatients: results one year after treatment with drugs and/or interpersonal psychotherapy. Arch Gen Psychiatry 38:51–55, 1981

27. Forsythe W, Fedmond A: Enuresis and the electrical alarm: a study of 200 cases. BMJ 1:211–214, 1970

28. Shaffer D: Notes on psychotherapy research among children and adolescents. J Am Acad Child Psychiatry 23:552–561, 1984

SECTION I:

THE
PSYCHOTHERAPEUTIC
PROCESS
WITH CHILDREN

◆ ◆ ◆ ◆ ◆ ◆ ◆

1 Children With Separation Anxiety Disorder

Richard A. Gardner, M.D.

INTRODUCTION

The separation anxiety disorder is one of the "purer" clinical entities in child psychiatry. When seen in its full-blown form it is hard to miss the diagnosis. Not only does the purity of the disorder contribute to the ease with which it is diagnosed, but the psychodynamic processes that are often contributory also have a uniformity and consistency that is unusual. Because of its relative purity, the therapeutic approaches to this disturbance are also more readily standardized. Like other childhood disorders, the facility with which it can be treated varies. Some cases can be dealt with quite easily, but in others the pathology is deep-seated and the family contributions are so formidable that it may be impossible to treat the child successfully. In this chapter I describe in detail the psychodynamic patterns I have found to be most consistently present and the psychotherapeutic approaches I have found to be most efficacious.

At this point, clarification of the terms *fear, anxiety,* and *phobia* is warranted. The term fear is generally used when there is a specific entity that is the focus of the fear. The fear reaction has survival value: It enhances one's efficiency to remove oneself from a danger. The term fear is warranted when it is the general consensus of observers that the individual is justified in experiencing the response and that the danger is real. The main difference between the *phobia* and the *fear* is that in the phobia the general consensus of observers is that the fright reaction is either totally inappropriate or grossly exaggerated. The phobia usually involves the use of pathological mechanisms such as displacement, avoidance, projection, and symbolization. In *anxiety* the individual does not have a specific mental representation of the feared object. The individual is often at a loss to know why the fearful reaction is taking place. *Anxiety attacks* or *panic attacks* (I use the terms synonymously) frequently occur without warning. Most often, the individual is at a loss to explain why the attack occurred at that point and cannot usually pinpoint specific precipitating factors. Many psychoanalysts hold that anxiety is the result of the threatened eruption into conscious awareness of unconscious thoughts and feelings about which the individual feels guilty. Although an analyst myself, I do not believe that the traditional analytical explanation holds for many of the patients I see who exhibit anxiety and panic states. I believe that there are a wide range of individuals with regard to the sensitivity of the fear reaction. Some people have a high threshold for elicitation of the flight response and others a very low threshold. Those with a low threshold may have their fear mechanisms triggered by innocuous or minimal stimuli, sometimes stimuli that are unrecognized by the person. In some cases there may be no external stimulus at all; rather, the mechanisms are brought into play in a manner similar to a seizure. Here there are basically biochemical, neurophysiological, and metabolic mechanisms that are operative, and this disorder can truly be viewed as a purely biological entity in these patients. In others the psychoanalytic explanation appears reasonable.

In 1941, Johnson and colleagues (1) introduced the term *school phobia* (Gordon and Young [2]). The term appeared warranted because the child's fear of school was clearly psychopathological and far beyond any realistic danger that the child could describe. Prior to that time, school phobia was not generally recognized as a discrete disorder. Rather, it was included among other school problems, especially those involving refusal and truancy. The term school phobia has applicability because the child will focus on the school as the source of the fear. In addition, because it is not really the school the child is basically afraid of, the distortion warrants the utilization of the term phobia. In some cases the child is less certain about the exact nature of the fear. The child may resist going to school, but cannot say exactly what it is in the school situation that causes the fear. The child does not present with the usual array of rationalizations for not attending (to be discussed below) and does not delineate specific factors in the school that he or she is afraid of. There is, however, a morbid sense of fear as the child approaches the school house. This nonspecific fear is more justifiably called anxiety. In 1957, Johnson suggested that school phobia was a misnomer in that the basic fear is not of the school but of separation from the mother and that "the essential problem lay in an unresolved, mutual dependency relationship between mother and child" (3). The child is not consciously aware of the fact that the basic fear relates to separation from the mother and a variety of other factors to be discussed below. Psychoanalytic theory holds that anxiety results from the threat that these unconscious thoughts and feelings will erupt into conscious awareness. The school situation increases the likelihood of such eruption, and the anxiety is related to this threat.

Because of these considerations, the term *separation anxiety disorder* has been substituted for school phobia. This is also the term used in DSM-III-R (4). Because the school is the consciously feared object for many of these children, I do not believe it is justifiable to discard the term school phobia entirely. We have not discarded the term agoraphobia with the argument that for patients who are agoraphobic, the fear of open places is merely a displacement and is symbolic of factors having little to do with open places. Accordingly, in my discussion, I will occasionally use the term school phobia and otherwise use the term separation anxiety disorder. I prefer to retain the original term because there are situations in which it appears to be the more applicable, that is, when the child focuses specifically on the school. I will also use the term separation anxiety disorder because there are children who do not focus on the school and the primary symptomatic manifestation is diffuse anxiety. Some children will state that they fear that something "bad" (not necessarily defined) will happen to their mothers while they are in school. Here the separation anxiety element is apparent and the psychodynamic significance of this particular response will be discussed below. In some cases, of course, it is unclear as to which term is warranted. Accordingly, I shall use the terms fear, phobia, and anxiety when referring to these children. Physiologically, however, they are identical. It is the cognitive and emotional concomitants that determine which of the terms is the most appropriate.

It is important to differentiate between school phobia and truancy. Eisenberg (5) states that the school-phobic child is frequently a good student; the truant is a poor student. Truants openly acknowledge their dislike for school; children who are school-phobic wish (at least ostensibly) they could attend. The truant avoids *both* home and school, whereas the school-phobic child stays at home. Moreover, the truants fabricate excuses to cover up their behavior; children with school phobia draw attention to their inability to leave home and to stay in school. Hersov (6), Gardner and Sperry (7), and Coolidge (8) provide useful presentations of the psychodynamics of school refusal.

The literature (DSM-III-R) (2,4) shows an equal incidence among boys and girls. The pooled results of many studies further indicate that there is no birth order pattern (2,9). Coolidge and colleagues (9) found children with school phobia to be of above average intelligence; however, they generally perform at an average level for the suburban population from which they were commonly drawn. Finally, there is some evidence to suggest that the incidence is higher in upwardly striving economic classes in which there is strong concern for education and achievement. The concerns of lower economic groups are different and the emotional problems of their children manifest themselves in other areas (10).

THE TYPICAL CLINICAL PICTURE

Primary Manifestations

Clinically, the picture that the therapist sees appears to justify the original term school phobia. The most salient feature is fear of going to school—to the point of panic. The closer the child gets to the school, the greater the fear. However, if the mother accompanies the child into the school there is little if any panic. And if the mother were to be allowed to stay in the classroom with the child, there would generally be no fear. This is pathognomonic of the disorder.

Most often, the fear of school does not exist in isolation. Refusal is a common concomitant. Generally, the younger the child, the greater the fear element; the older the child, the greater the refusal element. But even the younger, panicky child will usually exhibit a refusal element. An adolescent is more likely to present as school refusal and may even rationalize the fear with professions of refusal. If the adolescent stays at home when not in school, then the fear element is probably dominant. However, if the adolescent spends time with friends outside the home, then the disorder should more properly be referred to as a school refusal problem or truancy. In the latter case, the term school phobia, or separation anxiety, is not appropriate in that the child is not exhibiting the characteristic dependent tie to the mother. When leaving the home in the morning the child frequently complains of a variety of physical symptoms: headache, nausea, vomiting, diarrhea, fever, stomachache, low grade fever, and so on. (These somatic symptoms have led Schmitt [10] to refer to the school phobic as "the great impostor.") These symptoms are usually physiological concomitants of the fear. Typically they are indulged by the mother, and it is difficult, if not impossible, to convince her that no physical disease is usually present.

School-phobic children usually rationalize their not going to school with explanations such as: the teacher is mean, they are bullied in the classroom, the school is boring, the janitor scares them, the bathroom smells, the work is too simple, the work is too hard, and so on. There may be a core of truth to many of these complaints. However, the classmates are going to school in spite of these discomforts and indignities; the child with a separation anxiety disorder does not. Furthermore, attempts to reassure such children that things are not as terrible as they envision are of no avail. They remain adamantly unconvinced and will create new rationalizations if one is successful in dispelling previous ones. Often the child does not genuinely know exactly what he or she is afraid of and will state so: "I don't know what I'm afraid of; I'm just scared." This may be an honest answer because the child may not be consciously aware of the underlying psychodynamic factors (to be discussed below) that are contributing to the anxiety.

Some children, if they can stay in the classroom, are still quite tense. They may have great difficulty concentrating on what the teacher is saying. This may be related to general anxiety, or they may be preoccupied with fears of harm befalling their mothers. They may fantasize about their mothers becoming sick or being injured, or may just have general fears that something terrible will happen to their mothers while they are in school.

Associated Features

Children with a separation anxiety disorder will often exhibit a wide variety of other fears. They may fear visiting other children's homes. Sleep-away camp is often unthinkable, and even summer day camps may be out of the question. Fear of the dark or of animals is common. They may be afraid to go on errands in the neighborhood when other children their age are eager for such growth experiences. Commonly, they are usually more fearful of new situations than other children their age.

In addition to their fears, these children tend to be demanding, coercive, and manipulative. This is especially the case with regard to the school situation. Upon being cajoled or pressured into going to school a child may state, "If you make me go to school, I'll jump out of the window." Unfortunately, the parents of these children tend to take such threats more seriously than is warranted. There is a grandiosity to these children that relates to the pampering and indulgence their parents provide. Often they act as if they were the masters and their parents the slaves. Coolidge and colleagues (11) emphasize these children's exaggerated sense of infantile omnipotence. Leventhal and Sills (12) propose that a central personality characteristic of these children is their grandiose and unrealistic self-image engendered by the parental overprotectiveness. Their aggrandized self-image is threatened in the more egalitarian school situation, so they crave to retreat home where their narcissistic gratifications can be indulged.

Precipitating Factors

Often, the precipitating factor is a situation that threatens the mother-child symbiotic tie. The mothers of these children are typically overprotective, and the central factor is the pathological relationship between an overprotective mother and an overdependent child. Sometimes the threat to the relationship is realistic; sometimes it is only fantasized. Any situation that can potentially result in a disruption of this tie can be a precipitating factor. Commonly, a mother's illness may provide the threat—especially when hospitalization is required. The birth of a sibling may threaten the bond because of the extra attention that the newborn requires. Parental divorce can precipitate the disorder. Even though the father may be the one who leaves the home, the child cannot but reason that if one parent can leave, perhaps the other can do so as well. The death of a significant figure may serve to precipitate a school phobia. The death of a grandparent, for example, may bring about the child's realization that we are all mortal—even mother. Sometimes the precipitating event can be the transfer to a new school or the moving of the family to a new neighborhood. It is important to appreciate that the precipitating event is not the sole factor in bringing about the symptomatology. It is best viewed as "the straw that broke the camel's back." One often obtains a history of milder fears of school attendance in earlier years.

THE FAMILY PATTERN

I present here the typical family pattern of the child with a separation anxiety disorder. It is important to appreciate that I am condensing typical features from a variety of children with this disorder. One rarely sees a "pure" form. Each family will have its own special variations. However, the pattern I describe here is common enough to be considered typical.

The Mother

It is the mother-child tie, much more than the father-child tie, that is of significance in understanding the separation anxiety disorder. More than anything else, these mothers are overprotective. They do not allow their children to ride bicycles on streets where the children's peers are being trusted to do so or to swim in deep water when other children their age are permitted. Running errands to distant neighborhoods is not allowed. Summer camp may be unthinkable. Day camps, however, may be permitted. There may be a general atmosphere of secretiveness in the home which, in subtle ways, is a manifestation of the maternal overprotectiveness. The child may not be told about disturbing events that occur in the family, such as serious illness, divorce, or job loss.

The basic message that such mothers are giving to their children is this: "The world is a dangerous place and only I can protect you from the calamities that may befall you if you venture forth into it. If you do go forth without me, you may die!" This is the common element that lies beneath all of the aforementioned overprotective maneuvers. Thus, there is a fundamental conditioning element in the separation anxiety disorder. Focus on the underlying psychodynamics (to be discussed in detail later in this chapter) often absorbs the attention and interest of the analytically-oriented therapist. Although focus on these underlying psychodynamics is important—even crucial—to successful treatment, one should not lose sight of this important conditioning factor in the separation anxiety disorder.

The mothers of these children are often phobic themselves. They may be agoraphobic and/or claustrophobic and serve as models for their children's phobias. The grandparents' role is often significant. The key figure generally is the maternal grandmother, upon whom the mother is significantly dependent. Although the mother may be in her 30s or 40s at the time of the referral, there may not have been a day in her life when she did not either see or have telephone contact with the maternal grandmother.

Commonly, the maternal grandmother overprotected the mother during childhood so that one observes the mother's adult manifestation of the dependent tie that she still has with the maternal grandmother.

The Father

The father of these children is typically passive. He generally views the mother as a "supermother" and is unaware of the depth of the pathological relationship between the mother and the school-phobic child. He generally supports the mother's rationalization that other mothers are neglectful. He generally subscribes to the traditional view that mothers should be in complete control of childrearing and fathers should be the breadwinners. There is usually little conflict between the parents with regard to childrearing in that the father submits to the mother's "authority" in this area. He may rationalize such submission by subscribing to the "united front" theory that states that it is very bad for a child to observe parents disagreeing. By complying with this dictum he justifies submitting to the mother's will.

Such a father is often so dependent on the mother that he can be viewed as just another child in the household. He may be phobic himself and thereby serve as a model for the development of phobic reactions in the child. He may reiterate the mother's warnings about the dangers in the world. He does this with less conviction than the mother but parrots her warnings as a manifestation of his desire to please her. The weakness of such fathers makes them poor models for identification by their children and does not engender in their children a sense of security. This further contributes to their youngsters' separation anxieties and feelings of vulnerability in their relationship with a world they have come to view as hostile and dangerous.

UNDERLYING PSYCHODYNAMICS

As is true of all forms of psychogenic pathology, the psychodynamic factors are multiple and complex. I present here those that I consider to be the most important. Again, they relate to the typical cases I have seen. It is extremely important for the examiner to explore these with an open mind and not enter a clinical evaluation with the preconceived notion that any one of the factors I describe here is necessarily operative. The likelihood is that some of them will be; but the likelihood also is that others will not be present in a particular family under consideration.

The Conditioned Component

As I have mentioned, these children have often been programmed for many years with the notion that the world is a dangerous place and that mother is the only one who can protect them from the catastrophes that await to befall them if they are to remove themselves from her protection. An important reason why such children fear going to school is that, for the first time, there is an enforced separation from the mother. Although the school doors are not actually locked, there is formidable pressure for the child to remain there. In the school situation such children are captive. They are exposed to the dangers they have been taught await them when not under mother's protection. And they cannot readily run home to reassure themselves that their mothers are not suffering some calamity if this is one of their concerns.

This aspect of the psychodynamic factors contributing to the development of the child's school problems is justifiably referred to as a conditioned component of the school fear. It is just one manifestation of the generalized fears that the child has been taught to experience. The desensitization aspect of the therapeutic program addresses itself to this contribution to the child's symptomatology.

The Complementary Psychodynamic Patterns of the Mother and Child

At this point I present what I consider to be a central psychodynamic pattern in the etiology of the separation anxiety disorder. To the best of my knowledge, this formulation has not been presented elsewhere, with the exception of my own previous publication (13). It comes from my observations of these children and their parents over many years.

To understand better this somewhat complex formulation, it is best to begin with the mother. As mentioned, she is often still dependent on the maternal grandmother. Consciously or unconsciously, she did not wish to leave the home of the maternal grandmother, but submitted to social pressures to leave home and marry. However, she did so with a psychopathological compromise in which she still maintains her dependent tie to the maternal grandmother. She may live close to the maternal grandmother or, if not, she still maintains very strong and frequent ties. Not only did she basically not wish to marry, but, in addition, she did not wish to assume the role of child rearer. Basically, she wished to remain a child in the home of her own mother. Accordingly, she resents the burden of raising her child and is basically angry at him or her. (Coolidge and colleagues [11] emphasize this factor in the etiology of this disorder.) She cannot allow herself to accept these unloving feelings because of the guilt they would evoke in her. She deals with her hostility toward the child by reaction formation. Each time she envisions some calamity befalling the child, she gratifies in fantasy her basic wish that the child die. But she is too guilty to accept the fact that she harbors such death wishes within herself and so transforms the wish into a fear (an extremely common mechanism). It is not, then, that she *wishes* the child to be harmed, but that she fears that the child would be harmed. To fear a child's death is socially acceptable; to wish it is not. But the fantasy provides partial gratification of the wish, whether or not she views it as a wish or a fear. She tries to keep the child constantly at her side in order to reassure herself that her hostile wishes have not been fulfilled.

When I say these mothers harbor death wishes toward the child, I am not saying that they actually wish the child to be dead. Our unconscious minds utilize primitive mechanisms to represent thoughts and feelings, mechanisms that often "exaggerate to make a point." Visualizing the child as dead is a way of symbolically representing the hostility the mother harbors toward the child. It must also be appreciated that the mother's "death wishes" are really only one aspect of her feelings toward the child. Like all human relations, the mother-child relationship is ambivalent. Deep loving feelings are present as well, and the mother of a school-phobic child would generally be devastated if her child were to die—the intense hostility notwithstanding.

The anger the mother originally felt at the prospect of rearing a child becomes intensified over the years as the demands on her increase. She becomes increasingly angry at the child because of the drainage of her energy and increasingly guilty over the direct expression of such resentment. Accordingly, there is a build-up of the reaction formation mechanism that serves, as mentioned, to allow for a fantasized expression of hostility without concomitant feelings of guilt.

Interestingly, an almost identical psychodynamic pattern develops in the child. The child is basically angry at the mother for a number of reasons. Being kept by the mother from activities that other children enjoy produces social stigmatization. The children's excessive dependency on the mother is a source of frustration and irritation. The basic impairments in the mother's capacity to be a parent are a source of deprivation for them. So deprived, these children become angry. They are not getting the same degree of healthy attention and affection as are children being reared in more stable homes. However, they cannot directly express this anger. They are much too dependent and fearful to do that. After all, mother is their protector from the dangers that await to befall them "out there." If resentment were to be expressed openly toward her they might lose her and then be exposed to the malevolent forces that ever await to pounce on unprotected children. And the children too come to deal with their hostility in the same way as their mothers. Specifically, they use repression, reaction formation, and fantasized gratification. Each time they envision calamity befalling the mother, they satisfy in fantasy their own hostile wishes toward her. By turning the wish into a fear, they assuage their guilt. They must be ever at their mother's side in order to reassure themselves that their hostile wishes have not been fulfilled. In this way, mother and child develop very similar psychodynamic patterns.

In this situation other difficulties develop that contribute to the entrenchment of the pathological tie, which is basically a parasite/host relationship.

The parasite and the host ultimately come to hate one another. The host comes to hate the parasite because its blood is being sucked. And the parasite grows to hate the host because it is ever dependent on the host and, at the whim of the host, may be "flicked off" and then may die. Although the host gains the gratification of benevolence, altruism, and other ego-enhancing feelings, the basic resentment may counterbalance these benefits. Although the parasite may gain the gratifications of a "free meal," there is a precariousness to the situation that compromises this gratification. The frustrations associated with being in such a situation may ultimately produce anger in both mother and child. And the anger so engendered in each feeds back into the aforementioned psychodynamic patterns.

In short, then, the mother and child exhibit complementary psychopathology. However, more than complementing one another, the psychopathology is almost identical. It is almost as if the child's psychopathology is a rubber stamp of the mother's. Accordingly, a therapeutic approach that focuses on the child primarily, if not exclusively, is not likely to be successful. The forces in the mother that contribute to the maintenance of the pathological tie are great and are not likely to be altered significantly by a therapeutic program restricted to working with the child alone. What I describe as "new" in this formulation is the basic similarity between the psychodynamic patterns of the mother and child. The mechanisms of repression, fantasized gratification, and reaction formation are well-known mechanisms and have been described in a wide variety of psychogenic disorders.

Further Factors in the Mother's Overprotectiveness

There are other factors that are psychodynamically operative in the mother's overprotectiveness. The mother may be overprotective as a way of compensating for basic feelings of maternal inadequacy. Another factor that contributes to the mother's overprotectiveness relates to vicarious gratification. Each time she ministers to the child she is vicariously gratifying her own dependency needs. She is psychologically giving to her projected self. Each time she indulges and infantilizes the child she vicariously gratifies her own desire to be the recipient of such indulgence.

Displacement and Projection of Anger

Coolidge and colleagues (11) describe other factors that contribute to the repression and projection of anger. They postulate that the hostile fantasies of the child are projected onto the world and make the school a particularly dangerous place. Such hostility, however, is projected indiscriminately and other areas are considered dangerous as well. The researchers also consider the mothers of these children to be inordinately uncomfortable with their children's anger. They harbor residua of their own childhood view that anger can destroy. Their overprotection serves to suppress and eliminate all overt expression of such anger. They may view the expression of anger to be devastating and may not be able to conceive of love and anger as coexisting. They may be significantly impaired in providing disciplinary and punitive measures because of their fear of their children's angry response. These attitudes contribute to the children's suppression and repression of hostility. Projection and displacement of hostility is commonly described in articles on school phobia.

Other Psychodynamic Factors

Sexual inhibition problems in the parents may contribute to the child's separation anxiety disorder. These "supermothers" may be so invested in their children that they have little investment in other activities, such as sex. And their passive-dependent husbands may relate to their wives in a mother-son pattern in which sex has little place. The mothers may be threatened by a sexual relationship with an adult male, but may be more comfortable with the milder sexuality of the mother-son relationship. In such situations the male child is used as a sexual-sensual surrogate by the mother. The processes by which this arrangement takes place are usually unconscious. It thereby warrants being a psychodynamic factor.

Another factor contributing to a child's separation anxiety disorder is the basic fearfulness of the parents. Having two parents who are both fearful is likely to contribute to feelings of insecurity in the child as he or she cannot rely upon either parent for strength and guidance in dangerous situations. The parents' primary way of dealing with danger (both real and fantasized) is by avoidance and flight. The dependency of the mother on the maternal grandmother deprives her of the reputation of being a strong, independent parent—something the healthy child very much needs. In addition, the passive-dependency of the father on the mother also deprives him of the reputation of being a strong parent. Even the maternal grandmother, who may be viewed as the matriarch, is basically a frightened person who is ever seeing danger in the world and fleeing from or avoiding it.

Another psychodynamic factor relates to the pampering the child receives at home. The child is often viewed by the mother as "God's gift to the world." And the child tends to view himself or herself similarly. In school, however, no such idolization of the child is evident, and therefore the school situation may be intolerable. As benevolent as the teacher may be, she is not going to indulge and pamper the child to the degree that occurs at home. The teacher may then come to be viewed as mean and rejecting by both the child and the mother. And this, of course, is considered to be another reason why the child should not go to school.

Concluding Comments Regarding the Psychodynamics

I have described what I consider to be the primary psychodynamic factors in the separation anxiety disorder. As mentioned, the therapist does well to appreciate that many of these factors may not be operative in a particular family being evaluated and treated. It is likely, however, that at least some of them will be. Each family must be considered distinct and unique and entitled to its own constellation of psychodynamic factors. To begin with the assumption that any particular pattern is automatically applicable may not only result in inadequate diagnosis, but will compromise significantly any treatment program based on such misapprehensions. I cannot emphasize this point too strongly. I sometimes refer to this phenomenon as the utilization of "applied psychodynamics." The caveat is an important one, especially for the novice therapist, who often compensates for lack of knowledge by applying to the patient any psychodynamic formulation that appears reasonable.

THE GENERAL STRUCTURE OF THE PSYCHOTHERAPEUTIC PROGRAM

Analytically-oriented and behavior therapists often view themselves as being proponents of contradictory theoretical persuasions, and they often provide therapeutic approaches that are exclusively consistent with their theories. I do not believe that such conflict is invariably necessary. Treatment of these children is a prime example. Some desensitization is warranted, not only for the conditioned fears that these children exhibit, but even for the phobic and anxiety factors in which there are complex psychodynamic contributions. A desensitization experience may still be helpful even when psychodynamic factors are operative. When the conditioned factor is contributing (as it most often is in these children), there is even a stronger argument for desensitization experiences in the therapeutic program. I will discuss below this aspect of the treatment in greater detail. These contributing factors do not exist in isolation, but interact with one another. Similarly, the therapeutic program does not involve directing one's attention to these items separately or seriatim, but addressing oneself to each factor and even to many together, as the situation warrants.

Desensitization

At this point, the reader is probably aware that my approach to the understanding of the separation anxiety disorder is that it is primarily psychogenic and that the primary approach to its alleviation should be psychotherapeutic. Although I emphasize the psychodynamic approach, I do not confine myself to a strictly individual psychoanalytic program. I work extensively with families in order to deal with the parental contribution to the child's disorder.

Principles of cognitive therapy are also incorporated into the therapeutic program, especially as they relate to the correction of distortions that are contributing. Furthermore, behavior modification techniques are also utilized, but in a more natural way as part of the normal course of the treatment rather than in a strict, formal manner in which objective assessment of changes is reported. And, when I believe they can be useful, I will also prescribe selected medications. Accordingly, in discussing the treatment approaches here I will focus primarily on the psychotherapeutic, but will comment as well on the role of other therapeutic modalities.

Waldfogel and colleagues (14) emphasize the importance of early intervention as it relates to prognosis. The longer most diseases remain untreated, the poorer the prognosis. This is especially the case for the school phobia. The longer one allows the symptoms to become entrenched, the more difficult it will be to get the child back to school. Children with separation anxiety disorder require an intensive therapeutic program. Optimally, they should be seen two to three times a week. Intensive work with the family—especially the mother—is crucial. As mentioned, without her active involvement the likelihood of successful treatment is very low. Ideally, the mother should be in treatment as well; however, she often has little insight into the fact that she has psychiatric problems and therefore has little motivation for meaningful therapy. In such cases she should be engaged on a counseling level. But even there, the therapist may meet with resistances—both conscious and unconscious. Although the father's participation in the treatment program is also advisable, my experience has been that he is most often unavailable. But even when he is available, his passivity and dependence on the mother make him an unlikely candidate for meaningful input into a therapy designed to bring about family change.

At the outset I attempt to lay down some very firm rules. The sessions are scheduled after school. I advise the parents that attempts must be made to get the child to school on time every morning. If, for whatever reason, the child does not make it in the morning he must return to school after the lunch break. After school we can discuss what happened during the day and the reasons why the child is having difficulty. The parents are also instructed not to indulge the child at home if panic becomes so great that he or she has to return home. Commonly, these children are allowed to watch television, play games, or otherwise enjoy their home activities. This only entrenches the problem. The parents are advised to create an atmosphere of "solitary confinement" as long as the child is home during school hours. They are urged to accept no excuse for not going to school. They should be discouraged from taking seriously minor complaints about physical illness and accepting as valid symptomatic complaints such as headache, dizziness, nausea, and stomachache. Only the most overt and definitely observable manifestations of physical illness should be accepted as a reason for the child's not going to school. And even then, it is preferable that the decision be made by the pediatrician or family doctor, rather than the mother or father.

The parents should be advised to push the child to the point of mild panic when urging him or her to go to school. They have to be helped to desensitize themselves to the bloodcurdling screams and suicidal threats that these children may utilize in order to avoid the school situation. They have to be helped to appreciate that the fear element is only part of such antics and that the coercive element is usually very much there. The therapist must impress upon the parents that there should be no day on which there are not at least two attempts made (morning and lunch time) to get the child to school. Leventhal and Sills (12) place great emphasis on the power struggles that are a necessary part of the treatment of these children.

All this is part of the desensitization program and necessary to initiate at the outset. As mentioned, an important contributing factor in the development of the separation anxiety disorder is the conditioning process. The child has been programmed to view the world as a frightening place. Accordingly, a program of systematic desensitization is warranted as a direct therapeutic approach to this aspect of the problem. I do not, however, believe that there should be rewards given to the child. The reward for staying in school should be the ego enhancement that comes from having overcome the fear and the knowledge that one gains from the educational process. The reader may consider this a somewhat idealistic goal, especially for children who are school-phobic. However, I believe that providing material rewards for academic performances is dangerous business. It directs the child away from the primary purpose of education—which is to learn for the gratification that knowledge provides.

In school, as well, the desensitization component of the therapeutic program should be utilized. This requires the dedicated cooperation of the school. The program that I prefer is one in which there is a progressive diminution in the time that the mother is allowed to remain in school. In addition, I do not suggest that attempts be made to get the child to go into his or her regular classroom from the outset. Rather, I suggest that the child first be brought to a resource room or other place where he or she can join a small group of children being tutored. Ideally, there should be two or three students in such a group.

In addition, if possible, it is preferable that one of the students be a classmate, someone who is in the child's homeroom class and requires resource room supplementation. It is generally easier for a child to remain in school as part of such a small group than to enter into a classroom that may contain many children. The child receives more attention in the resource room and is more likely to develop a relationship with the teacher as a substitute for that which he (she) has with the mother. Of course, there are many differences—especially the fact that the teacher is not likely to be anywhere near as indulgent as the child's mother.

Over time, the child should be encouraged to remain in the resource room for increasingly longer periods. Finally, attempts are made to have the child return for short periods to the regular classroom. Here, accompanying the classmate from the resource room to the homeroom can be useful. The classmate then becomes a transitional person, somewhat similar to the resource room teacher. Progressively longer periods of toleration of the regular classroom routine are then encouraged.

Unfortunately, the cooperation that one gets from the parents of these children often leaves much to be desired. In every session they may come in with yet another excuse for not having followed the aforementioned recommendations. They may misinterpret, forget, and distort the instruction to the point where the total program may be subverted. The number of rationalizations is endless: "He had the sniffles yesterday and I didn't want to send him to school with a cold," "I felt his head and I'm sure he had a temperature," and so on.

Attempts to help such mothers appreciate that they are rationalizing and that they basically are contributing to the perpetuation of the child's illness often prove futile. I often try to impress upon such mothers that nothing terrible will happen, even if the child does come down with an illness while in school. Attempts to impress upon them that the worst that can happen if the child becomes ill in school is that he or she will be returned home, is not generally responded to with receptivity. Rather, I am viewed as being insensitive, uncaring, and even defective when it comes to practicing good medicine. However, because I am "only a psychiatrist," my naiveté in this area is generally tolerated. In some cases, one can enlist the aid of the father. However, most often he too is swept up in the mother's delusion that she is a "supermother" and that my advice would only be followed by the most negligent of parents.

As mentioned, the aid of the school is important. The school's cooperation varies. Some schools quickly provide home tutoring for the school-phobic child. School personnel then need not involve themselves in the kind of desensitization program that is such an important part of these children's treatment. By allowing the child to remain at home they merely intensify the problem, in that the child's mother is now being given educational and legal sanction to keep the child at home. There is probably no better way to entrench the pathological tie between the mother and the child.

A not inconsequential effect of home tutoring is that the child's education suffers inordinately. It is rare that such tutoring is provided for more than a fraction of the educational exposure the child receives in school. Accordingly, the child falls even further behind, and the home tutoring thereby increases the likelihood that he or she will be fearful of returning in the future. Sometimes the school needs a doctor's statement that the home tutoring is necessary for medical reasons. I have never signed such a recommendation, and cannot imagine myself ever providing one. Hippocrates's caveat *Primum non nocere* is certainly applicable here: "Above all, do not harm."

The school should be asked to tolerate to a reasonable degree these children's antics and disruptions. They may consider the aforementioned program to be inhumane and may view the therapist who recommends it to be at best insensitive and at worst sadistic. There is no question that pressuring these children into going to school may be viewed as cruel; however, it is no more cruel than giving an infant injections that may cause pain, but may protect the child from a host of dreaded diseases. There are times when school authorities have appeared to agree with my recommendations, but have signified their acceptance of the program with comments such as "Well, you're the doctor" and "You must know what you're doing." Such "compliance" with the desensitization program may be disheartening, but it may be the best one can obtain from certain school personnel.

Factors in the school itself may be contributing to the disorder. The child may be reacting to realistic fears such as those induced by harassment or attacks from older students or maltreatment at the hands of a sadistic teacher. Sometimes such children will exhibit panic comparable to that seen with school-phobic children. Bolman (15) emphasizes the importance of the examiner's looking carefully into the school situation in order to assess its possible role in the disorder. Children in this category, like those who exhibit truancy, do not suffer separation anxiety and this can be an important differentiating diagnostic criterion. In these situations the therapist should do whatever possible to bring about changes in the school personnel and related factors in order to ameliorate the child's symptoms.

Behavior Modification

Lazarus and colleagues (16) have developed a therapeutic program based on the learning theory approach. It incorporates a combination of classical and operant conditioning procedures. When avoidance behavior is motivated by high levels of anxiety, classical counterconditioning techniques are used. These include reciprocal inhibition methods such as conversation from the therapist designed to encourage and relax the child. When anxiety is minimal, and avoidance behavior is apparently motivated by secondary reinforcement (i.e., parental attention at home), operant conditioning is used, such as providing various rewards contingent on school attendance. The program is a complex modification of systematic desensitization: the child is presented with a series of anxiety stimuli, such as approaching school, but not attending. These stimuli gradually approximate the source of the phobic reaction. The child is thus eventually able to attend school without the phobic anxiety previously experienced. The secondary gains generally shift to rewarding the appropriate behavior, thus reinforcing the child's willingness to stay at school.

As mentioned, I incorporate the principles of behavior modification into the therapeutic program. Most important, I utilize extensively desensitization via instructing the mother to strongly encourage the child to go to school and enlist the aid of school authorities to place reasonable pressures on the child to expose himself or herself to the anxiety-provoking situation. My primary criticism of those who utilize exclusively behavior modification is that they are not giving proper attention to the complex underlying psychodynamic factors that are operative in bringing about this disorder. I prefer to utilize such behavior modification principles in a natural way, in the course of the therapeutic program.

Psychotherapy With the Child

The therapeutic approaches discussed thus far direct their attention to the symptomatic manifestations of the disorder. I view these as necessary parts of the treatment, but not central elements in the therapeutic approach. The therapist's primary attention should be directed to the underlying problems that are at the root of the disorder. With regard to the psychodynamic factors, there is the danger that the therapist will view the central underlying problems in a somewhat oversimplified fashion. To restrict oneself to the overprotection/overdependency problem is to take a narrow view of the child's difficulties. To focus on the phobia or the school is also to take a restricted view of the child's difficulties. These children are not simply fearful of their long list of objects and situations. Rather, they are basically afraid of life. The world for them is indeed a dangerous place and they feel themselves helpless to cope with all the menacing forces that lie in wait for them. Our goal in therapy, then, is not only to get the child back to school. The goal of therapy is to help these children reach an age-appropriate level of independence—especially with regard to separation and independence from the mother.

Regarding the individual work with the child, I generally begin each session with the mother and child together. This is my usual procedure. For the child with separation anxiety disorder, however, I try to confine such joint meetings to a very short period at the outset of the session. As described elsewhere (17) I generally work closely with parents and refer to my primary therapeutic approach with most children as *individual child psychotherapy with parental observation and intermittent participation*. However, there are certain situations in which close ongoing work with the parent and child together is contraindicated. Children with separation anxiety disorder are in this category. To keep the mother in the room with the child throughout most of the session is to perpetuate the very psychopathology one is being asked to alleviate. This does not mean, however, that one should not allow the mother to step into the room at any point. She can be a valuable source of information and provide other forms of therapeutic assistance. Accordingly, the compromise I make is to have the mother in the room during the first few minutes in order to get any information that she may be able to provide me. After that, she is asked to sit in the waiting room, and I generally do not have further contact with her during the session unless the situation warrants it.

The main goal of treatment is not simply to get the child back to school. It is to help the child reach the level of independence and maturity that is appropriate for his or her age. I try to help the child mature in *all* areas of functioning whether they be in the home, neighborhood, or school. I try to help him or her learn better ways of adapting to the realities of life. The child needs to be helped to grow up in all major areas of functioning. If, for example, the child complains about being picked on by other children, I will discuss in great detail the various ways that children can handle those who try to scapegoat them. Any enhanced knowledge or competence that I can help my patients gain is likely to be therapeutic. The child has to be helped to appreciate that cowards and brave people are quite similar in that both suffer with initial fears. Cowards submit to them; brave people force themselves to tolerate their fears while doing the thing that they know they must do. It is to be hoped that this advice will not only contribute to the child's tolerating school anxiety but, even more important, tolerating the inevitable fears that we all suffer when we enter new and strange situations—especially those that are challenging. I try to help the child tolerate and squelch the fears most people have of asserting themselves and encourage proper and appropriate self-assertion. I try to help the child appreciate that the discomforts associated with such self-assertion are generally far outweighed by the benefits to be derived from such expression. In general, I encourage direct expression of thoughts and feelings as a preferable method for dealing with the problems of life.

Regarding the central anger problem, this may be harder to deal with in treatment. I consider it to be more deeply repressed (both for the patient and the mother) and not as accessible to conscious awareness and discussion. However, this does not preclude my providing messages (via the mutual storytelling technique [17], The Talking, Feeling, and Doing Game [18], and other techniques described previously) that relate to the problem. I try to help reduce children's guilt over their anger. I attempt to do this by advising them that angry thoughts and feelings toward parents are normal and that all human relationships are mixtures of both loving and hateful feelings. I may point out that the main difference between them and others is that they feel worse about their anger than others, but they do not differ from others in regard to the presence of angry thoughts and feelings. I also attempt to help them appreciate that angry thoughts and feelings cannot bring about their realization.

I take the opportunity to express my views on the subject of magic and include the fact that thoughts are not magical and cannot make things happen in the world outside of the head in which the thoughts reside. For a younger child I might in the course of play therapy make comments along these lines: "This boy was really angry at his friend who had now become his enemy. He was so angry that he wished him dead. But no matter how hard he wished him dead, he still didn't die. No matter how hard he strained his brain, the other kid still stayed alive. He kept wishing it for hours—praying that it would happen—but nothing happened. At least a thousand times he said, 'I wish he was dead'—but the other kid still remained alive. The enemy didn't feel any pain and he didn't even suffer with a scratch—even after all those thoughts and wishes. It took all that to help the boy realize that *thoughts can't harm!*"

I try to help children appreciate that all human relationships are ambivalent, including the relationships children have with their mothers. I try to help them alter internal dictates regarding anger, dictates such as: "Good boys never get angry at their mothers or fathers," and "Curse words are bad—especially if you think them about your mother or father."

On a number of occasions my therapeutic work has resulted in the child's returning to the school, to the point where there has been minimal if any anxiety. I have accomplished this without significantly delving into the underlying anger problems. The parents and the child at that point have raised the question as to whether further therapy is warranted. It may come as a surprise to some readers that I will not place great pressure on the parents to keep the child in treatment at this point. The primary factor that motivates people to remain in treatment is psychological pain. When there is less pain there is less motivation for treatment. In child therapy, the pain is rarely the child's. Most often it is the parents'. When the child is attending school and both the parents and child have learned to tolerate the separation, they may have little pain. One might argue that recurrence is likely if the underlying problems—especially those around anger—are not worked through. My experience has been that this is not the case. Perhaps the anger theory (and that's basically what it is) is wrong. Perhaps the desensitization program was all that was needed. Or, perhaps the messages I have provided regarding the central anger issues have operated to bring about the changes without there being much conscious awareness on the part of the child and the parents that these factors have been operative in bringing about the therapeutic change.

The therapist who pressures the parents into keeping the child in treatment because of the belief that the underlying problems have not been worked through (especially if "working through" must include conscious awareness of underlying psychodynamics), may be doing the family a disservice. The increasing resentment caused by such pressure may compromise the relationship between the parents and the therapist. And this can often interfere with the progress of the treatment. In addition, it may "sour" the child on therapy and therefore reduce the efficacy of the treatment. Such souring may make it more difficult for the child to reenter treatment if it is warranted in the future. These experiences with the anger elements in the separation anxiety disorder lend support to my original speculation that the conditioning element may be more important than the anger factor in bringing about the separation anxiety disorder. Further experience in the treatment of this disorder should enable us to make more definitive statements regarding this issue.

The Use of Medication

It would appear that anxiolytic agents would be the drugs of choice in the separation anxiety disorder. I do prescribe such drugs, but I am careful to point out to both the parent and the child that they can only serve a minor role. Believing as I do that underlying family problems are central to the development of the disorder, I do not wish to convey the notion that the whole problem can be dispelled by a drug. The drug that I have most frequently used is diazepam (Valium). I generally start the child on 2 to 4 milligrams in the morning and at lunch time. I then progressively increase the dose—often to the sublethargic level. Although anxiolytic agents may contribute somewhat to the reduction of the child's anxiety, one runs the risk that they will interfere, as well, with the learning process because of the lethargic side effects one sees with higher doses. I will generally tell these children that the medication will probably help them to be less scared, but that they cannot expect it to solve the whole problem. I emphasize that their own willpower will be required and that we will have to discuss after school some of the family problems that are contributing to their fears.

Gittelman-Klein (19) and Gittelman-Klein and Klein (20) are strong proponents of the use of the tricyclic antidepressant imipramine in the treatment of the separation anxiety disorder. They consider these agents to be capable of blocking the peripheral physical manifestations of the panic state. Gittelman-Klein and Klein point out, however, that psychotherapy is also warranted in the treatment of these children. Although my own experience with imipramine in the treatment of the separation anxiety disorder has been limited, I have not been significantly successful with its utilization. I have not found it to be as effective as diazepam in reducing the symptomatology.

Family Therapy

Although the parental contribution (especially the mother's) is an important consideration in the development and perpetuation of the separation anxiety disorder, it is not always wise to utilize a family therapy approach. Although the psychopathology of the parent and the interrelationship between the parental psychopathology and the child's should clearly be dealt with, placing the child in a family therapeutic setting is likely to perpetuate the symbiotic ties. Because of this consideration many hold that family therapy is contraindicated in the treatment of the separation anxiety disorder. I am not in agreement. I believe that there is a reasonable compromise, namely, devoting some of the therapeutic time to individual work with the child and some of it to family therapy and other kinds of family involvement. In this way the child can have experiences of separation and yet the interpersonal problems can also be dealt with in the optimum way.

Skynner and Robin (3) propose a therapeutic approach focusing on the family dynamics. The major goal is to enable the family to overcome the pathological situation by achieving insight into the underlying psychodynamics of their interactions. They have devised a number of techniques designed to adapt to the maturity, ego-strength, and motivation of the parents. Where possible the parents act as the agent by which the crucial challenge (i.e., understanding the pathology of the mother-child relationship) is presented to the child. One or more therapists meet with the child and parents together to provide insight and interpretation. Alternative methods, employed in cases where the parents lack the ego-strength to recognize and verbalize these therapeutic insights, include participation of the therapist to supply the missing parental functions. Davidson (21) and Malmquist (22) also describe family therapy approaches to the understanding and treatment of separation anxiety disorder.

RESIDENTIAL TREATMENT

One could argue that residential treatment is strongly indicated for children with separation anxiety disorder because it provides an enforced separation from the mother and is thereby useful in breaking the symbiotic tie. This is a powerful argument in favor of hospitalization. However, I believe that there are many factors that argue against such placement. Elsewhere (23) I have described in detail my views on hospitalization of children. Placing the child in such a setting removes him or her from the particular school to which the therapist is trying to help the child adjust. The school in the residential setting is part of the same protective environment and even when attended is not likely to be as anxiety provoking as going off to one's own school outside. Also, it is not likely that the school in the residential center or hospital is going to be as demanding or as adequate as the school to which the child has been going.

There is an artificiality to the environment of a hospital that is very different from that of the home, neighborhood, and school. The child is deprived of working through, in the natural setting, a wide variety of other fears that are probably present along with the school phobia. Placement in a hospital deprives the child of opportunities for working through these problems in the natural setting.

REFERENCES

1. Johnson A, Falstein E, Szurek SA, et al: School phobia. Am J Orthopsychiatry 11:702–711, 1941
2. Gordon DA, Young RD: School phobia: a discussion of aetiology, treatment and evaluation. Psychol Rep 39:783–804, 1976
3. Skynner A, Robin C: Applications of Family Techniques to the Study of a Syndrome: School Phobia. New York, Brunner/Mazel, 1976, pp 306–328
4. American Psychiatric Association: Diagnostic and Statistical Manual of Mental Disorders, 3rd Edition, Revised. Washington, DC, American Psychiatric Association, 1987
5. Eisenberg L: School phobia: a study of communication and anxiety. Am J Psychiatry 114:712–718, 1958
6. Hersov LA: Refusal to go to school. J Child Psychol Psychiatry 11:137–145, 1960
7. Gardner GE, Sperry BM: School problems-learning disabilities and school phobia, in American Handbook of Psychiatry, Vol II. Edited by Arieti S. New York, Basic Books, 1974, pp 116–129
8. Coolidge JC: School phobia, in Basic Handbook of Child Psychiatry, Vol II. Edited by Noshpitz JD. New York, Basic Books, 1979, pp 453–463
9. Coolidge JC, Brodie R, Feeney B: A ten-year follow-up study of sixty-six school phobia children. Am J Orthopsychiatry 34:675–684, 1964
10. Schmitt BD: School phobia—the great imitator: a pediatrician's viewpoint. Pediatrics 48:433–438, 1971
11. Coolidge JC, Tessman E, Waldfogel S, et al: Patterns of aggression in school phobia, in The Psychoanalytic Study of the Child, Vol XVII. New York, International Universities Press, 1962, pp 319–333
12. Leventhal T, Sills M: Self-image in school phobia. Am J Orthopsychiatry 34:685–695, 1964
13. Gardner RA: Separation Anxiety Disorder: Psychodynamics and Psychotherapy. Cresskill, NJ, Creative Therapeutics, 1984, pp 18–22
14. Waldfogel S, Tessman E, Harhn P: A program for early intervention in school phobia. Am J Orthopsychiatry 29:324–333, 1959
15. Bolman WM: Systems theory, psychiatry, and school phobia. Am J Psychiatry 127:25–32, 1970
16. Lazarus AA, Davison GC, Polefka DA: Clinical and operant factors in the treatment of school phobia. J Abnorm Psychol 70(3):225–229, 1965
17. Gardner RA: The Psychotherapeutic Techniques of Richard A. Gardner. Cresskill, NJ, Creative Therapeutics, 1986, pp 364–464
18. Gardner RA: The Talking, Feeling, and Doing Game. Cresskill, NJ, Creative Therapeutics, 1973
19. Gittelman-Klein R: Pharmacotherapy and management of pathological separation anxiety. International Journal of Mental Health 4:255–270, 1975
20. Gittelman-Klein R, Klein DF: School phobia: diagnostic considerations in the light of imipramine effects. J Nerv Ment Dis 156(3):199–215, 1973
21. Davidson S: School phobia as a manifestation of family disturbance: its structure and treatment. J Child Psychol Psychiatry 1:270–287, 1960

22. Malmquist CP: School phobia: a problem in family neurosis. J Am Acad Child Psychiatry 4:293–319, 1965
23. Gardner RA: Psychotherapy With Adolescents. Cresskill, NJ, Creative Therapeutics, 1988, pp 734–742

2 Self-Destructive Preschool Children

Paul V. Trad, M.D.

ecent studies indicate that suicidal behavior may occur prior to adolescence. Some believe that young children are developmentally incapable of committing suicide because children lack the cognitive capacities to engage in and understand the permanent quality of this type of action. However, statistics reveal that suicide among 5- to 14-year-olds occurs every year. For example, in 1988, suicide among 5- to 14-year-olds occurred at a rate of 0.7 deaths per 100,000 people, or 243 children (1). The rate of suicide in the preadolescent population is the lowest of all age groups in the United States and has remained consistent, in contrast to the rate of suicide among adolescents, which has risen considerably. Moreover, children who suffer from a psychiatric condition, and especially those who are eventually hospitalized, have been found to have a higher suicide rate than children in the general population (2). Although the statistics for preadolescent suicide are not as dramatic as and do not receive as much of the media's attention as the statistics regarding older children, the interpretation of self-destructive tendencies that are manifested by the preadolescent population needs to be examined by using a developmentally oriented perspective.

Even more prevalent than outward self-destructive displays may be the incidence of annihilating fantasies among this young population (3). For example, suicidal ideation and nonfatal acts have been found to exist in preadolescents at the rate of 12% to 19% of the children in community samples and more than 75% of children who are psychiatric inpatients (4,5). One approach that has enabled researchers to devise models that test for the presence of suicidal ideation and behavior in young children is developmental psychopathology. The developmental perspective contrasts adaptive and maladaptive manifestations that emerge throughout childhood (6–8).

Although the impulse to commit a suicidal act is universal (9–11), a number of forces are at work in most individuals to check this urge. Some specific factors that have been found to be linked to suicidal ideation and behavior in young children include depression (12), depression with conduct disorders (13), antisocial behaviors (14), firesetting (15), and aggression (16–18). Furthermore, by adopting a longitudinal point of view, researchers have begun to predict the emergence of suicidal impulses and thus trace their etiologies (19). In this respect, suicidal behavior has been found to be correlated with a number of dimensions that encompass all facets of life: physiological, emotional, intellectual, social, cultural and economic (20–23). Other correlates include gender, family instability, and parental suicidal behavior (24). For example, Kosky has noted that suicidal behavior in young children appears to be strongly associated with the male gender, personal experiences of significant loss, academic underachievement, marital disintegration between the two parents, and past or current intrafamilial violence, including physical abuse of the child (25,26). These findings represent the areas of the research that need to be performed in order to better determine the nature of suicidal behavior among youths.

Two additional factors that may contribute to the development of suicidal ideation in young children involve impulsivity and self-esteem (27). First, impulsivity may play an important role in the self-destructive tendencies of young children more so than in their adult counterparts. Young children do not yet possess the self-regulation necessary for controlling their impulses. The child's developing capacities for self-control and self-regulation also contribute to the child's impulsivity in that these capacities coordinate attention and response in the developing child (28). Although some theorists have suggested that this dimension is a result of temperamental forces (29), other researchers concur that affective and cognitive regulation play an important role in a child's ability to control impulses (30). With regard to the child's affective capacity, researchers have documented instances in which overwhelming emotions were the cause of suicide (7). Mischel and Mischel (31) studied a group of children ranging in age from 4 to 11 years. These researchers observed that the younger children often sought immediate gratification even if they had to create self-defeating strategies in order to do so, whereas older children developed more primitive strategies or abstract ideation to control their impulses. These findings suggest that older children will be able to withstand more stress than younger children before they feel compelled to yield to their impulses.

Although suicidal behavior in children may be, to a degree, an impulsive act, even very young children are capable of engaging in intentional behavior. Shultz and colleagues (32) have distinguished between intentional and mistaken behavior. Intentional behavior refers to those acts that are performed to achieve a particular outcome, while mistaken behavior refers to a mismatch between the behavior and the intention. Kosky (25,26) has reported that in a recent survey of suicidal children, most children were serious in their intent. That is, they told the therapist they wanted to die and yet they were secretive in their purpose. Thus, children who exhibit suicidal tendencies may understand that suicidal acts will hurt them but nevertheless engage in self-destructive behaviors because they do, in fact, want to hurt themselves.

Another factor that may contribute to suicidal ideation and behavior in young children involves self-esteem. It appears that suicide among populations of all age groups generally results from a change in body- and/or self-image (33,17); likewise, Pfeffer (34) has suggested that children engage in suicidal behaviors to eradicate a negative self-perception. Self-perception is tied in part to processes involving the attachment bond and separation-individuation. The attachment bond with the caregiver can produce a positive self-concept. As attachment strengthens, so does the sense of self (35). Similarly, separation-individuation results in self-efficacy and self-esteem. If either of these processes are disrupted, a negative self-perception may result. Although the young child's limited verbal abilities restrict the quality of empirical data that can be obtained about their self-concept, studies of latency age suicidal children have revealed that their death wishes are accompanied by feelings of loss of the ideal self or of disappointment at their inability to satisfy ego ideals (36), as well as by low self-esteem (16). Thus, the developmental approach may enable researchers to obtain additional insight into the etiology of self-destructive behaviors in young children.

Among the most promising insights gleaned from the developmental approach has been the finding that self-destructive manifestations during childhood often emerge from feelings of hopelessness engendered by a chaotic family situation (37). Suicidal ideation may represent for the child a means to accomplish separation and/or individuation from the family (38) or may constitute a method for gaining a sense of control over environmental challenges (7,8). The belief that psychopathology is a means of adaptation to a frenzied world and an attempt to achieve a cohesive sense of self are very important insights derived from developmental psychopathology (39). The following case history of Alexi, which documents a preschooler's 3-year struggle to overcome self-destructive behavioral patterns, is dominated by the theme of domestic turbulence.

Three forms of self-destructive fantasy and/or behavior emerged. During the first few months of therapy, Alexi revealed a fascination with the annihilating effects of fire during fantasy interludes that punctuated the sessions. The patient also reported dreams with a fire motif and displayed a cigarette burn he had "accidentally" inflicted on himself. In the second year of treatment, a more dramatic self-destructive fantasy of Alexi's surfaced involving a desire to jump from the window of the therapist's office. The expression of this fantasy, which was combined with Alexi's physically aggressive behavior, was inevitably preceded by a period of cognitive disorientation, during which the patient became unresponsive to the therapist's queries and seemingly oblivious to his environment. Finally, a fantasy involving physical assault with a knife dominated during the opening months of the final year of treatment.

Because the patient was engaging in self-destructive behaviors without comprehending the permanency of their potential outcomes—i.e., death—he was considered suicide-like. In other words, because he lacked the specific intent to die, his self-destructive impulses only resembled actual suicidal tendencies. Once the full import of the patient's suicide-like ideation became evident, therapeutic goals and strategies were formulated to circumvent the normative developmental orientation that causes preschool-age children to be oblivious to the consequences of self-annihilating activities. For example, it was conveyed to the patient that the therapist as a rational authority figure would not collude with desires to indulge in self-destructive ideation. Another strategy involved tutoring the patient in alternative methods for managing overwhelming feelings that emanated from an excessively fused relationship with the maternal figure and a tenuous relationship with a distant paternal figure.

Also, in order to overcome the patient's misconceptions about the ramifications of his self-destructive fantasies, the therapist relied upon play techniques. This stage of therapy was designed to elicit from the patient an overview of who he believed himself to be. Each time a fantasy was expressed, the child would be gently confronted with the issue of what would happen if the self-destructive behavior were to be performed. Special emphasis was placed on conveying such notions as "finality" and "irreversibility" which, as researchers have pointed out, are inaccurately understood by preschoolers (40,41).

The therapist continued with suggestions that the child consider the result if the doctor could not fix him, and thus moved the child to a more realistic representation of self-destructive ideations. As the treatment progressed, the patient displayed an ability to regulate ideations in a more adaptive fashion. Sullivan's (42) notion of "detailed inquiry" was particularly useful during this stage of the therapeutic process. In keeping with the therapeutic goals, the patient exhibited increased willingness to engage in conversation with the therapist about what stimulus had triggered the fantasy; correspondingly, the self-destructive ideations themselves became less potent and were less likely to be transformed into physical behaviors.

During the final year of treatment, the patient became fascinated with the story of Goldilocks. He repeated this story to the therapist at virtually every session, and with each recitation he became more captivated by details pertaining to the main character's ability to find household possessions that were "just right" for her. Interest in this particular fairy tale was interpreted by the therapist to be an assertion that the patient was adjusting to his proper position in his own family. This interpretation was related to the patient and, hence, "termination," the final therapeutic stage, was completed. This phase coincided with events in the family that enabled the patient to separate somewhat from the maternal orbit and to resolve previous hostilities towards his father.

CASE HISTORY

Alexi G. was a $3\frac{1}{2}$-year-old male of normal height and slightly below average weight. A comprehensive physical examination revealed no organic abnormalities. The patient had been referred for consultation because of disruptive outbursts in nursery school during which, according to teacher reports, he had threatened to "kill" his father. The child's mother reported destructive behavior, particularly a fascination for playing with fire that dated back 3 months.

This coincided with the time the child's father departed from the household. In addition, Mrs. G. reported that Alexi had begun to show signs of fitful sleeping patterns, coupled with a tendency to lapse into sullen, inexplicable silences.

Conversations with the patient's mother during the first few months of treatment revealed that the child was the product of a third, unplanned pregnancy. Throughout the gestation period, Mrs. G. had considered having an abortion. Her marriage to the patient's father occurred during the seventh month of pregnancy, largely as a consequence of family pressure. The marital union was troubled from its inception. The patient's mother reported financial problems, coupled with alcoholism and gambling on the part of her husband. Mrs. G. also confessed to amphetamine and marijuana use during the pregnancy, in direct contravention of her obstetrician's cautions. She gained an excessive amount of weight prior to delivery and told of a deep postpartum depression that lingered for approximately 1 year. The delivery was by cesarean section, during which Mrs. G. experienced brief anaphylactic shock due to the anesthetic. Although the patient was initially breast-fed, this behavior was discontinued after the fourth week when a cyst was discovered in Mrs. G.'s left breast. On several occasions, Mrs. G. voiced regret that the child had not been a girl.

According to the patient's mother, her husband had lived with the family only intermittently during the first 3 years of the patient's life. Quarrels between husband and wife were frequent, often involved physical abuse, and were witnessed by the patient. On one such occasion, Mr. G. had set fire to the family photo album with a cigarette lighter in the presence of the patient. He had stomped out the fire with his feet, scattering the charred ashes around the living room. Mrs. G. reported that she had become "hysterical" during the episode, but that the patient had seemed "fascinated" and had watched the events unfold "like he was hypnotized."

Mrs. G. also expressed profuse affection and concern for the patient. She commented that each morning they "worked out together in [her] bedroom." After the exercise sessions, the patient's mother would take a shower, while her son would "lie on the bed waiting for me." The patient's mother also reported that when the patient exhibited his periodic outbursts or played with fire, she had devised a method of "calming him down." She would bring the patient into the bedroom, where both mother and son would lie on the bed and sing songs, while Mrs. G. stroked her son's hair and "held him close." This ritual seemed to have a "soothing effect," she reported, and the patient often fell asleep in her arms.

At the initial interview, the patient was reticent about engaging in conversation, although intermittently he smiled directly at the therapist in a seductive fashion, while batting his eyelashes. Occasionally, he would approach the therapist very closely, belly extended outward. When asked to draw some pictures, the child was cooperative. He drew several human figures, with detail appropriate for his developmental status. Of particular note was the sketch of a wrestler with exaggerated teeth and disproportionately large clenched fists, which the patient demonstrated by clenching his own fists in the air. At this first session, the patient unexpectedly began emitting a barrage of profane language in a ritual-like fashion. Upon being questioned, he abruptly changed the subject and commented that fire engines passed by his house at night, disturbing his sleep.

During the first few months of therapy, the patient returned to his preoccupation with fire during stream of consciousness ramblings. He related several dreams involving burning houses with "children laughing." In each of these instances, the patient seemed aware of the fact that his affective response was inappropriate for the details of the dream, and he would look at the therapist in a challenging manner.

During the third month of treatment, the child entered the therapist's office without greeting and gravitated immediately to the toy cabinet. In slow, measured movements, he began to systematically remove some toys. Each time an item was removed, the patient would hold the toy in the therapist's direct line of vision. As the therapist acknowledged each toy, the patient would replace it in the cabinet and reverse the position of the cabinet's sliding doors. The therapist began to verbalize this behavior, suggesting to the patient that his motions suggested an exercise in revealing and concealing.

At the next session, the patient appeared agitated and disoriented. He ignored the therapist for the first few minutes and began playing with the blackboard eraser, chanting "it won't erase; it won't erase." After pounding the eraser against the blackboard for several minutes, the patient became enveloped in a cloud of smoke. As the chalk dust grew denser, the patient blurted out, "I burned my finger with Daddy's cigarette." When the therapist asked to see the injury, the patient approached cautiously and extended his left index finger, displaying a fresh scar. After allowing the therapist to inspect the injury for a moment, the patient jerked his finger away and began speaking of the "fire engines" he had heard the previous night. Then, leaning forward in a stance of confidentiality, he reported a dream in which "100 cops and 100 robbers" were battling in a "big garage." Soon the garage burst into flames.

"One hundred firemen" arrived, followed by "100 magic snakes." The snakes were "magic," the patient explained, "because they disappeared whenever the firemen looked at them." This dream was reported in animated tones.

Following the conversation, the patient rose abruptly. He seemed oblivious to the therapist's further queries and instead, moved to the center of the room and began spinning around in chaotic motions. Without warning, he began to run to the window, hurling himself against the sill and slapping the palms of his hands against the window panes. In a clear and distinct tone, he yelled "I'm going to jump," several times in rapid succession. The therapist rose and approached the patient, who seemed oblivious to inquiry about the incident. Eventually the patient left the window area and returned to the middle of the room where he began playing calmly with a toy truck.

Thereafter, behavior involving the window was repeated at virtually every session for the next several months. At these times, the therapist verbalized his observations about the patient's behaviors, providing the patient with an objective account of his actions: "I see that you are thinking about hurting yourself and jumping out of the window." Initially, the patient ignored requests to discuss this behavior with the therapist. As treatment progressed, the therapist's queries were met with a barrage of profane language and physically aggressive acts, in the form of punching and biting the therapist's arm. In response to this aggression, the therapist first interpreted for the patient his behavior: "Your violent and destructive behavior makes me think that you must be feeling very angry." The therapist then asked the patient to express why he was feeling angry. The therapist then set limits on the patient, encouraging him to express his anger but not to act on it. Gradually, the patient was able to respond to inquiries about what would happen if he jumped from the window. To aid the child in understanding consequences of destructive behavior, the therapist suggested that the child throw a doll from the window. The child retrieved the damaged doll and examined it, thereby gaining an understanding of the irreversibility of his destructive behavior. This was videotaped, and the therapist later viewed the tape with the child, stopping for discussion at different points. For example, the videotape would be stopped where the therapist and child had left the office and the screen was, therefore, empty. To assist the child in differentiating between reversible and final phenomena, the therapist would ask questions:

"Why is the office empty?"

"Because we went to get the doll," the child responded.

"What will happen next?"

"We will go back to the room and fix the doll," the child answered.

"If you jumped out of the window, what would happen?" the therapist continued.

"You would fix me."

"What if I could not fix you?"

"I would not come back."

"How do you feel when the room is empty?" . . . and so on.

To help the child identify his feelings prior to his window approach, the therapist would stop the tape and ask the child to think about what he was thinking and feeling at that time. This technique of reviewing the tape of himself gave the child an opportunity for a more objective examination of his motivations and his behaviors as well as their consequences. Additionally, it set the stage for development of alternative methods of response and action. By the fourth month after this manifestation first surfaced, the child was able to express a complicated scenario describing what occurs when someone jumps from a window.

As the child's window-running behavior began to abate over the next few months, it was replaced by another form of involvement with the window. Periodically, during the middle of the session, the patient would interrupt his play activities and slowly walk to the window, where he would stand quietly looking out. Upon being questioned, he responded that he was "looking for Daddy."

During the second year of therapy, the patient engaged in a repetitive fantasy about knives. He commented that he had cut himself "from the belly button up" and would pull up his shirt, tracing an imaginary scar over his abdomen. Upon being questioned, he noted that the injury had been an "accident," because the knife just "popped" in his hands. Intermittently, he would report that his father had "lots of knives" and a "big moustache," similar to the therapist's moustache. By the end of the second year of treatment, the fantasy involving the knife had diminished, with the patient reporting that his father had taught him karate, which could "block the knife" from "hurting people."

During the third and final year of treatment, the patient engaged in his own variation of the Goldilocks fairy tale. He emphasized details of the story involving the character's ability to find a place that was "just right" for her within the bears' household. The patient appeared to derive pleasure from telling the therapist this story and became especially enthused at the tale's conclusion, when he would disengage from the chair, approach the therapist, and urge him to repeat in unison the phrase "just right." This conveyed the child's readjustment of his place in his own family, which included delineation of boundaries that allowed individuation from his mother and the start of resolution of hostilities toward his father. By this juncture, teacher and parental reports indicated that the child's disruptive behavior and profane outbursts had ceased. The patient was also reported to be able to engage in cooperative play activities with peers. His frenetic "window crashing" behavior and fantasies pertaining to fire and knife cutting had also remitted. Psychotherapy was terminated shortly thereafter, although monthly assessments by a family therapist were maintained. ·

ISSUES FACED BY THE CHILD

A number of etiologic theories are useful in analyzing this case. First, based on the patient's age, developmental status, and family configuration, it appears likely that a network of Oedipally charged emotions had triggered some of his self-destructive ideation. Undifferentiated closeness with the maternal figure was suggested by Mrs. G.'s report of morning exercise sessions with her son, and episodes of quelling his outbursts by lying on the bed and holding him "close." This pervasive closeness to the maternal figure was not buffered by the countervailing presence of a paternal figure since, as reported by Mrs. G. and confirmed by the patient, Mr. G. was only a sporadic occupant of the household. When a child is raised in an anxiety-ridden environment such as this, he will have difficulty developing a sense of inner security and self-esteem (39).

In addition, maladaptive features of the mother-child dyad exacerbate this problem (43). Given this scenario, self-destructive ideation may have accomplished a variety of goals for the patient. Through self-annihilation, he could symbolically disengage himself from his mother's grasp. Moreover, by jumping from the window, the child might fantasize a reunion with his father, thereby assuaging pangs of guilt he experienced at being too closely involved with his mother. It should be remembered that as the erratic window-running behavior began to abate, it was superseded by a less dramatic form of "window gazing," during which the patient expressed a desire to look for his father. In these sessions, the therapist suggested to the patient that he go to the window and describe what he sees. By doing this, the therapist encouraged the patient to verbalize his thoughts. This "window gazing" also served as a reality test; the therapist could verify the patient's observations. Finally, the patient may have fantasized that by leaping from the window, he would precipitate a reunion between his parents, enabling him to expiate any guilt he experienced from the close fusion with the mother.

Mahler and colleagues' theory of separation-individuation (44) offers a supplemental explanation for the self-destructive ideation predominating in this case history. According to this theory, the most noteworthy event occurring during the first 2 years of life is the child's separation—both physical and psychological—from the caregiver. In this case, the maternal figure harbored deep ambivalence toward the patient. The puerperal period was fraught with blatantly self-destructive behaviors, such as drug and alcohol abuse, whereas the postpartum period was colored by depression and an interference with breast-feeding patterns. Although these factors alone are not necessarily indicative of trait-psychopathology, in this instance a pattern emerged, with Mrs. G. alternatively blaming her son because her body was "fat and unattractive" and her breasts had become "lumpy and full of cysts" ever since her pregnancy, and then profusely declaring affection for her son. This combination of factors is a common precursor of the formation of a defiant, oppositional personality (39). Additionally, painful and anxious interactions between parent and child may result in an inability to separate (39) or a child's regressing to a simpler life stage (i.e., infancy) (45).

Given this evident ambivalence, it is probable that the patient's sense of self-esteem was undermined. As a result, while the patient yearned for separation from the maternal figure—along with its concomitant sense of autonomy—separation simultaneously represented a disruptive event, because distance from the secure orbit of the mother reminded the patient of his undeveloped sense of individuality. Suicide-like behavior patterns may thus have symbolized a dramatic effort by this patient to disentangle himself from the maternal field. This form of separation may have been chosen for two reasons: first, because the maternal figure thwarted normal efforts by the child to differentiate; and second, because the patient's father, by leaving the house after burning the family's mementos in such a violent and tempestuous fashion, may have conveyed the notion that separation is accomplished through impulsive behavior.

Seligman (46) and colleagues (47) proposed a theory of learned helplessness to explain why particular individuals perpetually replicate self-destructive behavior patterns in almost ritualistic fashion. According to this theory, individuals who are subjected to repeated episodes of uncontrollable stimuli eventually come to adopt a self-denigrating attitude that incorporates feelings of incapacity at altering external events, along with a pervasive mood of loss of control. This overwhelming mood of depression then interferes with cognitive and affective patterns. Occasionally, when the experience of depression reaches unendurable levels, the individual may engage in impulsive behavior in a desperate effort to stave off the debilitating repercussions of negative affect.

Also, Mrs. G.'s predominantly depressed mood was most likely transmitted to her son, whose perception of negative affect may have been compounded by the realization that separation from the caregiver would likely be an impossible feat. Plagued by feelings of hopelessness and emotional depletion, the patient engaged in self-destructive behavior as a means of surmounting debilitating affect. This theory is given credence by the fact that immediately prior to engaging in the window-crashing behavior, the patient would inevitably become acutely disoriented, incapable of performing even simple tasks or responding to the therapist's queries.

Tauber (48) discusses the concept of "disordered affect" in terms of a pervasive element that is evident in all aspects of the patient's personality. Disordered affect is the clinical state in which an intolerance for uncertainty and independence is coupled with a circumscribed sense of joy and other positive affect. The first phase in its development is described as "ambivalent attachment." In this phase, the caregiver's emotional ambivalence generates in the patient contradictory desires. The patient fears being alone and seeks the caregiver to help him in negotiating the environment; however, at the same time, he wants to avoid the caregiver, who triggers feelings of rejection and powerlessness with each new contact. In the second phase of this disorder, the patient creates an elaborate defensive structure to protect himself from his mother. This structure takes the form of a narcissistic orientation that may become exacerbated as the individual enters a necrophilic phase, characterized by fantasies of extravagant self-destructiveness. Disordered affect is manifested in all interpersonal relationships as well as in feelings for the self. It results in the tendency to veer away from uncertainty, aliveness, and any form of independence, for these states are unduly anxiety-provoking.

In accordance with this, Tauber (48) asserts that the goal of psychotherapy is to foster a commitment to living through loving and being loved as well as through logic and reason. In this manner, the therapist will aid the patient in tolerating vagueness and insecurity. Tauber adds that the path to "disordered affect" more often than not begins with an affective disturbance in the mother-child dyad (49,50). From its first appearance, the child's desire for healthy individuation is quickly quelled by the mother. The child, as a protective measure, then develops an abnormal degree of narcissism that consciously allows him or her to believe that it is the mother who needs the child and not vice versa. This veil, however, is merely a mask that hides the child's total dependence upon and inability to separate from the mother. The final step of this maladaptive relationship is the "disordered affect" that, according to Tauber, is characterized by "blurred—or even outright—fantasies of outrageous destructiveness" (48, p. 295).

Alexi's relationship with his mother quite clearly follows this trend; it began with Mrs. G.'s disappointment in her son's sex and her resentment of his having "ruined" her body. These sentiments were expressed both overtly and subtly to Alexi; however, they alternated with affirmations of love and devotion (i.e., Mrs. G.'s method of "calming" Alexi). Alexi's mother led him to the belief that, without her, he would be totally helpless and ineffectual. This belief, though, conflicted with Alexi's intense (yet healthy) desire to separate from his mother. As a result, Alexi became unable to cope with any degree of uncertainty and exhibited what Tauber calls disordered affect "a negation of life."

Thus, the goal of the therapist in Alexi's case was to "grasp the human condition" by understanding the maladaptive nature of the mother-child relationship. In addition, the therapist had to "give and receive love" by accepting Alexi unconditionally and teaching Alexi to trust him. He also had to "help Alexi develop the powers of reason." This was accomplished through confrontation with the consequences of fulfillment of Alexi's fantasies. Finally, the therapist had to help Alexi "acknowledge what is alive against its illusory representations and to tolerate uncertainty and insecurity" (48). Evidence of this accomplishment was Alexi's fascination with the Goldilocks story at the end of treatment—his assertion that everything was finally "just right."

ISSUES IN THE TRANSFERENCE RELATIONSHIP

The first sign that a therapeutic alliance had developed was in the third month of therapy when the child removed several toys from the cabinet, one by one, and showed them to the therapist. Upon receiving recognition of his actions, the child replaced each toy, closed that side of the cabinet, and removed another toy from the other side of the cabinet. By doing this, the child was testing the therapist to make sure that he was paying attention to the child's actions. Although the child's behaviors may not have been given attention at home, the child began to realize that the therapist, in contrast to his caregivers, was a person who would acknowledge his actions.

This behavior, in essence, indicated to the therapist that a relationship with transferential innuendoes was being developed. It resulted in the child's ability to trust the therapist and, hence, facilitated his ability to cope with the lack of a father figure within his home and the pervasive closeness of his relationship with his mother. Evidence of this outcome can be seen by the fact that the toy removing and replacing activity immediately preceded the session in which the child first displayed his suicidal behavior, implying that he felt secure enough with the therapist to share his fantasies through behavioral displays with him.

The Parents' Symptomatology

The symptomatology in this case may be delineated into two distinct categories. One constellation of behaviors, predominating during the first year of treatment, indicated an ambivalent posture toward the caregiving figure coupled with an impaired sense of self-esteem and autonomy. The second symptom cluster, which emerged with heightened intensity as treatment progressed, embodied a series of self-destructive manifestations. These two groups of symptoms were reminiscent of features listed under Oppositional Disorder and Major Depressive Episode in DSM-III-R (51). By the third and final year of treatment, most of this symptomatology had receded. Remaining dysfunctional symptoms at that time most closely fit the definition of Dysthymia in DSM-III-R.

With respect to the first category of symptomatology, the patient's initial response to the therapist revealed a tendency to engage in manipulative behavior. He was hesitant about engaging in conversation, but intermittently approached the therapist in a seductive fashion, displaying a suggestive facial expression and thrusting his body forward. The patient's ambivalence towards caregiving figures was demonstrated by outbursts of profane language directed against both parents. Comments with respect to the patient's mother were demeaning, while his remarks with regard to his father were tinged with aggressive intent. Although it is likely that the patient was in part repeating fragments of parental arguments during these outbursts of profanity, nevertheless he appeared to derive a degree of pleasure from engaging in verbal abuse directed against both parents, as revealed by laughter and smiles. Inappropriate body image was displayed through drawings of male figures with exaggerated teeth, forearms, fists, and genitals. Although the patient identified most of these figures as being his father, he occasionally commented that the sketches were self-portraits.

The second category of symptoms emerged towards the end of the first year of treatment. It is the therapist's contention that only after a secure transference bond had been forged did the patient trust the therapist sufficiently to reveal this symptomatology. Manifestations here involved a fixation on fantasies involving fire and burning imagery. The patient's apparent fascination with fire was also converted into physical behaviors, as confirmed by his mother's reports of burning toys and by his own display of a finger scar. These behaviors were likely connected with his father's burning of the family picture album. The patient also expressed an undisguised desire to jump from the window. Although this fantasy wish was not converted into physical reality, in the therapist's presence the patient would repeatedly fling himself against the sill of the window, often slapping the palms of his hands against the window panes. Initially, the patient ignored the therapist's queries about this behavior. Marshall and Doshi (52), in a study done with preschool-age children, found that normal preschool children did not project their real-life problems in doll-play fantasies but could use their imagination to act out situations. These researchers concluded that children with manifest problems may act out these conflicts without resorting to fantasy play. In this regard, children who act out their conflicts in this particular fashion may be viewed as being at a greater risk for taking self-damaging behaviors out on themselves. Thus, their inability to separate object from meaning places them at a higher risk for acting out self-destructive wishes.

ISSUES FACED BY THE THERAPIST: COUNTERTRANSFERENCE IDENTIFICATION

The transference bond that developed between Alexi and the therapist was instrumental in revealing Alexi's symptomatology. However, the countertransference feelings that this relationship evoked were just as significant.

First introduced by Freud in 1910, the concept of countertransference refers to the affective states in the therapist arising as a result of the patient's influence on [the therapist's] unconscious feelings (53). Based on the belief that the therapist evokes past conflict for the patient, the theory of counter-transference postulates that, correspondingly, the patient would evoke emotional content from the therapist's past. Although it can be initially perceived as an obstacle to the therapist's objectivity, with time countertransference can come to be viewed as a potentially valuable tool (54). As Schowalter (55) explained, if the therapist could learn to recognize and interpret the therapist's responses to the patient, eventually the countertransference feelings would serve to inform and guide the therapist.

Tower (56) was another researcher who praised the power of countertransference in facilitating the therapeutic relationship: "[countertransference is] the vehicle for the analyst's emotional understanding of the transference neurosis" (56). In other words, countertransference permits the therapist to emotionally experience the affective state of the patient. Tower also believes that the treatment milieu between patient and therapist is, at its most profound level, essentially a prototype of the mother-infant relationship, involving libidinal exchanges and complex unconscious, nonverbal channels of communication. It is therefore up to the therapist to be aware of, and attuned to, the workings of his own unconscious in order to help the patient work through his or her internal conflicts.

Two main varieties of countertransference have been noted by Springmann (57)—therapist-induced and patient-induced. Patient-induced countertransference emanating originally from the patient constitutes a component of the patient's intrapsychic configurations and should be utilized as interpretable material. Therapist-induced countertransference, however, is ultimately destructive to the therapeutic relationship and must be resolved by the analyst alone, without involving the patient. The therapist must therefore exert every possible effort to distinguish between the responses being evoked by the patient and those emanating from the analyst's own unconscious.

The milieu of child analysis, as Kohrman and colleagues (58) assert, is particularly prone to evoking countertransference. The child, by directly demanding responses and actions, tempts the therapist to postpone interpretation in order to either take action or to discharge the action impulse through excessive passivity. In addition, as Kohrman and colleagues caution, children can evoke regressive responses in the therapist that in turn cause him or her to identify with the child.

Children's proclivity toward action rather than verbal expression often acquires an aggressive dimension, as Anna Freud (59) has noted. Alexi exemplified this tendency when flinging himself against the windowsill or burning himself with a cigarette lighter, and when vividly describing his self-mutilation fantasies. Because the character of these actions was so vivid and powerful, the therapist's countertransference feelings became equally intense. However, as Kohrman and colleagues (58) noted, when the child does choose to convey affective states verbally, these verbalizations are more frequently accompanied by an appropriate action. In other words, their implicit instinctual drive becomes more immediately evident than with adults, and the responses they evoke in others are therefore more potent and intense.

Moreover, as Kohrman and colleagues (58) suggested, this action orientation of the child, although allowing the therapist to observe drive gratification, also means that the child will not relinquish his efforts to achieve gratification as readily as will an adult. Thus, in relation to the therapist, children will occasionally engage in seductive, coercive techniques or outright assault. This observation is especially pertinent to Alexi's case. Alexi was capable of attempting to seduce the therapist to his point of view, smiling enticingly and moving his body in a manner not generally seen in children. In the first few months of therapy, he would also hit the therapist on the arm if he was not allowed to do something or if an indication was made that his behavior was unacceptable.

It may be argued that once the therapist has alerted himself to the intensity of countertransference phenomena with young children, his task will be more easily accomplished than with an adult. The child's drives may be more directly expressed and therefore stronger, but they emerge on the surface more readily and in a purer form. Thus, once the therapist can analyze the countertransference with a modicum of skill, he can devise strategies for overcoming the powerful urges that the child cannot resist.

In Alexi's case, for example, the therapist found himself identifying with Alexi's plight and vulnerabilities. Every time he discovered himself overidentifying with Alexi's problems and resurrecting his own childhood memories, he was forced to analyze his feelings in an attempt to understand why they had arisen at that particular point within the treatment situation (8). The therapist was able to utilize a dream he had about Alexi, in which the little boy was in danger, to alert himself to the depth of the incipient psychopathology between mother and son. Ultimately, it was this knowledge of the overpowering force Mrs. G. exerted on Alexi's unconscious, coupled with the child's equally powerful empathic desire to fulfill his mother's wishes and gratify his own desires, that enabled the therapist to position himself as a buffer between parent and child and to devise strategies that would promote Alexi's adaptive separation from his mother's orbit.

Finally, Bernstein and Glenn (60), writing on the subject of the child analyst's emotional reactions to his patients, classified a series of typically encountered emotional reactions:

1. Countertransference;
2. Transferences to the patient;
3. Identifications or counteridentifications;
4. Experiencing the patient as an extension of the analyst's self; and
5. Reactions to the patient as a real person.

The first two categories were discussed earlier. It is this last category, according to Bernstein and Glenn, that is most crucial for achieving progress within the therapeutic setting. Within the therapist's reactions to the patient as a real person, there are empathetic reactions that can generate insight into the patient's emotional conflicts and evoke affective states that may be used during treatment.

Identification or counteridentification, first discussed by Fliess (61), alludes to the analyst's emotional responses that arise when identifying with the patient. Because the child psychiatrist, as Bernstein and Glenn (60) indicate, often works both with the child and the parents, and because a child can evoke submerged or buried memories more readily than adult patients, child patients can often exert a stronger pull than their adult counterparts on the unconscious processes of the therapist. Such was the case with Alexi's therapist, who became acutely aware of the times when Alexi evoked responses that he identified with based on his own individual experience.

Counteridentification, on the other hand, refers to the therapist's reaction to the patient's own identification with the therapist. This phenomena often includes a regression to a state in which the self and the object representations are poorly differentiated. In children, who tend to rapidly identify all adults with their parents, counteridentification renders the child psychiatrist susceptible to maternal or paternal feelings.

Viewing the patient as an extension of oneself can be even more insidious in that the therapist may imagine himself to be the parent of his patient or may view the child as a narcissistic extension of himself. According to Bernstein and Glenn (60), if this interference is serious, the analyst may regress and begin to envision a fusion with the patient as both parent and child. Such intense transferences are possible between therapist and child patient and must be short-circuited by the therapist through careful analysis and interpretations of feeling of identification with the patient.

THERAPEUTIC STRATEGIES

In addition to the strength of transference bonding between child and therapist, child therapy differs from its adult counterpart in the strategies of analysis and treatment.

Cognitive Interventions

During play, the child learns to master and organize past or current experiences and thoughts into a complex symbolic network, by having opportunities for expression and control over what may be uncontrollable and/or fearful circumstances in real life. By scaling thoughts down to these symbolic play enactments, the child masters the conflict through a true reorganization of thought. In the case of Alexi, the therapist's support helped him to practice and represent as a means of replacing direct acts (e.g., jumping out of the window) with expressive channels of a more adaptive nature. As treatment progressed, however, the patient was able to discuss the ramifications that "jumping out of the window" would entail. Although the patient seemed immune to notions of finality and irreversibility, consistent with his developmental status (41), as treatment progressed he became more adept at projecting the consequences of such self-destructive tendencies. Through reality-testing—for example, encouraging the child to explore, in depth, what would happen if his self-destructive ideations were acted out in the real world—the child developed cognitive skills useful for interpreting his behaviors and thoughts. In asking questions about real-life consequences of actions, the therapist strove to keep interactions at the highest cognitive level at which the child was capable of operating. Sometimes the therapist used methods of reasoning that he knew were slightly beyond the child's operational level, in an attempt to stimulate growth of the child's cognitive skills. This approach was rewarded by the progression of the child, whose cognitive limits expanded in fresh and vivid ways, especially during the second and final years of treatment. Other authors, such as Habermas (62), documented the therapeutic and cognitive value of working with children at, and slightly beyond, their most mature level of functioning. In this case, the outcome was the child's ability to separate fantasy of self-destruction from corresponding physical behaviors.

The patient's final indication of self-destructive ideation was revealed in his fantasy pertaining to knives. The imaginary wound on his "belly," described to the therapist in intricate detail, suggested a desire to fantasize about annihilating behaviors. Nevertheless, unlike the previous self-destructive manifestations, the knife fantasy was accompanied by no outward physical behaviors suggesting a proclivity to convert the imaginary sequence into physical behavior. Moreover, in conveying this fantasy, the patient generally maintained a coherent conversation with the therapist, indicating an ability to share the experience almost completely.

Family Interventions

Weiss (63) explains that the therapist not only interacts with the child but with the parents as well. Parental figures and teachers are indispensable, albeit sometimes biased, sources of information. It is from parents that the therapist can learn not only about the child's overt symptomology, but also about underlying dynamics at home that may have provoked the child's difficulties. For example, it was the interactions and discussions with both Mr. and Mrs. G. that helped the therapist unravel the family dynamics that led to Alexi's pathology.

The therapist conducted regular monthly family sessions with both parents in the presence of Alexi. In these sessions, the therapist discussed with both parents how they interpreted Alexi's development and behavior, and how they were coping with their son's aggressive impulses. The therapist confirmed that the parents were setting limits on these aggressive impulses. In order to ensure the success of his sessions with Alexi, the therapist attempted to verify that the family was supporting Alexi's progress rather than continuing to engage in behaviors that might reintroduce to the patient self-destructive impulses.

Physical Activity

Physical activity, both of the child and the therapist, is another technique that differs drastically from adult therapy. Whereas in adult therapy both therapist and patient face each other, or more traditionally, the patient lays on a couch, it is children's physical activity that can convey an infinite array of messages to the child therapist. Alexi's running to the window, his play fantasies with fire trucks, and his drawings all illustrated the conflicts he was grappling with internally but not yet able to verbalize. Thus, the child therapist must move away from adult-type verbalizations and concentrate on the child's more visually imagistic world in order to fully understand and interpret the young patient.

Gift-Giving

Finally, according to Weiss (63), gift-giving is one aspect of child therapy that is virtually unique. There are, according to Weiss, two forms of gift-giving that can occur: the child finding an object or toy in the therapist's office and asking to have or borrow it, or the child giving the therapist a gift. Weiss described this phenomenon as having great significance in terms of the communication between child and therapist.

At the beginning of Alexi's therapy, he would occasionally take toys from the therapist's office. The therapist did not respond to Alexi's behavior as others had previously. He asked Alexi instead, "How do you think the other children would feel if there were no toys to play with?," repeating the question every time he noticed a toy missing and encouraging Alexi to verbalize the reasons for his behavior, until Alexi eventually stopped taking toys. Another significant gift incident occurred near the end of Alexi's treatment, when he gave the therapist a statue of Saint Joseph. Significantly, Joseph, the caregiver and nominal father of Jesus, was not his biological father. In the same way, Alexi seemed to view the therapist as a kind of substitute parent—one who was helping him tame his impulses—and giving the statue to the therapist was Alexi's way of communicating this view.

The relationship with child and parents, the importance of the child's physical activity, and gift-giving are all factors unique to child therapy. As such, therapists working with young children must recognize the distinctive patterns of behavior such patients will exhibit and plan a treatment strategy that encompasses these important factors.

DISCUSSION

A $3\frac{1}{2}$-year-old male was referred for treatment after reports that the child was unable to socialize adequately and engaged in verbal outbursts involving profanity and patricidal wishes. Several months after psychotherapy was initiated, the child revealed several self-destructive fantasies and accompanying behaviors, including wanting to burn himself, to cut himself with a knife, and to jump from the window. This case substantiates notions that suicide-like behavior can occur in preschool-age children.

Moreover, it suggests that preschool children are capable of harboring fairly sophisticated self-destructive ideation patterns and occasionally engaging in behavior manifestations that indicate that fantasy wishes are actively being converted into self-destructive activities. For example, another case in which a preschool child manifested self-destructive ideation patterns was the case of Jason. Jason's mother was a substance abuser who was severely beaten by Jason's father when she was 5 months pregnant. Jason's father was in jail at the time of the referral. The reactions of Jason's mother to Jason's behavioral difficulties was limited; frequently she slapped him, and at other times she simply ignored him or withdrew from him altogether. Jason's grandmother became his primary caregiver.

Jason was referred to treatment at the age of 3 years and 10 months, when he began exhibiting maladaptive behavior at his nursery school. His nursery school teacher noticed that he began exhibiting unprovoked aggression toward his classmates and could not tolerate transition from one activity to another. In addition, he talked incessantly, was unable to sit still or sleep at naptime, and indicated to his teacher that "grandmother was using a knife." When his statement was clarified with Jason's grandmother, it became clear that the child had witnessed a confrontation between his grandmother and his mother, during which Jason's grandmother brandished a knife toward her daughter.

Jason's self-destructive fantasies were evident from the first session, when he made a block into a gun and said he wanted to shoot himself. Asked what would happen then, he answered, "Then I'd be dead . . . and then my Mommy would come and wake me up." Hostility toward the members of his family was evident during play. After a month of treatment, Jason demonstrated some ambivalence about his self-destructive ideas: "I don't want to be dead . . . I'm thirsty." He began to openly express a need for attention. He also began to tell the therapist about episodes of abuse and to express hostility toward his caregivers. As he continued to open up to the therapist, it became evident that there was a corresponding escalation in the expression of Jason's self-destructive behaviors immediately after some anger at others had been expressed. However, there was also a growing awareness on his part of his deliberate wish to hurt himself. Eventually he was able to make a clear connection between his feelings of hostility toward others, his guilt about these aggressive feelings, and his desire to harm himself. He began to respond to firm limit-setting and showed some concern for himself, in spite of repeated attempts at reckless behaviors. His aggressive tendencies became more subdued and were often accompanied by feelings of insecurity when he realized the potential outcome of his intentions.

To sever the transition between self-destructive fantasy wish and physically annihilating behavior, the therapist's task is to reorient the child's displays of cognitive deficit. Particular attention should be given to the fact that developmental status precludes such young children from inculcating concepts like "finality" and "irreversibility" with respect to self-destructive behavior. Thus, the therapist must function as a surrogate, providing appropriate vicarious cognitive and affective responses for children exhibiting these destructive behavioral patterns. Family configurations must also be examined in these cases as the most likely catalyst of the child's distorted thought processes. As in this case, it is important to assess whether caregiver alignments are appropriate to facilitate the child's resolution of Oedipal feelings and expression of autonomy. Finally, tutoring the child in strategies for overcoming negative affect—in this instance, triggered by maternal depression and paternal abandonment—is vital for ensuring that self-destructive patterns do not resurface during the early school years.

REFERENCES

1. National Center for Health Statistics: Monthly Vital Statistics Report, Vol 39: Advance Report of Final Mortality Statistics. Washington, DC, National Center for Health Statistics, 1988
2. Kuperman S, Black DW, Burns TL: Excess mortality among formerly hospitalized child psychiatric patients. Arch Gen Psychiatry 45:277–282, 1988
3. Cohen-Sandler R, Berman AL: Diagnosis and treatment of childhood depression and self-destructive behavior. J Fam Pract 11:51–58, 1980
4. Pfeffer CR, Plutchik R, Mizruchi MS, et al: Suicidal behavior in child psychiatric inpatients and outpatients and in nonpatients. Am J Psychiatry 143:733–738, 1986
5. Pfeffer CR, Lipkins R, Plutchik R, et al: Normal children at risk for suicidal behavior: a two-year follow-up study. J Am Acad Child Adolesc Psychiatry 27:34–41, 1988

6. Trad PV: Infant Depression Paradigms and Paradoxes. New York, Springer-Verlag, 1986
7. Trad PV: Infant and Childhood Depression: Developmental Factors. New York, John Wiley, 1987
8. Trad PV: Psychosocial Scenarios for Pediatrics. New York, Springer-Verlag, 1988
9. Zilboorg G: Differential diagnostic types of suicide. Arch Neurol Psychiatry 35:270–291, 1936
10. Rosen G: History in the study of suicide. Psychol Med 1:267–285, 1971
11. Rosen G: History, in A Handbook for the Study of Suicide. Edited by Perlin S. London, Oxford University Press, 1975, pp 2–14
12. Friedman RC, Corn R: Follow-up five years after attempted suicide at age 7. Am J Psychother 39(1):108–113, 1985
13. Puig-Antich J: Major depression and conduct disorder in puberty. J Am Acad Psychiatry 21:118–128, 1982
14. Shafii M, Carrigan S, Whittinghill JR, et al: Psychological autopsy of completed suicide in children and adolescents. Am J Psychiatry 142(9):1061–1064, 1985
15. Jacobson RR: Child firesetters: a clinical investigation. J Child Psychol Psychiatry 26(5):759–768, 1985
16. Pfeffer CR, Conte HR, Plutchnik R, et al: Suicidal behavior in latency age children. J Am Acad Child Psychiatry 18:679–692, 1979
17. Pfeffer CR: The Suicidal Child. New York, Guilford, 1986
18. Pfeffer CR: Self-destructive behavior in children and adolescents. Psychiatr Clin North Am 8(2):215–226, 1985
19. Trad PV: The Preschool Child: Assessment, Diagnosis, and Treatment. New York, John Wiley, 1989
20. Dublin L: Suicide: A Sociological and Statistical Study. New York, Ronald Press, 1963
21. Gould RE: Suicide problems in children and adolescents. Am J Psychother 19:228–246, 1965
22. Curran BE: Suicide. Pediatr Clin Amer 26:737–746, 1979
23. Maris RW, Lazerwitz B: Pathways to Suicide: A Survey of Self-Destructive Behaviors. Baltimore, MD, Johns Hopkins University Press, 1981
24. Fritz GK: Attempted suicide in a five-year-old boy. Clin Pediatr 19:448–450, 1980
25. Kosky R: Suicide and attempted suicide among Australian children. Med J Aust 1:124–126, 1982
26. Kosky R: Childhood suicidal behavior. J Child Psychol Psychiatry 24:457–468, 1983
27. Trad PV: Treating Suicidelike Behavior in a Preschooler. Madison, CT, International Universities Press, 1990
28. Vaughn BE, Kopp CB, Krakow JB: The emergence and consolidation of self-control from eighteen to thirty months of age: normative trends and individual differences. Child Dev 55:990–1004, 1984
29. Buss AH, Plomin R: A Temperament Theory of Personality. New York, John Wiley, 1975
30. Kennedy H, Moran GS: The developmental roots of self-injury and response to pain in a 4-year-old boy. Psychoanal Study Child 39:195–212, 1984

31. Mischel W, Mischel HN: The development of children's knowledge of self-control strategies. Child Dev 54:603–619, 1983

32. Shultz TR, Wells D, Sarda M: Development of the ability to distinguish intended actions from mistakes, reflexes and passive movements. Brit J Soc Clin Psychol 19:301–310, 1980

33. Tishler CL, McHenry PC: Parental negative self and adolescent suicide attempts. J Am Acad Child Psychiatry 21:404–408, 1982

34. Pfeffer CR: The family system of suicidal children. Am J Psychother 35:330–341, 1981

35. Ainsworth MDS: The development of infant-mother attachment, in Review of Child Development Research. Edited by Caldwell BM, Ricciuti HN. Chicago, University of Chicago Press, 1973, pp 1–94

36. Ackerly WC: Latency-age children who threaten or attempt to kill themselves. J Am Acad Child Psychiatry 6:242–261, 1967

37. Cohen-Sandler R, Berman AL, King RA: Life stress and symptomatology: determinants of suicidal behavior in children. J Am Acad Child Psychiatry 21(2):178–186, 1982

38. Ekstein R, Friedman SW: The function of acting out, play action and play acting in the psychotherapeutic process. J Am Psychoanal Assoc 5:581–629, 1957

39. Siegel LI: Sullivan's contribution to child psychiatry. Contemporary Psychoanalysis 23(2):278–298, 1987

40. Piaget J: The Psychology of Intelligence. Totowa, NJ, Littlefield, Adams, 1976

41. Speece MW, Brent SB: Children's understanding of death: a review of three components of a death concept. Child Dev 55:1671–1686, 1984

42. Sullivan HS: The Interpersonal Theory of Psychiatry. New York, Norton, 1953

43. Winnicott DW: Playing and Reality. Harmoundsworth, England, Pelican, 1974

44. Mahler M, Pine F, Bergman A: The Psychological Birth of the Human Infant. New York, Basic Books, 1975

45. Hall CS, Lindzey G: Theories of Personality. New York, John Wiley, 1970

46. Seligman MEP: Helplessness: On Depression, Development and Death. San Francisco, CA, Freeman, 1975

47. Seligman MEP, Maier SF, Solomon RL: Unpredictable and uncontrollable aversive events, in Aversive Conditioning and Learning. Edited by Brush FR. New York, Academic, 1971, pp 347–400

48. Tauber ES: Symbiosis, narcissism, necrophilia: disordered affect in the obsessional character, in Affect: Psychoanalytic Theory and Practice. Edited by Cantor MB, Glucksman ML. New York, John Wiley, 1983, pp 293–309

49. Tauber ES: Symbiosis, narcissism, necrophilia: disordered affect in the obsessional character. J Am Acad Psychoanal 9(1):33–49, 1981

50. Tauber ES: Preoccupation with immortality expressive of a negation of life. Contemporary Psychoanalysis 18(1):119–132, 1982

51. American Psychiatric Association: Diagnostic and Statistical Manual of Mental Disorders, 3rd Edition, Revised. Washington, DC, American Psychiatric Association, 1987

52. Marshall HR, Doshi R: Aspects of experience revealed through doll play with preschool children. J Psychol 61:47–57, 1965

53. Freud S: The future prospects for psycho-analytic therapy (1910), in The Standard Edition of the Complete Psychological Works of Sigmund Freud, Vol 11. Translated and edited by Strachey J. London, Hogarth Press, 1967, pp 141–151
54. Tauber ES: Exploring the therapeutic use of countertransference data. Psychiatry 17:331–336, 1954
55. Schowalter JE: Countertransference in work with children: review of a neglected concept. J Am Acad Child Psychiatry 25:40–45, 1985
56. Tower L: Countertransference. J Am Psychoanal Assoc 14:528–537, 1965
57. Springmann RR: Countertransference: clarifications in supervision. Contemporary Psychoanalysis 22:252–277, 1986
58. Kohrman R, Fineberg HH, Gelman RL, et al: Techniques of child analysis: problems of countertransference. Int J Psychoanal 52:487–497, 1971
59. Freud A: Normality and Pathology in Childhood. New York, International Universities Press, 1965
60. Bernstein I, Glenn J: The child analyst's emotional reactions to his patients, in Child Analysis and Therapy. Edited by Glenn J. New York, Jason Aronson, 1978, pp 375–392
61. Fliess R: Countertransference and counteridentification. J Am Psychoanal Assoc 1:268–284, 1953
62. Habermas T: Social-cognitive aspects of therapeutic interactions. J Am Acad Child Psychiatry 26(5):770–773, 1987
63. Weiss S: Parameters in child analysis. J Am Psychoanal Assoc 12:587–599, 1964

3 Timid and Withdrawn Children

Richard S. Briggs, Ph.D.

Timid, withdrawn children are less noticeable than their more aggressive peers, but not necessarily less in need of therapeutic help. Unfortunately, because they do not speak loudly through behavior, their difficulties can be more easily overlooked. It is a common experience for clinicians to become concerned about a quiet, withdrawn sibling of a more aggressive child who has been referred for treatment. Typically, the parents are in the midst of worry and frustration over their aggressive child, and feel relief that the quiet sibling is offering no problem. The child may experience a similar "benign neglect" in the classroom, where his reticence is taken for good adjustment. Nevertheless, such children comprise a consistent minority in the consulting room. Even as patients, they do not command the same level of attention in the recent clinical literature as do children with attentional problems or children with aggressive behavior. One purpose for this chapter is to focus attention on a group that all too effectively manages to avoid it. A second purpose is to consider their particular characteristics and requirements as patients. This chapter will focus on the adaptation of psychodynamic play therapy and parental counseling to the treatment of timid and withdrawn children.

The children who are the subject of this chapter are between the ages of 6 and 12. Psychotic children will not be considered, nor will children whose primary diagnosis is a phobia or a learning disability. The children included share a tendency to avoid social contact, athletics, and more aggressive activities. They participate in solitary activities, such as daydreaming, hobbies, reading, playing solitary games, and watching television. They are inhibited in verbal and emotional expression. Their interests and play themes are often immature. Many preserve an attachment to certain toys of early childhood, sometimes through their twelfth or thirteenth birthdays. Alone, they can be quite expressive, sometimes acting out inner dramas. Startled parents may come upon such children in the midst of a dramatic monologue, gesticulating energetically.

The spectrum of diagnoses encompassed by these children goes from avoidant disorder, or separation anxiety disorder to obsessive-compulsive, schizotypal, and Pervasive Developmental Disorder. Commonly, these children have additional deficits, which may include learning disabilities and lags in motor development. Such handicaps probably contribute to the tendency toward social withdrawal, either directly by interfering with a child's skills and hence his or her peer activities, such as games and sports, or indirectly, by intensifying a feeling of being different and inadequate.

As may be evident from the diversity of children included in my category of those who are timid and withdrawn, I do not propose any single etiology for this pattern of behavior. Equally, in this chapter I will not attempt to offer a comprehensive account on the treatment of specific syndromes, such as Pervasive Developmental Disorders. I take the position that timidity and withdrawal are broad patterns of interpersonal adaptation that develop out of a complex set of factors. These factors differ from child to child, yet have considerable overlap. I will give a sketch of what I see as common elements below.

Interest in a broad pattern of adaptation, such as timidity and withdrawal, may appear to run counter to recent efforts to identify discrete diagnostic subgroups that may be differentiated by symptom cluster and by specific biological dysfunction. These subgroups include childhood depression (1), anxiety disorder (1), and obsessive-compulsive disorder (2,3). Obsessive-compulsive disorder in particular shows considerable overlap with the pattern of timidity and withdrawal (1,2,3). The responsiveness of obsessive-compulsive disorder to clomipramine treatment lends credence to the argument for a specific underlying biological deficit (4). But the delineation of such specific factors at a biological level is consistent with the articulation of larger patterns of interpersonal adaptation at a psychological level.

Numerous authors have described basic patterns that have a similarity to timidity and withdrawal. Quay and LaGreca (1) argue that multivariate statistical studies support the existence of a broad-band internalizing dimension that encompasses indicators of anxiety, depression and social withdrawal. Thomas and Chess (5), in their seminal work on temperament and behavior disorders, delineate a pattern in children who are slow to warm up that appears to have a similarity to patterns of timidity and withdrawal. Studies of nonclinical populations have also identified children who exhibit a pattern of inhibition from an early age (6,7,8).

Kagan and colleagues (7,8) see behavioral inhibition as an enduring characteristic of certain children, influenced by biological factors. In their own longitudinal study, they claimed that inhibited children have a stable, higher heart rate than uninhibited children in unfamiliar situations and in circumstances of mild risk. Studies of traits such as inhibition and withdrawal have not lead to any definitive conclusions. There is no commonly accepted definition of terms such as inhibition and withdrawal. It is difficult to know how the children in Kagan's work, for example, might compare to the clinical population considered here, who are generally an older group. Nevertheless, these studies do suggest the possibility of an innate disposition toward timidity and withdrawal that may well apply to children seen in treatment.

Within psychoanalytic theory, children who show significant deviation in their behavioral tendencies are often understood as manifesting a deviation in drive endowment (9). Timid, withdrawn children could be characterized as lacking in aggressive drive, thus exhibiting a deficit in their engagement of their world, as well as lacking initiative. Although this conceptualization stresses biological determinants, it rests on a theory of drive discharge that is inconsistent with contemporary neurophysiological knowledge (10,11). Psychoanalytic ego psychology, on the other hand, can offer an understanding of timidity and withdrawal that is independent of drive discharge. Holt (10) has shown that, although the concept of ego structure emerged from the drive/defense paradigm through Freud's tripartite division of psychic functioning, it does not require a concept of drive discharge. Rather, ego structure requires the postulation of wishes, obstacles to these wishes within and outside the individual, conflict, and defense. Thus, from this perspective, timidity and withdrawal can grow out of psychic conflict. They can be seen as ego mechanisms that may serve various defensive purposes. For example, Anna Freud's (12) account of defense mechanisms in children offers a characterization of inhibitions as defenses against phallic, exhibitionistic wishes or against Oedipal, competitive strivings.

Bowlby's (13) work on attachment and separation offers another perspective on patterns of timidity and withdrawal that, broadly speaking, is also consistent with psychoanalytic theory. Based on experimental work with primates, ethological studies of animals in the field, and clinical investigations of mothers and children, Bowlby postulates an innate, fundamental need for attachment. Disruption in the early experience of attachment can be manifested in various patterns of clinical dysfunction. Bowlby describes three types of fear behavior in man and animals:

1. Reduction of distance from protective persons or objects—that is, attachment behavior;
2. Increase of distance from threatening persons or objects—that is, withdrawal; and
3. Immobility in relation to threatening or protective objects—that is, freezing.

Thus, timidity and withdrawal constitute a possible pattern of attachment in which there is a threatened loss of the attachment figure, the presence of a threatening figure, or the combination of a threatening figure and an attachment figure in the same person.

Other theorists, such as Mahler and colleagues (14), have postulated that patterns of relatedness, such as timidity and withdrawal, may have evolved from the particular characteristics of the mother/child attachment during the first 2 years of life. Unlike Bowlby, their emphasis is on the hypothesized internal representations of self and other that the child forms in the process.

Sullivan (15) also gave pride of place to the nature of the parent-child attachment in his understanding of subsequent problems in living. Sullivan was particularly impressed by the destructive effects of unmanageable levels of anxiety in the transactions between mother and child, and how anxiety in the mother is a contagious process that affects her child. The experience of anxiety in the parent-child dyad is a paradigm for those experiences that disrupt the processes of learning and growth. Timidity and withdrawal are instances of what Sullivan called security operations; that is, patterns of behavior that, while hampering the child's openness to new experience and learning, nevertheless serve to protect him or her from exposure to potentially frightening levels of anxiety. Sullivan was one of the first clinicians to propose that the child's pattern of coping—what Sullivan called security operations and the self-system—grew out of the nexus of moment-to-moment interaction between the child and significant others. Sullivan's theory is less rooted in an evolutionary determinism than is Bowlby's and is less wedded to an inevitable developmental unfolding of specific psychosexual stages. Rather, it stresses the particularity of the child's experience of others from birth through adolescence. Sullivan was a precursor of current trends in developmental research, as exemplified by the work of Stern (16).

In my opinion, each of the perspectives on timidity and withdrawal have something to offer in considering the difficulties of an individual child. The clinical literature and my own observations of timid, withdrawn children support the likelihood of a constitutional contribution to this pattern, at least in certain children. Disturbances in attachment, whether in Bowlby's (13) ethological framework, or in the object relations frame of Mahler and colleagues (14), appear to be a definite feature of certain timid, withdrawn children. Other children, or the same children at other times, show clear indications of conflict between impulses and defenses. Sullivan's focus on anxiety in the moment to moment interplay between the child and significant others seems particularly germane. Virtually all timid, withdrawn children that I have observed are quite reactive to the emotional state of others and can quickly withdraw in response to any perceived negative feeling.

COMPOSITE PORTRAIT

Although there is much individual variability among timid, withdrawn children, there are qualities common to most of them. The following descriptions are based on my clinical work with these children. Generally, they are slow to warm up to a therapist, but do become quite attached over time. They demonstrate this attachment in subtle but clear ways. These may include a routine comment at the end of the session that reassures them of the time and place of the next meeting. Such children show a strong attachment to one or both parents, more consistently the mother. The capacity to become attached is clear, but the attachment per se does not appear as an obstacle to the pursuit of other activities. These children generally separate from parental figures relatively easily. They are not school-phobic in general, although on occasion they may attempt to stay home to avoid certain frightening or challenging situations in school. Parents or adults continue to serve a type of protective function for them. For example, such children may prefer to engage an adult during school play periods. But the attachment itself appears to be a relatively secure experience, and one that the child can draw on as an inner resource in the physical absence of the caretaking person.

One or both parents of these children are often visibly overanxious. They can become preoccupied with their child's difficulties and communicate a sense of much inner tension. They may take a specific symptom of their child and build it into a case for something quite frightening. One parent became convinced that her child suffered from Tourette syndrome on the basis of a minor mannerism that he developed for a brief time. The parents can quickly become emotionally distraught and filled with feelings of guilt. These reactions are not specific to the child, and often appear in connection with unrelated matters.

These children generally show a very quick, although surreptitious concern about others' emotional state, and, in particular, the nature of their impact on the other person. These reactions can imply a rather exquisite sensitivity to others. Immersed in their own fantasies or play, they may suddenly become aware of the other's presence. Such awareness may suddenly color a child's face, cause a startled reaction, or emerge as a hurried apology, question, or hesitation.

Such children have limited involvement with peers—either no close friends or, at most, one or two children with whom they have ongoing but rather specific, limited contact. Some of these children do not particularly attract the attention of peers, or do so in a nominal way that does not lead to any particular deepening of the relationship. Others are the scapegoats among their peers and encounter considerable teasing. When friendships develop, the friend may be expected to participate in restricted ways that are dictated by the timid child. These may include scenarios to be enacted, or toys, such as cars, trucks, and human figures, to be used—actions that take place along very rigid lines. Children who lack the patience and/or willingness to participate, as well as those with a larger compass to their interests, will tire of these restraints rather quickly.

Timid, withdrawn children thus exhibit a very strong need for control of the other. Their activities are often developmentally immature, with an emphasis on make-believe with predictable sequences of events and outcomes. This contrasts with their age-mates, whose interests tend to be more directed to the mastery of skills and novel experiences in the actual world. Timid children are very active daydreamers, sometimes with elaborate imaginations. They do their best in relationships with like-minded children.

After a considerable period of work in therapy, aggressive themes occur frequently in the play of such children. Some portray punitive reactions to relatively minor aggressive or defiant acts, in the context of play. Others will offer elaborate schemes involving violent activity perpetrated against some specific enemy, commonly another child or a teacher. Although fears of their own aggressiveness and fears of retaliation for it do figure prominently in the work with these children, conflict over aggressive impulses does not appear to be their central psychic struggle. Rather, these children generally fear the expression of all feelings and impulses. The boundary between emotional experience and taking action is not secure for them, and they demonstrate a need to restrict spontaneity in most directions. The prominence of aggression itself in their play activities may result from years of excessive inhibition. The frustration associated with the pattern of timidity and withdrawal can be inferred from the spontaneity and expressiveness that often becomes commonplace in their play activities later on in therapy.

These children appear to lack a consistent sense of self. Frequent comments and play themes point to a devalued self, characterized by ineffectiveness, peculiarity, and alienation from others. There is often a large gulf between a fantasized self that emerges in play and the sense of self that accompanies daily life. Although the self may be experienced as impotent, paradoxically, the child may have a greatly exaggerated anticipation of his or her impact on significant others, particularly parents.

The observations and suggestions offered in this chapter are drawn from extensive psychodynamic play therapy with the type of children just described. In the course of characterizing a rather typical sequence of evaluation and therapy, I will make reference to illustrative cases. Although each case has its unique features, the examples were chosen to represent common circumstances and dilemmas in working with such patients.

THE COURSE OF THERAPY

The need for a thorough, extensive evaluation is never more apparent than with timid, withdrawn children. Such children may appear to lack obvious difficulties. Because they are withdrawn and relatively hidden, their symptoms may be private or obscure. A parent's concern may seem unwarranted, possibly a result of excessive anxiety, but it may reflect an acute perceptiveness concerning his or her child. In my experience, parents have quite correctly persisted in the request for an evaluation on several occasions, in spite of reassurances from a teacher or a pediatrician that the child had no difficulties.

Individual sessions with the child are the core of the evaluation. The child should be seen several times concurrent with other types of data gathering, such as parent interviews, family sessions, and possible contact with extended family members. This evaluation period may be the beginning of therapy as well, and it should be conducted in that spirit. The therapist needs to create an atmosphere of exchange and involvement in the individual sessions. Timid, withdrawn children are unlikely to take the initiative, and when faced by a relatively quiet, nondirective therapist, can shrink further into themselves. But they can also shrink back in if someone presses them too hard. The therapist's task is to convey his or her liveliness, interest in the child, and willingness to play, without pressing too hard or being intrusive.

It is important to clarify the child's understanding of why he or she has come to therapy early on in the process. It is common in families with such children for things to remain unsaid, out of excess concern for causing upset, and, as a result, for serious misunderstanding to persist. The therapist can offer a simple description of what he or she understands to be the child's difficulties, and then explain the therapist's role as a person who talks and plays with children, and helps them with their feelings. With this introduction, the therapist can draw the child's attention to the various play materials available and encourage exploration of them. If the child does little more than sit quietly, the therapist might consider introducing the child to puppet play. It is a rare child who will not respond to a silly-looking cloth figure on the hand of an adult. Puppet play is a wonderful medium to begin learning about the child's impulses and conflicts in relation to others. But the therapist should not rely on play alone. During the first or second session, the therapist can ask questions about the child's life at home, feelings towards parents, relationships with siblings, fears and wishes, school experience, friendships, and preferred activities. All of these questions cannot be answered at once. Several sessions may be necessary to begin discussing even some of them. The central matter for the therapist is to keep in mind what he or she would like to know, even though the time to ask may be months off. The goal of the evaluation procedure just described is to assess the nature and extent of the child's difficulties, assess the apparent need for treatment, and make preliminary plans about the treatment structure. In addition, the clinician ought to have formed hypotheses about what has contributed to the child's difficulties.

In my experience, timid, withdrawn children do very well in psychodynamically grounded play therapy. Although reticent about talking, timid children often have an active inner life, as I have already described. Play therapy provides a natural context for the gradual unfolding of this inner life. In bringing this fantasy life into the therapy, the timid, withdrawn child begins to act in a more forward, more courageous manner than is customary for him. This alone can be a significant change. The fantasy material, once introduced, can become a powerful medium for deepening the therapist's understanding of the child, and the child's self-understanding.

The individual play therapy sessions should be combined with regular parental sessions as well as frequent telephone contact. In order to effect a change in the child's social isolation, and to ensure that appropriate opportunities for social development occur, the therapist needs to enlist the parents as active participants. The child can not effect these changes independently. The experience gained in more active social participation can be crucial for forward movement in the therapy. Witenberg (E. Witenberg, personal communication, 1982) has suggested that new insight commonly depends upon previous change in behavior and consequent change in experience.

Although timid, withdrawn children are ideal candidates for play therapy, they are, paradoxically, often poor players. They are frightened of novelty and constrict their spontaneity and expression of feeling. Their own imaginative world is highly private, and quite often rigidly structured. They are rarely spontaneous, expressive players. They certainly shy away from interaction with the therapist.

In the timid child, it is the particular combination of a guarded inner world of fantasy and a relatively poor ability to play that dictates the particular adjustments necessary in the treatment. The initial goal is to encourage the development of the play process. In the beginning, timid children often engage in repetitive, unexpressive activities, such as building a structure or drawing some favorite object a number of times from different perspectives. These activities do not involve the therapist. Fred G., an 8-year-old boy whom I will describe more fully below, began his therapy by setting up a dollhouse with human figures and other items, then rearranged them in several ways. He spent the remainder of the session looking through other play materials.

It is important to have a diversity of play materials for such children. With certain children (see Chapter 6 on children with attention-deficit hyperactivity disorder), materials should be restricted to a minimal amount that is conducive to their projective use. In the case of timid, withdrawn children, however, the greater the diversity of materials, the greater the likelihood that a play process will develop. I want to emphasize that is the important goal. The therapist need not worry about the meaning of the play, certainly at the beginning, so much as its elaboration. Board games and other highly structured activities are worth avoiding. The therapist might be well served by putting such materials out of the way when seeing a timid, withdrawn child. If the child simply avoids the play materials entirely, then the therapist may have no choice but to attempt a conversation. Any number of topics may be valuable, as long as the child does not feel as if he or she is being grilled with questions. At this juncture the therapist might bring the board games back out of the closet just to get some activity going, rather than sitting silently. Frequently, however, timid, withdrawn children are more able to talk than to play, and more able to talk to adults than to peers. The encouragement to participate in play therapy addresses the core of their difficulties.

Usually, the child will become engaged with something in the play materials that has struck his or her fancy. The therapist may have to maintain a very low-key presence during this period. Timid children need ample time to investigate a new environment and to reassure themselves that the therapist's intentions are benign and supportive. It can be similar to sitting still in the presence of a frightened animal—to reassure the creature that there is no danger present. This phenomenon appears to fit Kagan and colleagues' (7) assertion that certain children have a consistently higher level of physiological arousal in unfamiliar settings. They appear to need a much longer period of time to feel safe and to be willing to venture forth.

The therapist's principal adversary in this waiting game is his or her own impatience and/or anxiety. It is hard to do nothing and feel you are earning your keep—especially hard if, at one's back, one hears the urging and questioning of an anxious parent. The therapist's most immediate feeling is likely to be a sense of inadequacy for not doing enough, or irritation and anger, if attempts to intervene are consistently rebuffed. It can become very difficult to maintain a sense of purpose in such circumstances. The therapist who stays engaged during this period may start to convey an anxiety and impatience that is similar to what the child has experienced from one or both parents. Alternatively, the therapist may withdraw and turn his or her attention to personal fantasies and daydreams, such as the possibility of pursuing a different career. But if the therapist can stay engaged without doing anything, then it is precisely this stillness and absence of overt tension in the therapist that offers an initial therapeutic benefit to the child.

Eventually, if the child realizes the setting holds no hidden hazards and develops a sense of security, play is likely to become more expressive. The therapist will begin to get more clues about principal fears and conflicts in the child's life. Timid, withdrawn children are not prone to expand play themes freely. More typically, small actions can adumbrate a whole world of meaning. But, by paying particularly close attention to the child's behavior, the therapist may be able to help the child elaborate on a theme.

The therapist's participation in the play process becomes, over time, a crucial mechanism for therapeutic work. In contrast to treatment in which the therapist assumes a more passive, interpretive attitude, he or she should actively seek ways to extend the interactive process. There are several reasons for this. First, the therapist often needs to teach the child how to play. Second, the therapist can act as a model for allowing greater freedom of nonthreatening emotional expression—that is, an expressiveness in play that does not result in a complete loss of self-control. These first two processes are the essential elements in cognitive/behavioral interventions with such children. Third, the child's emotional experience of playful engagement carries the potential of repatterning the child's moment-to-moment experiences of ease and anxiety in intimate involvements with another person. Fourth, by becoming a part of the child's external representation of his internal conflicts, the therapist can "speak to" the possible solutions the child sees as available to him for his psychic dilemmas. Fifth, the therapist's ability to interpret these conflicts to the child is enhanced by his or her intimate involvement with these issues.

CLINICAL ILLUSTRATION

Fred G. was an 8-year-old boy who had virtually no friendships with other children and appeared to avoid social contact. He was close to his younger brother, but he also appeared envious of his brother's athletic abilities and wider sphere of social contacts. His parents described Fred as fearful of new situations, and timid even in areas where he had achieved significant competence. For example, he was a good swimmer, but he refused to go into the deep end of any pool. Fred preferred quiet, sedentary activities and resisted his parents' efforts to involve him outside the home. Fred was delayed in his motor development, which interfered with his acquisition of important skills, such as throwing a ball and riding a bike. He also manifested a pattern of motor excitability, which included hand flapping and spontaneous sounds.

In seeking therapeutic help, Fred's parents had become particularly concerned about Fred's pattern of rituals and required sequences in his behavior. These compulsive behaviors included an absolute insistence on going to bed and on arriving in school at a set time, an unvarying sequence of activities in the morning leading to school (such as going in and out of his room twice before having breakfast), and certain ritual verbal exchanges with his mother and grandmother. In addition, Fred usually insisted on wearing certain articles of clothing. If he was unable to complete things in just the way he wanted, he developed a panicked, desperate reaction and could not be calmed. The parents had long noted this tendency, but they believed his insistence on these routines increased markedly after his mother took on a full-time job.

Interviews with his parents also revealed how fully Fred had turned toward an inner fantasy world. Mrs. G. was convinced that Fred had an imaginary companion. She noted that Fred often appeared engrossed in conversation by himself, as though interacting with another person. His parents also described his fascination with shows and performances of all kinds. This interest ran the gamut from a type of obsessive preoccupation with television—he memorized the day and time of virtually every program—to a startling expressiveness in imitating song and dance routines while alone.

Fred's parents identified several, potentially traumatic aspects of his development. These included two surgical procedures for strabismus that required hospitalization and that Fred found very frightening. Fred had several rather intimidating experiences with other children when he was quite young. These included being beaten and bitten by a neighborhood boy. More recently, Fred had been diagnosed as having scoliosis.

The meetings with Fred's parents helped to give a better picture of the parents' role in their son's difficulties. Mr. G. was a very retiring man who preferred sedentary activities. Although he cared deeply for Fred, he had not found a common ground for their relationship. In a separate individual session, Mrs. G. confided in me that she saw her husband as emotionally fragile—someone who would become highly distraught over minor mishaps, and virtually become nonfunctional in his anxiety and self-recrimination. She acknowledged that, as a consequence of this experience with him, she had kept most of her concerns about Fred to herself. She felt that her husband, in order to shield himself from the distress he might have felt, overlooked any of Fred's difficulties and was therefore less in a position to help him. Mrs. G. described how she relied much more on her own mother for conversation and advice concerning Fred and other matters. She also felt that she and Fred turned more to each other, solidifying the bond between them.

Mrs. G., although highly involved with Fred, did not function as a reassuring presence who could help him better cope with the world around him. A highly anxious person, Mrs. G. was easily suffused with feelings of pain and worry.

Fred lacked secure parents who could help him accommodate his burgeoning impulses and reassure him that they could act as guard rails to prevent him from going too far. Instead, he had a father who found it necessary to withdraw as a means of regulating his own emotional life. He had a mother who was available emotionally but who quickly became suffused with anxiety herself and was prone toward a calamitous view of things. He and his parents showed a high level of sensitivity to each other's behavior and a mutually induced anxiety. Both parents, gentle, caring, and humane though they were, could not offer Fred much inspiration for pluck and feistiness. Mr. G. bemoaned Fred's absolute adherence to rules, yet was very tied to such structures himself. In his own right, Fred appeared to be a boy with a true gift for isolation, who could entertain himself for hours with his own imaginings.

It was clear that Fred was a troubled boy who showed difficulties in several spheres. The extent of Fred's disturbance was less clear. He was a quite bright, imaginative boy who, in spite of his isolation, retained the general affection and respect of his age-mates. He had a quality of self-possession that was not entirely obliterated by his general awkwardness and apprehensiveness. He could entertain himself with a rather idiosyncratic set of interests for extended periods of time. But he also appeared so immersed in his own world that it raised questions about his capacity to remain reality oriented.

Fred's behavior included noteworthy obsessive-compulsive and schizoid features. Was Fred also an innately timid boy, an extreme on a spectrum of timidity? Were Fred's compulsive symptoms the sign of a discrete, biologically based dysfunction, such as an obsessive-compulsive disorder? Quite possibly he could be characterized in these ways as well. In spite of the complexity of factors that can be identified in Fred's case, however, he represents much that is typically seen with timid, withdrawn children.

In our initial sessions, Fred said very little. He was reasonably content to be together, but he wanted no overt interaction. He set about playing with a dollhouse and human figures, identifying the characters, but with no elaboration, and then went on with other structured activities, such as drawing schoolhouses. I made occasional comments about these activities, but mostly just sat quietly. At one point, Fred reached for a toy gun, pointed it at a large clock on the wall, and pretended to shoot it several times. I had noticed that, in his drawings of schools, clocks figured prominently on the walls. After each make-believe shot, Fred looked in my direction. I then picked up another toy gun, and with emphatic movements, pretended to shoot toward the clock as well. Fred smiled slightly, grinned more mischievously, and pretended to fire at the clock again. I repeated my own actions. He grinned. I made a comment about how good it would feel to get rid of all the clocks. I made no reference to his own concerns about time, to his possible wish that time would not bring our meeting to an end, or any direct reference to his aggressive feelings. I wanted to encourage his participation in interactive play and chose to be more of a participant than a commentator, fearing that any drawing of attention to his behavior might well inhibit it.

Fred's reluctance to engage me directly became even more understandable as I gained a fuller picture of how limited his relationships were with his peers. He had no ongoing friendships. When Fred's mother invited a boy to play with him, after 30 minutes he would beg her to take the boy home. He was at a loss as to how to involve himself with others. So much of his attention went to private fantasy, that, unless he could find some specific way to include another boy in it, he would rather be alone.

Not all timid, withdrawn children are as restricted in their activities as Fred was. Some blossom in creative play during therapy sessions. Todd is a boy I will describe briefly as a contrasting example to Fred. A 7-year-old, he came to therapy following the death of a sibling. His parents' primary concern was Todd's reaction to the loss of his brother—to wit, a reluctance to talk about it, a denial of much overt sadness or anger, but occasional extreme temper tantrums. Todd had always been a timid child who had little social contact outside the home, except for what occurred during his day at school. Todd literally refused to take any initiative in our beginning sessions. He politely demurred when I explained that he could choose to do whatever he wanted. At first, I took the path of least resistance, and made suggestions. He started on a quiet note, with puppet play that could be described as genteel. As long as I got us started, he was at ease in playing with me. From the beginning, he showed an imaginativeness in his play, inventing characters and exploring a variety of play materials, and he included me in the unfolding plots. But his play was benign and gave little hint of the rage his tantrums revealed, nor of the deep sadness occasioned by his brother's loss.

I kept taking as much license as I could with the characters Todd assigned me. My characters became more provocative. For example, if I were a driver stopped by the police, I would make sarcastic remarks. Todd loved it. His reluctance to choose an activity at the beginning became a game, with mock stubbornness on both our parts. We were able to laugh together about all this pseudo-politeness. He responded quickly and with enthusiasm to my expressiveness. He developed a puppet character who owned a dog. The man was benign, most of the time, but the dog was unpredictable and vicious. The play became quixotic and violent in its expressiveness. Todd's transformation from a highly polite, constricted, timid child into a loud, completely captivated, aggressive participant was truly impressive. He developed themes of loss and death with much rapidity once he found his new voice in our sessions. This behavior was quite specific to the therapy. In the rest of his life, he maintained his normally reticent manner.

Fred and Todd, though different in important ways, went through similar processes in the beginning stages of treatment. Reticent and emotionally constricted at first, they eventually developed an expressiveness in sessions not characteristic of their ordinary behavior. Both children appeared to be affected by my own expressiveness and participation with the play materials. Once involved in an active way, these children began to express a powerful aggressiveness. At this early stage, the therapist's task is to nurture this nascent vitality and outward movement. The therapist is fully in the relationship, with a spontaneous, improvisational participation.

Interpretive comments and the introduction of extraneous material can easily deaden this vitality in its early stages. For example, Fred would withdraw in a dazzlingly quick fashion whenever I offered any interpretative comments that attempted to draw a connection between the play themes of the moment and his own conflicts. A similar thing happened when I introduced material reported to me by his mother. In one dramatic example, Mrs. G. had informed me that Fred was deeply distraught about his brother's involvement with a group of children, who played on a baseball team. Mrs. G.'s anxiety and her portrayal of Fred's upset moved me to raise the topic in my sessions with him. Fred confirmed his mother's report and described his feelings in more detail, but did not want to discuss it further. For the rest of the session, he drew floor plans of buildings, an activity that he engaged in occasionally that appeared to be a safe alternative to more interactive, expressive play. For the next several weeks, Fred continued to do nothing but draw floor plans, retreating altogether from any spontaneous exchange, and relinquishing a whole set of play themes that had developed between us.

During the long period when Fred was drawing floor plans, I found that sitting in the room with him could become insufferably dull. I had to be there, if only to wait, or possibly to endure my punishment for violating our private world. The therapist can feel a very strong motivation to do something in this situation to get things moving, to make contact with the child, or to simply alter the monotony. Yet, any initiative taken will likely prompt the child to withdraw further. During these periods, the therapist lives through this conflict, maintaining a waiting attitude, and continuing to find ways to stay in contact with the child. There are often little signs indicating that more is going on than the overt behavior suggests. This sign might simply be a smile upon entering the consulting room that quickly vanishes in some type of isolated activity. I found it useful to imagine myself to be an ethologist, like Jane Goodall, studying some particularly reclusive, fearful primate. I reminded myself of the great patience and time that the ethologist's work requires. But I also kept myself engaged by occasional innocuous comments, such as, "Oh; that looks like a large classroom," in response to what Fred was drawing, or by moving around the room to get a better look at what was being done. I found it useful to keep my lines of communication out there, and Fred would now and then acknowledge the remark and make some comment of his own about what he was doing. The treatment of children like Fred depends on the therapist's capacity for active waiting.

In spite of setbacks, timid, withdrawn children do become more open and courageous if the therapist can stay with them. For Fred, this openness included enacting various performances, such as singing and comedy routines, becoming a famous person, acting out the part of someone seeking envious revenge against a famous person, playing the part of a doctor, and playing the part of a murderer. Ultimately, he created a complex portrait of the major themes in his emotional life.

Fred's play themes included a classroom scene involving two students and a very stern teacher. One student usually did the correct thing, and another continuously misbehaved. Fred usually assigned the misbehaving character to me, while he would play the part of the teacher. The bad boy, Joseph, would never have his homework done, would usually talk to another boy during class, and, when reprimanded, would talk back to the teacher. I would improvise insulting or sarcastic remarks, which Fred delighted in, and he would then attack me (as Joseph) with great ferocity. He would stomp around the room in a seeming paroxysm of anger, dish out severe punishments, call my mother at home, and call in the school principal. Fred suggested certain lines, which often included a curse word or a scatological reference that he would not actually pronounce, but would identify by context or spelling. If I then correctly guessed my assigned word, and said it, he would erupt in giggles.

Fred was fascinated by bad, defiant, and scatological behavior. Although at first he did not play these parts himself, they became staples of our work. In this play, Fred enacted what was most likely a central inner drama. In his normal life, he steered clear of the bad boy's behavior by a wide margin. In fact, Fred's father told me that he wished, when he told Fred to be careful of the new grass, that, for once, he would just thoughtlessly walk across it. Mr. G. often found himself in the peculiar position of setting rules that he hoped in part his son would break. Yet, Fred harbored a desire to give life to his own Joseph, the bad boy—to express his tendency toward aggressive, challenging behavior. In the person of the stern teacher, Fred voiced the powerful self-punitive attitudes he experienced toward his own misbehavior. But he also expressed the rage that accompanied the painful frustrations in his life. Through the teacher, Fred also displayed a completely uncharacteristic motoric freedom. The teacher's aggressive gestures and vigorous movement contrasted with Fred's own constricted posture and his handclapping when excited. Eventually, Fred began experimenting with "bad" words, rather than assigning them to me. He would blurt out a curse, sometimes in the role of a puppet character, and on occasion, on his own.

Clearly, Fred made use of our relationship to explore the multiple facets of his personal conflicts. He also used the freedom and security of our relationship to experiment. In so doing, he created a kind of shared mythology, a set of well-defined characters and themes. Fred's longing for attention and admiration became clear in the personas of the performer, the rich man, and the powerful politician. His sadistic, self-punitive rage became manifest in Mr. O'Donnell, the teacher, and in a few other authority figures in the play. Others, such as Joseph, the bad boy, gave voice to a range of aggression that included envy and murderous hostility.

Once he and I had participated in the evolution of these themes and characters, we were able to discuss them in an interpretive manner. Within this shared world, I could suggest, for example, that because the performer had no friends, he must be very lonely, and that he may long for others' attention and love through his performance. We talked about how the bad boy's friend in the classroom envied his freedom to express his anger and rebelliousness but was fearful of acting that way himself and risking the rage of Mr. O'Donnell, the teacher. This type of interpretive exploration became possible only after, more than a year into therapy, Fred and I had a very solid rapport and a host of shared experiences.

Often, timid, withdrawn children nurture a highly private fantasy world that they are very reluctant to reveal, and, in fact, may never bring forth in therapy. This fantasy world can express a primitive, infantile level of psychic organization. These children will devote an extraordinary amount of time to the elaboration of their imaginary worlds. Much after he and I had developed our own realm of imagination, with recurrent themes and characters, perhaps after $1\frac{1}{2}$ years of treatment, Fred began to make references to such a private world. The central characters in this fantasy were a family with two parents, a brother named Verturt, and a sister named Wee Wee. These characters were never enacted within the therapy, but it became clear that Fred had created a very detailed fantasy of their lives. The principle themes were misbehavior of a primitive kind, involving feces and urine (one character would fall into feces; a character would pee on another) that expressed a primitive rage and retaliation. The structure was similar to our schoolroom play in that there was one good figure, Verturt, and one bad, Wee Wee. In this world, however, the bad child, the younger sister, was never punished, whereas the older, virtuous brother always got into trouble. After Fred made me his confidant, he would gossip about the lives of these characters as if they were actual people. But it also appeared that Fred introduced me to these characters as part of a long ritual of saying goodbye to them. In making them public, he was probably ready to give them up.

The therapist's ultimate role is to help the child understand himself more fully and to recognize unnecessary limits he imposes on his own behavior. To this end, it is important that the child come to understand the relationship between the themes—the beliefs and emotions of the play—and his own life. Often, when the therapist makes such connections explicit (that is, offers interpretations of the child's play as expressions of personal conflict), the child quickly stops what he is doing. The interpretation appears to heighten the child's self-consciousness, and he or she reacts with inhibition. This inhibition might be useful with aggressive children, but with timid, withdrawn children, it is precisely the reaction one would hope to avoid.

The therapist's observations and interpretations are less likely to inhibit the play if they are made within the play metaphors. Fred and I explored his conflicts over loss of control and aggression versus fear of destructiveness and retaliation. Similarly, we examined his wish for fame and celebrity status versus feelings of loneliness and insignificance. This exploration felt mutual, but it was an integral part of further elaborating the characters we had created. We both knew we were discussing Fred, but we stuck to an implicit agreement that we would pretend otherwise.

Interpretations that explicitly refer to the child's own life may fare better if they are not closely tied to the immediate play activities. Toward the end of Fred's sessions, he often spent a less active period, asking me questions about various matters or relating certain incidents in his day. I could use this time to suggest interpretations rising out of the preceding play, but not too closely attached to it. In one instance, I suggested that his impulse to be more aggressive frightened him because he feared losing control and causing damage. Then I commented that in the preceding 40 minutes, he had been more aggressive than he usually allowed, and nothing harmful happened. His experience of increased spontaneity and free expression of aggression within the sessions gave him the basis for accepting such an interpretation.

As the therapy evolves, and as the child's playful engagement has become more firmly established as a key aspect of the relationship, the therapist can afford to assume an increasingly interpretive role, including interpretations of the child's transferential feelings. In addition to their experience of angry, hostile feelings, such children develop very powerful, positive attachments, as well as idealizing attitudes towards the therapist.

In their relationship to the therapist, timid children can find relief from the painful loneliness that is a consequence of their retreat from social contact. In this relationship, the child has brought forth an emotional self, with longings and hostilities, and has succeeded in preserving the attachment. Commonly, the child may develop transferential feelings for the therapist as an idealized, wished-for parent. The child may also see the therapist as a true friend, possibly the only one he has ever experienced.

Sullivan (15) characterized the first true friendship for a child as the chumship. According to Sullivan, the chum is the child's first true experience of a collaborative relationship that involves intimacy, reciprocity, and a selfless concern for the well-being of the other person. Sullivan viewed the chumship in preadolescence as crucial to the development of a capacity for adult intimacy. It is through the chumship that the child learns about the process of an intimate relationship with another. It also provides the child an opportunity for new learning regarding interpersonal relatedness. The child's self-system, shaped in the crucible of family life to protect the child against disabling anxiety, is open to change through the chumship.

Of course the therapist is not a chum to a child. The relationship is not one between peers and, it lacks the reciprocity essential to the chumship. But the therapeutic relationship can include elements of the chumship, in positive and negative ways. On the positive side, the child may develop an unprecedented ease in chatting with the therapist about various interests and feelings. He or she may bring things in to show the therapist, and may, in turn, feel emboldened to ask the therapist personal questions regarding the therapist's interests and opinions, including preferences in cars, sports, politics, and other matters. The child may express curiosity about the therapist's childhood experiences, as a basis of comparison with his or her own. This latter type of question in particular seems similar to what a child might do with a chum. The child may, in effect, fantasize that he or she and the therapist have a chumship that requires disregarding the time gap in the occurrence of their childhoods. In essence, the fantasized chumship is a type of transference relatedness. Of course, the therapeutic relationship serves purposes that have much in common with chumship, in offering a child an opportunity to relinquish certain rigid self-restrictions and blocks to new experience that are elements of what Sullivan called the self-system. The child goes through a process of unfolding personal possibilities that can be integrated into a wider life. In this respect a chumship transference may be beneficial; in a child of Fred's age, it can become a precursor to development of a genuine chumship in preadolescence.

On the negative side, the timid, withdrawn child may turn to his relationship with the therapist as an alternative to seeking chums in his actual life. The therapeutic relationship does not pose as many conflicts and challenges as does a relationship with a peer. Several timid, withdrawn children have explicitly identified me as their only friend and have seemed relatively content with that arrangement. Thus, the therapy itself can become an obstacle to the child's expansion of his social world. I think this possible development is more likely if the therapist interacts with the child in the ways I have suggested. In effect, my recommendations emphasize the role of the therapist as playmate and as facilitator of certain kinds of interaction. This can be very rewarding and reassuring to the child, but it can also contribute to the child's sense of the therapist as his one true friend.

The therapist can discourage this tendency by becoming more actively interpretive. The more the therapist says about the connections between their mutual experience in the sessions and the child's conflicts in life, the more clearly will he define the therapeutic relationship as a setting in which to work on things, rather than an end in itself. As the therapist addresses the transference aspects of the relationship, he can draw the child's attention to his desire for a chum, and suggest that he and the child might talk more about how to develop such a relationship.

The parents' participation in the therapy is crucial for timid, withdrawn children. At the beginning, the therapist may choose to see a child's parents on a weekly basis. One alternative is to arrange parent sessions with another therapist, but, in my experience, the coordination of effort is better when one person works with both parents and child. The therapist is likely to ease the parents' own anxiety by developing realistic goals and strategies for helping them help their child. Often, the parents' apprehension and sense of urgency have acted as roadblocks to their effectiveness. Sometimes, by learning more about their child's particular strengths and weaknesses, especially outside the home, the parents make discoveries that improve their outlook. Fred's parents learned that he enjoyed performing in various classroom events—skits and plays—and they discovered that, although he was socially isolated, he was much better liked than they expected. In my view, excessive anxiety in the parents constitutes a major disruptive factor in emotional development for timid, withdrawn children. To the extent that the therapist can intervene to alleviate parental anxiety, the child is that much more likely to experience a reduction in his own anxiety, and an improvement in his coping mechanisms.

The child's parents can also function as key participants in furthering the child's involvement in activities that develop social and other skills, and that promote greater assertiveness. As I have already stated, individual therapy is often insufficient for timid, withdrawn children. Their vulnerability to anxiety and their impulse to withdraw are such fundamental ingredients in their personality structure that the novel experiences of the therapy need to be reinforced by opportunities in the child's life. The therapist can act as a consultant to the parents who themselves become behavior therapists, arranging appropriate challenges in the child's life. In my experience, parents of such children often show a general willingness to help, but have a remarkable difficulty thinking of even the simplest strategies to intervene with their child.

Fred's treatment illustrates how well things can go when a combined effort is made. His parents' participation made a significant contribution, as did therapy Fred received for his motor delays. At the point of termination, Fred had succeeded in developing several friends on his own, had started playing a musical instrument, and was participating more actively in age-appropriate pursuits.

As I stated earlier, it is my view that timidity and withdrawal are broad patterns of interpersonal adaptation that encompass a range of diagnostic entities. Fred represents one particular set of difficulties; he cannot be taken as representative of the entire spectrum of timid, withdrawn children. But Fred's case was unusual in including so many elements that a therapist sees with timid, withdrawn children. In other cases, one may be impressed by the issue of conflict over impulses, the child's complex attachment to one or both parents, or the important contribution of constitutional factors, such as physical and developmental problems. All of these factors were evident with Fred.

Fred's case also illustrates how important it is for the therapist to assume an active, engaged role with these children and with their parents. A more passive, interpretive, or limit-setting role will not work. The therapist must mix it up with the child and help him learn how to play through encouragement, invitation, and example. At the same time, the therapist must exercise patience and be prepared for a very gradual unfolding of the child's capacity for play. The therapist must also help the parents become active therapeutic allies who can help moderate anxiety and encourage experimentation and growth in their child.

REFERENCES

1. Quay HC, LaGreca AM: Disorders of anxiety, withdrawal and dysphoria, in Psychopathological Disorders of Childhood, 3rd Edition. Edited by Quay H, Werry JS. New York, John Wiley, 1975, pp 73–110
2. Judd LL: Obsessive compulsive neurosis in children. Arch Gen Psychiatry 12:136–143, 1965
3. Rapoport JC: Childhood compulsive disorder. J Child Psychol Psychiatry 27:289–295, 1986
4. Flament MF, Rapoport JC, Berg CJ, et al: Clomipramine treatment of obsessive-compulsive disorder. Arch Gen Psychiatry 42:977–983, 1985
5. Thomas A, Chess S: Temperament and Development. New York, Brunner/Mazel, 1977

6. Bronson GW: Fear of visual novelty. Developmental Psychology 2:33–40, 1970
7. Kagan JJ, Reznick JS, Clarke C, et al: Behavioral inhibition to the unfamiliar. Child Dev 55:2212–2225, 1984
8. Reznick JS, Kagan K, Snidman N, et al: Inhibited and uninhibited children: a follow-up study. Child Dev 57:660–680, 1986
9. Alpert A, Neubauer P, Weil AP: Unusual variations in drive endowment. Psychoanal Study Child 11:125–163, 1956
10. Holt RR: Drive or wish? a reconsideration of the psychoanalytic theory of motivation, in Psychology Versus Metapsychology: Psychoanalytic Essays, in Memory of George S. Klein (Psychological Issues, Monograph 36). Edited by Gill M, Holtzman P. New York, International Universities Press, 1976, pp 159–197
11. Klein GS: Psychoanalytic Theory: An Exploration of Essentials. New York, International Universities Press, 1976
12. Freud A: The Ego and the Mechanism of Defense. New York, International Universities Press, 1966
13. Bowlby J: Attachment and Loss. New York, Basic Books, 1969
14. Mahler M, Pine F, Bergman A: The Psychological Birth of the Human Infant. New York, Basic Books, 1975
15. Sullivan HS: The Interpersonal Theory of Psychiatry. New York, WW Norton, 1953
16. Stern DN: The Interpersonal World of the Infant. New York, Basic Books, 1985

4 Paternal Absence: Psychotherapeutic Considerations in Boys

Owen W. Lewis, M.D.

There are many reasons for a father's permanent absence from home. Divorce, an accidental death, death following an illness, or incarceration, for example, entail very different circumstances for the spouse, the family, and of course, the child. These circumstances will inevitably affect a developing child in very different ways. These differences notwithstanding, paternal absence in and of itself has a major developmental impact on a child.

Fatherlessness does not necessarily produce psychopathology and is not a cause for psychotherapeutic intervention. Nevertheless, the effects of a parent's absence on the process of a child's psychotherapy are significant, regardless of the disorder for which psychotherapy has been undertaken. The approach I present in this chapter differentiates the problem of paternal absence from the problem of paternal loss and absence on the process of psychotherapy. To this end, the psychotherapies of several children, each of whom lost contact with his father at a very young age, will be presented. In this way, absence can be examined without the compounding problems entailed by loss. To further minimize the complexity of the problem, only the treatments of boys have been selected. From these treatments, the technical adaptations particular to the treatment of the fatherless boy will be articulated. Many of these principles will also apply to circumstances of experienced loss and absence, although in such circumstances the issue of loss may at times overshadow the issue of absence.

DEVELOPMENTAL HAZARDS OF FATHERLESS SONS

Before discussing the various treatment issues, some of the literature pertaining to the developmental hazards of fatherlessness for boys will be highlighted. A clinician approaching the treatment of a fatherless child brings to the treatment an anticipation of a problematic development because of the unavoidably powerful meaning of fatherlessness itself to the clinician. Some broader understanding of the developmental impact of fatherlessness is therefore necessary. In general, there are conflicting concepts deriving not only from such divergent sources as individual clinical case reports and well-sampled, nonclinical studies, but also from the nature of the problem itself. As Chiland (1) states, " . . . Nothing can be said about 'the father' in general. Something can be said about a particular father conjoined with a particular mother, and about an absent father only in relation to the qualities of the mother" (p. 371).

There have been numerous studies recently of the role of the father in "normal" child development. Extrapolation of these findings to the individual fatherless child can be misleading. Although a given function may be ascertained to derive from the father, alternate pathways toward its achievement are often possible. For instance, one of the father's roles in the infant's cognitive development has been studied in intact families by Brooks-Gunn and Lewis (2), who found that pictures of fathers were correctly labeled by all infants in their study by 18 months, a time when only some of the pictures of mothers were beginning to be labeled by these infants. These findings were explained by the effect of the mother referring to the (temporarily) absent father during the day and by the effects of distance in fostering object representation. Does the single-parent infant lose this particular effect on cognitive development? It clearly depends on individual circumstances. The child exposed primarily to only one caretaker may not benefit from this effect, although the child raised in a household with a working mother and another caretaker may.

Although several aspects of the father's role in normal development will be noted, normative generalizations must be applied carefully to the individual child. The clinician in assessing an individual case should determine if and how the given function may have been achieved. Areas to be considered include pre-Oedipal development, latency, and gender identity. The role of the father in Oedipal development will not be reviewed, because this has been the cornerstone of classical psychoanalytic thinking.

A major role for the father in the separation and individuation process has been described by Mahler and Gosliner (3), who note, "The father is a powerful and perhaps necessary support against the threat of re-engulfment of the ego into the whirlpool of the primary undifferentiated symbiotic stage" (pp. 209–210). Abelin (4) describes the practicing subphase in which the mother is taken as "home base" and father comes to stand for distant, "nonmother" space that fosters an elated exploration of reality. The father may also be necessary for resolution of the ambivalent rapprochement crisis. Meerloo (5) has similarly described the father as a bridge to the outside. Herzog (6) notes the importance of the father for pre-Oedipal boys in the modulation of aggressive drives and fantasies.

Ross (7) holds that, although the father plays a vital role in fostering self-identity in the second year, he plays an equally important role in a child's assumption of his or her sexual identity in the third year. Tyson (8) believes that a boy needs to identify with the father as a sex-role model both in the urethral stage when he gains mastery of bodily functions and during the phallic-narcissistic stage when overexposure to female genitals may affect a boy's body image. The development of sexual identity is not solely dependent on the presence of a father. Other factors include the mother's attitudes (9,10); the presence of siblings (11); and the presence of father surrogates (12).

Results from more systematic research cannot be applied directly to the clinical situation, because sexual identity encompasses a wide spectrum of behaviors and attitudes, and paternal absence may occur under many circumstances. Hetherington (13), for instance, found that sex-typed behaviors were diminished among 9- to 12-year-olds who were without fathers prior to the age of 5 but not among those who were without fathers after the age of 5. In a sample of $3\frac{1}{2}$- to 5-year-olds, Reyes (14) found that social development was unaffected by father presence, absence, or surrogacy. In a comprehensive review, Biller and Borstelmann (9) state, "There are data indicating that paternal masculinity, paternal nurturance, and paternal limit setting can be important factors in the masculine development process. However, taken separately, no one of these factors seems sufficient to ensure that the boy will become masculine" (pp. 348–349). Furthermore, they conclude, "Children who are paternally deprived, however, are more likely either to take a defensive posture of rigid adherence to cultural sex role standards or to avoid expected gender-related behaviors" (pp. 349–350).

During the latency years, the father-son relationship provides for an important mentorship (7) that, in succession from the Oedipal relationship, parallels the boy's earlier rapprochement with mother. The father helps the child discover new skills, "to explore and experiment in the service of competence rather than be driven, or inhibited, by some competitiveness" (7, p. 249). Sarnoff (15) notes that such help bolsters the child's self-esteem and that children need to overvalue their fathers to deal with their own humiliations. Other functions include introducing and interpreting reality limitations to the family and strengthening problem solving by a relative intolerance for ambiguity.

Although studies of normal development contribute to an understanding of the effects of fatherlessness, there are numerous reports linking problematic development to fatherlessness directly. Effects have been noted in the areas of delinquency, mental disorders, and academic performance.

Freud's understanding of the role of the father in superego development formed the cornerstone of Aichorn's (16) understanding of delinquent, and often fatherless, adolescents. Although innumerable reports corroborated this view, more recent studies have considered other factors associated with fatherlessness. Herzog and Sudia (17) for instance, note that although a correlation of delinquency and father absence exists, other equally important factors include stress in the home, a depressed family income, and poor maternal control. Rutter (18,19) has shown that intrafamilial conflict before divorce may be more pathogenic than the change to a single-parent family. In a comprehensive review of the subject, Adams and colleagues (20) conclude, "Effects of father absence appear to relate to delinquent behaviors mainly in white middle-class males" (p. 202).

The presence of other mental disorders has also been associated with the absence of the father, including psychoneuroses, anxiety, depression, suicidal behaviors, and schizophrenia. Although Adams and colleagues (20) state, "We see that paternal absence has been associated with psychiatric illness generally" (p. 214), they also find that methodological flaws in most studies and the compounding factors of familial discord and poverty in father-absent families make etiological determinations difficult.

Finally, father absence has been associated with poor academic performance. This impact has been attributed to a variety of factors including cognitive style and self-confidence in problem solving, but it should also be noted that authoritarian paternal behaviors tend to be associated with reduced academic competence as well (21). In general, there are contradictory findings. Radin (21) notes, "Non-death-related father absence appears to be most damaging to the intellectual functioning of boys when the absence occurs before the age of five" (p. 308). In a study of lower-class white boys who were in the fifth grade, Santrok and Wohlford (12) found that although the departure of the father within the previous 3 years most severely affected a son's academic performance; those with the very earliest father loss were the next most severely affected academically. On the other hand, Adams and colleagues (20) come to a different conclusion in their review of the studies correlating fatherlessness with poor academic performance, stating, "The evidence suggests that fatherlessness counts less than social inequity does" (p. 143).

INTRODUCTION TO CASES

I will present a brief synopsis of each case so that in subsequent sections it can be referred to without repetition.

Dan

Dan's difficulties developed rapidly over several months at the age of 10 following the disloyalty of his best friend. The boys' families took a short vacation together, and the friend, after what should have been a minor squabble on the first day, ignored Dan in favor of another child. Before this time Dan had shown no particular difficulties, had maintained adequate friendships, and had done well scholastically and athletically. Following the incident, he became increasingly nervous and found himself wanting frequent re-assurances from peer and adult friends. He found this state quite uncomfort-able, and it distracted him from schoolwork. He was aware that his need for reassurance was unreasonable and that the most sympathetic reassurance would not ease him.

Dan became wary, if not tearful, at the mention of his father. He knew a few facts regarding his father: that his father had left within weeks after he was born, that his father had been opposed to his mother's pregnancy, and that his mother's decision not to terminate the pregnancy was related to his father's departure. He knew, too, that his father had children from a first wife and had also married a third time. In addition, Dan was aware of the child support given to his mother. His only "contact" with his father had occurred about a year before the commencement of treatment. On this occasion, having ex-pressed curiosity about his father, his mother gave him the father's number. Dan called, and as he identified himself, his father hung up.

There were other male figures in Dan's life. He had contact with maternal grandparents on vacations and a weekly visit with a male friend of his mother's whom he referred to as his other dad. Dan's mother had never remarried and, to his knowledge, was not dating.

Dan's mother was a thoughtful woman who could anticipate many of her son's difficulties. She led an active and satisfying professional life that rarely interfered with her time with her son.

Jared

Jared, at 11, had never been a particularly popular boy. His friendships were always somewhat marginal, never progressing to a real chumship, though he certainly desired friends. He was, however, quite engaging with his mother's adult friends. He was generally shy, was a good student, and had a particular interest in electronics and gadgets.

He knew that his parents in the first few months of his life had fought, even physically, and that his mother had fled with him in one arm and a single suitcase in the other, in the middle of the night, to escape his father. He had some regular contact with his paternal grandparents, which afforded him bits of news regarding his father. Over the years he had received an occasional birthday or Christmas card from his father. These he saved. Other than that, he had no contact with his father until he was 11, the summer prior to the initial psychiatric consultation. His father appeared unannounced at his grandparents' beach house while he was visiting, took him for a fast and terri-fying ride in an open, low speedboat, returned him to his grandparents, and left.

Over the next few months, Jared became socially withdrawn, declining all after-school play dates. He continued to function well academically but found himself increasingly teased at school—probably provoked by his shyness—about his weight (he was slightly overweight) and his intelligence. He was less able than ever to defend himself. He also began to object to his mother's going out on evenings or weekends without him and became more demanding of her time. At home, he spent many more hours than previously on his electronic devices and motorized gadgets.

Jared's mother was an intelligent professional woman who was caring though a bit impatient with Jared's immaturities. She had never remarried and dated sporadically. Jared had no siblings.

Mike

Mike was 15 when he was referred by his boarding school for psychiatric evaluation. The school was undecided about his starting a new term. He had passing grades but was not working up to his intellectual potential. He was defiant at times, rude on occasion, though also friendly and engaging. He was not a troublemaker, though he frequently ignored rules.

Mike had a brother who was a year older. When Mike was two and living in Europe with his family, significant discord erupted between his parents. His mother, who was independently wealthy, apparently refused to turn over her assets to her husband. There were now frequent episodes of violence by the father against the mother. Whereas Mike's brother showed regressive behaviors at the time, Mike frequently attempted to protect their mother and attack their father. Fearing a further escalation of violence, Mike's mother returned with the children to live near her family in the United States. She obtained a divorce, and there was never any subsequent contact with the father.

At the age of 10, Mike was sent to a boarding school because his mother had difficulty handling her sons. He felt lonely at the time but relieved to have had the company of his brother. Otherwise, his adjustment was average. Mike made friends easily and had good social skills. His brother did not show either a good social or academic adjustment, had frequent rage attacks at home during vacations, and was hospitalized with a diagnosis of a personality disorder when Mike was 12 and subsequently sent to a therapeutic school.

During his probationary semester, Mike returned home every other weekend and had a psychotherapy session. His grades improved to the point where he made honor roll, and his behavior likewise improved. Curiously, however, on the day before Christmas vacation, he openly smoked marijuana in the dormitory corridor and was caught and expelled. Because of the difficulty of finding a new boarding school quickly, his mother and he were forced to resume living together.

Mike's mother had not remarried and did not date. She felt generally that her skills as a mother were limited and, to her credit, was forthright about her limitations. She genuinely regretted not having been able to care for her sons at the time they were first sent to boarding school and regarded Mike's return as a second chance. She was a bit eccentric in style. She denied the consideration that she had agoraphobia although she often remained in her house for days or weeks at a time.

TECHNICAL CONSIDERATIONS

Although there is clearly no consensus of opinion or evidence regarding the impact on development of a father's abandonment, from the vantage point of an individual psychoanalytically oriented psychotherapy, which seeks, essentially, to elucidate personal meaning to the individual, the effects of fatherlessness are profound. The disparity between some of the research cited previously and the individual "research" of a single case stems from the fact that not all emotional difficulties will express themselves as measurable psychopathology. Although Dan, Jared, and Mike did not seek treatment because of fatherlessness, the effects of their fatherlessness in their treatments required special technical adaptations. Areas to be considered include the concept of "father hunger" and its relation to personality development, the role of the therapist in relation to developmental stages generally (and specifically to Oedipal development), the therapist's role as real and transference object, the role of the mother in the treatment, conflicts with the mother, and common countertransference issues.

The Concept of "Father Hunger"

Herzog (6) introduced the term "father hunger" to describe a tenacious affective state of longing experienced by more than 70 children of divorce studied by him. He states, "Father hunger appears to be a critical motivational variable in matters as diverse as caretaking, sexual orientation, moral development, and achievement level" (p. 174). Adams and colleagues (20) take exception to this view, stating, "One seldom misses or craves something one has not savored, so 'father hunger' is most felt by those who have had a father previously" (p. 327). They believe that the experience of longing can occur only as an innate urge to reinstate a former gratification. As a consciously experienced affect, only Dan (among the three boys I have discussed here) expressed such feeling. However, if one looks for unconscious manifestations of such longing, it will become apparent that all three boys were affected by the fathers they did not know.

The relationship with the absent father was experienced as a void. In this respect, these children knew themselves to be different from other children in their milieu. Although at times they felt varying degrees of longing, for the most part they did not dwell on what they did not have. This might appear in relating an episode about a friend and the friend's father, wistfully lingering on a detail or two about their interaction, but not imagining themselves in such a relationship.

On the other hand, a relationship was also unconsciously construed from what they did know of their fathers, however slight this knowledge was. Whatever bits of biography they gleaned, there was one prominent episode that each boy knew: the events of the abandonment. In the initial history-taking, the mothers of these boys recounted the events that occurred at the time of the fathers' abandonments. For the most part the boys' knowledge about their fathers was sparse. But in the initial interviews, each boy recounted a story of being abandoned by his father that paralleled the story told independently by his mother. This meant, of course, that the story was both communicated to each boy and was important to him. A further finding, however, became apparent: that each "story" revealed certain personality characteristics that were similar to the presenting personality problems of each boy. It is possible to speculate that although the boys may not have "missed" the fathers they did not know, their personalities evolved from the particulars of how they lost their fathers, thus allowing the fathers a permanent place in their lives.

Jared's mother took flight with him in the middle of the night. She escaped from a man presumed to be dangerous. Jared's single subsequent experience with his father (in the speedboat) confirmed this view, but even prior to that episode, he seemed to be a shy and timid boy who avoided confrontations. One could say that he was always anticipating and avoiding a dangerous "other." Although Mike's mother also fled her husband with Mike and his brother, it was not before Mike had made a stand and staged his own counterattacks. Mike was seen as a somewhat rebellious boy who was always taking his stand against authority. This behavior was more evident in relation to men; he expressed disapproval to women by merely disregarding them. One could similarly say about Mike, then, that he was always anticipating a dangerous "other" but was on guard and ready to protect himself. Dan's father left his mother in her final months of pregnancy, visiting just once after he was born. In his view, his father was not interested in him. Characterologically, Dan was extremely sensitive to rejections in his friendships, expecting that others would act toward him as his father had. He was always deliberating whether to officially promote a friend to best-friend status, or to demote a friend because he was feeling slighted. In short, he was always anticipating a rejecting "other" over whom he had little control.

Essentially, what is suggested here is that the "story" of the abandonment constitutes each boy's main experience with his father and thus forms the basis of his internalized object relationship with him. This, in turn, forms a cornerstone in the evolution of the boy's personality. Viewed in this way, father hunger becomes a pervasive albeit often unconscious theme in these boys' lives. The chief complaint that brought them to treatment can be seen as an unconscious attempt to address this fact of their lives. The void of their conscious experience of their fathers is unconsciously no void at all.

In these circumstances, one need not wait an extended period of time until sufficient trust in the therapeutic relationship is developed to allow the "deepest" conflicts to become manifest. From the start, the therapist should work on the presenting problems in the context that a relationship with a new object represents a reworking of the conflicts related to the boy's abandonment by his father. An appreciation of this characterological displacement leads to a judicious restraint in addressing the abandonment more overtly—it is being addressed anyway.

The Therapist's Role in Relation to Developmental Stages

In her discussion of childhood mourning, Sekaer (22) notes that as a child passes through subsequent developmental stages, the significance of the absence needs to be reworked in accordance with the new and normative stresses. In the same way, the abandonment by a father can have a different impact on a child, depending on the current developmental stresses.

For example, Mike's relationship with his mother had been problematic. She was experienced as inadequate in the early years and rejecting when she sent him off to boarding school when he was 8. As previously noted, the difficulties that led to the consultations were treated in an infrequent psychotherapy (every 2 to 3 weeks), which allowed him to remain at boarding school. At the end of a superior semester, he flagrantly abused a rule and was expelled. The meaning of this attempt to sabotage his progress soon became clear. For the first time in 5 years, Mike would be living with his mother. Initially, he appeared indifferent to this change. Soon, however, he was complaining about the rotten "Egg McMuffins" she made for him every day for breakfast. Some months later he found the very same sandwiches to be all right. From this and other considerations it became clear that his therapy, which began intermittently, facilitated his return home. As Blos (23) notes, early adolescence involves a necessary regression to pre-Oedipal drives and conflicts. The presence of the therapist allowed Mike to return to his mother and to accept previously interrupted gratification of his needs for nurturance. Here, the therapist functions as Mahler and Gosliner (3) and Abelin (4,24) suggest the father functions during the process of separation and individuation—to prevent engulfment in dependency gratifications.

The other two boys demonstrated similar developmental "uses" of the therapist. Dan, cautiously at first, then eagerly, tested out swear words, dirty jokes, and finally asked questions about sexual concerns. Although his mother discussed sex freely with him, he noted that he always felt a little funny about it. His questions seemed to have less to do with a need to know specific answers than with a need to observe how a male discussed sex. After several months of tame conversations in therapy, Jared soared out of the elevator one day on roller skates (as the therapist was passing) and bashed into him with gusto. Such "accidents" subsequently became more commonplace. He sorely needed such rough-and-tumble play. Here the therapist was being used to help the child modulate aggression in a manner described by Herzog (6) fitting the pre-Oedipal boy.

The general technical consideration follows that the presence of the therapist in the child's life may allow the child to experience—through the therapist, either directly or indirectly—the fulfillment of a developmental need. It is as if the family is reconstituted with the presence of the therapist. This can elicit the mother's unresolved transferences from the ex-husband, a topic I will discuss subsequently. When the therapist functions in a role to symbolically complete the family and fulfill a development need in the child, there is rarely a necessity to interpret this. Rather, if any further intervention is needed, it should be in the direction of advising the parent to seek additional figures who may fulfill this need.

Oedipal Conflicts

Most reports in the literature focus on the Oedipal development of children paternally abandoned at or near the Oedipal stage. These discussions may or may not have bearing on children abandoned by fathers in the earliest years. Meiss (25), in describing the analysis of a 5-year-old boy whose father died when he was 3, discusses the conflicts that center on the boy's view of the father as an avenging figure not subject to subsequent revision. Neubauer (26), generalizing from the analysis of a girl whose father left the house just prior to the Oedipal stage, also noted a tendency to view the absent father as overly punitive or overly idealized. Both noted some degree of superego deviation, as did Kestenbaum and Stone (27) in their report of the effects of paternal deprivation in girls. Burgner (28), in reporting on 13 children who were father-deprived during their preschool years, notes pseudo-Oedipal behavior, referring to the effects of early triangulation, a persistence of attachment to the primary object, and a pseudo-latency.

The ubiquity of the Oedipal complex has been questioned by some researchers. As Adams and colleagues (20) have noted:

Oedipal problems may be at the core of a fatherless child's neurotic patterns when there has been some exposure to a dreadful father; but if there has been no father to internalize and to stimulate the child's internal representations, the child's difficulties will have to be chalked up more sensibly to pre-Oedipal or non-Oedipal forces. (p. 326)

To judge from the cases of the boys presented here, these children did seem to experience Oedipal conflicts—as evidenced, for instance, by the fluctuating transferential admiration and denigrating competition. It is possible that it is the attachment of a child to a male therapist that precipitates the Oedipal conflicts. I will discuss this in the next section.

Superego deficiencies, fantasies of parricide or of incest with the mother, and persistence of a dyadic attachment to the mother have been emphasized in the Oedipal conflicts of boys who have experienced the loss of a father. Although these considerations are applicable in some circumstances to the boy abandoned early by his father, the negative Oedipal development in such boys has not been emphasized. Negative Oedipal development refers to the libidinal attachment of a boy to his father. As Blos (23) has pointed out, this facet of development usually again becomes manifest in the de-repression of early adolescence. Father hunger is a complementary concept referring more generally to the affects of longing. For the boy with little or no actual experience with a father, these desires may remain active and overt during latency.

Dan, for instance, after several months of psychotherapy during which his therapist had become quite important to him, began to establish play situations that put him in physical contact with the therapist. He would race to the therapist's chair at the start of the sessions, declaring he was to sit in the "superior" seat and his therapist in the "inferior" seat. When the therapist did sit in his own chair, Dan would climb over the back and wind up in the therapist's lap. In response to this wish for physical contact, he would attempt to make himself undesirable by threatening flatulence or trying to get the therapist to smell his "smelly" feet and place his feet in the therapist's lap. He had a fantasy that behind the closet door was a luxurious bedroom where the therapist took his girlfriends. This fantasy of the therapist as a sexually mature male was followed by taunts that the therapist couldn't even get an ugly girl. Some days the therapist was "shrinkie-dinkie," other days he had a "hippopotamus butt" and an "elephant thing." Although these fantasies and feelings were quite exciting to Dan and his acting on the wishes had to be curbed by the therapist at times, there was also a process of identification at work. The fantasy of the bedroom behind the closet door, for instance, followed Dan's telling his therapist a "secret": that he really liked a girl in his class but was afraid his friends would tease him for this. It appears, then, that the Oedipal compromise functioning at this point in his latency was still subject to modification, specifically with isogender sexual wishes giving way to a more solid masculine identification. Follow-up during late adolescence, of course, would be necessary to know the definitive outcome of his sexual identification.

The more overt competitive impulses should be handled in a way that conveys the therapist's approval of the boy's winning as well as the therapist's pleasure at winning and sustained self-esteem at losing. Dan, for instance, objected strongly to the therapist's keeping his own notes about him. The issue was becoming something of a power struggle as Dan demanded to read his file. However, he took readily to the therapist's suggestion that in their own notebook they jointly write notes describing each session in the last 5 minutes of each session. At a certain point, Jared wanted to play cards or checkers and was sullen and distressed when he did not win. Eventually he came to enjoy the competition itself, regardless of who won. Finally, another aspect of competitiveness involves the child's wish or demand to know something personal about the therapist. Although I will discuss this more fully in the following section, refusal on the therapist's part to appropriately gratify some of these wishes often results in a more general sense of defeat for the fatherless boy. For example, the therapist on one occasion stalled about answering a personal question of Dan's whose subsequent associations were to his most immediate social failures at school.

The Therapist as Real or Transference Figure

Male therapists, and possibly female therapists as well, cannot enter into the life of fatherless boys without functioning in many respects as real figures. Burgner (28), in reporting on the analytic treatments of 13 children abandoned during the preschool years, writes, "With these children the importance of the analyst as a real person should not be minimized" (p. 314). She also stresses the necessity of helping such children with real, external difficulties as opposed to limiting the work to the analysis of internalized neurotic conflicts.

Failure to heed one's role as a real person in such a boy's life can lead to a disruption of treatment. For example, after Jared had been in treatment for over a year, his shyness, depressions, preoccupations with his father, and separation anxiety from the mother had improved. Many of the sessions were spent with his showing the therapist his ingenuity with mechanical or electronic gadgets. Although this was clearly a transference manifestation of his relationship with his father (about all he knew of his father was that he was a good mechanic), these interests represented an attempt to please his father that was fully unconscious and thus not subject to interpretation. One day, at a time when the therapist was preparing to move his office from the hospital where he met with Jared, some 2 hours after a session, the therapist entered a public bus that Jared had entered ahead of him. As he passed him the therapist said "hello" and proceeded to the back of the bus. This was the last the therapist saw of Jared, despite several phone calls and a meeting with his mother. In retrospect, Jared had probably been shadowing the therapist, knew his schedule, and had arranged this "chance" meeting. Unable to speak about the feelings behind such action, he had unwittingly arranged for a repetition of the rejection from his father. Had the therapist, on the other hand, taken more time with him on the bus, allowing for more of a real relationship, the outcome may well have been different. Countertransferential anxiety in regard to the intensity of Jared's need for his father probably accounted for this error.

The importance of the therapist as a real figure can be seen in the previous example. Yet therapy is never as simple as functioning as a real person in a child's life. As Anna Freud (29) has noted,

> The child who enters analysis sees in the analyst a new object and treats him as such, so far as he has a healthy part to his personality. He uses the analyst for repetition, i.e. transference, as far as his neurosis or other disturbance comes into question. (p. 38)

On the other hand, Adams and colleagues (20) have pointed out that a child without experience with a father cannot bring this lack of experience into the transference. They also state, "Fatherless children need effective therapists, not father substitutes, when they come for psychotherapy," (p. 328) and advise, rather, that the therapist encourage the child and the mother to make more contacts with "real objects." The issue, however, is not as simple as transferred versus new experience. What must also be considered is the capacity of the child for an essential object relationship with a father figure when he has not experienced the primary object relationship. In other words, there will be a certain resistance to the experience of intimacy by the child with the therapist, based not on an avoidance of repressed conflict with the object but on the absence of the primary paternal object relationship and an avoidance of an attachment that will awaken feelings of what has been absent. Thus, the technical implications of these considerations will involve an alternating use of oneself as a transference and a real object, with an ongoing assessment of how the therapist as real object has been experienced. This is perhaps the single most important technical aspect in work with father-absent boys. The following examples will clarify this point.

Mike was having difficulty organizing his work habits for school. He wanted to do well but couldn't seem to bring it off. He asked his therapist one day what kind of student the therapist was at his age. The point of the question was not whether or not the therapist could relate to his predicament, but rather whether it was yet necessary at his age (fifteen) to have developed good work habits if one intended to go on to college. Mike had no model of achievement, either in his absent father or in his mother. The therapist answered the question directly and affirmatively. The effect of this soon led Mike to work with a tutor. Here, Mike learned something from the therapist by learning about him and used it effectively. This contrasts to another episode from his treatment. Mike had observed that when he left his sessions he had "a funny feeling like depression." Several sessions later, while discussing a rock concert he was going to attend, he asked what rock groups his therapist had heard when he was younger. The therapist mentioned several groups, then, remembering he had attended the 1969 Woodstock Festival, he mentioned this too. Mike became quite curious about many details about the festival and spent the rest of the session asking the therapist about it. This was the first time he had expressed more than passing curiosity about the therapist's life, and through the specific questions about the festival had a greater sense of an aspect of the therapist's life. Although this seemed to apparently please Mike, he missed the next session and forgot to call. This was the first time he had completely overlooked a session. By the following session he had "forgotten" everything that had been said. It became clear that at this point he could not allow himself this gratifying curiosity about the therapist. It was not until some 6 months later, while discussing Mike's detachment—a trait Mike was beginning to notice himself—that the therapist could interpret the above event, which was far from forgotten.

In general, then, the therapy must address not only the patient's wish to know the therapist and the therapist's acting as a real person, but must also address the patient's specific resistance to knowing the therapist as a real person—which reflects, in these cases, the underdeveloped capacity for such object relatedness. As the capacity for object relatedness to a paternal figure is expanded, the patient's capacity for benefiting from the example and advice of a therapist will increase, as will his ability to make use of his interpretations.

I have described aspects of Dan's Oedipal development. Also to be considered are the effects of the therapist as a real figure in this aspect of his development, and the child's reaction to the therapist in this role. On one occasion, Dan spoke with some contempt about a friend's father who took his 10-year-old son to what he referred to as a "pornography show." His envy was obvious and easily interpretable. After minimal denial, he asked the therapist if he had ever gone to a pornographic movie and if so, when. The therapist first asked him if he discussed these things with his mother or his "second Dad." Mike responded that he had with his mother, yes, but she was a woman; with his "second Dad," no. The question seemed to be a request for information about how he should handle his sexual curiosities. The therapist answered that, when he was a teenager, he had first seen a pornographic movie. Dan at first thought this was too young, but on reconsideration decided it was better than at age 10. Although he was pleased to have this information, later in the session he began a new round of "shrinkie-dinkie who couldn't get a mule." The information he wanted also brought the awareness that the therapist had a sexual life. Although this served to stimulate the Oedipally derived conflict that the therapist had more information than he did, it also stimulated his awareness that, unlike his friend who had a father who would teach him about pornography, he did not. The therapist must differentiate between resistance to these affects and resistance to the emotional conflicts of the Oedipal stage. The latter involves a resistance to conflicts within an object relationship, the former to the evolution of the object relationship itself. Very different technical interventions would follow.

Thus, in considering the role of the therapist as a real and as a transference figure, and the necessary fluctuations between these technical positions, the boy's capacity for meaningful relatedness to the therapist as a father figure is both challenged and assessed by the therapist's interactions as a real figure. The development of this capacity must proceed not only by interpretations of resistance to the transferential figure, but also of resistance to a relationship with the real figure.

A related issue concerns the choice of gender of the therapist. If one views the affects of father-hunger in fatherless children as an individual, rather than a more ubiquitous, issue, one will not view the gender of the therapist as crucial, a position advocated by Adams and colleagues (20). But if father-hunger is seen as a more ubiquitous affect, and if character development is regarded in relation to father absence, the gender of the therapist becomes crucial. This is not to say that there are not other transferences that would need to be worked out, but the transference to the male therapist by the fatherless boy can hardly be neutral. If the treatment, by external necessity, must be a limited one, the choice of a female therapist for a fatherless boy will allow more focused work to proceed. Otherwise, a male therapist is to be preferred.

The Mother's Role

Atkins (30,31) has significantly underscored the mother's role in the child's development of a relationship with his or her father. He states, "The way mother 'prepares' her child may well affect the separate, yet related, relationship that the child develops with the father" (30, p. 146). Depending on her attitudes, and the effects of what Atkins calls "transitive vitalization," minimal actual contact with a father can flourish into a full relationship.

These same considerations hold true for the father-absent boy in relation to his therapist. The extent to which the child's mother has maintained angry or resentful feelings toward the abandoning father, and the extent to which she will foster a significant relationship for her son outside of hers will often determine whether or not the son can allow the therapeutic relationship to become meaningful to him. It is exceedingly important, therefore, to carefully assess the mother's attitudes in advance. The essential question is whether the mother is prepared to see the therapist as a new object or whether she will use the therapist as a new figure relatively free from her transferences to her ex-husband. The extent to which the mother has promoted "father substitutes" is often indicative of her future reactions to the boy's relationship to the therapist. The mother who remains actively embittered should be referred for treatment herself. The mother who is anxious about the son's separation as a result of a new significant relationship needs to be included to a greater extent in the treatment. In some cases, the therapist will have to meet for extended periods of time with both mother and child, understanding that such an expansion of the dyad leads to greater separation. The involvement of Dan, Mike, and Jared with their treatments was due first and foremost to their mothers' unconflicted facilitation of the treatments.

The Child's Conflicts With His Mother

Although fatherless boys certainly experience a range of conflicts that defy generalization, essential conflicts directly involving the mother will be difficult to approach. Because the relationship with the mother usually represents the primary object tie, threats to it lead to more dangerous and overwhelming anxiety. This is not to say that these boys have unusually harmonious relationships with their mothers. In fact, there may be more than the usual amount of fighting as an attempt to disrupt the dyadic closeness. But the essential conflicts become repressed simply because awareness of them leads to a greater sense of abandonment.

One essential conflict with the mother usually involves the unacknowledged blame the boy feels toward her for having lost his father. Although Jared was overtly clinging toward his mother when he was at his most distressed, analysis revealed that he was enraged at her for losing his father. Mike, on the other hand, criticized his mother openly and at times mercilessly, but his rage centered not only on what he wanted from her that she wasn't providing (namely, a more normally run household), but also on the fact that it was only from her that he could get this. His fantasies about how he would raise his own children were no consolation to him. Dan approached the issue tangentially. He spoke of a favorite great-uncle who had died 2 years before because his great-aunt took him to the doctor too late. It was only after telling this story several times that he recognized his feelings of blame toward his mother for his father's abandonment of him.

Such feelings of blame towards the mother will be expressed only later in treatment. The child will need not only to have developed a sense of trust and security with the therapist, but also to have internalized important aspects of this new relationship.

Countertransference

There are two main sources of countertransference reactions in work with fatherless boys. The first involves bringing personal ideas and emotions regarding fatherlessness to the treatment. Adams and colleagues (20) take the position that fatherlessness is viewed as natural by many children, though this view is infrequently shared by therapists.

A second source of countertransferential difficulties lies in the therapist's personal response to the manifest aspects of father-hunger. These responses may involve either an underreaction, as perhaps occurred when the therapist met Jared on the bus, or more commonly, an overreaction. Nontherapeutic outings or home visits or bringing more than the usual number of treats to a session are indications of an overreaction. The dangers are twofold. One is that the involvement may overwhelm the child's capacity for involvement or stimulate his fantasies of the therapist's involvement beyond the therapist's willingness or capabilities. This will lead to disappointment and dejection, which are difficult enough to handle as transferential affects without the encumbrance of real expectations that have an established precedent. The second danger of such overinvolvement is that it deprives the child of the chance to expand the number of real male figures in his life once he begins to desire such relationships. In short, these countertransferential reactions will obscure the therapist's judgment regarding shifts between his dual roles as real and transference figure.

It is important to pace one's therapeutic involvement and to assess carefully each increment. Mike's treatment began with a consultation every 2 to 3 weeks for the first 6 months. It was only when he returned home after expulsion from his boarding school that therapy began on a twice-a-week basis. He would not have tolerated any more rapid a commencement. Dan initially began his treatment on a once-a-week basis. After 3 months and many statements that he never had enough time to tell the therapist everything, treatment was increased to twice a week. For at least the first 2 months, however, of twice-a-week treatment, he was far from joyous. Now that he had the extra session, he complained about the trip to the office and became quite critical of the therapist. It is clear that he was attempting to fend off a growing attachment to the therapist, but at times these new objections threatened to disrupt treatment. Given that he rarely saw his second Dad more than once a week, and sometimes not as regularly as that, one can appreciate that the meaning of two therapy visits per week has an entirely different significance than it does for a boy who has a father at home. More time can be construed by the child as a desire of the therapist's for increased intimacy. This brings its own increased resistances.

CONCLUSION

Adams and colleagues (20) in their comprehensive review of the subject report, "Since fatherlessness is not a homogeneous state, not much is written about therapy with fatherless children and adolescents" (p. 320). Given the disparate circumstances of father absence, and the timing of these circumstances in relation to developmental stages, generalizations both about development and treatment must be made cautiously. The approach taken here focuses on the absence of a father and not on the loss of a father. The themes and techniques of the treatment of a father-absent boy will apply to the treatment of a boy who has lost his father with respect to how the absence functions in his life and in the therapy. What has not been addressed here are the technical aspects of dealing with a loss itself.

The acute problem that brought Dan, Jared, or Mike into treatment has be seen as an exacerbation of an already present character style that in turn has been shown to be related to the absence of the father. It is said that the unconscious knows no negation; similarly, it contains no void. What is consciously felt or known as a void has more specific unconscious content. Thus, one can see the character style of these boys evolving from the story of the abandonment of the father. It is their attempt to hold onto the father.

This understanding of the unconscious elaboration of early paternal absence leads to certain specific modifications of therapeutic technique. Chief among these are the therapist's dual roles of real and transferential figure. Analytically oriented psychotherapists are schooled in tracking the patient's resistance to the transference. Therapists will be less likely to consider and monitor the patient's resistance to the emergence of the real relationship. The new real relationship is no gift. It awakens a sense of what might have been. Pleasure in the new relationship can occur only after therapeutic work on these affects. After each introduction of some aspect of the therapist's real life, whether by personal anecdote, an opinion, or by a direct response to a question, the overall quality of relatedness must be reassessed. Has the child become withdrawn, belligerent, or more involved with therapy and curious about the therapist? These shifts within the therapeutic relationship in response to knowing more about the therapist are an essential locus of observation. By this type of work, the relationship with the nearly nonexistent father is removed from the character style into a new relationship with the therapist. In the process a new and essential object relationship is created. The therapist ultimately is not a father substitute, although he may function at times in this way. He makes it possible finally for the child to have more meaningful flexible relationships that can approximate the father-son relationship—one of admiration and competition, of guidance and friendship.

REFERENCES

1. Chiland C: A new look at fathers. Psychoanal Study Child 37:367–379, 1982
2. Brooks-Gunn J, Lewis M: "Why mama and papa?" The development of social labels. Child Dev 50:1203–1206, 1979
3. Mahler MS, Gosliner RJ: On symbiotic child psychosis: genetic, dynamic and restitutive aspects. Psychoanal Study Child 10:195–212, 1955
4. Abelin E: The role of the father in the separation-individuation process, in Separation Individuation. Edited by McDevitt JB, Settlage CF. New York, International Universities Press, 1971, pp 52–69

5. Meerloo JAM: The psychological role of the father: the father cuts the cord. Child and Family 102–116, 1968
6. Herzog JM: On father hunger: the father's role in the modulation of aggressive drive and fantasy, in Father and Child: Developmental and Clinical Perspectives. Edited by Cath SH, Gurwitt AR, Ross JM. Boston, MA, Little, Brown, 1982, pp 163–174
7. Ross JM: In search of fathering: a review, in Father and Child: Developmental and Clinical Perspectives. Edited by Cath SH, Gurwitt AR, Ross JM. Boston, MA, Little, Brown, 1982, pp 21–31
8. Tyson P: The role of father in gender identity, urethral erotism, and phallic narcissism, in Father and Child: Developmental and Clinical Perspectives. Edited by Cath SH, Gurwitt AR, Ross JM. Boston, MA, Little, Brown, 1982, pp 175–188
9. Biller HB, Borstelmann LJ: Masculine development: an integrative review. Merrill-Palmer Quarterly 13:257–294, 1967
10. Money J, Ehrhardt AA: Developmental differentiation, in Man and Woman, Boy and Girl. Baltimore, MD, Johns Hopkins University Press, 1972, pp 176–194
11. Seegmiller BR: Sex-role differentiation in preschoolers: effects of maternal employment. J Psychol 104:185–189, 1980
12. Santrok JW, Wohlford P: Effects of father absence: influences of reason for and onset of absence. Paper presented at the annual meeting of the American Psychological Association, Miami, FL, September 1970
13. Hetherington EM: Effects of paternal absence on sex-typed behaviors in Negro and white preadolescent males. J Pers Soc Psychol 4:87–91, 1966
14. Reyes TF: Father absence and the social behavior of pre-school children. Dissertation Abstracts International 39(1-A):185–186, 1978
15. Sarnoff CA: The father's role in latency, in Father and Child: Developmental and Clinical Perspectives. Edited by Cath SH, Gurwitt AR, Ross JM. Boston, MA, Little, Brown, 1982, pp 253–264
16. Aichorn A: Some causes of delinquency and some causes of delinquency (continued), in Wayward Youth. New York, Viking, 1935, pp 37–61, 63–71
17. Herzog JM, Sudia CE: Children in fatherless families, in Review of Child Development Research: Child Development and Social Policy, Vol 3. Edited by Caldwell BM, Ricciuti HN. Chicago, IL, University of Chicago Press, 1978, pp 79–92
18. Rutter M: Maternal deprivation 1972–1978: new finding, new concepts, new approaches. Child Dev 50:283–305, 1979
19. Rutter M: Long-term consequences: possible mechanisms, in Maternal Deprivation Reassessed. Harmondsworth, England, Penguin, 1972, pp 79–119
20. Adams PL, Milner JR, Schrepf NA: Fatherless Children. New York, John Wiley, 1984
21. Radin N: The role of the father in cognitive, academic, and intellectual development, in The Role of the Father in Child Development. Edited by Lamb ML. New York, John Wiley, 1982, pp 36–51
22. Sekaer C: Toward a definition of 'childhood mourning.' Am J Psychother 41:201–219, 1987
23. Blos P: Phases of adolescence, in On Adolescence. New York, Free Press, 1962, pp 52–156

24. Abelin E: Some further observations and comments on the earliest role of the father. Int J Psychoanal 56:293–302, 1975
25. Meiss ML: The oedipal problem of a fatherless child. Psychoanal Study Child 7:216–229, 1952
26. Neubauer PB: The one-parent child and his oedipal development. Psychoanal Study Child 15:286–309, 1960
27. Kestenbaum CJ, Stone MH: The effects of fatherless homes upon daughters: clinical impressions regarding paternal deprivation. J Am Acad Psychoanal 4:171–190, 1976
28. Burgner M: The oedipal experience: effects on development of an absent father. Int J Psychoanal 66:311–320, 1985
29. Freud A: The relationship between child analysis and adult analysis, in Normality and Pathology in Childhood. New York, International Universities Press, 1965, pp 25–53
30. Atkins RN: Discovering daddy: the mother's role, in Father and Child: Developmental and Clinical Perspectives. Edited by Cath SH, Gurwitt AR, Ross JM. Boston, MA, Little, Brown, 1982, pp 139–149
31. Atkins RN: Transitive vitalization and its impact on father-representation. Contemporary Psychoanalysis 20:663–676, 1984

5 Aggressive Children

Constance L. Katz, Ph.D.

DEVELOPMENTAL AND DIAGNOSTIC ISSUES

When we speak of the behaviors such as destroying property in a fit of rage, attacking others, or taking oneself as the object of attack in a tantrum, we are, of course, speaking of symptomatic behavior in a child. As such, these behaviors may reflect many varied meanings and origins in different children, and suggest different diagnostic pictures. It is also possible that destructive behavior in the same child may have different meanings at different times, or be a normal manifestation. As Anna Freud has pointed out, between the ages of two and three, many children have "temper tantrums" that, over time, moderate in terms of duration, intensity, and frequency (1). These displays may be considered a normal developmental event in the life of the child of this age, showing vigor of will, need for the release of intense affect, and incapacity to satisfactorily express feelings verbally.

In pathological development, though the child ages, he retains the emotional lability of the younger child. One sees the persistence of tantrums and the inability to withstand progressive degrees of frustration. With increased age, the child also becomes capable of doing greater damage during a destructive outburst and becomes harder to physically control. If the problem is not resolved early and becomes severe enough to frighten parents and/or teachers, such children may be institutionalized when they become too powerful for one person to restrain (2,3). In children who have sufficient ego development, we may see the attempt to suppress tantrums through the rigid control of spontaneous behavior and the inhibition of motor activity. For these children, even sports can be considered dangerous activities, involving the potential destruction of the self or others. The occasional eruption of aggressive behavior may nevertheless occur under conditions of sufficient stimulation of aggression, prompting a new effort at rigid self-control.

Children with chronic problems in containing destructive impulses usually do not engage in symbolic play. It has been my impression that such children are too frightened by their fantasies to create play from them. Helping such children to play is the sine qua non of a therapy that will help them gain control over motor expressions of aggression.

We may identify a complex of related, constructive events in the life of the child that enable him or her to moderate rageful impulses, at least so that he or she is not compelled to give vent to them as a motor discharge of destructiveness or assault. With the existence of a strong attachment to a caregiver, and under the conditions of adequate gratification of impulse as well as adequate and age-appropriate frustrations (4–6), children begin to give up the pleasure of immediate gratifications of many sorts (e.g. physiological pleasures, exploratory urges, greed, and destructive impulses). They do so not from cognitive understanding of the superiority of one set of behaviors over another, but out of the need to please the caregiver and to retain the caregiver as a loving, protective, and therefore gratifying object. The "good-enough" caregiver, by definition modulated in his or her affect, permits the child to transcend the normally polarized views of toddlerhood wherein the caregiver is seen as being either all-good (at moments of gratification) or all-bad (at moments of frustration). Over time, and after many instances of the parent's mostly remaining steady and nonpunitive in the face of trying moments in child care, the child forms an internalized mental representation of a benevolent caregiver who is essentially constant in physical availability and emotional benevolence. This representation sustains the child both during separations from the caregiver and during the inevitable frustrations of the socialization process. The child "knows" that the frustrating parent is one and the same as the gratifying one and that hurting the parent in a moment of frustration hurts the gratifying parent as well as the depriving one (5,7). This process has been called the development of emotional or libidinal object constancy. The beginning of the ability to integrate both good and bad perceptions of individuals has been dated at about age three (5,8). Klein called the transcendence of splitting as the achievement of the "infantile depressive position" (9). For Mahler, it represented the culmination of the stages of separation-individuation, and the beginnings of emotional object constancy. Sullivan, in describing the polarizations of early childhood, noted that many adults retain a tendency to bifurcate their experience of others, tending to persist in seeing them as all-good or all-bad, and the task of fusing these perceptions is often a lifelong one. We may note reflections of this form of splitting in our cultural myths and beliefs, which portray the deeds of individuals as the actions of heroes or villains.

When parenting is inconsistent or harsh, when parents are emotionally unavailable, or when events such as prolonged and traumatic separations in early childhood are part of a child's early history, that child does not have the opportunity to learn that a parent can be essentially benevolent even though there are occasional "misses" of good parenting. The child will be unable to tolerate limits and frustrations that are part of the socialization process, with a faith that these are in his or her best interests. Splitting, the normal cognitive and perceptual mode of early childhood, now accrues a defensive function. It appears that in order to retain some hope in the reality of a good parent, the child sees him or her as all-good either in a fantasy distortion, or when the parent is being gratifying.

During times of frustration or disappointment, the child lacking emotional object constancy seems not to remember that individuals who frustrate may also be benevolent. Therefore, there is no experience at these moments that anything worthwhile will be lost if the object is hurt or even destroyed. The object is seen as evil and deserving of great punishment. It is critical to recognize that, without therapy, this developmental deficit leaves the child no way to develop beyond the use of splitting mechanisms in relationships that may be potentially constructive but do not represent primary attachments. It is the purpose of the therapeutic interventions described later in this chapter to help advance the child toward the development of emotional object constancy through use of the transference, and toward the related development of the ability to verbalize affect and engage in symbolic play.

A therapist often sees, as a consequence of inadequate parenting, an intensification of the child's narcissistic vulnerability. Trying to understand the relationship between narcissistic injury and aggressive activity has been part of the quest to determine what kinds of aggression might be understood as reactive as opposed to instinctual (8,10,11). In these children, rage reactions may be easily evoked by small slights. Children react to anticipated or imagined narcissistic injury, thereby inducing rejections, confirming their perceptions of others, and making them feel justified in their rage. Highly aggressive institutionalized children with profoundly turbulent histories and extreme narcissistic vulnerabilities have been well-described by Willock (2,3).

It appears that physically abused children have a higher probability of becoming aggressive than do neglected children. In one study, 50% of a sample of physically abused children, as opposed to 31% of neglected children, had been designated as "unmanageable" and were put into a second foster home placement (12). Predictor variables for the open expression of aggression in these children included being a victim of physical abuse; displaying themes, fantasy, and verbalization of depressed mood; needing foster home replacement; and repeating first grade. However, being the object of physical abuse was the most powerful single factor determining overt aggressive behavior. It is noteworthy too, that depressive expression and ideation are not mutually exclusive of open aggression. An explanation for this is offered in a later section, as part of my discussion of the problem of failure to develop self as well as object constancy.

A history of chronically depriving parenting of the abusive variety is not the only route to the development of problems in modulation of aggression, although child cases seen in clinics and outpatient hospital settings are often noteworthy for the degree of turbulence, deprivation, and abuse sustained by children in their earliest years. I am thinking instead of the many instances of

wild children brought into therapy by well-meaning parents who confuse benevolent parenting with extreme permissiveness, which is often actually a
guilty submission to the child. Some of these parents use extensive reaction
formations against aggression and are unable to feel or express the desire to be
normally firm with children. Some of them chronically suppress their anger
but explode at their children when the children escalate in destructiveness,
unconsciously hoping to force parental limits. This picture certainly suggests
long-standing problems with the expression of aggression in these parents,
who—after a lifetime of curtailing their own angry or even assertive responses—need to deal with a child who may have become the "container" of
aggression for the family. The situation repeats itself cyclically, as the parents'
guilt over an explosion at the child serves to reinstate their inappropriate permissiveness. In addition, I have also seen special efforts to be "easy" with the
child made as an attempt at reparation to children for deprivations sustained
earlier in childhood for which the parents feel guilty. The following vignette
illustrates some features in the family background of an aggressive, suicidal
boy. These include the mother's characterological difficulties with anger, her
feelings of guilt, the probable contribution of an early trauma in the infancy of
the boy, and the additional variable of the aggressive boy's identification with
a verbally explosive father. The family was a middle-class, professional family.

Mrs. A. had a severe depressive episode following the birth of her second child
and was eventually hospitalized for several months when the baby was 8 months
of age. The event that precipitated the hospitalization involved the mother's
briefly putting a pillow over the infant's face one day when he was crying and
she was unable to soothe him. We may speculate that these events (i.e., the
emotional loss of mother to depression, the trauma of the brief suffocation, and
the physical loss of her when she was hospitalized) greatly hindered the boy in
the task of consolidating a sense of trust in his mother, and that the frustrations
of these several months stimulated some extra measure of rage in him.

The mother, who had raised a daughter of school age, saw the birth of the son
as locking her into an unhappy marriage with a childish and verbally abusive
man. She was frightened about aggressive feelings toward her infant son, and
quite guilty about her feelings toward him both before and after her return
from the hospital. She continued to assume a masochistic position with regard
to her husband, and took an appeasing stance toward her second child as well.
The boy was eight when he was brought for treatment for destructiveness and
suicidal threats and gestures. (He also had a corollary problem in separating
from his mother in various situations.) Although the boy needed her presence
very badly in many situations in which he would otherwise be terrified, she was
afraid to use her power to help him establish some controls, fearing that limits,
physical restrictions, or withdrawal of love or privileges would anger him and
make matters worse.

Research into patterns of parenting that correlate with high levels of aggressiveness has been consistent with these psychodynamic formulations. Parents who physically punish children have highly aggressive children (13, 14, 15). Parents who use other forms of discipline, such as withdrawal of affection, have children low in aggressive displays. The highest level of open aggression existed in children with permissive parents who intermittently exploded and hit their children.

Although I have described various familial configurations that impede the child in moderating the expression of intense affect, it is important to note the possible existence of constitutional or temperamental factors that could exacerbate an individual child's problem. At the extreme, it is apparent that significant neurological impairment would make the establishment of controls over intense affect a difficult task. Chess, Thomas, and Birch identify three temperament types in normal children. Although each type poses certain risk factors depending on what responses they elicit from figures in the milieu, they imply that children with high activity levels in combination with high intensity of affect are at particular risk for behavior disorders (16,17).

An in-depth presentation of the many perspectives for viewing the etiology and manifestations of aggressive behavior is beyond the purview of this chapter. For this purpose, the reader may consult Bandura and Walters (15) for a discussion of the social learning theory of aggressive behavior, Freud (18) for a discussion of aggression as drive, Aronson (19) for a review of theories of aggression from a sociologist's perspective, Magid and McKelvey (20) for a consideration of problems associated with aggression in psychopathic youngsters, and Schiavi (21) for a review of the biological aspects of aggression.

Inasmuch as I have been describing children who have failed to achieve the developmental milestone of emotional object constancy with its various corollary achievements, it may be inferred that the usual diagnosis of these children would be that of borderline personality disorder. We may see destructive behavior in chronically psychotic children as well, but my focus here will be on those children that may be only intermittently psychotic and who may be worked with in an office setting (as opposed to a therapeutic milieu). Because the symptoms of destructiveness, attack, or self-injury in these children indicate deficits in early development, we assess these behaviors and treat them differently than we might the same symptom in a neurotic child who is momentarily stimulated beyond his capacity for control or who is testing limits. Neurotic children are different with regard to the intertwined issues of attachment, degree of superego development, and inhibitory potentials. That is, they can weather disappointments in those to whom they are attached, they can tolerate feelings of having been wrong or bad and want to make reparation, and they can express anger at times in a symbolic fashion (i.e., through words, play, or other fantasy outlets). Although all children are narcissistically vulnerable, our work in the treatment of these children will have to make special note of the extreme vulnerability of aggressive borderline children, as well as their devaluation of and desire to be sadistic toward those who have hurt or disappointed them.

TECHNICAL ISSUES IN THE MANAGEMENT OF DESTRUCTIVENESS WITHIN THE THERAPY SESSION

Maenchen has written of her experience in having to limit a wild, attacking girl in therapy, and her impressions of the sense of failure experienced by many therapists when interpretations alone fail to help a child control destructive behavior (22). She notes a hesitancy to report cases in which children had to be managed with means other than verbal ones, and an apologetic attitude on the part of the therapist when he or she cannot manage children's aggression with the use of verbal means alone (see also Redl and Wineman [23]). Probably many of the "techniques" we learn for dealing with aggressive outbursts are adequate for the neurotic child. Interpreting, reinstating a protection or defense, setting limits, or offering a toy or doll on which the child may displace aggression—these techniques all can work for the less disturbed child. These children have symbolic means available to them for expressing aggression (i.e., play and words) and are motivated to preserve relationships, expecting that they will be mostly rewarding. If they have an occasional loss of control, they are therefore responsive to the mild efforts of a benevolent adult to serve as an auxiliary ego and/or superego.

When children have failed to achieve emotional object constancy, they have also failed to achieve self-constancy and need to make strenuous efforts to maintain a sense of flawlessness in order not to turn aggressively on themselves. The common clinical picture of highly aggressive children who are also suicidal attests to the breakdown of such efforts at times. (Suicidal threats and gestures are also maintained by powerful secondary gains, as the child invariably learns to manipulate his caretakers with these threats.) The therapist's interpretation of the probable cause of the child's aggression is invariably experienced as a painful criticism and narcissistic injury. It has several potentials: to disorganize the child, to arouse further hostility against the therapist, or to stimulate self-destructive feelings. Offering a substitute toy as the target for aggression is not acceptable because the child, in the throes of raging against the all-bad one (in this case the therapist), wants the satisfaction of punishing him or her directly—not a substitute. These children have been called "sublimation-deaf" (23, p. 93). For the same reason, verbally setting limits is not effective with them.

Developmental progress for the destructive or assaultive borderline child requires the physical restriction of motorically expressed aggression within the session, whether it be directed toward the therapist, the therapist's possessions, or the child himself. Therapy usually requires, for a time, the active participation of at least one parent, both in the child's sessions and in regular sessions with the parent(s). The presence of the parent in the session is often mandated by the child, who may be afraid of the retaliatory anger of the therapist, but it is also useful to the therapist, as two people are often needed to contain one wild child. Additional parent sessions are necessary to help the parent change styles of parenting that may have contributed to the development of the child's problem and to maintain therapeutic movement outside of the office. This dual involvement of the parent(s) in the child's therapy (i.e., in the child's session and in the parents' sessions) helps to maintain the prime importance of the parents in the child's life. This is narcissistically important for the family, provides therapeutic and modeling opportunities to the parents, and has side benefits in reducing the resistance of the parent to the child's therapy. The child's developmental progression to emotional object constancy is ideally achieved, in this view, with both the parents and therapist congruently. This is in contrast to the situation in which emotional object constancy is thought to be achieved with the therapist first, and then transferred, as is the case with adults (11, Chapter 6; 24).

The therapist's restriction of the child's physical destructiveness is critical for several reasons, aside from the obvious one of preserving the therapist and his or her possessions. It establishes the adults as authorities that the child cannot control, and therefore relieves the child of the burden of having too much power, and the consequent experience of loss of protection. If accomplished in a nonpunitive manner (i.e., the child is restrained, not hurt), it preserves the therapist and parent as "good objects" in the face of the child's aggression, a requirement for the development of emotional object constancy. It permits the child and parent to have a modeling opportunity for nonpunitive but firm and self-protective behavior in the face of provocation. It allows a space for the therapist to verbally express his or her understanding of the general issues involved in the child's need to thrash out and/or be destructive, as well as to hint at particular issues the therapist may be aware are operating for the child at that moment. But perhaps most important of all, the removal of the possibility of expressing aggression through physical means establishes the condition for the child to begin to express it through other means— games, fantasy, and verbal communications—and therefore to begin progressing developmentally in a cognitive and affective mode.

The child who is destructive is invariably deficient in the ability to verbally communicate feelings and the motivations for them. In the midst of a tantrum or while being prevented from continuing a tantrum, such children grunt, moan, or scream, but seldom use denotative language. The arrest in development of the child is clearly illustrated by his or her reliance on a mode of affective expression typical of the child up to age two. (Buxbaum [25] may be consulted for a fuller discussion of the relationship of speech to aggressive control.) In their sessions, such children act as if any verbal reference to feelings is simply a further stimulus for aggressive discharge, suggesting that originally too much aggression was stimulated to be easily contained by resources available at that point to the children's psyches. Other factors such as the family's habitual failure to communicate affect and/or the use of physical aggression as a mode of object relations (26) would support an adjustment in which motor discharge remained the primary way of handling intense feelings. The failure to engage in fantasy play is usually characteristic of these children, who prefer games involving large muscle activity (e.g., basket-shooting). Although these children do need active play in their schedules, not providing such opportunities in the session encourages other form of expression.

To summarize, therapists need not feel apologetic about physically restraining the child. They must recognize that if the child is permitted to bully and tyrannize others, he or she will never achieve the more advanced developmental position of control over physical aggression and expression of it in verbal and/or symbolic ways. Although a firm physical curtailment of destructiveness may be considered a "parameter" in the therapy of neurotic children who are momentarily out of control, it is a critical aspect of the therapy of the chronically out-of-control child.

At those times when the child is becoming destructive or attacking and must be restrained, the therapist may speak, in language the child can understand, of the issues identified in the previous discussion and may, in essence, urge the child on to a more advanced level of affective expression. The following listing of verbal interventions is not offered in an order intended to be sequentially presented in treatment or to indicate that these interventions must be addressed separately from each other. They are simply listed for the sake of clarity of presentation.

1. The therapist's regret that he or she (or the therapist and the mother or aide) must "manage" the child physically, but that the therapist will help control the child's arms and legs until the child can get control of them all alone. (It is the arms and legs that need controlling, not the feelings themselves.) "Maybe this difficult time will pass soon."
2. The therapist's suggestion that if the child's wild feelings could be put into words, the child might not have to use his or her arms or legs so wildly. When the therapist has an idea of what distressed the child, he or she may venture a statement linking the source of the distress to the destructive display, if the therapist thinks the child can tolerate it. At first, this will have to be in general terms, rather than in terms specific to the patient. This is necessary because of the nature of the patient: he or she is a child who has not developed direct or symbolic ways to express feelings and problems, and the therapist will probably not yet have a way to understand the problems from the child's point of view.

3. The therapist's awareness that something is (worrying, bothering, angering) the child, and that the child has not been able to express these feelings. If the therapist knew what bothered the child, perhaps he or she could make things better for the child in the future.
4. The therapist's insistence that everything and everyone in the office be safe ("I have to feel safe, your mom has to feel safe, you have to feel safe if we are going to get our work done here"). Emphasizing "you have to feel safe" is an important therapeutic statement. The child may think about how he or she would feel about being attacked and perhaps begin to understand that others may feel the same way. The statement therefore encourages the development of the capacity for empathy, and ideas of mutuality in relationships. Mutuality, in turn, begins to make possible valuing and wishing to preserve the object from attack and destruction.
5. The therapist's conviction that if the child succeeds in being destructive or hurtful, he or she will later feel terrible about the damage done, and it will be difficult for the child to continue to feel comfortable in the relationship. Here the therapist stimulates both ego and superego functioning in the child, by reminding the child of a cognition that was lost in the process of splitting: that the devalued, worthless object of the moment is, at other times, a valued, important object that the child will feel guilty about injuring.
6. The therapist's recognition that this behavior must be the kind of behavior that is making so much trouble for the child with others. The desire to help the child with this problem can be expressed at the time the therapist judges that the child can tolerate feeling this degree of exposure. For patients at the beginning of treatment, and for many aggressive children well into treatment, the "help" with concrete problems may have to wait until the child is able to symbolize them in play or fantasy. Although play offers the child an outlet for aggressive feelings, it also gives the therapist data with which to figure out what the child's ideas and perceptions are.

It is not, of course, possible to speak to the child throughout the containment process. The therapist may be protecting himself or may need to ask for the parent's help; the child may be screaming or may be difficult to grasp. However, a relative hiatus usually occurs during which some of these ideas can be spoken, even if in a pressured and anxious manner. The therapist's stress is inevitable and not necessary to hide; the child knows that he is subjecting the therapist and others to a difficult moment, and this may be alluded to directly by the therapist, as an honest acknowledgement of induced feelings. Such connections are useful for the out-of-control youngster. Of course, these issues may also be broached at opportune moments in the session when the child is not throwing a tantrum.

These issues apply in a general sense to all children who are chronically destructive. There are other aspects of aggressive displays that apply to particular children and that may be addressed as the therapist feels the child can tolerate hearing them. Maenchen (22) described aggression as a defense against feelings of weakness—what has been called the "macho" defense. Anna Freud saw some tantrums as anxiety attacks because the child was being deprived of a way of protecting himself against something he feared (1, p. 111) Sometimes children feel guilty and, in behaving badly, are arranging to have a punishment. At other times, they may be seeking mastery over unpredictable displays of aggression toward themselves by adults. In an effort to make life more predictable, the child provokes the aggression on his own terms. Finally, I must mention those instances when the child, in being restrained, relaxes into the body of the therapist. The child wishes for physical closeness and uses his destructiveness as a way to achieve it, perhaps not having any other way of obtaining an "embrace."

I have objections to two "management" techniques for aggression that have been described informally to me by other professionals. One is the use of the hospital aide who steps in to contain the child who is becoming physically aggressive. The therapist steps aside until the child is calm. The second involves ending the therapy session when the child becomes destructive. Both methods sacrifice the opportunity for the therapist to deal directly with a problem the child also has with others. The first deprives the therapist of the opportunity to make a personal statement as the recipient of the aggression, and for the momentarily devalued therapist to remind the child that the child feels differently about the therapist at other times and might want to preserve him or her for those occasions. On the positive side, it does permit the session to continue once the child is in control again and therefore rewards him for regaining self-control. The second method punishes the child for being aggressive by depriving him or her of the session. The therapist is unable to comment on the (potential) achievement of self-control. It teaches the child a way of ending the session when upset, but it is a manipulative way; and because the therapist is not in session, there is not really a chance to comment upon the possibility of these wishes and the child's possible belief that this is the way to get what one wants (i.e., forcefully). While the child is being restrained, there is, of course, no chance to address any of the six issues noted previously, because the child is off somewhere else with his or her tantrum.

COUNTERTRANSFERENCE ISSUES

In the classic report of their work with aggressive and predelinquent children in a group home, Redl and Wineman (23) expressed the dismay felt by counselors when a child "turned" aggressively on them:

In such moments, the child also loses—temporarily—all relationship he has had before to the adults around him and the ego is suddenly stripped of all channels of communication. This makes us powerless. Neither fear of consequences or of law, nor authority, nor respect, seems to have any effect, and even the ties of love and friendship where they have been developed, are out of commission. In fact, this is the hardest part to take: the adult so proud of his successes in establishing a "good relationship" of some sort with the "children who hate" will suddenly see it gone completely. The child will lash out at his most beloved counselor as he would at the most hated policeman. (p. 452)

The authors provide a good description of the bewilderment and hurt feelings the therapist may feel during the times the child, now seeing the therapist as the "bad" object, turns aggressively on him or her. In settings in which the therapist has sole responsibility for the containment of aggression, a destructive child can, paradoxically, make the therapist feel out of control. He or she may question an action, or lack of action, and may feel guilty about the intensity of hurt or angry feelings he or she experiences. There is inevitable stress, as the therapist struggles to moderate his or her own reactive impulses enough so that a therapeutic strategy may be devised. As I suggested previously, this stress will be apprehended by the child, so it is best for the therapist to acknowledge it directly and use it, by helping the child to see the effects his or her behavior has on the relationship with the other. Often, insights into the child's behavior or into a way of coping will come later and will be useful for another occasion.

Another type of challenge confronts the therapist once the child is improving and beginning to play symbolically. The therapist needs to have the fortitude to permit the grotesque imagery, sadistic and masochistic fantasy, and antisocial feeling that may be expressed in play at this point. These issues will be illustrated in the next case.

CASE PRESENTATION: LARRY L.

Larry was $6\frac{1}{2}$ when he began what was to be a 4-year psychotherapy. Psychotherapy was recommended by his teacher, who noted his chronic teasing of other children. He was often inattentive and seemed to be off daydreaming. With his mother, Larry talked about wanting to be killed, and he performed potentially self-destructive acts such as running into the city streets. Tantrums, often involving destruction of property, occurred several times a week, when Larry became convinced of some favoritism from his mother toward his younger brother, Derek. Of himself, Larry said that when he was older, he wanted to be a bully, and when he grew up he wanted to kill people.

Larry's mother had a comfortable pregnancy with him. His father and she were eager to have a family. His mother stayed home full-time and would carry Larry close to her in a Snugli. She described him as an easy, friendly, curious, and healthy child. She dated the beginning of his emotional distress to the time when his younger brother was born, when Larry was two. At that time she felt overwhelmed with the task of having two very young children to care for, the older of whom was used to easy access to his mother. She hired a housekeeper and put the woman in charge of Larry—an abrupt and traumatic change for him. Mrs. L., frustrated by Larry's now-increased neediness of her, began to be impatient with him and would send him to his room alone occasionally. Once, she locked him in the bathroom when he refused to nap while she was busy with the new baby.

Larry's father was a well-meaning but emotionally constricted man who was unable to speak of his feelings or even acknowledge them. He was involved with the children through tasks that he would perform at the times when he was home (e g., making the children breakfast, taking them to school). However, he could not "talk" with the children other than to state task-related communications. Larry's mother engaged with the children more affectively. Both parents had a conscious aversion to aggression in any form and wanted to be "permissive" parents. His mother was quite guilty about her treatment of Larry after Derek was born and now tried to reason with him rather than restrict him when he was disobedient. The boys learned that they could disregard her and, as they got older, began to mock her.

Some of Larry's behavior toward his mother was no doubt an identification with his father, who would not engage in open conflict with his wife but would do things as he wished. He, too, found it easy to disregard his wife's expectations or wishes. This engendered a fair amount of tension between the parents, and for a time, parent sessions were added to the therapeutic plan. There were many times when Mrs. L. felt at her wit's end with Mr. L. and threatened to leave him. He did not seem to really understand what bothered his wife and was inclined to see her as overreactive.

The parents dealt with affect in sharply different ways: the father was affectively isolated, the mother easily brought to tears and feelings of blameworthiness. She readily felt tortured by "mistakes" in the past or by her explosions in the present. Such a familial configuration abets the child's tendency to polarize his perceptions of others but becomes very confusing. It would have been impossible for Larry to understand, for example, why his denigrated mother was also the parent with whom he felt more comfortable. The father, whom Larry referred to as "The Angel," made an implicit request not to be troubled with the messiness of feelings.

Larry was brought to therapy by his mother, whom he wanted to stay with him inside my office. He sat on my couch rigidly shaking, hands clenched into fists, jaw clenched into a grimace, mute and looking terrified. His mother went over to him embraced and soothed him, and eventually he calmed down enough to look through the toys. He examined the toys but did not play with them. I asked him if he knew why his mother had brought him to see me. When he did not answer, I indicated that his parents thought that he could be happier, and that this was a place where children got help with bad feelings. This turned out to be a mistake.

Although Larry did not respond in the session, upon leaving he told mother he did not want to come back again. My reference to feelings must have been terrifying to him, and his mother's preparation of him for his first sessions in which she too, mentioned his feelings, probably set the stage for his terrified reaction inside my office.

Several days later, I was waiting in my office for Larry and Mrs. L., who were late. I looked out of my window on the eighth floor, and saw Larry running about on the sidewalk and then onto the busy avenue, eluding his mother's grasp. Eventually, he permitted her to catch him, and she brought him up to the waiting room. I entered as Larry picked up an object from the table and moved to fling it. I was able to grab it from him and direct him and his mother into the office, where he grabbed a paperweight and was about to throw it at the window. This time, he was held down by both of us. I indicated I knew he was upset about having to see me, and that I could see he was angry. I wondered aloud if he could tell me about it instead of showing me. He never spoke to either his mother or me, but grunted at first, as he struggled with us. As he calmed down, he began sobbing. I brought over a plastic inflated "Boppo" doll, thinking that he might need to use it later, but he proceeded to bite into the plastic and chew it, while sobbing. I tried to soothe the boy, telling him that I would try very hard to make my office a comfortable and safe place for him, as it had to be for all of us, and that I thought it would never feel as bad again as it had today.

Larry left the session in his mother's arms. As she asked me about the next appointment, he burst out, "If I have to come back to see Dr. Katz, I will really kill myself," and thrust his head into the edge of a cabinet against the office wall.

I needed a few minutes to recover my equanimity before greeting my next patient. Later, I wondered if I could work with Larry. I thought that my office was not well set up for a child who might be wild often, as it was an office also used for adult patients. I was frightened by his linking psychotherapy to suicidal threats. I thought that he might need to be hospitalized at some point, and that it might be better for him to see someone with admitting privileges.

I telephoned the mother that evening to find out how Larry had been after the session. She reported him to be extremely calm and loving. I was heartened by the fact that the session, despite its turbulence, had not disorganized him in his "outside" life. He continued to have a calm week, although he persisted in his suicide threats regarding having to come back. Meanwhile, I had reconsidered my doubt about working with him, and I decided that it would be best if the boy did not manipulate me into ineffectiveness with his suicidal threats, as he had his mother. I realized that I did not really know that his aggression would be unmanageable for me and his mother.

Perhaps it was because Larry was secretly happy that the adults had finally taken charge and not permitted him to rule them that Larry no longer threatened he would kill himself if he had to see me. For my part, I steadied myself before each session and reminded myself to be very careful of how I alluded to feelings. When Larry refused to talk, Mrs. L. and I would talk about the family's week, and Larry would shortly join in contemptuously correcting her presentation. However, he literally could not speak without becoming motorically agitated. He jumped up and down or spun around in the revolving chair; alternatively, he clenched his fists, jaw, and entire body. In an early session, he confirmed the correctness of my decision to make him come to sessions by telling the story of elephants who were afraid of mice. When I commented, "Those mice must think it's a pretty crazy world, if large powerful creatures are afraid of them!" he said nothing, but scrutinized me as if he suddenly understood the metaphor by which our work would be accomplished.

We settled on a schedule of therapy that involved two sessions a week for Larry and one session a week for the mother (and sometimes the mother and father). It seemed necessary to have regular parent sessions in order to help the mother get the domestic scene in some order and to help her understand what she experienced in the sessions with the boy. Mrs. L. became a good observer of her son, both in and out of the therapy sessions. It was also valuable to me to get messages from her on my telephone answering machine about the events in Larry's week.

Larry did not use dramatic play until the end of the first year in therapy. However, he began telling me about movies and telling me about monster figures like Dr. Doom. He preferred bad guys to good guys. He could not speak of anything interesting to him without alternating between the agitated, active states and the rigid, clenching ones. After a time, I was able to comment that these behaviors showed that he had many feelings inside that he did not let out into words. His mother reported that, at home, he enjoyed mocking me and imitating these statements about feelings.

In those first few months, Larry was both better and worse at home. He talked to his mother more, but also had more tantrums and once attempted to strangle his younger brother. In the sessions, he had only occasional tantrums but restricting him required strenuous efforts on the part of both the mother and myself. During these moments, I would address the issues outlined previously and express the hope that some day we would be able to talk about the problems that made him so upset. The tantrums might be followed by Larry's cursing at his mother. Although his mother was at first upset by this, she was helped to see this as a "way station"—the beginning, for an aggressive child, of expressing rage in a verbal mode. It was clear, however, that our work at that early stage would depend on Larry's finding some metaphors through which he might express his problems.

The metaphor became apparent when Larry told me the story of Bruce Banner, who, when angered, turned into the Hulk, a large frightening creature who would destroy property and frighten people, but who nevertheless was very attached to his great strength. For several weeks we talked about the Hulk, and eventually the three of us made up a tape of how Bruce Banner overcame the effects of the bad gamma rays. It involved giving up the awesome strength of the Hulk but left Bruce strong enough to take care of any situation calling for great strength. Larry took the tape home and listened to it there. Periodically, in his sessions, he would ask to listen to the tape and smile as he did.

The Frankenstein story was another important one for Larry. The Frankenstein monster killed the master's son, because he was angry that the master went away and left him alone. This scenario permitted me to make many comments about the monster's rather human feelings (e.g., his love, hurt feelings, the connection between being hurt and becoming destructive, and the displacement of aggression), statements that were well tolerated by Larry. Clearly, Larry had been finding ways to symbolically deal with conflicts over his excessive power, the price he paid for it, and his attachment to this power as a compensation for his helplessness in preventing the loss of his mother's attention and the abrupt loss of omnipotence.

Although the activities I have described were the "pure gold" of therapy with Larry, it should be emphasized that they were interspersed with much motor activity, occasional tantrums, and much talk about grotesque scenes of horror and bodily damage and adulation of characters of evil. He needed toys with which to express his rage and his feelings of being grotesque and defiled. It took fortitude for both his mother and myself to permit him to use a stage knife on his own body, put on grotesque makeup, or use play blood on his body to enact scenes, over and over, of being wounded and falling dead. Only over time did the proportion of motor activity to symbolic activity decrease. As we discussed the characters and movies about which Larry spoke, he became less destructive.

Larry weathered his first long summer break well. His teacher reported that his concentration had improved and he had friends. Although he refused to talk of feelings in his session, he talked progressively more with his mother and told his father he didn't like him. He now conveyed hostile fantasies to his mother with worry rather than with pride, a sign that his superego had moderated sufficiently for him to tolerate the anticipated experience of guilt. For example, with much anxiety he asked her, "What if a 6-year-old should kill a 9-year-old?"

Eventually, the methods I used in Larry's therapy became more inclusive than at the beginning of treatment. They included the moderation of his aggression through verbal reconstruction (e.g., early feelings about his brother) and some interpretation. During the second year, he felt safe enough to indicate that he no longer needed his mother in his sessions. Larry still required his mother to come into the office at times when he was angry at me, however.

During the third year of Larry's treatment, many sublimations of aggression developed (e.g., an interest in making explosions in after-school science, a desire to manufacture explosives as a career, and an interest in reading about guns). A major achievement was that he overcame his tendency to be accident-prone. This enabled him to become quite graceful and proficient in several sports, which in turn, enhanced his social life.

The fourth year of therapy was a turbulent one, because Larry was insisting on stopping therapy and was furious at his mother for making him stay. He insisted that he did not need therapy and never had. There were many times when his mother was back in the office, because he could not discuss this topic without her being there. Although he would become enraged and go from cursing her to begging her to let him stop therapy, he never came near to making a destructive or assaultive gesture. He was embarrassed that a friend had stopped therapy and he hadn't. The context was complicated by the fact that his father had decided to leave his mother and to live with a new woman and her infant. I thought it was important to go through these transitions with Larry in treatment, but eventually we set a termination date.

Several important matters were accomplished in this treatment, although Larry remained a sensitive boy, easily distressed by his own imperfections and, when greatly disappointed, inclined to excoriate others for their weaknesses. That is, he was still vulnerable to becoming polarized in his experience of himself and others. However, he had friends, had become focused at school and was achieving well, had some success with girls (which was very important to him), and had found outlets for his aggression.

CONCLUSIONS

I have tried to focus on some special aspects of therapy with the highly sensitive, easily wounded, aggressive child, and to show that when a child lacks emotional object constancy, aggressions against the self may be as much a part of the clinical picture as outwardly directed aggression. Therapy with such a child requires the therapist to gently advance the child, but to be able to retreat from interventions that stimulate further aggression. Toys are needed to help the child express sadistic and macabre feelings that have been motorically discharged previously. The relationship with the family is critical to the success of the treatment; the parents have to be willing to do some relearning, and participation in the session is often helpful for child and parent, as well as a necessary help for the therapist and often desired by the child. A guiding principle for such "acting out" problems is that the conditions must be created that require the child to begin to express feelings symbolically, and when this fails, the therapist needs the emotional stamina to respond to the tantrums within the session. A powerful emotional bond is created among the participants in these scenes (usually mother, therapist, and child), because the therapist implicitly conveys the message: I will endure this with you; things can be different.

During a final advisory session with the parents, I had suggested that Larry be encouraged in pursuits that would be vehicles for the expression of feelings. He seems to have spontaneously turned to writing, with much admiration coming from peers for his stories. His most ambitious story involved a planetary disaster followed by humans successfully putting the world back together again—an optimistic metaphor for a boy who had experienced both the disruption of family life and the ending of a 4-year relationship with a therapist.

REFERENCES

1. Freud A: Normality and pathology in childhood: assessments of development, in The Writings of Anna Freud, Vol 6. New York, International Universities Press, 1965
2. Willock B: Narcissistic vulnerability in the hyperaggressive child: the disregarded (unloved, uncared for) self. Psychoanalytic Psychology 3:59–80, 1986
3. Willock B: The devalued (unloved, repugnant) self: a second facet of narcissistic vulnerability in the aggressive, conduct-disordered child. Psychoanalytic Psychology 4:219–240, 1987
4. Kohut H: Restoration of the Self. New York, International Universities Press, 1977, pp 63–139
5. Mahler M, Pine F, Bergmann A: The Psychological Birth of the Human Infant: Part II. New York, Basic Books, 1975, pp 39–108
6. McDevitt JB, Mahler M: Object Constancy, Individuality and Internalization, in Self and Object Constancy. Edited by Lax R, Bach S, Burland J. New York, Guilford, 1986, pp 11–28
7. Pine F: Libidinal object constancy, in Developmental Theory and Clinical Process. New Haven, CT, Yale University Press, 1985, pp 102–107
8. Sullivan HS: The Interpersonal Theory of Psychiatry. Edited by Perry HS, Gawel MS. New York, WW Norton, 1953
9. Klein M: A contribution to the psychogenesis of manic-depressive states (1935), in Contributions to Psychoanalysis, 1921–1945. London, Hogarth Press, 1948, pp 282–310
10. Parens H: Toward a reformulation of the theory of aggression and its implication for primary prevention. Emotions and Behavior Monographs 1:87–114, 1984

11. Kohut H: Thoughts on narcissism and narcissistic rage (1972), in The Search for the Self: Selected Writings of Heinz Kohut. Edited by Ornstein P. New York, International Universities Press, 1978, pp 615–658

12. Timberlake EM: Child abuse and externalized aggression: preventing a delinquent life style (1979), in Exploring the Relationship between Child Abuse and Delinquency. Edited by Hunner RJ, Walker RE. Montclair, NJ, Allanheld, Osman & Co, 1981, pp 43–51

13. Sears R, Maccoby E, Levin H: Patterns of Child Rearing. Evanston, IL, Row-Peterson, 1957

14. Maccoby E: Social Development. New York, Harcourt Brace Jovanovich, 1980

15. Bandura A, Walters R: Social Learning and Personality Development. New York, Holt, Rinehart, & Winston, 1978

16. Thomas A, Chess S, Birch H: Temperament and Behavior Disorders in Children. New York, International Universities Press, 1969

17. Chess S, Thomas A: Temperament in Clinical Practice. New York, Guilford, 1986

18. Freud S: Beyond the pleasure principle (1920), in The Standard Edition of the Complete Psychological Works of Sigmund Freud, Vol 18. Translated and edited by Strachey J. London, Hogarth Press, 1948, pp 7–64

19. Aronson E: The Social Animal. New York, Freeman & Co, 1988

20. Magid K, McKelvey C: High Risk. New York, Bantam Books, 1987

21. Schiavi PC: Sex chromosome anomalies, hormones, and aggressivity. Arch Gen Psychiatry 41:93, 1984

22. Maenchen A: The handling of overt aggression in child analysis. Psychoanal Study Child 39:393–405, 1984

23. Redl F, Wineman D: The Aggressive Child. New York, Free Press, 1957

24. Lax R: Libidinal object and self constancy enhanced by the analytic process, in Self and Object Constancy. Edited by Lax R, Bach S, Burland J. New York, Guilford, 1986, pp 271–290

25. Buxbaum E: Remarks on aggression. J Child Psychotherapy 7:167–174, 1981

26. Frankel S: The management aspect of psychotherapy with aggressive children. Child Psychiatry Hum Dev 7:171–185, 1971

6 Children With Attention-Deficit Hyperactivity Disorder and Their Parents

John D. O'Brien, M.D.

Much has been written on the etiology (1–3), diagnosis (4–6), and pharmacologic treatment (7–9) of children with attention-deficit hyperactivity disorder (ADHD). However, the same cannot be said about psychotherapeutic work with these children. In this chapter, I will focus on the psychoanalytic psychotherapy of ADHD children and their families.

GENERAL PRINCIPLES

Before one begins to address the issues involved in treatment of children with ADHD and their families, there are several general principles that must be carefully considered. All of these principles need to be kept in mind before a therapist embarks on any course of treatment.

The first and probably the most important principle is that the children and their families have been aware of and attempting to cope with the problems of ADHD for a long time prior to seeking treatment. Although most of these children are not diagnosed until their school years (most frequently in the third grade), the children and their families have been dealing with the symptoms since the children were preschoolers. During the preschool years, the standards for behavior are determined almost exclusively by the family, usually with a great deal of tolerance. However, when the children begin school the standards become different, and failure to live up to these standards is neither well tolerated nor overlooked.

> Johnny was a 7-year-old second grader who was referred by the teacher because of poor academic performance, inattention, and restlessness. He was a ADHD child who during one of his sessions talked about when he was in the day-care center (age 3–4 years) he was "a paster not a cutter." Although he first described this with a sense of pride, later he secretly admitted to me that he had a terrible time trying to cut and that both he and the teacher had given up, making him instead chief paster. He felt bad that he could not do what the other children did. His mother and father well remembered their attempts with him

and how this had been the beginning in a long series of failures for their child. "Even at that age he couldn't seem to get himself going in the right direction," said his mother.

As Rappaport (10) has eloquently stated, ADHD children often do not have the ego functions at birth that enable adequate adaption to their environment. The ego function disturbances interfere with the early infant-mother relationship, because the children do not respond appropriately to the mother. The mother, then, may become unsure of herself and feel she is doing something wrong. She may tend to overprotect her children or become less responsive to them. All of this may lead to a difficulty in establishing basic trust. From the very beginning, mothers and children sense something is wrong, and the children, because of their deficits, may not stimulate the natural desire to interact with them more, thereby leading to a diminution in the interplay that aids further ego growth. The mothers secondarily react to this defectiveness, and the combination of the two leads to the children's inability to develop a sense of being "all right," which is the basis for a sense of identity.

> Mrs. A. was the mother of Adam, who was referred at age six because of his hyperactivity and his having failed first grade. Adam was the second of three children. His mother was very verbal and intelligent. In discussing Adam's developmental history, she remarked, "Something was wrong from the very beginning. I never got the sense of gratification I did with the other children. It always seemed we were out of tune." She admitted she didn't interact with Adam as much as the other children, and although she had always felt "at a loss with him," this feeling had become worse as he had gotten older.

These vignettes illustrate that the neurological difficulties affect the tasks of development for the children and mothers from the very beginning. Both children and parents have had to deal with the problem for many years. The long-standing problems have occasioned defenses to be erected that need to be dealt with in the psychotherapy of the family and the children.

The next general principle that needs to be highlighted is one implicit in the first. The children are affected in all areas of functioning. School difficulties, especially reading difficulty, often become the focus of attention with these children. However, ADHD children are often affected in areas of functioning beyond the school such as the home and the playground. In fact, there are some children whose disability is manifested mainly in the motor area. Often these children do well academically, except perhaps in writing, but have serious difficulties in sports or manual arts. These children suffer as much from the trauma of not being able to do as their peers on the playground as the nonreader does in the classroom. For the purpose of emphasis, reading disabled children have been dichotomized from poorly coordinated children. In fact, many of the ADHD children fall into the middle of the spectrum and have both learning problems and coordination difficulties.

> Richard was a 9-year-old boy who was seen because of poor academic performance. Richard was not doing well in a very good public school system. The academic failure was of utmost concern to his wealthy, articulate, successful, and ambitious parents. However, in treatment a very important theme arose one day when Richard tried to play with a yo-yo. The simplest maneuvers were beyond him, and as I watched him try again and again with tears welling in his eyes, I felt the profound helplessness, frustration, and sense of failure he had experienced in this area. Richard did everything, including getting sick, to avoid the family tennis outings. These outings, his fears of gym, and his attempt to find some sport with which he might succeed became the themes of our sessions for months to come. He said that day, fighting back tears, "I would rather do a trick with this yo-yo than read a hundred books." What must be kept in mind is not only what the parents see as the problem, or what the therapist believes is the area of greatest need for the future but, above all, what the child sees as his major difficulty and what is most important to him.

The third general principle is that children exist within a matrix, the two most crucial elements of which are the family and a setting for learning such as a school or day-care center. It is essential that the entire family be perceived of as sharing in the problems and successes of the child with ADHD. This includes not only parents but, most importantly, siblings. Obviously, the family and mainly the parents are the first teachers of the children: not only do they impart knowledge, but they also give structure to experience, communicate attitudes about learning to the children, stimulate the children (or not, as the case may be), and, above all, convey a sense of all-rightness to the children. Siblings play a crucial role in the workings of a family and must be included in any therapeutic endeavor, however briefly. The other matrix for the children, generally the school, requires the therapist's input in formulating an individual educational plan for the children.

In this chapter I will not consider extensively either the therapist's role in educational planning for the children or the use of medication. Although my focus will be on the psychotherapeutic interventions with the family and the children, this does not mean that proper educational intervention or medication is not important. Indeed, the first areas of therapeutic endeavor should be the appropriate school placement of the children, techniques for enhancing learning, and dealing with behavioral difficulties in the classroom. Medication is an important part of the therapist's armamentarium, and often a necessary one. From my clinical experience, three criteria have been devised for the use of medication. If the children are so hyperactive and distractible that they cannot sit still or concentrate for a short period of time in the office on a one-to-one basis, medication should be used quickly. If no special education program or classes are available, or if placement in such a class would take months, rapid institution of medication may be helpful. Also included here is the situation in which parents may want to try to keep the children in a regular classroom with medication. However, parents are advised that the medication should only be given on an experimental basis for 4 to 6 months, and if no significant improvement occurs, the children should receive special education. Finally, if the children have been in an appropriate special class placement for 6 months and are not making progress, then medication may be useful. Time is of the essence because many of the children who come for assessment are already 2 years behind grade level. Further delay causes further difficulties.

FAMILY CONSIDERATIONS

Parental Reactions to Referral

This discussion of treatment will begin with intervention with the family. What must be kept foremost in mind is the fact that most of the parents of ADHD children are not seriously psychiatrically disturbed. Most frequently, they are reacting (sometimes quite defensively) to the social and academic deficits of their children. What must be addressed initially is the stance of the parents regarding the referral of the children. The stance can vary from great concern that something is very wrong, to blaming the school system, to seeing the fault as residing in the children. Gardner (11) has divided parental responses into acute and chronic reactions of adaptation. The evaluation of these reactions is essential. The reactions themselves fall into several overlapping categories. The first is concern—the parents are anxious about their child's problem and are truly looking for an answer. Frequently, this is accompanied by frustration, for they have tried many things that often have not worked and have seen many consultants. Guilt is a frequent concomitant, and they are quite concerned that they have done something wrong. The therapist must investigate this concern to see if the children have been overprotected by the family or any of its members. Generally, such overprotection is the product of a normal but undifferentiated response to the children. The overprotection stifles areas of competence and usually leads to further difficulties for the child, which I will address later in this chapter.

A second reaction by the parents is that of blaming, which may be subdivided into blaming their children and/or the school. The parents often believe that the school is inadequate and produce a litany of complaints about it. There is little attempt to see the children as they are; the deficits are so threatening that the parents must find someone or something to blame. One of the most destructive mechanisms used is that of blaming the children. This can reach delusional proportions in some parents, who come to see their children as willful, lazy, and deliberately trying to thwart the school and the family. This is a common reaction in more primitively organized families. It is important for the therapist to be empathetic with the parents and to recognize their frustrations and attempts to cope with the situation. When parents talk about the children as if they were in a power struggle with them, the stage should be set to discuss at a later date the possibility of the parents reacting with physical punishment and abuse. The therapist should mention how frustrated parents must feel and how angry they must be that their efforts have come to naught and should convey an understanding of their feelings. Subsequently, the therapist can bring up the idea of anger and make reference to his or her experience that parents who usually feel angry often seriously punish the children. In this way, the issue of corporal punishment can be dealt with directly. Most of the time, parents believe that the therapist understands, and they frequently express their profound sense of helplessness in the situation by asking "But what else could I do?"

> Arturo was a 9-year-old boy who was referred for poor academic performance, frequent fights in school, lying, and stealing. His mother and father were very angry. They felt he would not listen to them, and he was impossible to handle both at home and in school. Arturo's mother said, "He is a bad child; he is inhabited by the devil and will continue to do evil things." When asked if she really believed that, she answered, "I have prayed for him and I have taken him to an exorcist already." It was also obvious that the child had been beaten severely on several occasions. The therapist told Arturo's parents that the boy's actions were due to his illness and they must stop hitting him.

Parental Reactions to the Results of the Evaluation

Parents react to the results of the evaluation in various ways generally related to their original feelings about the referral. The evaluation is a crisis for the family, for though they may be aware that something has been wrong for a long time, the diagnosis of ADHD confronts them with the reality. Their suspicions and fears that something is seriously wrong with their children have been confirmed. The primary issue that has to be worked through is the loss and subsequent mourning of the idealized child. All the expectations with which the children have been imbued or burdened require reexamination by the parents. Most parents have a set of expectations or standards for their children, and, realistic or not, these must be dealt with by the therapist.

> Larry was an 11-year-old who was referred by his father. The boy was doing poorly in school and had serious coordination problems and few friends. His father's dream was for Larry to be a concert pianist. Larry tried very hard to accommodate to the sometimes subtle, sometimes overt pressure put on him to

accomplish this. However, try as he might, his fine motor coordination difficulties made him unable to play well. When he began to practice, his father would attempt to help him, and a fight would break out. Everyone felt terrible afterwards, especially Larry.

After much discussion with both Larry and his father, the piano was abandoned. For their own reasons, however, each wanted Larry to play a musical instrument, and at my suggestion Larry took up drums and became quite proficient. I chose drums because they do not require the degree of fine motor coordination Larry obviously did not have. Interestingly enough, at a 5-year follow-up, Larry had used his drumming talent to enable him to get in contact with other people. He, as the coleader of a band, not only met many people but "was being paid for it, too."

It was necessary for Larry's father to mourn the child who might have been and to realistically appraise his child with ADHD. For Larry's father, it was necessary for him to feel sad before he could resolve the loss and go on to constructively work toward a solution.

In some families, the children have been recognized as handicapped and have been blamed and debased because they cannot do or be like other children. This image, too, must be confronted. Parents must be helped to see the positive aspects and accomplishments of their children and must also see the children in a realistic light.

When people deal with any crisis, they can have several reactions. Usually, anxiety is the first reaction. When they first hear that their child has ADHD, parents describe themselves as feeling unreal or being numb. It is very important to realize that many people have difficulty in assimilating information at this time; information has to be repeated several times before it sinks in. It is important for the therapist to point this out to the parents and to be available for questions afterwards. The therapist should urge the parents to go home and talk it over together, sharing not only the content of what was said but also their feelings. With those parents who have blamed their children, it is very important that the therapist state clearly that the children are not doing this volitionally and are not trying to thwart their parents or anyone else. This will have to be stated again and again.

Along with their anxiety, parents of children with ADHD often feel a mixture of guilt and anger. Many times they will ask what they did wrong and try to get immediate relief. This may be accompanied by an angry attacking stance in which the therapist or the school is blamed. Some parents want a second opinion; this is their right. Often a therapist will withdraw when he or she sees a professional opinion has been rejected. However, the therapist should try to help the parents find a reasonable person for a second opinion. Parents should be reminded that there is a limit to the number of opinions sought. It is essential to clearly explain why a specific intervention is being recommended. The anxiety surrounding the diagnosis must be discussed and worked with openly; all the clarity in the world will still not alleviate all the anxiety, and parents must be given a chance to ventilate their frustration and ask questions. It is not uncommon for the anxiety of making the unknown known to further solidify previous unhealthy patterns. Thus, an overprotective parent may become more intrusive and overinvolved in a child's life. This tendency should be discussed with the parents and examples in their behavior pointed out.

Most often the parents get through their initial shock and anxiety over the ADHD diagnosis. They then begin to acknowledge the problem and try to resolve it. Sometimes they become overwhelmed and helpless, abrogating their responsibility in dealing with their children by saying, "Whatever you say, doctor." This cannot be done with children who have ADHD, because active participation by the parents in the children's educational and psychological treatment is essential. In some rare cases, the children may be openly rejected and the parents may suggest that they be sent away to school or a residential treatment center. The therapist must then reassure the parents that prognosis is good with appropriate treatment, and making such a decision at a stressful time may be a mistake.

With the advent of acknowledgment, the parents can be actively enlisted into their child's treatment program, and realistic planning can begin. Not only the areas of difficulty but also the strengths must be stressed. The major principle for working with ADHD children is to build on their strengths and work on their weaknesses.

Given a thorough diagnosis, it is important that the therapist give concrete suggestions about handling difficult situations and tell the parents what to expect from their children.

Issues Regarding Siblings

After the parents and their children have been given the assessment results, a few family sessions should be initiated. This is essential because the entire family helps to shape the children, and the children shape it in turn. There is no question that a child with ADHD often becomes the focus of attention—both positive and negative—in a family. Siblings can be a source of strength and comfort to a child with ADHD, or they can be negative, provocative, or ashamed of their sibling. Frequently, with the help of the therapist, the parents may have changed their perceptions of and attitudes toward their child with ADHD, and the other children in the family are confused by and possibly resentful about the changes or the perceived "double standard." Often siblings are afraid that what the child with ADHD has may be contagious or is hereditary. One child once said with great anxiety that he feared waking up one morning and being like his brother. In some instances, the siblings have been approached by a former teacher who currently has the child with ADHD in her class. The teacher asks them what is wrong or why their sibling isn't doing well. This puts the siblings in an impossible situation; some siblings have even expressed the fear that their sibling with ADHD would die from the condition.

One of the most significant experiences that occurs in a family is the scapegoating of the child with ADHD. As one older sister told me, "I know just how to press his button and get him started." There are many undercurrents in a family of which the child with ADHD is not aware or is unable to grasp. Also, a child with ADHD can easily be used as a diversion. In one such family, an older female child was acting out sexually while the family was preoccupied with their son who had ADHD. Whenever attempts were made by the parents to talk with this girl (and the attempts were minimal), she would direct attention to her brother, either by discussing her worries about and her reaction to her brother or by setting up a situation that would result in his disruption of the household.

It is necessary to get the parents and the siblings to understand the effects of the syndrome on the whole life experience of the child with ADHD and to enlist their aid and active participation in the treatment process.

Greta was an 8-year-old girl who was referred for poor school performance and withdrawn behavior. The child was tested by a psychologist and was believed to have an emotional problem. Family therapy was recommended. During the psychiatric evaluation, Greta was unable to find her way to the office, although this was her third session. Also, when she was called, she was unable to tell from where the sound came, became quite anxious, and began whirling in the hall. She had serious organic deficits. The parents lived in a two-story house, and it was not only very common for her mother to call Greta from a different story but also to give her specific tasks to do. Greta's mother could not understand why Greta could never follow through on these tasks. One suggestion to the parents was that whenever they spoke to her, they should look directly at her and give only one direction or suggestion at a time.

It was pointed out to the mother that, given Greta's illness, it was not reasonable to expect Greta to be able to do the tasks. However, when she did a task it was suggested that the parents show approval verbally and/or physically. Greta's mother believed her husband had withdrawn from their child, leaving the entire burden of working with Greta on her. Greta had difficulty tying her shoelaces. Daddy was urged to take one of his big shoes and work for a short time (limited to 5 minutes) nightly on the task of putting the shoelaces in and tying them. It was meant to be a great fun game for both of them. No matter how she did, Greta was to get a reward for trying. The reward was more time with either parent doing something she liked. Within several weeks, Greta was able to lace and then tie her own shoes, to the tremendous satisfaction of all.

Such success was extremely important for the parents, because not only could they see their child as successful, but they saw that they had an active role in the success. This was the beginning of dealing with their overriding feelings of helplessness.

CONSIDERATIONS RELATED TO THE INDIVIDUAL CHILDREN

General Considerations

In this section, I will focus on the individual psychotherapy of ADHD children. The first issue to be considered is under what circumstances and why does a therapist undertake individual psychotherapy with ADHD children. Obviously, appropriate school placement and work with the parents and family is always necessary. But when is individual psychotherapy needed? The main criterion I will suggest is the presence of a negative self-image (low self-esteem). This self-image either is not changed by the success that occurs through environmental alterations, such as a special class and family changes, or so paralyzes the children that they cannot actively participate in their own treatment program—that is, either they will not try a new approach or they actively undermine attempts by the educator to help them. Generally a waiting period of 6 months is used to see how they adapt to the educational program devised for them and to see how the family resolves the crisis of the evaluation. De Hersch (12) has written that within the first two school years, children form an image of themselves as learners. Usually, ADHD children who are diagnosed after the age of seven or eight need individual psychotherapy, because they have become so traumatized in so many areas by repeated failure that their self-image of badness has become internalized.

ADHD children have difficulty with all stages of psychosocial development: the learning disability, hyperactivity, and distractibility interfere with most if not all developmental tasks. Children with ADHD may develop many types of emotional disorders as they try to master the stages of normal psychosocial development while attempting to cope with the frustrations and failures they experience in all aspects of life.

The core psychological problem for these children is that of poor self-esteem. The children have a sense something is wrong with them—that is, they are not like other children. They seem always to be in trouble with their parents, their teachers, and themselves. They can't even get their bodies to work the way they want them to.

One child who I have mentioned previously described it this way: "I try to get my fingers to work right; my mind screams at them but nothing seems to work. There are times I get so mad I would like to cut them off." Another very bright ADHD child poignantly remarked, "I guess I can't blame my parents for being disappointed in me; I can't even get myself to work right." This lack of trust in and control over one's body is devastating to the child's self-concept.

Because of failures and frustrations in accomplishing the tasks of development and poor interactions with parents and peers, children with ADHD feel angry and devalued. Very often these children become depressed, which is expressed (depending on the age of the children and their personalities) in various ways, such as irritability, aggression, or the more classic symptoms of depression. Much of their anger may be turned inward; the children see themselves as bad, stupid, and unable to do anything correctly. These feelings are based on a body of real experiences with themselves, and also with the reactions of their parents, who may debase them or blame them because of their disability.

Specific Defensive Maneuvers

The following reactions or symptomatology are seen as attempts made by the children to defend against low self-esteem—attempts made to protect these fragile human beings. Often these defenses only make the situation worse and lead to a further decrease in self-esteem. The children are aware of their difficulties in survival, and there is an excessive sense of helplessness both in understanding and coping with their experiences in the outer world and in organizing and controlling their inner worlds. The types of emotional problems developed are based on the personalities of the children, their resources (which is greatly affected by their age), and their families.

The first common mechanism of defense is withdrawal or avoidance. With a body of previous failures, children with ADHD approach any new situation, especially the learning situation, with fear—fear that they will be humiliated and frustrated again. In school, they find themselves unable to keep up, and they are often teased by their classmates. Their fear and frustration mount, and they often refuse to try anything new. They may then refuse to do any work at all. This reaction must be seen as a product of fear and not of defiance.

When parents misinterpret their children's refusal as defiance, they will punish the children and may even beat them. This can lead to a vicious cycle of increasing parental demands, withdrawal by the children, and parental anger, followed by increasingly severe punishments. Teachers often describe children with ADHD as willful and lazy and say that things would get better if only the children tried harder. Implicit in this is the idea that the children are in control of the situation and only their obstinacy prevents them from learning. Again, the children are penalized with extra work and seen as quitters. These children may end up avoiding any or all situations that may lead to possible humiliation or rejection. Their repertoire of behaviors and interests diminish. One of the most dangerous situations is withdrawal into fantasy and isolation, which can reach severe proportions. The children get little gratification from the world of school, so they enter a different one, a world they create. In this way, they become even more unavailable for learning. Satisfaction and relief come chiefly from the world of make-believe.

> Victor was a 9-year-old third grader who was referred because of poor school performance and daydreaming. After an extensive workup, Victor was diagnosed as having ADHD, with a learning disability that put him 2 years below grade level. He constantly fantasized about being the best baseball or tennis player. His world was populated by sports figures that he wanted to be like. He had few friends and little social life. Much of his school time was taken up with daydreaming. After several months in treatment, Victor said that his daydreams took him out of class and made him feel better. In his fantasies he could be the strongest, the fastest, the best; most of all, he didn't feel so stupid. Fantasy enabled him to escape from the hard reality of his severe learning problems but led him further away from his teacher and from other children. He functioned much better at home. He had no symptoms of depression. However, after about 6 months, as part of the process of treatment Victor became quite depressed when he had to confront his disabilities.

Another mechanism used is functioning at a more immature or infantile level than expected for one's age. The children play the games of younger children and play with younger children. In this fashion they avoid the demands of their peer group with which they are sure they will be unable to cope. Such regressions can become quite severe.

Overcompensation is another defense, and in this situation children frequently use aggression. The children overcompensate for their deficiencies by seeing themselves as leaders, controlling, manipulating, or bullying other children into their mold. Generally ADHD children have some areas of adequate functioning, and these are used to control the group. The children feel very powerful, and in this way they can deny their inadequacy. Usually, however, this leadership is of the bullying, domineering type, with much impulsive behavior and little ability to stick to a plan for any length of time.

Some children use denial. The choice of this defense usually means that a parent (or parents) is also using the same mechanism. Here, the children deny—with family support—that they have any difficulties, or they deny that these difficulties have anything to do with them. They say the difficulties are the fault of the school, or the other children who distract them, or a poor teacher.

The following mechanism may be seen as a type of avoidance, but it is used so frequently and so well that it deserves to be specifically mentioned. Clowning helps the children deal with their deficiencies in academics or sports by drawing attention away from these areas through jokes, tricks, and so on.

(Some children divert attention by asking to leave the room for water, acting up before they can be called upon, etc.) The children save themselves from ridicule by ridiculing themselves first. They play the role of clown and get a peculiar type of acceptance, one based on people laughing at them and not with them. The situation is set up by the children as if they chose the clown role and thus have mastery over the situation. They declare that they chose this role because it is fun for them. However, this role seriously undermines their self-esteem.

Although the next mechanism is not a common one, it bears mentioning because it has been labeled school phobia: somatization or hypochondriasis. The children develop pain on school days or during certain classes and need to see the school nurse. Because of their feelings that their bodies don't work correctly for them, these children frequently have an overconcern about their bodies, especially their brains. This leads to the final common mechanism of defense, which is the use of the syndrome itself as a defense. The children rationalize their failures by saying that they can't help making a mistake or being disruptive because they are brain damaged or "a retard." Thus, they are free of responsibility.

Techniques of Therapy

In discussing the use of psychotherapy in the treatment of children with ADHD, one must keep in mind a very important fact put quite succinctly by Weil (13): "Such neurotic-like disturbances represent direct consequences of the dysfunctions and are not the end result of unconscious elaboration like the truly neurotic symptoms, although they may amalgamate with the latter" (p. 60). These children's basic problem is not neurosis, and the technique of psychotherapeutic intervention is not at all like the technique used with neurotic children. These children had a real body of experience that results from and confirms their disability. For children with neurotic difficulties above and beyond ADHD, those issues must await the interventions targeted to ADHD. If attempts are made by the therapist to deal with neurotic issues initially, treatment usually founders.

In contrast to the technique with neurotic children, regression should not be fostered or permitted with ADHD children, at least, certainly not during the long introductory phase of treatment. As Smith (14) has written, "This regression in the child's play could, and often should, be prevented if the therapist were to provide more structure" (p. 258). Such regression usually leads to disorganization, from which ADHD children have great difficulty recovering. It also leads to a further loss of control. The children see themselves as damaged and unable to keep themselves together. Thus, regression—even so-called therapeutic regression—leads to a further diminution in their self-esteem.

A few words about interpretation: ADHD children often are not able to use interpretation to achieve insight. In fact, interpretation may be seen as permission to act out impulses. Gardner (15) devised the Mutual Storytelling Technique, which uses stories to transmit insight, values, and standards of behavior. Using this strategy, the classical psychoanalytic interpretation need not be employed. Gardner's discussion abounds with numerous examples of this technique.

The treatment truly begins when the therapist presents his findings to the children with ADHD. It is essential for the explanation to be as clear as possible for the children, commensurate with their capabilities to understand. The use of analogies and concrete examples are essential—for instance, the analogy related to trains and motors. The children are told that their brain is like a motor that is set too fast. If people are riding on a train and looking out the window, when the train is traveling at 90 miles per hour they can see nothing outside the window except a blur: however, if the train is slowed down to 30 miles per hour, they can see the scenery. The therapist's job, their parent's job, and the children's job is to try to get their motor to slow down so they can do more things well.

Some therapists (16) say that these children can be treated with an open playroom technique—that is, the children are introduced into a playroom and asked to choose their own toys. In my experience, this has not been helpful. In fact, such an approach has been quite disconcerting to hyperactive children and in that sense destructive to them.

> Ralph is a 10-year-old who was referred because of hyperactivity and for having kissed another boy. He had been evaluated by another psychiatrist and was referred for treatment. After speaking with him for about a half-hour, he was brought into the playroom. Here he became completely disorganized and ran from toy to toy, not really playing with any of them. At this point, the playroom experience was terminated. Succeeding sessions with Ralph were held in a room with a limited number of toys.

Although their reactions may not be quite as dramatic as in Ralph's case, most children with ADHD have not been able to tolerate an open playroom setting. The therapist should tell them that they will play together and that they may choose two or three toys that will be gotten for them and brought to an office that is not filled with things. A space where there are not many things that may distract them and where the therapist can structure the play is best for ADHD children. If the children cannot make a choice, then the therapist should choose two or three types of toys—generally clay or play dough, pencil and paper, a dollhouse, or a toy from which it is easy to get a result, such as "Fantasy Film." In working with these children, nothing succeeds like success. Because these children have a low frustration tolerance and trouble delaying gratification, brief, result-producing experiences are most helpful. If a child becomes angry and withdraws from the game or breaks toys, the therapist and child can talk about the child's sense of frustration and anger and with whom he or she is angry. If this is resolved, both return to the game, and the therapist becomes more actively involved in its accomplishment.

The therapist cannot play a passive role; he must actively engage with the children in a supportive manner. Concrete accomplishments should form the basis for interventions. Emphasis is put on the positive and on successes as much as possible. If there are negatives to be discussed—and there always will be—the therapist and the child can focus on how to avoid or get around them. In time, the focus becomes the problem of getting something accomplished in the session. Once this has occurred, this success is related to the school experience in a manner that compares what the child has accomplished in the treatment and what he or she had done at home or in school. The therapist can make remarks such as "You can do it here; I wonder if you can try the same thing at school" or "Do you think you can teach that to your mother and father?" In this manner, not only is the child urged to reproduce these accomplishments for others, but he or she is also encouraged to be assertive. The child begins to feel less helpless and begins to talk more about his or her inner feelings and torment. Often a great deal of rage emerges; this must be carefully structured, because the child can easily become disorganized with deep emotions, and the therapist must take active steps to organize and channel these feelings.

A point should be made about language. Many children with ADHD have language deficits and cannot articulate well or facilely. Therefore, they are more likely to express themselves motorically. It is important for the therapist to recognize this style, allow for it, and then talk about the experience. Frequently, when these children try to verbalize, this often tenuous function is easily overwhelmed. The children must therefore be taught that they can use words effectively.

Generally, after anger and frustration have been expressed, sadness comes to the fore. The children talk about other kids picking on them and the feelings of worthlessness that result. As with any patient in a session, they are allowed to ventilate; yet the therapist should comment on the accomplishments and successes he or she has seen and that have been reported by teachers and parents. For example, a statement such as "this has been in the past but now such and such has happened" can be made. This is not to argue the children out of their feelings but to point out that there is a new body of experience that forms the basis for their competence and is in direct contradiction to their past experiences.

In treatment, children with ADHD must come to terms with their deficiencies and try to change them if possible. Following that, a realistic appraisal of their strengths and weaknesses must be made. Much as their parents had to mourn the loss of the idealized child, ADHD children must mourn the loss of an idealized image and replace it with a more realistic one.

Obviously, the therapist must be more structuring, more active, and more supportive at the beginning of treatment and possibly for a long time. There also is a more didactic component in the treatment of ADHD children than there is in treating neurotic children. Mastery in the session should be accomplished and then transferred to outside situations.

In conclusion, it is essential in the treatment of children with ADHD to find or create areas of good achievement and of pride and pleasure. This is necessary to salvage the children's self-esteem and to work with parents and children to recognize the areas of good functioning so that the children can rely on these and the parents can supply the needed support and acknowledgment to tackle areas of deficiency.

REFERENCES

1. Haenlein M, Carl WF: Attention deficit disorder with hyperactivity: a specific hypothesis of reward dysfunction. J Am Acad Child Adolesc Psychiatry 26:356–362, 1987
2. Rosenthal RH, Allen TW: An examination of attention, arousal and learning dysfunction of hyperactive children. Psychol Bull 84:689–715, 1978
3. Wender PH: Some speculations concerning a possible biochemical basis of minimal brain dysfunction. Life Sci 14:1605–1621, 1974
4. Silver LB: Playroom diagnostic evaluation of children with neurologically based learning disabilities. J Am Acad Child Psychiatry 15:240–256, 1976
5. Silver LB: The minimal brain dysfunction syndrome, in Basic Handbook of Child Psychiatry, Vol II. Edited by Noshpitz J. New York, Basic Books, 1979, pp 416–438
6. Wender PH: Minimal Brain Dysfunction in Children. New York, Wiley Interscience, 1971
7. Gittleman-Klein R, Klein DF: Methylphenidate effects in learning disabilities. Arch Gen Psychiatry 33:655–664, 1976
8. Kupietz SS, Winsburg BG, Richardson E, et al: Effects of methylphenidate dosage in hyperactive reading disabled children, I: behavior and cognitive performance effects. J Am Acad Child Adolesc Psychiatry 27:70–77, 1988
9. Rapoport JL, Buchsbaum MS, Weingarner H, et al: Dextroamphetamine: its cognitive and behavioral effects in normal and hyperactive boys and normal men. Arch Gen Psychiatry 37:933–943, 1980
10. Rappaport S: Behavior disorder and ego development in a brain injured child. Psychol Study Child 16:423–450, 1961
11. Gardner R: Psychogenic problems of brain injured children and their parents. J Am Acad Child Psychiatry 7:471–491, 1968
12. de Hersch K: Studies in tachyphernia, IV: diagnosis of developmental language disorders. Logos 4:3–9, 1961

13. Weil A: Learning disturbances with special consideration of dyslexia. Issues in Child Mental Health 5:52–66, 1977
14. Smith HF: The elephant on the fence: approaches to the psychotherapy of attention deficit disorder. Am J Psychother 40:252–264, 1986
15. Gardner R: The mutual story telling technique in the treatment of psychogenic problems secondary to minimal brain dysfunction. Journal of Learning Disabilities 7:135–143, 1974
16. Axline V: Play Therapy. New York, Ballantine Books, 1969

7 School-Age Psychotic Children and Their Parents

Joseph Youngerman, M.D.

T wo hundred years ago, in the humanistic blaze of the French Revolution, Philippe Pinel, who struck the chains from the mentally ill in Paris, examined a mute, unkempt, unsocialized pubertal child found abandoned in the rugged woodlands west of Provence and diagnosed as an incurable idiot this "wild child of Aveyron." Undeterred by his professor's gloomy pronouncement or the gawking disinterest of the general public, Pinel's student Itard undertook the systematic enlightenment of this feral child, outlining to France's Minister of the Interior a comprehensive treatment plan that included goals for sensory, affective, cognitive, social, and language development. Five years later Itard lucidly recounted his far-reaching efforts to educate and civilize this "savage child" in a foster-care setting on the outskirts of Paris (1). The scope of this therapy and the faith in the enlightenment of mankind that sustained it remain a compelling first paradigm for the therapy of profoundly disturbed children today, whether the principal diagnosis be social deprivation or mental retardation or psychosis.

Although we now look for guidance to psychoanalytic experts rather than Enlightenment philosophers and would eschew some of Itard's reported interventions (such as holding the patient out the window to invoke fear or locking him in a dark closet for seclusive punishment), we would recognize all too easily the intensity of the therapeutic struggle, the elation of reaching a totally isolated and alienated youth, the frustrations in finding techniques to keep him engaged and moving toward the world of people, the disheartening moments of unexpected regression, and the enormously impressive though poignantly limited achievement.

In the comprehensive sense, treatment of psychotic children regularly includes a whole service delivery system of special schools, residences, and hospitals, the all-important context or milieu in which the individual treatment is provided. In this chapter I will not weigh such varying treatment programs, which usually reflect administrative and political decisions at a level beyond the power of the individual therapist. I will not directly review the continuing search for etiological factors and diagnostic precision either, though it naturally affects treatment decisions. For example, children diagnosed as autistic are often treated in designated programs separate from other less clearly delineated but seriously disturbed children. This is so even though we have come to recognize an autistic spectrum rather than an autistic disorder—a multiplicity of pervasively developmentally disordered children rather than a single diagnosis that describes a homogeneous population responsive to a uniformly defined treatment.

In working with the heterogeneous array of children called psychotic, we recognize that symptom picture and developmental level prescribe the focus of treatment (2,3). Precision is critical in delineating, for each individual child, what is particular in terms of both limitations and strengths. For the treatment question *par excellence* is always how can this unique child be approached, engaged, led backward to understand the inception of the trouble and led forward to resume less compromised development. Under this broad rubric, psychosis is viewed as a process, a profound derailment of the normal developmental trajectory that encompasses the wide range of affective and cognitive, intrapsychic and interpersonal, playful and realistic growth; and treatment is another broad and intersecting process. In this chapter, my focus will be on that therapeutic intersection, or more specifically on what the therapist does with the child, and with the child's parents, within the bounds of the office.

CONCEPTUAL MODELS OF THERAPY

Although our etiological models abound with intricacy and our diagnostic schemas canonize complexity, it is curious how limited a conceptual model of therapy we ordinarily use in our treatment of seriously disturbed children. Somehow our standard conceptualization of treatment remains the individual therapist analyzing the individual child, with a premium on verbal interpretations—not that we actually work this way as therapists. We know our patients are not neurotic adults in psychoanalysis even as we make repeated reference to a "psychoanalytic" model that posits a primary disturbance within the mind and fantasies of the child. A striking example of this disparity between oversimplified standard theory and richly complex praxis is presented in Ekstein and colleagues' classic "The Psychoanalytic Treatment of Childhood Schizophrenia" (4,5). Ekstein schematically presents an intricately drawn blueprint of individual psychoanalytic therapy between analyst and patient. However, his painstaking work with the parents of psychotic children, which he emphasizes as clinically essential to therapeutic success, is simply not included in the graphically elegant diagram.

Historically, it may be helpful to recall that emulation of the psychoanalysis of adults was the starting point for child analysts. Melanie Klein (6) was quite strict about the necessity of excluding parents from play therapy at the very outset, in order for the analytic transference to develop; Anna Freud (7), on the other hand, allowed for an initially modified period of preparation of the child for analysis. Nonetheless, whether strict or modified, the model was the adult analytic situation. Apparently, the explicit involvement and implicit support of the parents was blurred by the fact that the early child patients were often the children of the early adult patients. Child analysts from Burlingham (8) to Bornstein (9) emphasized the vital importance for the child's therapy of the mother's attitude toward treatment. Traditionally, if the mother were not in analysis herself, she might be seen weekly in so-called "ancillary" or "collateral" sessions by a social worker. Intensive therapy with one or both parents was a fundamental part of the paradigmatic work with psychotic children reported by Szurek and Berlin (10). Though repeatedly recognized in practice, therapy with parents that was conducted at a different time and place or by a different therapist than the child's therapy continued to be conceptualized as a parameter in the individual psychoanalytic work with the child. Thus, individual psychoanalysis, though initially constructed for adults with Oedipal conflict resolution in mind, became adapted to the exigencies of psychotic children.

Pre-Oedipal treatment models gradually developed from the observations of the mother-infant dyad by Mahler, who noted in her own research with Furer on infantile psychosis how tardily the conception of a mother-child-therapist unit evolved, despite abundant clinical evidence prompting extension of traditional methods (11). Stern (12) has challenged and enlarged Mahler's observations by early infant research from which he has elaborated a theory of the interpersonal development of the self arising from the interactions between infants and mothers. Winnicott (13) also centered his theoretical perspective on the parent-infant dyad, from which individuals and reality emerge, and recorded an extended example of his clinical work with parents in *The Piggle* (14), published posthumously. Bergman and Escalona (15,16) had drawn attention to the unusual sensitivities of psychotic youngsters and introduced the crucial concept of fit between mother and child. They underscored how readily an ordinary mother might fail to fit the special sensitivities of a particular child who might then, as a consequence of the joint failure to fashion an adequate maternal stimulus barrier, develop a clinical psychosis. In another context—working with schizophrenic adults—Sullivan (17) had long ago posited the crucial significance of the interpersonal field in the developing child and in analytic therapy. These strands and others can be woven into a treatment model for psychotic children that emphasizes the interactive, interpersonal aspects of child development and child therapy, without neglecting the standard intrapsychic approach.

In a contemporary conceptualization of the treatment of child and parents as a unit, Ornstein (18) has proposed a treatment model termed child-centered family therapy: the parents supply the motivation; the child, the symptoms; and the family, the therapeutic environment for the symptomatic child. Individual sessions with the child are deemed diagnostic rather than therapeutic. The therapist instructs the parents on the basis of the in-depth understandings of the child's world gained during individual play therapy sessions. This conceptualization is specifically proposed for childhood disorders of the self, in which pathogenesis stems from failures in parental empathy rather than intrapsychic conflicts. Still, Ornstein notes that this new model also addresses a widespread disappointment with the individual play therapy model that has been incurred by the dilution of standard analysis into only once-a-week treatment with nonneurotic youngsters.

In contrast to family therapy theorists, who conceptualize children as simply the identified carriers of structural conflicts, Ornstein has advanced a proposal that avoids the common pitfall of relative neglect of the child's experience. On the other hand, for child therapists, this new model practically reduces child therapy to child diagnosis, with parental psychoeducation the new schema by which therapists can address the crucial need for parents to empathically understand their children's feelings and problems. How can this unified conceptualization of child-centered parent-participant therapy be extended to work with psychotic children, where failure of empathy by the parents is more clearly understood as a consequence rather than a root cause of the primary pathology?

PARENTS AS COPATIENTS AND COTHERAPISTS

Despite these theoretical underpinnings, the office therapy of children is rarely undertaken in the presence of their parents. The singular exception is the psychotherapy of infants and preschoolers, for whom Furman (19), Fraiberg and colleagues (20), Blos (21), Brinnich (22), and Loewald (23) all espouse conjoint therapy of mother and child. Of course, therapeutic preschool nurseries also not uncommonly use this joint approach. Particularly for psychotic children, there are numerous compelling reasons for the conjoint therapy of children with their parents. Theoretically, to treat psychotic school-age children as though they were psychologically individuated is to mistake the chronological for the developmental age of the child.

In practical terms, this means that psychotic children are frequently terrified initially to be separated from their parents, even if only by the door between office and waiting room. Conversely, psychotic youngsters who blithely separate from their parents to enter the office with a strange therapist are not achieving emotional separation but are instead demonstrating a lack of emotional attachment. Moreover, the primary parent of a psychotic child is intensely involved, by the sheer force of the symptomatology, in the life of her or his child to an extraordinary degree. Joint sessions between parent and child do not preclude separate sessions with the child or with the parent individually, but they establish the visible situation within the treatment setting that is so problematic at home. Moreover, the child, the parent, and not least of all the therapist are alerted to the irreplaceability of the primary parent. For the sake of efficiency, too, as Fraiberg and colleagues (20) and Blos (21) observed, conjoint therapy tends to move more quickly than traditional therapy; the interactions, or lack of interactions, are witnessed; and the maternal plasticity is engaged. As in marital or family therapy, only more so, the emotionally charged interactions between regressed partners are immediate and open to exploration and to understanding. The not-so-hidden hatred, the secret guilt, the exasperating frustrations, the helpless, hopeless withdrawals, the sudden shifts of tone and of empathy—all are therapeutically available, not just reported intellectually or defensively rationalized.

In previous reports (22,23) of conjoint therapy with nonpsychotic children, several limiting conditions have been defined. The child's behavior must be at least somewhat dystonic to the parent. Care must be taken lest the parent subtly encourage, or even openly provoke, the symptomatic behaviors of the child. The parent's need for therapy for marital, vocational, or personal issues not directly related to parenting must not be permitted to take over the session to the exclusion of the child. Clearly, joint parent-child therapy is no panacea.

Another major obstacle to joint therapy is, however, also a major advantage: the public presentation of the therapist. An initial reluctance to be seen has to be overcome. The therapist may feel awkward, self-conscious in failing to engage the child, or defeated in attempts to control the child's wayward behaviors. All this discomfort is the daily fare of the parents and is useful in cementing the empathic connection between parent and therapist. "Now you see what I have to deal with all week long" can be heard as "Now I see that you have the same trouble with my child that I have," releasing the parent from guilty self-disparagement. Yet the therapist persists where the parent has been overwhelmed and withdrawn, thus serving as a model and resource for the parent, an auxiliary ego or parent prosthesis, in the painful effort to reach the psychotic child. Everything experienced during the therapeutic hour parents may utilize at home, either explicitly or as an indirect catalyst for the discovery of their own ways of reaching their child.

THE THERAPIST AS COPARTICIPANT

In working with the psychotic child, the therapist must be active in setting limits and positive in initiating activities that can organize wild eruptions into coherent play. Better to intrude countertransference reactions in an obvious way during active participation in the play than to abstain under the guise of neutrality, for the therapist's traditional self-restraint may withhold from the disorganized child an essential catalyst that transmutes the play from inchoate disruptions into meaningful vignettes.

An illustration of the organizing power of interventions on both child and parent occurred in the initial work with a 7-year-old boy.

> Donald was the wildly disruptive child of two legal professionals, each of whom had previously experienced psychoanalytic therapy. Donald entered the office clinging to his mother, keeping his grip on her even as she sat down. From his maternal launch pad he then rocketed around the office, darting from window sills to cabinets to the backs of the armchairs before aggressively crash landing into his mother's lap. There was scant opportunity on my part for therapeutic inactivity as neutral observer. I was constantly called to protect Donald from self-injury by slipping and to protect his mother from injury by his jumping on her.
>
> At my rather counteraggressive insistence, Donald and I began throwing a sponge ball and then wadded up tissues at each other. These soft missiles were safer projectiles than Donald himself, and they at least kept him more or less on the floor. He quickly understood my attempt at a distracting game of catch as an invitation to unidirectional bombardment: scooping up the tissues like soft snow, he would fire multiple shots at close range. My role was to be hit, to try to win but to lose, to be killed off, to be blasted into smithereens. Without explicitly planning this transformation, I had changed the action in the session by interposing myself in a forceful but playful way between Donald's aggressive claims on his mother and his mother's depressive resignation to intolerable attack.
>
> Donald's wild leaps, from which I could barely protect him and his mother, had become organized into symbolic play in which I could definitely not protect myself from his blistering attacks of Kleenex tissue balls. There was a concomitant transformation from activity to affect: what went whizzing around were less and less the shots of matter and more and more the interjections of emotion—"mercy, mercy; please don't kill me again; I'll make you pay for that." Rage, frustration, exhaustion, pity, and self-pity could all be enacted in this play. Donald's responses were not startling alterations in behavior but slight ameliorations in the intensity of the dramas. A decided regularization of the frenzied battle gradually occurred: we knew what was going to happen and how it was going to be played out. Regularity, humor, and shared pleasure in the retelling had emerged.

To organize such intense and direct physical play so that it focuses on the real person of the therapist has intrinsic problems. Limiting the therapist's exhaustion and the child's aggression are the self-evident ones. It is one thing to stimulate interaction with a psychotic child, who surely has many defensive reasons why he may wish to remain undisturbed in his isolation. To channel that child's energy, once aroused, into more manageable and symbolic activities may prove quite difficult, but the therapist can productively count on arousing an intense sense of his or her own desperate energy.

As I have noted, sometimes the aggression can be shifted into more neutral physical games, such as playing catch or volleyball with a sponge ball. In other youngsters who lack the coordination and social interest, soccer or baseball may not catch on as substitutes for direct physical combat. For many children and therapists, puppets or action figures are another welcome alternative, which may need to be offered over several sessions before they catch on. In Piagetian terms, the therapist is trying to move the play from the sensorimotor into the symbolic. Though contrary to the notion of the observing, non-contaminating analyst, this active introducing of playthings is akin to a mother's animating of objects in an infant's world, the vitalization of teddy bears and cars that establishes a new realm of cherished creations or transitional objects (12,24).

At this stage in the therapy with Donald, the toy figures were repeatedly offered. Finally, a drama evolved in which the large dinosaurs would assault the small family figures, mashing and eating them one by one—repeatedly, relentlessly, untiringly—for an entire session. This scenario soon became difficult for Donald's mother to endure, sitting on the other side of the room. "That's just the way he is with the baby," she would sigh, in increasing distress. Prompted by the mother's discomfort as well as my own, I grew impelled to intervene actively in the play again, to stop Donald from perseverately destroying the family. "What can the family do?" I would ask, and I would receive the answer, "Nothing, they will all be destroyed." One by one, over and over again, they were.

I began to think up small strategies, such as hiding one here or there—all to no avail, of course. Donald's mother offered a few suggestions as well. Questions and interpretative guesses about the reasons for the dinosaurs' aggressive rampages were met with no signal of understanding or acceptance. Again a threshold is crossed: how many times can you witness the same destruction of the same family without intervening? Such repetitive play begins to lose all interest, just as it paradoxically commands increasing attention. It is so boring and yet so loaded, surcharged with rigidity and unbearable tension.

Feeling bored leads the therapist to question why the child is deadening the play: defensively, what needs to be hidden; constructively, how can it be disclosed? I began holding the family figures together to protect them from being swallowed individually by the dinosaurs. Dialogue was simple, again offered by the mother as well as the therapist: "let's stick together, this is terrifying, at least we have each other, it's not much but it's better than being all alone." Donald and the dinosaurs would ultimately defeat the little family, but delays and detours and digressions were increasingly tolerated. The play developed interest again. A competitive interactive play between child and therapist had emerged, with the battlefield consigned to the floor at Donald's mother's feet rather than to her lap.

The physical proximity still allowed for rich interactions. Donald never wanted to talk about events at home or at school, but my questions to his mother in the midst of the battles were partially tolerated. In terse interchanges she would describe the battles at home, while Donald consistently interrupted and argued. However, the battles of the dinosaurs raging at the moment gave a necessary distance to the battles that had raged at home and provided a possible means of communication. My dinosaurs could enact the constellations or strategies of the battles at home. No matter what I tried, my side was always defeated; but during the brief but invariably repeated battles, I could give voice to Donald's hopes and terrors, as I understood them from mixing his mother's descriptions of the home battles with his own maneuvers in the dinosaur battles. Of course, his mother understood that I was speaking about her son's feelings, and so did Donald, who would frequently shout at me to stop talking about all that. Manifold themes of parents and babies, involving birth and death, protection and abandonment, eating and killing, sibling jealousy and possessive dominance, were all played out with dinosaurs at Donald's mother's feet on the office floor.

The other theater of play and communication that continued to evolve used not toy figures but improvisatory actors. Its origin lay in my repeated interventions within the session to physically protect Donald's mother from his infantile assaults. Cuddling in her lap, he would become overexcited and provoke rejection by kissing, licking, biting, and slapping her face and stroking her breasts and thighs. Although this seemingly triangular interaction, in which a man pulls a boy off a woman, later achieved striking Oedipal clarity—when Donald told me to play king to his mother's queen—it started as a simple maternal substitution.

Not able to get Donald's mother to stop her son's desperate search and provocative rejection of her, I substituted myself for her. In my arms, Donald tried to bite and to hit me; and I defended myself, showing her how to restrain him safely. To this basic management of aggression, I added the absurdity of playing mother by rocking this 60-pound baby in my arms while carrying him around the room. This is hard enough to manage and ludicrous enough to provoke laughter and defuse the tense assaultiveness. What appeared mutative was this theater rather than my interpretive comments, which apparently were not heard in the midst of the fray or seemed irrelevant—or worse, even provocative of new outbursts.

As befits this drama of symbiotic duality, the actors could be easily interchanged. When Donald as baby was too ferocious to handle, I might become the baby, parodying his antics by clinging to him and threatening, demanding, cajoling, and raging, to everyone's relief and delight. Obviously, it was easier to control my own babyish tantrums than his. Still, Donald was not only reassured by this reversal but also frightened. I worried that my play was unduly upsetting my patient, but I was reassured by remembering that Winnicott had played the role of greedy baby to both the relief and the terror of the Piggle (14). The external sequence—of my tantrum seeming out of control, of Donald's terrified demanding that I stop, and of my prompt stopping—modeled what I hoped would be a developing internal sequence of rage brought under self-control and an interpersonal sequence of childish rage brought under parental control.

Another transition in the development of this theater was the use of props. The idea of maternal protection was first extended in a game of tag, in which Donald designated his mother and her chair as home base. How comforting to have a sanctuary! When I complained about not having a mother always available, I was instructed to use another chair as my base. Later I began complaining that my armchair was empty. Donald filled it with a folding chair on which he had previously reigned as king. When Donald assaultively attempted to embrace his mother, I could mirror and parody his actions by attempting to climb into the folding chair on top of the armchair, talking all the while about the difficulty of getting back into my mother's arms and body when I had grown so tall. Such improvisations were extravagant and arresting. Donald encouraged my actions, gleefully laughed at my failures, and informed me of the painful impossibility of once again becoming an infant in my mother's womb. His mother, who understood the drama all too well, was again relieved to see it enacted on a stage which was not her own body.

THERAPEUTIC PARENTING AFTER-HOURS

As with any child patient, only more so, the therapy of a psychotic child is assuredly not limited to the therapy hours. Much work is required outside of sessions by the child, the parents, the significant others in the family and the school, and by the therapist. Issues of parenting extend well beyond the interactions of the therapy hour to include every aspect of the child's basic daily routine. These include but are not at all limited to waking, dressing, eating, toileting, going to and returning from school (not to mention the added complexity of tripartite negotiations between school personnel, parents, and therapist), doing homework, playing and fighting with siblings, going to bed, and waking in the middle of the night. We know from inpatient units that any aspect of the daily schedule and any time during the 24-hour day may become the focus of intense struggles. To create a therapeutic milieu at home, many phone calls and meetings with both parents are essential. Between clear limits and compromising accommodations, between expectations of autonomous self-control and acceptances of current disabilities and dependencies, a plausible path that promotes normalizing development is continuously sought, found, lost, and relocated.

A quintessential paradigm for this process is the use of medication.

Whether to medicate or not, when, for what symptoms, for how long, and with what side effects must all be negotiated between and among parents, therapist, and child. Perhaps the fact that medication is given by the parents, and sometimes by the school, outside of the therapist's office adds to the unstated distortions. To recommend giving pills means to acknowledge that all the psychotherapy hours cannot help the child, so my child's condition must be incurable, reasons the parent. The mind/body or mind/brain split is polarized into a dichotomy of power in which the parents' feelings of impotence and guilt are readily projected onto the therapist: psychotherapy is powerless to change my child's mind; therefore, medication will be used to control his brain. Parental denial of the seriousness of the child's problems may be either overwhelmed into helpless submission to the medical authority or fanned into incredulous resistance to toxic chemicals or drugs.

Therapists, too, may develop strong countertransference positions, whether they refer their patient for a pharmacological consultation or prescribe the medication themselves. With a referral, the dangers of splitting are explicit, with hierarchical discoordination between therapists all too evident. On the other hand, in prescribing medication, the therapist runs more subtle risks while "changing hats" of surreptitiously establishing an internal split between doctor and therapist. Admonitions about the need for medication, considerations regarding effective dosage and regimen, and cautions about side effects such as tardive dyskinesia are so compelling that they may supersede explorations of the emotional meanings of medication for the parent and for the child. In brief, psychopharmacology may unnecessarily undermine or unwittingly obscure psychodynamics.

Parental perplexity is the accurate term Goldfarb and colleagues (25,26) have given to the surprising paralysis of parents of psychotic children when faced with managing the most ordinary parenting situations. In the Goldfarb examples, one child physically assaulting his mother and another masturbating under his mother's skirts were each quickly brought under control through a single clear injunction from the therapist to the mother: set limits. In my experience, even forceful intervention by the therapist into the interaction between parent and child has not been so rapidly efficacious. As part of the deeply entrenched accommodation of parent to psychotic child, parental paralysis in the face of the child's physical or sexual assaultiveness seems rooted in the parent's positive efforts to manage and to protect the child from overwhelming anxiety and panic.

Discussing parental perplexity directly is an evident therapeutic approach generally welcomed by parents who have been struggling with psychosis alone and without professional understanding or distance. Dissension between the parents on "the right way" to help their psychotic child behave normally is commonplace. Frequently, the mother struggling to manage is blamed by the father struggling to remain detached. Though resistance can be expected, simple family interventions that involve the father and relieve the mother, at least on weekends or in the evenings at bedtime, are often useful. One parent cannot readily substitute for the other, because only one is the truly symbiotic partner for the psychotic child. Nevertheless, the child may do quite well with the more distant parent, at least for circumscribed periods, as the more developmentally mature and independent aspects of the child are engaged. One danger of these good times with the other parent is the reinforcement of that parent's blaming attitude toward the primary parent: "I have no trouble with the boy, and neither would she if she treated him the way I do." Intensive parental counseling and frequent phone calls are the normal accoutrements of therapy with the psychotic child.

Indeed, therapeutic work with the parents can be the central aspect of therapy with psychotic children. Are the parents providing enough to meet the special requirements of their psychotic child? Are they providing too much? Is the home a suitable place for the child to live right now? Is a residential school, or hospital, really preferable? What can be done at home, and with what impact on the marriage and on the siblings, to protect and enhance the development of a particular psychotic child who requires special familial adaptations? These basic questions are always confronted in the therapy of psychotic children, whereas they are less common and less pressing in the therapy of less severely ill youngsters.

What are clearly most distressing are those irreconcilable situations that require removal of the psychotic child from the parental home. The bilateral ambivalence of child and family needs to be thoroughly explored to ensure successful placement—never a speedy or even finite undertaking. Hospitalization often serves as an acceptable bridge between home and residence, as it is more evaluative than definitive, engaging parents' desires for expert assistance and transient relief rather than their fears of permanent abandonment through placement.

Often the answers to questions about the child's home environment are surprising to our stereotypic notions.

One 11-year-old immigrant boy set fire to his mattress in a foster home in response to command hallucinations, after his mother had been hospitalized for an acute exacerbation of paranoid schizophrenia. Hospitalization of the child with haloperidol in minimal doses resolved his psychosis but not the more difficult question of where he should live. After extensive investigation over several months, it became clear that his mother was an exceptionally devoted and effective parent when restabilized on her antipsychotic medication. She had been fully able to make sure that he regularly attended a special class in the public schools. Her only failure was an aspect of her virtue: her devotion to this moderately retarded child had been complete but exclusive, lacking supportive connection to appropriate outpatient services and after-school programs.

Unfortunately, psychotic children not infrequently suffer the additional burden of having a psychotic parent. The commonplace identifications of child with parent—including physical characteristics such as color of hair, eyes, or skin; temperamental traits such as activity level, sensory sensitivity, adaptability, or withdrawal; and defensive styles such as obsessive, histrionic, paranoid, or depressive—achieve an uncommon intensity in these families. The child readily identifies with the more blatantly pathological aspects of the parent—with being sick, crazy, bad, or wild. In turn, the unstable parent may symbiotically identify the child as being "just like me" or projectively identify the child as being "totally unlike me."

The old family game of blaming the in-laws—"he gets that from your family; nobody has that on my side"—has been raised to a new level of reality by the current studies of the genetic determinants of affective illnesses, especially manic-depressive disorder. The psychoeducational approach to the gene structures elucidated in some families with bipolar illness may become distorted by young patients into a sense of fatalistic inevitability that they must suffer every step, and misstep, of their parent's illness. Identification is reduced to cloning or twinning. Not only did one pubertal child take lithium, the same medication as his mother, but he took it at the same dosage. Would he therefore have the same number of hospitalizations, he wondered? This new repetition compulsion, or biological predeterminism, can be seized upon by the child as a rigidly unbreakable identification with the ill parent. Unfortunately, therapeutic efforts to transmute this bond may become derailed by frustration into simplistic denunciations of the parent: "You don't have to be crazy like him!" Instead, the therapist must actively search for positive identifications to supplant the negative ones, or for positive attributes of the parent before the negative ones are delimited: "I am sure she loves you very much but right now she is so overwhelmed with her own problems that she knows that the best way to take care of you is to let someone who is not so sick be a substitute parent for a while." Such affirmations by therapists allow children to express their disappointments and to disidentify at a rate that suits their capacities (27).

THERAPEUTIC APPROACHES TO PSYCHOTIC THINKING

Not only identifications but each and every ordinary issue of childhood may become infused with and confused by psychotic thinking. To transform such thinking requires more than simple pedagogy or cognitive explanations. A therapeutic dialogue must be heard (28) and elaborated (29), founded on the entire trusting and facilitative therapeutic relationship (30). At first, the child's underlying thought processes are usually less troubling to the parents, and even to the therapist, than the child's obvious difficulty achieving some average expectable mastery of a developmental task. Gradually, the therapist develops a vague but educated hunch that psychotic ideation is admixed with the inexplicably intense struggle with a particular issue. Next comes the search for clues or fragments of this thinking, through questioning of both the child and the parents. Then the astonishing extent or shocking distortions of the psychotic perspective emerges, to be followed by patient and thoroughgoing clarification and interpretation.

For example, a child's psychotic thinking may imbue the ordinary childhood issues of separation and bodily integrity with quite unusual danger. More than routine parental attentiveness is then required simply to ensure the basic physical and emotional safety of such a child.

> One 9-year-old girl, Alice, who was living with her well-educated and psychologically sophisticated mother, was wantonly injuring her hands and feet with sharp objects. Since birth she had been physically inseparable from and closely identified with her mother, then just a teenager, who had shared a bed with her child in her grandmother's apartment. A year before referral, they had moved into their own apartment, which apparently delighted Alice. However, she had been somewhat distressed after her customary, but that year exceptionally prolonged, summer visit alone with her great-grandmother in the Antilles. She had missed her mother far more than usual.

> My initial evaluation had generated diffuse speculations, applicable across three generations, about a child's feelings of abandonment by and rage toward her mother. Not until several months later, during a lull in a checker game, were some specific and unexpected aspects of Alice's thinking about her self-injurious behavior disclosed. I had misidentified a certain move of hers, leading to a double jump possibility for me, as suicidal or, at the very least, underprotective. She seized upon my implication and vehemently corrected me: "You think I am suicidal! Who says I'm trying to kill myself! I cut myself just like my mother does. I watch her cut her feet, right on her heels, with a razor blade, but it never bleeds. Why do I always bleed when I cut myself?"

> When I asked how she understood her difference from her mother, Alice alluded to voodoo rituals and graveyard visits with her great-grandmother during the past summer. Much further work was necessary, both in verbal clarifications and in play enactments of death and resurrection, near-death, and resuscitation, to resolve these psychotic confusions. The environmental recommendations were notably simpler: for now, mother should not pare her corns in front of her daughter; and next summer, the girl's mother should accompany her on her sojourn in the Antilles or replace it altogether with day camp at home.

The resolution of sibling rivalry, or the sharing of parental love without feelings of catastrophic loss and rageful revenge, is another developmental issue that is particularly problematic for psychotic children. However we conceptualize the birth of a sibling—whether as an intolerable interruption of symbiotic omnipotence, of primitive narcissism, or of tenuous intersubjective relativeness—the therapist must be alert to the probability that a young child's behavioral repertoire of incessant fighting, regressive withdrawal, or clinging depression may conceal a fundamentally psychotic conceptualization of his relationships with parents and siblings.

> For example, Donald, the 7-year-old I had discussed previously, had been engaged in a protracted war against his little sister, an easy baby whom his mother saw as a veritable angel bedeviled by her big brother. Limits and bribes, reasons and remonstrations, promoted only transient cease-fires between the children. Therapeutic regressions enacted during the sessions were no more than temporarily effective. For a week or two, the home battles might ease. On several occasions, the sides were even reversed, with Donald becoming the good boy and his little sister becoming the jealous disrupter. All too soon, however, physically violent fights would recur.

> In this war-weary climate, Donald's mother had become increasingly exhausted and disheartened by the innumerable failed peace efforts, while his father had become increasingly involved—to the relief of his wife—in the supervision of the children. Finally, at the insistence of his wife and the invitation of his son, the father even became the one to bring Donald to therapy. Only at this juncture did Donald disclose to his father the extent of his psychotic thinking about his mother that lay behind his sibling rivalry: "Since I was the first baby, everything in the house belongs to me. I own all the toys. I let sister play with them, but she must give them back whenever I want them." Donald nodded in earnest ascent to his father's report of this conversation in the joint therapy session. "And your parents?" I asked him. "No," he replied immediately, "they don't play with toys." I rephrased my question: "Are your parents completely yours as well?" "Of course," he again replied without hesitation, "I was born first. Sister can borrow them, but she has to be ready to give them back, too."

> Having articulated the psychotic extent of his conception of primogeniture, Donald could then be engaged in a therapeutic discussion of the ideological basis for his unending holy war. It was evident that every previous truce had simply overlooked this distorted conception of his rights. His psychotic thinking is presented here not as the etiological prime mover nor as the singular entry point for therapeutic intervention. Rather, it is a fundamental organizer of his affect and behavior that needs to be presumed, looked for, and pointedly addressed in the midst of an otherwise irresolvable maelstrom.

THERAPEUTIC OBJECTS

The literal-mindedness of psychotic children also presents some special opportunities for therapeutic concreteness. In part, this is the domain of

Sechehaye's (31) symbolic realization—that ideal of the perfectly chosen gift from therapist to patient, like the perfectly timed interpretation, a transitional phenomenon that enables the patient to establish a new and continuing wholeness. On the more prosaic level, there are many ordinary things that therapists give patients, from appointment cards to prescriptions to bills, which also have symbolic meanings. With a child functioning on a psychotic level of organization who has unusual trouble maintaining whole object relationships, the therapist's giving of real objects that can be held during his absence has a special usefulness.

The usual treatment of such children within hospitals or day treatment programs, which enable the child to see the therapist in some capacity several times a day, regularly precludes the need for some special transitional object. In the individual therapy of a psychotic child, the drawings, scorecards, partially completed models, or paper and Scotch tape constructions—indeed, anything created or altered during the session—may serve as a much needed bridge between sessions. During longer interludes, such as vacations or before discharge, calendars marked with Xs are the standard way of organizing the passage of time. For children who can read, important ideas can be written down in the style of almanacs, or prayers, to be read and reread during the therapist's absence. Of course, even for the nonreader, postcards from the vacationing therapist can be read to the child by other staff or by parents. For some very disorganized psychotic youngsters, we have even resorted to the often caricatured tape recording by the therapist of central conceptions, therapeutic understandings, achievements of self-esteem, limits negotiated and promises contracted—a compendium of ego, superego, and self and object constructs voiced by the therapist as a sort of mechanized reminder and reliable positive "hallucination." Tape recordings by the child—whether with the therapist, such as a recording of a session, or during the absence of the therapist, such as a vocalized diary of events and emotions—serve as useful means of keeping the therapeutic relationship alive during long intersessions.

Indeed, the task of keeping alive an absent object of love and desire has been an issue for centuries. Poetry and pictures, lockets and trinkets have long been saved as memorabilia, although they are now all but superseded by snapshots and home videos. Whatever the family has customarily employed or the child selects can be used to keep alive the relationship with the therapist, or with the absent family during the child's residential placement.

One psychotic child was delighted to discover that the little golden heart on her mother's necklace was a locket that could be opened, but she was dismayed to find that it was empty. Rashly ignoring all remonstrations, she pulled out a lock of her hair, which proved too long to be fit into the tiny space. In a pique of desperation she then yanked out several of her own eyelashes, which she enclosed in her mother's empty locket, pledging her mother to save them for 10 years until she was grown. In this literal but psychotic way, she was attempting to fill her mother's empty heart with an enduring piece of herself.

CONCLUSION

In many ways, psychotic children are continually bidding for a secure place in the hearts of their parents, and of their therapists—at least until they can grow up into wholeness. As therapists, we must ever be alert to recognize their fragmentary attempts to create for themselves a sense of existing completeness, in part by imploring us to organize in our minds a cohesive sense of them. Such a therapeutic partnership with the child and the parents requires not only a visionary view of these children's potentials but a sober acceptance of their disabilities, which are frequently denied or exaggerated by the parents and depressively reified by the children. Constructing stable and realistic representations of themselves and others from fluctuating impressions and psychotic fragments thus becomes the enduring goal of the therapy for child, parents, and therapist alike.

REFERENCES

1. Itard JMG: The Wild Boy of Aveyron. Translated by Humphrey G, Humphrey H. Englewood Cliffs, NJ, Prentice Hall, 1972
2. Kestenbaum C: Childhood Psychosis: Psychotherapy, in Handbook of Treatment of Mental Disorders in Childhood and Adolescence. Edited by Wolman B, Egan J, Ross A. Englewood Cliffs, NJ, Prentice Hall, 1978, pp 354–384
3. Cantor S, Kestenbaum C: Psychotherapy with schizophrenic children. J Am Acad Child Psychiatry 25(5):623–630, 1986
4. Ekstein R, Friedman S, Caruth E: The psychoanalytic treatment of childhood schizophrenia, in Manual of Child Psychopathology. Edited by Wolman B. New York, McGraw-Hill, 1972, pp 1035–1057
5. Ekstein R, Caruth E, Cooper B, et al: Psychoanalytically oriented psychotherapy of psychotic children, in Child Analysis and Therapy. Edited by Glenn J. New York, Jason Aronson, 1978, pp 647–707
6. Klein M: The Psychoanalytic Play Technique. Am J Orthopsychiatry 25:223–237, 1955
7. Freud A: The role of transference in the analysis of children, in Introduction to Psychoanalysis: The Writings of Anna Freud, Vol 1. New York, International Universities Press, 1974, pp 36–49
8. Burlingham D: Child analysis and the mother. Psychoanal Q 4:69–82, 1935
9. Bornstein B: Emotional barriers in the understanding and treatment of young children. Am J Orthopsychiatry 18:691–698, 1948
10. Szurek SA, Berlin IN: Clinical Studies in Childhood Psychoses. New York, Brunner/Mazel, 1973

11. Mahler MS, Furer M: Observations on research regarding the 'symbiotic syndrome' of infantile psychosis. Psychoanal Study Child 29:317–327, 1960
12. Stern D: The Interpersonal World of the Infant. New York, Basic Books, 1985
13. Winnicott DW: The theory of the parent-infant relationship, in The Maturational Processes and the Facilitating Environment. New York, International Universities Press, 1965, pp 37–55
14. Winnicott DW: The Piggle: An Account of the Psychoanalytic Treatment of a Little Girl. New York, International Universities Press, 1977
15. Bergman P, Escalona SK: Unusual sensitivities in very young children. Psychoanal Study Child 3(4):333–352, 1949
16. Escalona S: Some considerations regarding psychotherapy with psychotic children. Bull Menninger Clin 12:126–134, 1948. Also in Child Psychotherapy. Edited by Haworth MR. New York, Basic Books, 1964, pp 50–57
17. Sullivan HS: Therapeutic conceptions, in Conceptions of Modern Psychiatry: The Collected Works of Harry Stahl Sullivan. Edited by Perry H, Gawel M. New York, WW Norton, 1940, pp 175–238
18. Ornstein A: The function of play in the process of child psychotherapy: a contemporary perspective. The Annual of Psychoanalysis 12(13):349–366, 1984, 1985
19. Furman E: Treatment of under-fives by way of their parents. Psychoanal Study Child 12:250–262, 1958
20. Fraiberg S, Adelson E, Shapiro V: Ghosts in the nursery. J Am Acad Child Psychiatry 14:387–421, 1975
21. Blos P, Jr: Intergenerational separation-individuation. Psychoanal Study Child 40:41–56, 1985
22. Brinnich P: Aggression in early childhood: joint treatment of children and parents. Psychoanal Study Child 39:493–508, 1984
23. Loewald E: Psychotherapy with parent and child in failure-to-thrive. Psychoanal Study Child 40:345–364, 1985
24. Winnicott DW: Transitional objects and transitional phenomena, in Collected Papers: Through Paediatrics to Psycho-Analysis. London, Tavistock Publications, 1958, pp 229–242
25. Goldfarb W, Sibulkin L, Behrens M, et al: The concept of maternal perplexity, in Parenthood. Edited by Anthony EJ, Benedek T. Boston, MA, Little, Brown, 1970, pp 411–420
26. Goldfarb W: An investigation of childhood schizophrenia: a retrospective view. Arch Gen Psychiatry 11:620–634, 1964
27. Schecter D: Identification and individuation. J Am Psychoanal Assoc 16:48–80, 1968
28. Khan M: Silence as communication, in The Privacy of the Self. New York, International Universities Press, 1974, pp 168–180
29. Ekstein R, Nelson T: The birth of the psychotherapeutic dialogue and the self. Psychiatr Clin North Am 4:533–549, 1981
30. Mohacsy I: Severe regression in an eight-and-one-half year old boy. Contemporary Psychoanalysis 12(4):455–476, 1976
31. Sechehaye M: Symbolic Realization: A New Method of Psychotherapy Applied to a Case of Schizophrenia. Translated by Wursten B, Wursten H. New York, International Universities Press, 1951

SECTION II:

THE PSYCHOTHERAPEUTIC PROCESS WITH ADOLESCENTS

✦ ✦ ✦ ✦ ✦ ✦ ✦

8 Adolescents With Borderline Personality Disorder: An Interpersonal-Systemic View

Leonard Israel Siegel, M.D., F.A.P.A, F.R.A.N.Z.L.P.

In this chapter, I will introduce an interpersonal-systemic (IS) view of borderline personality disorder (BPD) in adolescence. There will be an outline of diagnostic criteria from DSM-III-R (1) and other sources. This will be followed by a brief discussion of the psychodynamics and family system characteristics. I will also discuss outpatient individual psychotherapy and residential treatment including family and group therapies. I will then make comparisons between an IS approach and an object relations approach, especially as elaborated by Kernberg (12–14) and by Masterson (15–19).

IS theory is an attempt at an eclectic synthesis of the interpersonal theory of Sullivan (2) and the family systems theory of Bateson (3). A number of authors have attempted syntheses of various theories with systems theory: of Behavioral (4), Object Relations (5,6), Karen Horney's theory (7), Kohutian self psychology (8), and constructivist theory (9). As I will discuss later, the IS approach features the interpersonal therapeutic process of the cocreation of a new narrative by therapist and patient. This revised story of the patient's life accompanied by affective changes is considered to be the crucial agent for positive change. This theory has been found useful in outpatient psychotherapy with selected adolescents and in the design of residential treatment of economically disadvantaged families containing a borderline adolescent.

Freud (10) focused on the intrapsychic, on the conflict between libidinal drives, ego, and superego. Object relations theorists Klein (11), Kernberg (12–14), and Masterson (15–19) added a dyadic dimension. Sullivan shifted the focus from the intrapsychic to the interpersonal as well as developing his own concept of the Self as a System. Von Bertalanffy (20) and Bateson (3) shifted the focus from the dyad to systems with three or more people. Purist systemic family therapists such as Watzlawick (21), Haley (22,23), Minuchin (24), and the Milan group (25) tend to deny the relevance of all intrapsychic processes (26). IS theory attempts to marry concepts of individual and family

The author is indebted to Dr. Stephanie Whitmont for her help in the editing of this manuscript.

development, the Self, the primary family triangular relationships, the larger immediate family system, and the ecological context of the family in the extended family and neighborhood. IS psychotherapy—whether individual, marital, family, or group—focuses on the interpersonal and systemic and the elaboration of the self in the context of the family and the peer group. It centralizes the importance of the development of dyadic and group interpersonal skills and the linkage between such skills with self-image and self-esteem.

For adolescent or adult patients who are sufficiently verbal and introspective, the IS therapeutic style is relatively neutral and less active. For adolescent patients and their families who are least suitable for and most resistant to insight-oriented psychotherapy, the IS residential treatment approach is more active and more confrontational as well as more directively supportive. Sullivan advocated a more active style than the classical psychoanalysts; and family therapists are generally more active than the Sullivanians. Although IS therapy tries to utilize the minimal level of activity, it is an active therapy, with mirroring, reframing, and the construction of new narrative. IS therapy is based on the Sullivanian, Constructivist, Kohutian, and Systemic theory that there is no objective reality other than that which is cocreated by consensual validation between two or more people. There is thus no objectively true scientific metapsychology as claimed by classical and object relations psychoanalytic theorists. It is believed, therefore, that the therapist should not impose his own metapsychology on the patient. Instead, the therapist might rather cocreate a new and unique narrative specifically built for and with that singular patient. Such a new narrative includes a wider variety of alternative solutions than the patient's pretherapy story with its former limited choice of symptom-as-solution.

When this approach is used in a residential setting, the situation is altered. For example, there is an initial imposition from therapist to patient. In residential treatment, the staff tends to assume certain commonly held beliefs, rules, and regulations (e.g., violence is forbidden) and must limit the acting-out behavior that is characteristic of borderline adolescent patients and their families. The treatment-avoiding borderline adolescent patient characteristically cannot settle down long enough to define goals for change in interpersonal patterns until the frantic acting out is limited by residential and school staff joining forces with a strengthened parental hierarchical system.

DIAGNOSIS

Inherent in the diagnosis of BPD is the concept of personality or "character" structure. Personality structure refers to the constellation of defenses or "security operations" that manage anxiety and maintain self-esteem. When these security operations fail to maintain self-esteem accompanied by a sense of interpersonal connectedness, clinically apparent symptoms emerge, such as free-floating anxiety, despair, shame, and guilt. Furthermore, symptoms are formed, including depression, and security operations are elaborated, such as interpersonal power operations (manipulativeness). In instances where defenses are too brittle, the self disorganizes toward psychosis with transient delusional or hallucinatory experiences. In BPD, the personality is sufficiently resourceful to recover rather quickly from such micropsychotic experience. Central to the adolescent borderline personality is the use of the self-soothing functions of drug and alcohol abuse, compulsive sexuality, self-mutilating behaviors, and various forms of acting out. BPD may also be thought of as a condition on the margin between personality disorder and the manic-depressive disorders or on the border with schizoid and schizotypal conditions. Because there is a tendency toward aggressivity and brief forays into antisocial acting out, the borderline condition might also be located on the margin with the antisocial disorders (formerly labelled as sociopathy or psychopathy). Despite these excursions into the psychoses or antisocial states, the borderline personality seems to maintain a cluster of characteristics that offer a recognizable stability of personality, which usually continues from adolescence into adulthood.

Mainstream psychiatry, in the form of DSM-III-R (1), focuses phenomenologically on the symptomatology, whereas object relations psychoanalysts focus on the presumed underlying character structure, with developmental fixation at the early phase of separation and individuation with inadequate rapprochement experiences and resultant abandonment depression (15–19). Esman (27) and Gunderson and Singer (28) give a comprehensive review of the literature on BPD of adolescence.

DSM-III-R differentiates between personality traits and personality disorders as follows:

> It is only when personality traits are inflexible and maladaptive . . . that they constitute Personality Disorders. The manifestation of Personality Disorders are often recognizable by adolescence or earlier. . . . (1, p. 335)

DSM-III-R makes several important points about BPD. These include the idea that the diagnosis is appropriate for both adolescents and children when "the disturbance is pervasive and persistent" (1, p. 336). The citation above highlights the requirements of inflexibility and the maladaptive nature of personality traits as precursors to the diagnosis of Personality Disorder. Additionally, BPD is clustered with certain other types of Personality Disorders. These are the Anti-Social, Histrionic, and Narcissistic Personality Disorders, which share certain characteristics with Borderline Personality Disorder. For example, people with any of these disorders can appear dramatic, emotional, or erratic. This cluster specifically excludes patients who primarily appear odd, eccentric, or anxious and fearful.

The particular symptoms of borderline personality include an identity disturbance, emerging as disturbances of self-image, self-orientation, or long-term goals. Difficulty may be experienced with choice of career, values, friends, and lovers. The condition is marked by feelings of emptiness and boredom. Interpersonal relationships are unstable, and this is manifest in alternations between overidealization and devaluation. Patients are unable to maintain object constancy, and there is a low tolerance to being alone. There is a desperate attempt to avoid being abandoned, together with a tendency to clutch at others, which tends to provoke abandonment.

Other symptoms include affective instability, with mood shifts, intense anger, and failure to control the anger. Borderline adolescents have frequent displays of temper, with recurrent physical fights. They can show self-destructive impulsiveness in such behaviors as shopping sprees, drug abuse, reckless driving, casual sex, shoplifting, and binge eating. Dysthymic features are manifest in suicidal threats, gestures, and behaviors. Self-mutilation may occur, apparently serving to manipulate others and/or to counteract the borderline adolescent's feelings of numbness and depersonalization.

All of these symptoms may be accompanied by features of Schizotypal, Histrionic, Narcissistic, or Anti-Social Personality Disorders. DSM-III-R criteria for the disorder suggest that people with Borderline Personality Disorder are socially contrary and pessimistic and that they alternate between dependency and self-absorption. Finally, they may manifest transient psychotic symptoms, in which case they must be differentiated from those individuals with manic-depressive and schizophrenic disorders.

The Westmead Borderline Personality Project (29) uses the following diagnostic criteria, which combine the phenomenological and the psychodynamic. The patient must meet the following criteria:

1. Fulfill DSM-III criteria for BPD;
2. Satisfy dynamic nature of BPD, e.g., patient relates to therapist and significant others in a manner suggesting emotional developmental arrest in the first couple of years of life; history of absent or markedly disturbed relationships with parents or parent substitutes early in life. (29, p. 5)

In reference to DSM-III diagnostic criteria, Clarkin and colleagues (30) found that four of the features (impulsivity, unstable/intense relationships, intense/uncontrolled anger, and affective instability) occurred in 75% of the cases they reviewed. Other DSM-III identifying features were much less frequently found. A three-point diagnostic system is put forward by Kernberg (13), who proposes the following criteria for Borderline Personality: 1) identity diffusion, 2) the use of primitive defenses (such as projective identification), and 3) intact reality testing.

In my experience, the borderline adolescent tends to split others into either all-good or all-bad, rather than mixtures of good and bad. They may over-idealize the significant other at the beginning of the relationship and then shift to the other extreme of contempt when the relationship deteriorates.

These considerations suggest that the diagnosis of borderline personality in an adolescent is not as specific as some authors such as Kernberg (14) may claim. In the clinical workplace, young people with other conditions may attract this label. For example, it seems that Masterson (16) uses the diagnosis as a grab-bag category, including a wide variety of disorders such as anorexia nervosa, severe antisocial acting out, "Hippie" syndrome, and so on.

Psychodynamics

Masterson (18) is a seminal theorist and clinician who has written extensively on his ideas about the psychodynamics of the borderline adolescent. His central concept is one of developmental arrest, contingent on a specific, single traumatic period occurring during the separation and individuation phase of childhood. The trauma that results in developmental arrest is typically the mother's emotional unavailability at the time when the child is attempting to separate and individuate. The mother, because of her own borderline disorder, rewards regressive behavior in her child, and she withdraws emotionally from the child's efforts to separate and individuate.

Masterson indicates other situations that might represent a trauma with similar result. These include a long physical separation from the mother; a mother who is psychotic, depressed, or emotionally empty and unable to nurture; a mother who spends too much time away from home at work; or a mother who has had a long illness and dies.

Developmental arrest at the separation-individuation phase is associated with severe defects in ego functioning. These defects include poor reality testing (in evaluating subtleties of interpersonal flow), low frustration tolerance, inadequate impulse control, fluid ego boundaries, and the persistence of primitive defense mechanisms. The primitive defenses are age-inappropriate to the adolescent and include defenses such as splitting, projection, projective identification, acting out the wish for reunion by clinging, denial, and avoidance of individuation.

In Kernberg's work (13) the presence of "identity confusion" is crucial to the diagnosis. This rests on the borderline adolescent's reliance on primitive defenses, such as splitting and projective identification. Masterson (16) describes the behavior associated with these underlying mechanisms. Borderline adolescents show quite characteristic interpersonal relations. They relate to others as part objects rather than as whole objects. Object relationships fluctuate widely with minimal frustrations. Under stress or extreme affects, the borderline patient is unable to evoke the image of absent known persons. One result of this latter characteristic is the patient's inability to mourn. A borderline patient may react in a calamitous way to the therapist's vacation, assuming the therapist will not return. Such a patient may absent him- or herself from planned interviews. Other behaviors include the exhibition of emotional detachment, or acting out in sexually compulsive ways such as by rushing into marriage.

A central construct of Masterson's (16) theory is what he calls "abandonment depression." Abandonment depression has six component feelings: depression, passivity and helplessness, emptiness and void, anger and rage, guilt, and fear. Because many of these phenomena are said to be unconscious, at least initially, this suggests that Masterson's construct may have implications for personality structure as distinct from phenomenology per se.

According to the IS point of view, borderline children and adolescents have been experiencing recurrent negative parental appraisals, anxiety, and anger over the course of their entire development. They have been triangulated by parents who are unable to resolve their own individual and marital conflicts and unable to differentiate from their own families of origin. The developing child is part of a malevolent feedback system, tending in a cyclical way to provoke further negativity from significant others. By the time the child reaches adolescence, he or she has incorporated the parents' negative appraisal of the child's own need to differentiate. The borderline adolescent senses the parents' need to cling. In their turn, the parents experience escalating anxiety as the child/adolescent becomes aware of a growing need to differentiate from the family. Furthermore, as borderline adolescents begin to feel close, they become more anxious, and they may provoke the other person's anger or withdrawal (31). This, in turn, tends to confirm the borderline adolescent's self-revulsion.

Family Dynamics

In the Australian Redbank House (RBH) inpatient cohort (31), many of the parents in the treated families have psychiatric histories or long-standing personality difficulties. The patients and their families come from deprived backgrounds, whereas Masterson's families are mostly middle-class. RBH families experience extreme marital difficulties, financial stress, and/or chronic medical illness. They all share extreme limitation in communication, conflict resolution, and social skills. Social isolation is common among the RBH single parents, who have neither an adequate social network nor a functional relationship with their own families of origin. By the time the patient is in his teens, it is not rare for his or her mother to have collected a string of de facto relationships, and to have produced several children fathered by different men; frequently these are alcoholic, abusive men. Despite coming from a more deprived background, the family characteristics are similar to those described by Masterson (16), who tends to label the parents as well as their teenagers as having BPD.

Masterson also points to severe marital difficulties, financial stress, and chronic illness in the parents. He describes a stormy emotional life in the history of each parent as well as difficult friendship patterns. In fact, Masterson claims, in a multigenerational concept, that both parents as well as grandparents of the patients suffer from the borderline syndrome. However, he fails to consider the possibility of a major genetic component; this issue will be dealt with in a later section of this chapter. In general, however, these observations suggest that many of the characteristics of borderline families may be robust across class lines.

In the RBH cohort, there is characteristically a pattern of the clinging mother engaged in an enmeshed relationship with her adolescent child. The father is peripheral to this mother-adolescent "cocoon." It seems that the adolescent is afraid of preparing to leave home, whereas the mother is made anxious by her adolescent's normal tendency to separate (22). An alternate family pattern occurs when the parents are tightly bonded together, forming a solid coalition. Similar to families that display high expressed emotion (32) with schizophrenic offspring, these parents tend to be overly critical and hostile to their teenager. As pointed out by Zinner and Shapiro (33), some parents will maintain personal and marital stability by colluding to scapegoat the adolescent. Projective identification may be a central process in these cases.

Masterson (16) describes the clinging mother as demanding, controlling, and fostering a symbiotic tie with the child while colluding with the father in his distancing of the child. This type of mother needs to keep the child dependent in order to maintain her own emotional equilibrium. Masterson claims this type of mother has been unable to separate from her own mother.

These mothers tend to project onto the children the image of one of their own parents or other siblings. They are afraid of being abandoned themselves and must keep the child close. If a child tries to individuate, he or she is manipulated by threatened withdrawal of emotional support. Such mothers are emotionally available only if their children cling; they withdraw emotionally if the children attempt to separate. Threatened withdrawal of emotional support triggers a child's fear of abandonment, and the child develops abandonment depression. Masterson (16) suggests this process can be recognized by the age of three. Even if it does not appear early, it will emerge later, becoming manifest during adolescence.

Giovacchini (34,35) contends that mothers, because of their own self-absorption and need for symbiotic union, tend to relate to their children as "transitional objects," "dehumanizing and controlling them while failing to soothe them, so as to permit the establishment in them of internalized self soothing functions." (See 27, p. 324.) Winicott's concept of "transitional object," as used by Giovacchini, is congruent with Kohut's concept of the parent's use of the child as a selfobject.

Masterson's view of the pathogenic mother is congruent with an IS view with the exception that it tends to blame the mother. The IS model would describe a circular view wherein the withdrawn father pushes the mother and child together; the mother and child's coalition pushes the father away; the mother and child's anxiety is increased by the father's withdrawal; the father seeks satisfaction in his work or in extramarital affairs; and the father abandons responsibility and pushes mother and child together. In this view, all family members are viewed as both causes and results of a circular systemic process. Although he generally concentrates on intrapsychic processes, one of Kernberg's observations tends to confirm this circularity. Kernberg (13) points out how the intrinsic pathological processes of the adolescent induces complementary pathology in the parents.

Although most authors focus on the role of the mother, Anderson (36) emphasizes the necessary role of the father in normal development and points out that borderline adolescents have suffered from a lack of such fathering. In the RBH series, in a minority of the families, it is the fathers who are the most clinging of the parents.

Gunderson and colleagues (37) present another type of family organization, where "the rigid tightness of the marital bond functions to the exclusion of the attention, support or protection of the children" (p. 31). This structure is similar to Feldman and Guttman's (38) family with a "Literal Minded" parent, where the father is primarily involved with the mother and peripheral to the child. In my experience with such families, the tightly bound parental couple may be associated with a dysthymic, suicidal adolescent rather than necessarily a borderline one. In this situation, the goal of family therapy is to mobilize the healthier parent.

Wynne and Singer (39; Wynne [40]) point out that families with a schizophrenic offspring with a thought disorder do not use language for rational communication, but rather to avoid anxiety. In families with a borderline offspring, their communication deviance scores were intermediate between the scores of parents of schizophrenic adolescents and those of neurotic adolescents. This finding is compatible with the notion that borderline patients are intermediate in severity of symptomatology between patients who are schizophrenic and those who are neurotic.

Outpatient Psychotherapy

In this section, I will survey various approaches to individual psychotherapy for borderline adolescents, outline the indications for outpatient psychotherapy, and then contrast them to indications for inpatient treatment. I will describe the metapsychology of IS psychotherapy and outline the modifications necessary for treatment of borderline teenagers.

Many contributors, such as Masterson (18), Kernberg (13), Gunderson (28), and Giovacchini (35), agree with the following modifications to classical psychoanalytic technique for borderline patients: increased activity; more structure than with neurotic patients; increased tolerance of patients' hostility; setting limits on acting out; relating actions to feelings; focus on the here and now; and close attention to countertransference feelings (29). These modifications are congruent with IS psychotherapy for borderline adolescents, as I will describe later. Kernberg's approach tends to be confrontational in his interpretations of negative transference and his focus on conflict. He also makes direct interpretations of primitive defenses.

With Buie (41), the individual psychotherapeutic approach seems to be warmer and softer. This approach encourages positive transference and allows gradual disillusionment of the idealizing transference. Using role theory, Buie describes his work as follows:

> One way to envision this process is to imagine the therapy as melodrama. The patient takes on one role and assigns the therapist a complementary one. The therapist then identifies the various roles that appear in the therapeutic session. In the early phase of treatment, the roles may change rapidly, sometimes from minute to minute, and often with intense affect directed toward the therapist. Once the therapist begins to recognize these roles, the therapist can begin to identify them for the patient and to point out how these roles affect the patient's interpersonal behavior. (41, p. 24)

Buie emphasizes this approach as a way to help the patient harmonize split-off part object–part self representations manifested in the various melodrama roles. In the concept of multiple roles or selves as derived from family role allocations, the IS point of view is congruent with Buie's ideas.

There is an ongoing debate in the literature between proponents of supportive psychotherapy for Borderline patients and those who propose expressive, uncovering psychotherapy. Knight (42) used supportive psychotherapy for strengthening the ego, pointing out that deep interpretations were dangerous because of their regressive pull. Esman (27) has pointed out that a classical psychoanalytic approach to the treatment of borderline adolescents as described by Laufer and Laufer (43) is problematical in that some patients terminate prematurely or suffer from severe psychotic episodes. Others (42, 44–46) have observed that intensive individual psychoanalytic psychotherapy tends toward severe regressive reactions and negative therapeutic results.

Knight (42) clearly favored structure for borderline patients. Zetzel (44) limited session frequency to once a week. This was to decrease the intensity of transference and countertransference. She also stressed reality issues and the structuring of treatment hours during long-term therapy.

More recently, some clinicians have preferred a psychoanalytic, expressive, psychotherapeutic approach, with unmodified psychoanalysis for selected adult patients. The Menninger group (47) recommends expressive psychotherapy with very little "structure" (limit-setting/advice) during the therapy session. However, they combine such minimal structure during the session with complete, concomitant structure (hospitalization) to the extent necessary. A similar approach is currently followed at the Westmead Borderline Personality Project (29).

A modified psychoanalytic or expressive psychotherapeutic approach is used by Giovacchini (34,35,48) and Little (49) and also by Winnicott (50,51). Kernberg feels this modification should be sharply differentiated from psychoanalysis. He points out that the large majority of borderline patients are treated with a *mixture* of expressive and supportive techniques. If the treatment contact is less than twice weekly, then it is common to use supportive techniques alone. These are combined typically with crisis intervention and brief hospitalization.

It should be noted that therapist variables may be at least as important to outcome as treatment configuration. For example, Frank's (52) investigation found that "better" therapists get better results, irrespective of whether the psychotherapy is exploratory or supportive in nature. In brief, the more empathic, gifted therapists produce better outcomes.

The psychotherapy for the Borderline (young adult and adult) Project at Westmead Hospital in Australia offers an eclectic synthesis of the therapies of Kohut, Winnicott, and Sullivan (29). Some of the characteristics of this style of psychotherapy include development of a strong therapeutic relationship to buffer anxiety of change, emphasis on developmental arrest rather than defense/conflict theories, and provision of a therapeutic holding environment. In contrast to Kernberg's theory, there is sparse interpretation of negative transference; a positive idealizing transference is allowed to develop with the gradual process of "optimal disillusionment"(53) (i.e., the patient gradually notices discrepancies between his idealized image of the therapist and the therapist's actual characteristics). In the Westmead model, for example, the patient's disappointments with the therapist's vacations or canceled sessions are used as opportunities for self-understanding.

In the Westmead Project, the tasks of the therapist include

1. To stay as well attuned, empathically, as possible;
2. To link the meanings of current processes with the history of past developmental failures;
3. To avoid confrontations that would intensify disorganization of the self; and
4. To pay careful attention to the sequence of therapist's empathic failures, patient's affect shift, therapist's reparative efforts, and patient's steps toward self-reorganization.

This model is congenial with the IS outpatient psychotherapy model, except that the latter features a richer mixture of ideational and cognitive material utilizing inquiry, systemic formulations, and coauthoring of new narrative. The Westmead model is also congruent with the RBH IS approach to hospitalized adolescent borderline patients, except that with the latter, confrontation and peer pressure are used more intensively during residential treatment.

In discussing psychotherapy with borderline adolescents, Masterson (18) reports that these patients may initially show denial and a blandness of affect. He expects a gradual emergence of both depression and rage. I would suggest, alternatively, that the patient may have been consciously experiencing depression and rage for a long period of time, but he or she does not trust the therapist enough initially to reveal those feelings. About the work of therapy, Masterson has written:

> The patient works through the pathological mourning (rage and depression) associated with separation from the mother and, through the mechanisms of internalization and identification, forms a new intrapsychic structure based on whole object relations. (16, p. 28)

The Westmead self psychology version of this idea might be that the patient uses the therapist as a selfobject and internalizes some of his or her functions, such as soothing, mirroring, idealizing, and optimal frustration.

The following section consists of an outline of the basic principles of outpatient IS psychotherapy applicable to adolescents and adults with a wide variety of disturbances. This approach is modified in treating the borderline adolescent. As I mentioned previously, there is increased activity, more structure than for neurotic patients, limits on acting out, and increased confrontation of interpersonal reality issues to deal with projections and increased support. The borderline adolescent is never treated in isolation but rather in conjunction with his or her family, who themselves tend to act out and to avoid treatment.

Family work may consist of only one or two family or parental couple sessions or may include a longer series of sessions running in parallel with individual psychotherapy for the adolescent. Sometimes, this work is shared by a second therapist. If the parents can be helped to support the teenager's individual therapy and if the familial dysfunction does not undermine the adolescent's progress, then the therapist may concentrate on the task of individual psychotherapy. In working with the adolescent, the therapist keeps a finger on the pulse of the family processes and will organize a family session either with the same or another therapist. In dealing with the borderline adolescent's tendency to act out, the therapist must give clear-cut limits as to timing and frequency of sessions and issues of lateness or missed appointments. The therapist might need to establish consequences for such acting out, such as the need for the patient to transfer to inpatient treatment.

Outpatient IS individual psychotherapy may be helpful for moderately disturbed borderline adolescent patients who are capable of utilizing psychotherapy (i.e., those who are intelligent, verbal, and capable of insight). By contrast, poorly motivated teenagers who avoid treatment and are relatively nonverbal may require residential treatment. In IS outpatient psychotherapy there is an emphasis on maximizing the therapeutic alliance and on using sufficient gentle confrontation to jog the patient out of self-destructive patterns. The therapist will need insight to induce alternate ways of viewing the world sufficient for the patient to reorder priorities. For example, with a teenaged adolescent girl who is totally obsessed with a particular new love affair, the therapist develops with her some picture of what the girl's priorities will be 10 years into the future in terms of marriage, a career, children, hobbies, friends of the same sex, and so on. Such an inquiry may be characterized as "future oriented." This may reduce an overinvested focus on the current anxious attachment. Instead of traditional interpretations of unconscious conflicts, there is the cocreation of therapeutic formulations that consolidate the therapeutic alliance, promote feelings of being understood, and trigger change in both attitudes and actual behavior patterns. Systemic therapeutic formulations are thought of as "narratives" (54), coauthored by therapist and patient, chronicling the history and meaning of the patient's life, based on concepts of feedback and circularity.

Therapeutic formulations are intended to interrupt old repetitive, cognitive-affective self-system patterns ("stuck points") and, one hopes, to release new meanings and more adaptive solutions from within the patient. It is the therapist's responsibility to monitor the patient's underlying affect to evaluate whether genuine change is occurring.

The individual patient, as well as a marital couple or a family, creates his or her own narrative before, during, and after psychotherapy. The concept of narrative is congruent with Ferreira's (55) concept of "family myths" and Minuchin and Fishman's (56) concept of "family realities." An example of such a narrative at the beginning of treatment might be a patient's statement, "My brother is the smart one. I am the dumb one. He will be the professional and I will be the unsuccessful small businessman. You cannot trust people outside of the family. My family knows the value of a dollar; I will never be able to manage money. I will always be a little mixed-up and peculiar."

Systemic therapeutic formulations link present interpersonal patterns with transference patterns with multiperson loops from the patient's past. Such formulations or part-narratives may be thought of as chains of sequentially related linear interpretations that, when interconnected, describe circular self-reinforcing interpersonal patterns from the past, present—and future. The total narrative is a long novel. It is delivered in bits and pieces, rarely in one package. These bits and pieces are frequently referred to by patient and therapist in their conversation over the entire course of therapy. These narratives or stories might be thought of as intertwining themes that serve as the core for the patient's new life story, a story that is constantly being rewritten and enlarged over the course of psychotherapy. The point is not that it is a scientifically objective story but that it feels true enough to the protagonists to jog them into change and personal expansion (and this includes the therapist in the change process).

In Sullivan's concept of the "inquiry" (57) and Levenson's (58) modifications of same, the psychotherapist tries to build a clear picture of the patient's actual interpersonal and complementary self-system operations in progressively finer detail (instead of focusing exclusively on the patient's fantasies and past life as in traditional psychoanalysis). This process releases old, previously buried, possibly valuable tendencies; triggers new ideas, cognitions, and affects; and is, one hopes, associated with an expansion of self.

IS inquiry reveals a systemic two-or-more-person point of view. The therapist and patient cocreate a word-picture of the patient's interpersonal network, power relationships, communicational styles, role allocations, separation-individuation patterns, value system, and worldview. The inquiry avoids conceptualizing any one person in the network as being either villain or victim, such as "your mother's unrelatedness left you feeling alone, anxious, and unsupported" or "your father dumped his anger onto you." The systemic view, rather, conceptualizes people as influencing others and being influenced by them. The problem or solution is passed around in a recursive redundant loop in the family or network circle. Therefore, the questions in the detailed inquiry are characterized as "systemic questions." These stimulate new styles of thinking, new information, and, one hopes, change.

In IS therapy, none of these inquiries are posed merely to get more information for a future interpretation. Rather, the questions are designed to release alternative ways of viewing things from within the person being interviewed. Each question is simultaneously a question, a reframe, a new "think," and a stimulus for change. In other words, the question contains "interpretations." The complexity of the "interpretation" may range from simple mirroring, to second-order deductions, to dynamic, interpersonal, or systemic speculations.

In sum, the IS psychotherapist is active, yet aware of the danger of overactivity with attendant loss of neutrality. As does the interpersonal psychoanalytic model of Levenson (58) and others, IS therapy works and interprets interactionally. Beyond that, it features three-and-more-person circular processes, interlinking intrapsychic, interpersonal, and systemic implications, highlighting cross talk between affects, semantic allusions and interpersonal behaviors. The IS therapist conceptualizes a person as being both a product of and the producer of multiperson patterns. The person is carried along by contextual, interpersonal personality-molding forces. In comparison to interpersonal psychoanalysis, IS psychotherapy is more active and didactic of interpersonal, communicational, and conflict resolution skills. From the family therapy repertoire, IS therapy uses circular or "double description" questions (59). It sometimes uses, with children and adolescents, externalization and defeat of a symptom and, with all ages, the delineation of the conflict between two "careers" (e.g., between creative vs. alienating). IS therapy occasionally uses paradoxical restraining from change; it employs the self of therapist to trigger change, yet it strives to be less obviously manipulative than many family and behavioral therapies.

The usual frequency of sessions in IS therapy is once or twice weekly, and duration of therapy ranges from 1 to 3 years. This relatively low frequency coupled with an active style does not evoke as much transferential frustration as does a schedule of psychoanalytic psychotherapy that is less interventional and has sessions 3 or 4 times a week. In contrast with Masterson's (16) claim that therapy once or twice weekly is inadequate, it is the IS position that results between the two approaches are at least comparable. This issue is currently being systematically investigated (see the following section).

INPATIENT TREATMENT

Inpatient treatment is indicated when outpatient treatment has failed, when there is a clear-cut danger to life (i.e., either a suicidal or homicidal risk), or if the adolescent is at risk of being sexually or physically abused by family members. Admission is also necessary if the family is severely dysfunctional and unable to contain the adolescent's destructive acting out. If several outpatient approaches have failed and the adolescent seems to be running away from treatment, then a short-term inpatient commitment might be indicated, long enough for staff and other patients to convince the patient to volunteer for more definitive therapy.

In the RBH day hospital and inpatient program in Australia, with those adolescents who resist treatment, the plan focuses on motivating them for treatment. In a pragmatic sense, this involves defining, together with the patient, a legitimate goal for change. To avoid a symmetrical battle with the adolescent, it is important that the goal for change be different from the one defined previously by parents or teachers. This usually requires a redefinition of the basic problem; for example, "You have a real problem in keeping your friends" rather than "You drink too much alcohol." A redefinition avoids perpetuating an old family "stuck point." The task facing the therapist and staff is to develop a strong enough alliance for the adolescent to be willing to engage in change processes. If a good therapeutic alliance results, the adolescent will allow previously ego-alien material into his or her awareness. He or she can then make good use of confrontation when it is balanced with support.

Therapeutic work largely consists of negotiating a truce between the adolescent and the family, who have previously been at war. This is accomplished by helping parents and siblings to identify the adolescent's redeeming features and by helping the adolescent develop more positive behavior toward the family. The goal includes a better cognitive understanding of the circular sequence of events within their family. This process is greatly enhanced when the therapist constructively confronts the adolescent with his or her own contribution to repetitive, maladaptive peer and adult relationship patterns. This can be done in both group and individual therapy settings. For the patient, insight is thus added to corrective emotional experience and to learning new interpersonal skills.

Zinner (60) and Shapiro and colleagues (61) support the view that combined individual and family therapy is essential in both the inpatient or outpatient treatment of the borderline adolescent. They include the individual therapist in the family therapy session. This facilitates more realistic attitudes on the part of the adolescent and the family as well as the therapists and clarifies some projections and confused communications.

There are a number of adolescent inpatient programs described in the literature (26,62–68; for a review of the literature concerning family systems approaches to adolescent residential treatment, see Mirkin and Koman [69]). In his hospitalization program, Masterson (16) uses a two-component, individual psychoanalytic psychotherapy for the borderline teenager, and casework therapy with the parents. The crucial goal for the teenager's parents is to learn how to support their adolescent's separation-individuation process. Masterson points out that the borderline teenager's abandonment depression will come to the surface but only after his or her acting out is controlled. In an individual session, the adolescent will tend to deny problems, including denial of depression. Seeing the adolescent in therapy together with the family may dissolve this denial.

At Redbank House, the staff use a problem-oriented treatment plan for severely disturbed, economically disadvantaged borderline adolescent patients (31). This allocates responsibility for change to various therapeutic agents (e.g., the individual, the family, a therapy group, the school, and the treatment milieu). Usually treatment plans focus on specified behavioral goals rather than on subtle insights. The following case manager's notes about a male adolescent illustrate a treatment plan style:

Family therapy to focus on patient's bereavement over the suicide of his older sister, drawing parent/child boundaries between mother and patient (mother has been parentifying the patient).

Mother should confide her worries to friends rather than her son. The plans are to encourage the patient to socialize with his peers and to increase the amount of peer related activities. We are to encourage mother to listen to her son's concerns and needs, of which she tends to be unaware.

Referring to the same patient's individual psychotherapy:

Individual therapy will focus on grief work regarding the older sister, encouraging the patient to discuss his feelings and to express anger (which he tends to turn inward). The plans are for the patient to discuss his ongoing problems in relating to peers and for the staff to challenge his negative self-talk.

In this example, several therapeutic modalities run in parallel. Individual psychotherapy has dealt with issues of unspoken needs, fears, and conflicts. Family therapy has highlighted those same issues, plus others: aberrant roles, collusive relationships, and skewed beliefs. At the same time, group work has dealt with the adolescent's denial of responsibility, projections of blame onto others, and difficulties in communication. Meanwhile, the school has been influencing the adolescent's cognitive and academic skills, capacity to confront and be confronted, understanding of social rules, and ability to relate to authority figures. The milieu deals with all of these (70).

In both the Redbank House model and in the Mirkin and Koman (69) structural-strategic program, the family is always involved in the decision of admitting the adolescent for inpatient treatment. The family is called in for an emergency session when the adolescent runs away, assaults staff or other patients, or is involved in alcohol or drug abuse. The staff and parents review the management of the adolescent on weekends or holiday home visits. This process maintains the parents' leadership role as limit-setters as well as nurturers.

In his inpatient program, Masterson (16) initially works individually with the adolescents and separately with the parents. He subsequently brings the family members together for a conjoint interview. The purpose of this conjoint interview is as follows:

1. To expose the family myth, being the collection of family rationalizations designed to obscure psychopathology;
2. To restore more appropriate patterns of emotional communication in the family. The patient does now what he could not do before: express his rage and verbally work it through with the parents; and
3. To find more constructive ways of dealing with family conflict.

In contrast with these goals mentioned by Masterson, an IS approach does not seek to expose and interpret family myths (although the therapist privately takes note of these); furthermore, it promotes conflict resolution skills, which work to bypass the generation of rage. The Redbank House IS program is different from Masterson's program in other ways: The RBH program uses individual psychotherapy much less frequently, and its therapists actively attempt to trigger family changes that will benefit the index patient and prevent psychiatric disorder among siblings.

Group therapy, along with family therapy, is considered of high priority in the RBH residential treatment model. The group therapist prioritizes issues for each patient, bringing up issues that are important to that patient. Patients are encouraged to deal with each other rather than with staff exclusively, and staff are discouraged from carrying the ball for the patients. Patient-to-patient confrontation and support are thus facilitated.

According to Masterson (16), durable change is thought to occur only through a long-term, gradual process of internal reorganization; the psychotherapist makes up for parenting deficits, recaptures the early amnesia, and interprets unconscious conflicts. By contrast, IS therapeutic "conversation" construes the adolescent as making a crucial choice of life "careers," rather than undergoing a "cure" for a psychological "disease" or receiving supplements for inadequate or damaged psychic process. (See White and Epston [71]). Staff functions to orchestrate those peer and family processes that prompt adolescents to make changes. More generally, the entire therapeutic community is considered as one organismic system, and this includes patients and staff at all levels. This view is colored by social learning and family structural theory (24) as well as by concepts of the therapeutic community (70,72).

In brief, I propose that a new interpersonal system composed of peers, family, and staff reshapes cognitive and behavioral patterns in the adolescent. This may lead to a reorganization of personality. Some of the old "damage" is undone. Deficits are altered rapidly in a way that allows for the initiation of new behavioral and perceptual responses. In a similar way to IS individual psychotherapy, new adaptive responses are encouraged (reinforced) by the new interpersonal system. The therapeutic community structures an opportunity for the adolescent to adopt new perceptions and behaviors; subsequently, it supports and strengthens adaptive choices.

Outcome Studies

Masterson and colleagues (19) report 58% of patients who completed long-term inpatient follow-up treatment showed mild impairment 4 years after treatment, whereas 42% showed more serious impairment. Another group of investigators reported that adult borderline patients did only slightly better after long-term inpatient treatment than a group of schizophrenic patients and less well than a group of patients with affective disorder (70,73).

Stevenson and Meares (29) cite 10 outcome studies for treatment of adult borderline patients. They conclude that these studies indicate that "various forms of psychotherapy do achieve results that are superior to no treatment and to placebo treatments" (29, p. 4). They also point out that there are "few definitive studies on the question of specific treatments with specific problems" (29, p. 4). In the Westmead Borderline study, 59 patients were treated in Kohutian, Winnicottian, Sullivanian psychotherapy by registrar psychiatrists with weekly supervision. At 12-month follow-up after 12 months of treatment, the patients showed a significant reduction in impulsivity, affective instability, reduction in anger, and reduction in suicidal behavior. Thirty percent of the patients had improved to such an extent that they no longer fulfilled DSM-III criteria for the diagnosis of BPD. It was concluded that relatively short-term (1 year) psychotherapy is an effective treatment modality for patients with BPD.

Discussion

Various authors have discussed the diagnosis of Borderline Personality Disorder. The American Psychiatric Association presents a current, thoroughgoing definition (1) that is subject to ongoing revision. However, it is important to recognize the contributions made by many individual theorists and to acknowledge that these authors have come frequently from the psychoanalytic and psychodynamic tradition. Although many authors produce overlapping or similar concepts about borderline patients, I must argue that, in a pragmatic sense, diagnosis for BPD is not yet specific.

Gualtieri and colleagues (73) point out that children and adolescents are frequently labelled as borderline even though they do not fulfill DSM-III criteria for the disorder. The diagnosis seems to be made if the youngsters are severely disturbed and suffer from an intermittent, partial, or near-psychotic condition.

In the Australian practice, there is a reliance on DSM-III-R, plus particular exclusionary criteria. That is, the diagnosis is used to refer to severely disturbed teenagers of normal intelligence who have severe emotional and behavioral disorders, who are without organic brain damage, and who are clearly not diagnosed as manic-depressive, schizophrenic, or sociopathic.

Some family therapists (71) would prefer to "unlabel" the borderline adolescent, because labeling might tend to make the condition worse by adversely affecting the expectations of patient, family, and therapist. On the other hand, the diagnosis, if used with some reservations, might be useful as a shorthand communication between therapists, a clearer definition for research purposes, and a lever for the design of treatment plans.

In reference to individual psychodynamics and family dynamics, the psychoanalytic view tends to emphasize the intrapsychic at the expense of the interpersonal and family systemic factors. The family systems approach, on the other hand, tends to emphasize the systemic at the expense of the intrapsychic. A purist systemic approach tends to view the individual as a black box with inputs and outputs and no internal workings. The IS approach tends to synthesize the two viewpoints in the belief that subjective processes, such as the sense of self, may be legitimately considered as interactional circular loops in addition to multiperson informational loops.

As to psychogenesis, object relations theorists (such as Masterson [15,16]) tend to localize the traumatic events to the early developmental years, whereas the IS view tends to view the traumatic experience as persisting through all developmental stages and, furthermore, as being mutually reinforced by all family members (and sometimes by helping professionals). The IS view includes parental empathic limitations as triggering defects in self-image and self-esteem. Parental anxiety and hostility trigger persecutory expectations of being rebuffed that, in turn, tend to provoke being rebuffed in a cyclical, mutually reinforcing spiral (7). For inpatient treatment, the IS approach may be considered a refinement of Masterson's (16) practice of using individual, family, and residential approaches and Mirkin and Koman's (69) practice of integrating the family system within the therapeutic community system. The IS residential approach for deprived families prioritizes contextual family and peer group processes over individual psychotherapeutic processes. The IS individual psychotherapy approach is thought to be useful in outpatient psychotherapy with borderline adolescents who are sufficiently motivated, verbal, and introspective. The technique of IS psychotherapy sidesteps the question of a psychodynamic metapsychology. Instead, it promotes the practical usefulness of a cocreated narrative, which becomes the therapeutic lever for the patient into his or her long-term future.

In contrast to the Masterson (16) inpatient approach, which tends to run individual psychotherapy for the adolescent in parallel with counseling for the parent, the Redbank House inpatient program (2,31) (as well as the program designed by Mirkin and Koman [69]) involves the parents intensively in the treatment team, mobilizes the entire therapeutic and psychoeducational staff in a behavior- and attitude-reshaping process, and maximizes the employment of peer pressure.

There seems to be a dichotomy between intrapsychic change on the one hand and systemic change on the other regarding treatment goals. Masterson (16), for example, aims for radical personality change in the treatment of middle-class borderline adolescents. In contrast, we do not expect radical personality transformations, nor do we aim for thoroughly revamped families. Our initial step is to break through the adolescent's denial of having a problem. When the patient can define the problem, he or she can then set a specific goal. Using a guiding metaphor, we try to achieve a change sufficient for the adolescent to select a different "career" from the one with which he or she entered treatment. We find that a small change in the family system can evolve into larger, more durable changes over time. Particular subgoals for these patients might include increased self-esteem, improved reality testing, greater openness to feelings, increased awareness of needs, better assertive achievement of needs, improved self-identity, and improved goal-setting skills.

We frequently construe the family within a "marriage" metaphor. For example, we think of adolescents and their families as coming to us to request a "divorce," although we hope that several months of treatment will achieve a "trial reconciliation." Furthermore, we try for a "remarriage" in the outpatient follow-up period. This remarriage may then be used therapeutically as a new base for an orderly separation-individuation process for the patient. Of course, there are some families that are so severely dysfunctional, in spite of treatment, that it would be contraindicated for the adolescent to return home.

Another issue is the type of therapeutic contact best suited to the severely disturbed adolescent in a residential setting. I suggested earlier in this chapter that a closed, individual relationship carries advantages and disadvantages. It has the advantage of providing an opportunity to make up for missed developmental experience and to promote insight into unverbalized needs and conflicts; but it has the disadvantage that teenagers tend to be reluctant about self-disclosure in group and family therapy settings. If a histrionic tendency is present in the patient, this can be inflamed by an intimate therapeutic approach. The end result is an adolescent who insists on seeing his psychotherapist several times a day and avoids all group encounters. This, of course, is partially determined by therapist bias and countertransference. Furthermore, teenagers in individual therapeutic relationships tend to avoid forming an alliance with unit staff. This situation renders the usual defenses (splitting, denial, and protection) more difficult to manage than they would otherwise be. It seems to be more constructive to encourage teenagers to discuss personal issues in group and family sessions when they are adequately prepared to do so in individual therapy.

As to the decision to hospitalize the adolescent, an individual adolescent admission has certain therapeutic benefits. Usually the family is at a low point and is considering ejecting the teenager to a long-term institution. The family is in crisis, with an intensification of angry, contemptuous feedback between parents and teenager. An individual admission takes the pressure off the family, and its members begin to relax. The crisis is reduced and the admission is framed as a new beginning, rather than the end of the line (74). It is true that reduced pressure can also occur at the start of outpatient family therapy; however, the staff at Redbank House deal with the most severely disturbed families who have been referred because outpatient treatment has failed.

As for ecological factors, according to Sullivanian interpersonal theory and Batesonian systems theory, the adolescent's personality and interpersonal behavior are molded by his or her family and peer group. Consistent with this realization, teenagers in residential treatment programs benefit from a combination of family therapy and peer group therapy. Offer (75) demonstrates that disturbed adolescent development is associated with disturbed family functioning: the parents themselves, their marriage, and their parenting functions.

Haley (22,23) has described adolescent disturbance as arising in a family matrix. He points to the special difficulties of adolescents preparing to leave home and the central importance of the parents' maintaining leadership at this crucial stage. He indicates that adolescents normally test the hierarchical arrangement within the family. This is associated with adolescent turmoil in families in which the parents fail to adapt flexibly to their teenagers' movement toward adult status. Haley believes that psychiatric disturbance in the teenager is always the mark of confusion in the parental hierarchy.

In subscribing to a multifactorial as well as a systemic approach, I suggest the matrix of disturbance reflects factors beyond those arising strictly from family relationships. These include the quality of inherited intelligence and temperament as well as those neurological variables underlying perceptual and learning difficulties. Environmental and physical stressors of all types are among these factors. Such factors can prevent, delay, or detour the developmental tasks of adolescence. The main point is that they must be taken into account in formulating a detailed management plan for these patients.

CONCLUSIONS

The following points broadly summarize the conclusions of this chapter:

1. A review of the BPD literature indicates there is a lack of specificity about diagnostic criteria (e.g., the field does not yet enjoy diagnostic consensus).
2. Nevertheless, there is evidence of general agreement among theorists that family issues are seminal in the generation of the BPD condition, with different theorists focusing on different aspects of family functioning.
3. The relative value of an intrapsychic versus an interpersonal approach to therapy may be influenced by age, diagnostic, and treatment location variables (with IS theory suggesting the judicious use of both approaches).
4. Various intervention strategies are appropriate at different levels and at different times in the therapeutic process. A particularly useful strategy in my experience has been the evolution of a new unique "narrative" as a way of reframing and redirecting both individual and family symptoms.
5. A multivariable approach that construes all levels of the BPD system (from internal biological to external community-ecological levels) is required to fully understand and treat the individual with BPD. The IS approach construes subjective psychological processes as a legitimate circular loop in this overall scheme.

REFERENCES

1. American Psychiatric Association: Diagnostic and Statistical Manual of Mental Disorders, 3rd Edition, Revised. Washington, DC, American Psychiatric Association, 1987

2. Siegel LI: Confrontation and support in group therapy in the residential treatment of severely disturbed adolescents. Adolescence 87:681–690, 1987

3. Bateson G: Mind and Nature. New York, Dutton, 1979

4. Epstein MB, Bishop BS, Lewin S: The McMaster model of family functioning. Journal of Marriage and Family Counselling 4:19–31, 1978

5. Scharff DE, Scharff JS: Object Relations Family Therapy. London, Jason Aronson, 1989

6. Slipp S: The Technique and Practice of Object Relations Family Therapy. London, Jason Aronson, 1988

7. Wachtel EG, Wachtel PL: Family Dynamics in Individual Psychotherapy. New York, Guilford, 1986

8. Imber RR: Reflections on Kohut and Sullivan. Contemporary Psychoanalysis 20:363–380, 1984

9. Feixas G: Personal construct theory and systemic therapies: parallel or convergent trends? Journal of Marital and Family Therapy 16(1):1–20, 1990

10. Freud S: Introductory Lectures on Psychoanalysis. New York, WW Norton, 1966

11. Klein M: The Psychoanalysis of Children. London, Hogarth Press, 1932

12. Kernberg OF: Borderline personality organization. J Am Psychoanal Assoc 15:641–685, 1967

13. Kernberg OF: The diagnosis of borderline conditions in adolescence, in Adolescent Psychiatry. Edited by Feinstein S, Giovacchini P. Chicago, University of Chicago Press, 1978, pp 298–319

14. Kernberg OF: Borderline personality organization, in Comprehensive Textbook of Psychiatry, Vol IV. Edited by Kaplan HI, Sadock BJ. Baltimore, Williams & Wilkins, 1985, pp 621–630

15. Masterson JF: The psychiatric significance of adolescent turmoil. Am J Psychiatry 124:11, 1968

16. Masterson JF: Treatment of the Borderline Adolescent: A Developmental Approach. New York, Brunner/Mazel, 1972

17. Masterson JF, Rinsley DB: The borderline syndrome: the role of the mother in the genesis and psychic structure of the borderline personality. Int J Psychoanal 56:163–177, 1975

18. Masterson JF: From Borderline Adolescent to Functioning Adult: The Test of Time. New York, Brunner/Mazel, 1980

19. Masterson JF, Lulow W, Costello J: The test of time: borderline adolescent to functioning adult. Adolesc Psychiatry 10:492–522, 1982

20. Bertalanffy L von: General Systems Theory. New York, George Braziller, 1968

21. Watzlawick P: The Language of Change: Elements of Therapeutic Communication. New York, Basic Books, 1978

22. Haley J: Uncommon Therapy. New York, WW Norton, 1973

23. Haley J: Problem Solving Therapy. San Francisco, CA, Jossey-Bass, 1976

24. Minuchin S: Families and Family Therapy. Cambridge, MA, Harvard University Press, 1974

25. Selvini-Palazzoli M, Boscolo L, Cecchin G, et al: Paradox and Counterparadox: A New Model in the Therapy of the Family in Schizophrenic Transaction. New York, Jason Aronson, 1978

26. Evans RI: Dialogue with Erik Erikson. New York, Harper & Row, 1967

27. Esman A: Borderline personality disorder in adolescents: current concepts, in Adolescent Psychiatry. Edited by Feinstein SC. Chicago, IL, University of Chicago Press, 1989, pp 319–336

28. Gunderson JG, Singer MT: Defining borderline patients: an overview. Am J Psychiatry 132:1–9, 1975

29. Stevenson J, Meares R: Outcome study of psychotherapy in borderline personality disorders. Am J Psychiatry (in press)

30. Clarkin JF, Widiger JA, Frances A, et al: Prototypic typology and the borderline personality disorder. J Abnorm Psychol 92(3):263–275, 1983

31. Siegel LI, Radojevic A, Whitmont S: Systemic residential treatment for severely disturbed adolescents. International Annals of Adolescent Psychiatry (in press)

32. Falloon IF, Boyd JL, McGill CW: Family Care of Schizophrenia. New York, Guilford, 1984

33. Zinner J, Shapiro ER: Projective identification as a mode of perception and behaviour in families of adolescents. Int J Psychoanal 53:523–530, 1972

34. Giovacchini PI: The sins of the parents: the borderline adolescent and primal confusion. Adolesc Psychiatry 7:213–233, 1979

35. Giovacchini PI: The borderline adolescent as a transitional object: a common variation. Adolesc Psychiatry 12:233–250, 1985

36. Anderson R: Thoughts on fathering: its relation to the borderline condition in adolescence and to transitional phenomena. Adolesc Psychiatry 6:377–395, 1978

37. Gunderson JG, Kerr J, Englund DW: The families of borderlines: a comparative study. Arch Gen Psychiatry 37:27–36, 1980

38. Feldman RB, Guttman MD: Families of borderline patients: literal-minded parents, borderline parents and parental protectiveness. Am J Psychiatry (141)11:1392–1396, 1984

39. Wynne LC, Singer MT: Thought disorder and family relations of schizophrenics. Arch Gen Psychiatry 9:199–206, 1963

40. Wynne LC: Structure and lineality in family therapy, in Evolving Models for Family Change: A Volume in Honor of Salvador Minuchin. Edited by Fishman HC, Rosman BL. New York, Guilford, 1986, pp 251–260

41. Buie SE: Borderline personality in adolescents: diagnosis and treatment. Paper presented at the Highland Highlights Seminar, Asheville, NC, 1980

42. Knight RP (ed): Borderline states, in Psychoanalytic Psychiatry and Psychology. New York, International Universities Press, 1954, pp 97–109

43. Laufer M, Laufer ME: Adolescence and Developmental Breakdown. New Haven, CT, Yale University Press, 1984

44. Zetzel ER: Current concepts of transference. Int J Psychoanal 37:369–378, 1956

45. Zetzel ER: A developmental approach to the borderline patient. Am J Psychiatry 7:27–35, 1971

46. Friedman H: Psychotherapy of borderline patients: the influence of theory on technique. Am J Psychiatry 132:1048–1052, 1975
47. Ekstein R, Wallerstein J: Observations on the psychology of borderline and psychotic children. Psychoanal Study Child 9:344–369, 1954
48. Giovacchini PI: The borderline aspects of adolescence and the borderline state, in Adolescent Psychiatry. Edited by Feinstein S, Giovacchini P. Chicago, University of Chicago Press, 1978, pp 320–338
49. Little M: Transference in borderline states. Int J Psychoanal 47:476–485, 1966
50. Winnicott DW: Collected Papers: Through Paediatrics to Psycho-analysis. London, Hogarth Press, 1958
51. Winnicott DW: The Maturational Processes and the Facilitating Environment. International Universities Press, New York, 1965
52. Frank J: Persuasion and Healing: A Comparative Study of Psychotherapy. Baltimore, MD, Johns Hopkins University Press, 1973
53. Kohut H: The psychoanalytic treatment of narcissistic personality disorder: outline of a systematic approach. Psychoanal Study Child 23:86–113, 1968
54. Spence OP: Narrative Truth and Historical Truth. New York, WW Norton, 1982
55. Ferreira AJ: Family myth and homeostasis. Arch Gen Psychiatry 9:457–473, 1963
56. Minuchin S, Fishman C: Family Therapy Techniques. Cambridge, MA, Harvard University Press, 1981
57. Sullivan HS: The Psychiatric Interview. New York, WW Norton, 1954
58. Levenson E: The Ambiguity of Change. New York, Basic Books, 1983
59. White M: Selected Papers. Adelaide, Australia, Dulwich Centre Publications, 1989
60. Zinner J: Combined individual and family therapy of borderline adolescents: treatment and management of the early phase. Adolesc Psychiatry 6:420–427, 1978
61. Shapiro ER, Shapiro RL, Zinner J, et al: The borderline ego and the working alliance: indications for family and individual treatment in adolescence. Int J Psychoanal 58:77–87, 1977
62. Clark LP: Some practical remarks upon the use of modified psychoanalysis on the treatment of borderline neuroses and psychoses. Psychoanal Rev 6:306–308, 1919
63. Hendrickson WJ, Holmes DJ: Control of behavior as a crucial factor in intensive psychiatric treatment in an all adolescent ward. Am J Psychiatry 115:11–16, 1959
64. Marohn RD, Dalle-Molle D, Offer D, et al: A hospital riot: its determinants and implications for treatment. Am J Psychiatry 130:6, 1973
65. Rinsley DB, Hall DD: Psychiatric hospital treatment of adolescents: parental resistances as expressed in casework metaphor. Arch Gen Psychiatry 7:286–294, 1962
66. Rinsley DO: The adolescent in residential treatment: some critical reflections. Adolescence (2)5:83–85, 1967
67. Rinsley DO: Theory and practice of intensive residential treatment of adolescents. Psychiatr Q 611–638, 1968
68. Rinsley DO: The adolescent inpatient: patterns of depersonification. Psychiatr Q 45:1–20, 1971

69. Mirkin MP, Koman SL: Handbook of Adolescents and Family Therapy. New York, Gardiner Press, 1985

70. Jones M: The Therapeutic Community. New Haven, CT, Yale University Press, 1953

71. White M, Epston D: Literate Means to Therapeutic Ends. Adelaide, Australia, Dulwich Centre Publications, 1989

72. Stanton A, Schwartz M: The Mental Hospital. London, Tavistock, 1958

73. Gualtieri GT, Koriath V, Bourgondien ME: "Borderline" children. J Autism Dev Disord 13:1, 67–72, 1983

74. Menses G, Durrant M: Contextual Residential Care: The Application of the Principles of Cybernetic Therapy to the Residential Treatment of Irresponsible Adolescents and Their Families. Adelaide, Australia, Dulwich Centre Publications, 1986

75. Offer D: Normal adolescent development, in Handbook of Psychiatry. Edited by Kaplan HI, Freeman A, Sadock BJ. 1978, pp 115–126

9 Bulimia in the Older Adolescent: An Analytic Perspective to a Behavioral Problem

Judith Brisman, Ph.D.

ngagement of the adolescent with an eating disorder in the psycho-therapy process may at first glance appear to be a contradiction in terms. The bulimic teenager is rarely interested in self-exploration. The eating disorder is not experienced as part of the self but, on the contrary, as an interference in what is otherwise often considered a "normal" life. Moreover, the symptoms of bingeing, vomiting, and the various other means of purging are often powerful and destructive. One patient eats and vomits at least 10 times daily. Another eats leftover food out of garbage cans and has been ar-rested for stealing food. A third is physically addicted to laxatives; by the age of 18, she is taking 80 to 100 Ex-lax daily.

The question of symptom management is present from the onset of treat-ment. Can a psychodynamically-oriented treatment be pursued when a symp-tom as potentially destructive as bulimia dominates the clinical picture?

WHAT IS BULIMIA? THE ADOLESCENT'S EXPERIENCE

Since the beginning of her teenage years, Karen worried about getting fat. Fad dieting evolved into bouts of eating and then fasting, and by the time she was 16, Karen learned that if she vomited after eating she could avoid weight gain from what were now daily binges.

Karen's adolescence was complicated by factors other than her disturbed eating patterns. At 13, her family relocated to a new part of the country; Karen never adjusted to the move, and she spent the next several years without close friends and never dated. Her parents, at that time, were preoccupied with finding an institutional placement for Karen's younger brother, who was born with Down's syndrome when Karen was six. Additionally, Karen's father had had a history of colitis that had begun in his adolescence and had resulted in his hav-ing a colostomy at the age of 22. The family was a nest of assumed security from which departure was considered a threat both to the person leaving and to the family itself.

Karen's adolescent years were spent going to school (where she excelled), laboring at homework, and after dinner, spending evenings in front of the television with her family. Bedtime rules were nonexistent in this family. Instead, Karen, her 10-year-old sister, and her parents would fall asleep together in the family room until one by one, in the middle of the night, each would drowsily awaken from the family slumber and go to bed.

As the family slept, Karen sat in front of their resting bodies gorging as much food as she could eat, until she felt sick enough to make herself vomit. Then she would eat some more. Often she would eat and throw up two to three times before falling to sleep herself. This pattern lasted throughout Karen's teenage years and resulted in her finally seeking treatment at the age of 23 for what was, at that point, a daily regime of bingeing and vomiting.

As in Karen's case, bulimia is overtly characterized by frantic (often unpleasurable) eating followed by a purging of the food in an attempt to avoid weight gain. Although a binge usually consists of massive amounts of food—more than one can believe a person could consume—the bulimic patient can *feel* as though she has binged if she eats merely one bite of food beyond an amount previously planned. In these cases, vomiting may occur merely after the ingestion of a piece of melba toast, or for example, upon a small taste of a "forbidden" dessert.

The bulimic patient usually gets rid of the food intake by vomiting, but other means of purging can include laxative abuse, enemas, colonics, fasting, excessive exercising, or the use of diet pills, amphetamines, or cocaine to reduce one's appetite. There is always a chronic and severe obsession with food intake and dieting. In fact, sometimes all one sees is this obsession without the actual binge or purge. This type of obsessional thinking (when it exists without anorexic weight loss) in and of itself can also be indicative of a bulimic disorder.

Although almost every teenage girl in our culture goes through a period of overeating and/or dieting, for the bulimic adolescent the binge-purge cycle takes on psychological functions that extend beyond concerns regarding food and weight. Food is not merely used for pleasure; dieting or purging are not merely for weight control. For the teenager who becomes bulimic, food, dieting, and purging function as thwarted attempts to organize an otherwise unconsolidated experience of the self. Instead of being able to tolerate the shifts in experience, emotions, and identity that are hallmarks of the teenage years, the adolescent who develops an eating disorder is one who panics at these changes and prematurely organizes her sense of self around an external structure—in this case, weight and food intake.

For the normally developing adolescent, overidentification with heroes and cliques is a normal reaction to the role confusion and turmoil of adolescence. It is common to "install lasting idols and ideals as guardians of a final identity"

(1, p. 261). By late adolescence, however, these overidentifications are relinquished or modified. A coherent self begins to emerge in which conflicts and personality become more stable and the individual's inner values are clarified. The individual in late adolescence can move on, having more clearly limited and defined values and life tasks, to implement goals in terms of permanent relationships, roles, and career choices (2). But for the bulimic teenager, this is not so. The defensive position of early adolescence, that of overidealization and identification, is not relinquished. Instead, a "foreclosed identity" is assumed in which there is a reliance on fixed, idealized notions of whom one should be (3); an inner cohesion of identity is thus delayed. External standards (perfect looks, perfect weight, perfect behavior) are adopted as guideposts for identity and are relied upon as vehicles to define self-worth. As adolescence progresses, these external standards are clung to all the more strongly. In that regard, the bulimic woman in her early 20s, such as Karen, may present much like an adolescent. She has not renegotiated defensive positions as she is growing up, but instead continues to rely on early adolescent adaptations (idealization, overreliance on external standards, and consequent bulimic behavior) as thwarted attempts at mastering tasks central to her age.

For such a person, one of the major tasks of adolescence—that of separating from one's primary caretakers and forming a coherent internal identity—is thwarted. Separation is either never attempted or its failure is hidden beneath an identity of pseudo-independence. The bulimic adolescent fears parental attack if she is overtly rebellious or defiant. If she does react to her parents with hostility, the anger keeps her attached to her parents and does not allow for differentiation. As in Karen's case, with her late-night binges, often secretive eating is the only vehicle for attempts at separation. Only through ravenous bingeing behind closed doors (or in front of sleeping parents) can the person who is bulimic let out her angers, frustrations, needs, and desires without threatening family cohesion. More direct expression of conflict in a genuine attempt to define oneself as separate from other family members is avoided.

For the most part, in the bulimic patient there is a failure not only to differentiate self from others but also to distinguish one's internal life from one's outside actions. Object constancy and positive self-regard are lacking. Bruch (4) notes that anorexic teenagers demonstrate a lack of awareness of leading their own lives. This is also true for bulimic teenagers. "I know I'll have a good time at the party tonight" Karen would tell me. How does she know? Because she has reached her goal weight of 110 lbs. The desired weight will now define the day's events; nothing can rock that certainty. Self-worth and a sense of being defined by the scale cannot be shaken by feelings, personal interactions, or stray thoughts. One's "identity," as such, is impenetrable. Underlying self-doubt and confusion are masked (5) as the bulimic patient clings to the outward structure stereotypic of "perfect" female behavior and looks.

Underneath this structure, emotions rage and confusion reigns. Life in general feels overwhelming. Often food and purging are used to numb emerging feelings (6) or to desperately compensate for "feeling empty," an experience common to the bulimic patient who is so out of touch with her own feelings (7). For some, eating provides a semblance of nurturance in the face of a history of deficient caretaking. For most bulimic teenagers, however, the eating is a contained and isolated outlet for the tenacious drives, frustrations, and emotions common to adolescence that threaten the preservation of an identity built on sand.

Karen would tell me: "If I get upset, it gets in the way of my life." For Karen, life was a world void of spontaneous feelings and thoughts. Feelings are global, undifferentiated, and experienced as "not me." They are alien forces, potential sources of anxiety in their own right (8), and often the catalyst for a binge.

Thus an imprisoning structure of goals, plans, and predetermined behaviors is adhered to while the binge and vomiting serve to express the alien aspects of self and otherwise function to organize, however unsuccessfully, the bulimic patient's life. The central task of adolescence—that of experiencing complicated and conflicting aspects of one's self and integrating them into a firm identity—is thwarted. Erikson speaks of adolescent relationships and love as "an attempt to arrive at a definition of one's identity by projecting one's diffused self-image on another and by seeing it thus reflected and gradually clarified" (3, p. 132). What is mirrored back to the bulimic patient, however, is only one stereotypic aspect of herself. Like the witch in Snow White whose mirror reflects only the qualities of being "fairest of them all," so it is with the bulimic patient whose interpersonal "mirrors" reflect back only the "fairest" characteristics that others are allowed to see. A realistic appraisal of self is lost.

Allowing the bulimic teenager a partnership in which she can express the kaleidoscopic aspects of her personality and realistically assess who she is and what her effect is on others is the major task of treatment. In this regard, the therapy works to unlock the bulimic patient's stance of a "foreclosed" identify and to allow the adolescent a normative experience of identity crisis. Only as conflicting notions of the self are allowed to be expressed and to exist openly, side by side, can a more solid identity emerge and develop.

CURRENT TREATMENT APPROACHES— RESPONDING TO THE URGENCY

Treatment of the bulimic adolescent should involve a multidisciplinary approach in which adjunctive therapies such as pharmacotherapy, nutritional counseling, group treatment, and family intervention may play a role.

In this chapter, I focus on the individual psychotherapeutic relationship that provides the therapeutic hub from which other modalities are considered.

With regard to the individual psychotherapy of the bulimic adolescent, it is essential to note that two types of approaches have tended to dominate the literature. Either the focus of treatment is on symptom management, or a more classical analysis is pursued in which a structuring of the symptom is avoided.

For the most part, the urgency of the symptom and the desperation of the patient to be rid of the destructive eating behaviors have predominantly resulted in treatment programs aimed at abatement of the problematic behaviors. Therapy involves the development of coping skills and ego-building functions as substitutes for the binge-purge patterns. Feelings, thoughts, and events that may precipitate a binge are explored, and alternative means of handling internal and external stressors are considered. Contracts that encourage healthier responses and that limit the binge-purge behavior are made between therapist and patient (9–13). The goal of treatment is symptom abatement, with sessions focused on strengthening ego functions such that this goal can be achieved.

In contrast to the behavior-oriented treatment approaches, classical analysis of the bulimic adolescent encourages a primary concern with underlying pathology; there is an avoidance of managing the acting-out behavior (14). Eating and purging are viewed as defenses against analytic understanding, and the role of the therapist is to interpret the defense, not help structure the eating behavior. In fact, the philosophy of treatment is that direct concern about the binge-purge pattern may actually accentuate these masochistic maneuvers on the part of the patient (14).

This point of view endorses the belief that the eating disorder is reflective of underlying conflicts having to do with impulses for assertiveness, rebelliousness, aggression, and sexual urges that impinge on ego controls. When the eating behavior is handled without too much constraint in the treatment, the patient is able to verbalize and analyze the underlying conflict, thus leading to a natural abatement in the need for symptoms. In this regard, interpretation is the primary mode of intervention (15).

For the bulimic patient in general, and particularly for the bulimic adolescent, a strictly interpretive or predominantly behavioral approach often misses the point. Complexities of the patient's underlying pathology and the complicated interaction between patient and therapist are either ignored or misunderstood.

Giovacchini (16) notes that with difficult patients such as these, traditional analytic method may be in direct opposition to the patient's pathology. Analytic neutrality is experienced as a recapitulation of neglectful parenting, and classical techniques such as the use of the couch or free association are defended against, as they are felt by the patient to be nothing other than manipulations.

Bruch has cautioned against the use of a strictly interpretative approach with anorexic patients, in that it "represents in a painful way the interaction between patient and parents, where 'mother always knew how I felt'" (4, p. 336). (For a more complete exploration of treatment of the anorexic adolescent, see Chapter 10.) This is so for the bulimic adolescent as well. When the bulimic patient enters treatment, she is specifically looking for help in managing the symptom. To dismiss the patient's wish for this help in essence gives the patient the message that as analyst, you know better than she what is important to talk about. The patient experiences the dismissal of her wish for direct help as dismissal of the patient herself. This may be "grist for the analytic mill" for the patient who is already committed to the psychotherapeutic process. But for the bulimic adolescent in the initial phase of treatment, this can result in the patient, who may very well have benefited from analysis, dismissing therapy in turn. Or the patient may stay in treatment but may immediately comply to a role of satisfying the analyst's needs and not her own (a position familiar to but often difficult to detect in these patients).

The eating disorder itself is the only language the patient has developed to communicate that something is wrong. By jumping to another language, that of "underlying dynamics," not only is the patient missed but the profound impact the eating disorder may have on her day-to-day life is overlooked.

On the other side of the coin, a strictly behavior-oriented approach is not the answer. An emphasis on changing behavior without further exploration focuses on what the patient does, not on who she is (17). The therapist may unknowingly replicate earlier familial patterns in which the patient's "messy uncomfortable" parts are deemed unacceptable. In an effort to be cared for, the patient dismisses and avoids many aspects of her self. She has been encouraged to look good and act "good" at the cost of a deeper understanding of who she is or what needs may have prompted such behavior in the first place. If the therapist merely contracts with the patient to "clean up the eating disorder," the patient's history of looking perfect at the cost of being known is replicated (18).

Giovacchini (16) suggests that with these type of patients, variations on analysis are needed that allow the patient special affirmation that she is of interest to the analyst. These variations are not "extra-analytic" but are, in fact, an essential aspect of analytic work with the "difficult" patient.

In this regard, with the bulimic teenager, an approach is needed that responds to the patient's request for help in abating destructive eating patterns. However, analytic exploration need not, nor should not, be neglected. The question of what meaning the focus on food has to the patient becomes a crucial component of inquiry and allows for the engagement of the adolescent in the analytic process.

MODIFICATION OF TECHNIQUE: THE BEHAVIORAL CONTRACT IN AN ANALYTIC SETTING

A willingness on the therapist's behalf to discuss bingeing, vomiting, calories, and weight obsessions carries a particular importance for the bulimic teenager. The language of "food and weight" is the main (and often only) language the patient has for talking about herself, her fears, and her needs. It is the only way she has of telling you "what hurts." In the treatment of any adolescent, the analyst and patient must find an appropriate language with which to work together. As is often noted, adult patients in Freudian analysis speak and dream of penises, Jungian patients of shadows, and those in Frommian therapy of relatedness. However, therapists working with adolescents must learn the language of the adolescent (19). For the adolescent with an eating disorder, the language is that of food and weight.

Treatment of the bulimic teenager thus, by necessity, starts with discussions about eating.

The therapist initiates a detailed inquiry into the environmental and psychic factors that influence binge and purge behavior. These teenagers often present with the complaint that the binge "just comes over" them. A deeper probe into thoughts, feelings, and interactions that occur before the binge, while often met with resistance, can be the first step in which the patient understands the eating behavior to be self-initiated, protective, and a well-intentioned though poorly conceived attempt to cope.

Here there is a focus on prementational states of agitation and defective self-soothing operations. This does not preclude the presence of intrapsychic conflicts that influence the patient's behavior. However, the point is that at this stage, an exploration of such issues does not help.

As in a behaviorally-oriented treatment, the patient is asked by the therapist to note the thoughts, feelings, people, and events—internal and external—that precipitate a binge. Behaviors that can delay bingeing are considered. Can the patient write her thoughts in a journal? Call a friend? What avenues of self-soothing are available to her?

The patient learns to recognize that she has turned to food and purging as a way to soothe herself and a way to cope—particularly as a means of coping with unwanted states of agitation and affect. Tolerance for these states is at best minimal. Krystal (20) has suggested that with patients such as these, the preliminary work of analysis entails explanation, elucidation, and at times direct reassurance regarding the experience of emotions. For the bulimic patient, this means recognizing that emotions are signals to the self that should be listened to and utilized, not avoided through eating.

In the third session of treatment, Sarah, a 20-year-old binge vomiter, responded to my request that she write her thoughts in a journal before *one* binge by saying, "I didn't do it. You want to put a separation between me and my eating. I don't want that separation." Discussion resulted in Sarah's thoughtful consideration of her belief that no one (other than "food") was available to her: "I'm a floating entity, like a piece of dust, just passing through life. I'm not connected to anyone—except to food."

As with most bulimic patients, Sarah will need support in distancing herself from impulsive bouts of eating such that she can first feel the anxieties and depression that are now masked by her symptom. A primary goal of early treatment intervention is allowing the patient the experience of anxiety; this is usually well avoided as long as eating is an immediate response to internal stress. With that goal in mind, contract setting with the patient is an important aspect of early treatment.

The "contract" is a verbal agreement established between patient and therapist in which the patient agrees to abate or delay binge behavior for a period of time in between sessions. For example, a patient who binges and vomits two to three times daily may decide she will forego bingeing for one day or one morning prior to the next session. Someone who only binge-purges once weekly may contract to go the entire week binge-free. Ways of coping, interacting, or self-soothing are discussed and encouraged as alternates to the binge. As in Sarah's case, early contracting may consist of merely delaying eating, with journal writing used to intervene on impulsive acting out.

Although these early interventions are behaviorally-focused, the goal of contract setting is not merely symptom abatement. Treatment of the bulimic patient entails a complicated admixture of structure *and* regard for the patient's reaction to the structuring process itself. That is, the goal is not merely to set up contracts the patient is able to keep, but instead to understand what gets in the way of her keeping the contracts in the first place, or what allows for successes she was unable to achieve on her own (18).

For example, in Sarah's case, I will eventually want to know if, content aside, everything I suggest is met with a negative "I won't do it." (I know already that this is the pattern that existed with her mother.) Or on the other hand, suppose a patient does relinquish her symptomatic behavior. What has happened? Has the therapeutic work in fact minimized the need for the symptom? Is the patient worried about displeasing me as therapist? Is she "hanging on for dear life"—succeeding at treatment as she has succeeded in her career or on exams, with her looks?

The contract is not only a means of exploring the behavioral and psychic functions of the symptom, but it provides a vehicle of "relatedness" necessary for work with the teenager who has learned to avoid the substance of relationships at the cost of her own identity. Lewis (21) has discussed the need for the analyst to find a means of relating to the teenager that responds to the developmental needs present at that time. For example, the shared act of discussing stories about superheroes may be more effective for the pathologically re-gressed adolescent than an analysis of superego defenses. With the bulimic teenager who is severely limited in her ability to negotiate a relationship, the contract is a means of putting the therapist in the room with the patient, whether it is within the session itself or outside its limiting confines. By ex-ploring how the patient reacts to an agreement made with another person, opportunity for a real interchange is encouraged with an otherwise evasive patient. The point is to understand what the patient is doing with the thera-pist, not merely to explore the symbolic meaning of the binge-purge itself.

Initially, the structure of a contract is sought by the patient as a "cure" for the binge-purge behavior. Underneath the wish to stop eating and vomiting however is a desperation to disavow herself of experiences and emotions that are threatening to her makeshift ego. That is the real reason why she wants to make the bulimia "go away." What the therapist often sees, though, is that the structure initially grasped is all too soon rejected. Without other outlets for spontaneous expression of self (threatening as they may be), the contract is soon felt to be an imprisoning force that allows for "good" behavior, not "bad." Contracts are broken—and the real work of the analysis begins. The ever-present struggle between a wish for the structure through contracting and the fear of its suffocating, narrowing results has both psychic and transfer-ential implications. The therapist becomes mother—eager in her demands, requiring perfection, holding the threads of survival in her knowledge of "what should be done next." In that regard, the therapist is also threatening, engulfing, suffocating, and controlling. The patient insists on help and struc-ture, and she alternately spits it out.

Early in treatment, Karen asked to contract not to binge for 2 days in be-tween sessions. Because she entered therapy bingeing at least once daily, this was a significant change in behavior but one that both she and I felt she was ready for (in previous weeks, she had gone 1 day a week without bingeing).

At her next session, Karen reported to me the following dream:

> My mother and I are sitting next to each other on a couch, one that actually looks like yours. I see a mouse—you know I hate mice and so does my mother. When my mother sees the mouse, she pulls her feet up on the couch and yells at me to "get it!" I roll up my sleeves and swing at the mouse. Finally I get it in my hand. But then the mouse changes into this disgusting ferret. It grows in length and starts squirming around my arm. I'm repulsed by it—it's disgusting. I'm really scared, but I keep fighting it. I wake up in a sweat, disgusted and scared, but I notice that I wasn't hurt.

In the exploration of the dream, Karen felt that the ferret was "somehow like the bulimia, disgusting, scary." Issues of intrusion and her fear that the bulimia could get out of control were discussed. Only thinly disguised beneath her overt concern about bulimia lay Karen's more primitive and global fear that it was not just the eating disorder but her feelings that could get out of control. Karen's intolerance of her own affect was an important aspect of the dream.

It is important for me to note here, in light of this chapter's focus, that Karen quickly identified her mother in the dream as "possibly being you." She had kept the contract as she had agreed but felt angry and upset that she had been abandoned to fight the binge-purge "ferret" on her own. Although she was not hurt by the struggle, she was angry that I would "pull up my feet" and tell her to "get it" (perhaps to "ferret" out a solution?). The work with the contract had not merely put a wedge into her eating behavior. As importantly, it had opened the door for exploration of an issue that would permeate sessions for the duration of treatment—her wish for help, her fear of abandonment, and (ultimately) her fear of intrusions, which in alternate sessions would result in her telling me to "get out."

Fear of engulfment, terror at separation, the need to control one's own experiences as well as those of others, and the fear of letting go of these controls are major transferential issues that need to emerge with the bulimic adolescent. However, the bulimic patient's tendency to submerge conflictual material and present a superficial, foreclosed identity can thwart expression of these issues and stalemate psychic development. A "transitional space" (22) must be allowed for in which the patient can experience all aspects of her fears and wishes, without concern for the contextual demands of the therapeutic relationship. The patient is given the room to identify her present experience without having to focus on what is expected of her. In this way, foreclosure of identity is discouraged, opening doors for the consolidation of fragmented, dissociated aspects of the self.

"I don't know how I should be today" is how Karen often started a session. She needed to structure how she would "be" in the room with me in much the same way she structured her eating or imprisoned herself in a life replete with rules that defined her behavior.

"How would you say you are right now?"

"Confused, not sure where to begin. Last session I though was a good session, but I can't get back to those feelings."

"So you are feeling some pressure to pick up where we left off but you can't just like clockwork."

"Yeah," Karen would say. And then she would be surprisingly calm or off and running with something else she wanted to tell me.

Giving Karen the space to "not know," to not "be," perhaps to play, allowed her to retreat from expectations of what she felt I wanted—or from rules she set up to define herself—and to feel the freedom to say whatever might have been on her mind. Often these moments of pressured retreat were in response to times she has felt connected or close to me. She felt that I was pressuring her to continue this closeness; or perhaps her own wishes for fusion obscured contradictory needs to escape, to pull back, to distance herself. The space to *not* do either, to remain confused, opens the way for discussion of this conflict.

Karen often did "not know how to be" when she had broken a contract after a long period of sustained connection with me through our agreements. She was not merely embarrassed or ashamed of breaking the contract. She did not know how to negotiate the space between feeling close and feeling distant. She did not know how to voice the disappointments or fury she may have been feeling toward me. Breaking a contract was often her way of getting distance, doing what she wanted to do, not what she thought that *I* wanted her to do. In that sense, the contract is a vehicle to explore the ever-changing shift between longings for closeness and ego structuring and the need to distance and risk expression of more unacceptable parts of the self.

The work of treatment often involves the therapist's telling the patient how she is being experienced. "Is the reception therefore definitive of the transmission?" asks Boris of a patient's nonverbal communication. "I hope so! It is all I had (and have) to go on" (23, p. 103). Exploration of what the patient is doing with the therapist vis-à-vis the contract provides the bridge for the patient to bring into the therapy room what is often left out—the unacceptable parts of herself that threaten both breakdown of the tentative connection to another person and the stability of her fragile hold on a masquerade of an identity.

COUNTERTRANSFERENTIAL ISSUES AND THE INEVITABILITY OF BEING ALONE

Work with the bulimic adolescent inevitably involves specific transferential/countertransferential issues that should be listened for if they are not readily apparent in the work. These patients are hungry. Their demands to be nurtured are often painfully overt. What is the therapist's response to the patient's emotional "hungers"? Withdrawal? Resentment? A wish to supply the needed goods? Men and women therapists tend to respond differently to these patients' dependency strivings, with men therapists tending to be more withdrawn, yet more comfortable than women therapists with the patient's persistent dependency needs (24).

The therapist may also feel pulled not only to be the omnipotent source of pleasure, but alternately to be the critical demanding mother who is impatient with slow progress or bulimic behavior (7). As with most disturbed adolescents, issues of control are often paramount with bulimic patients. Acting-out behavior such as missed appointments, refusal to talk, or the omnipresent response "I don't know" may dominate sessions as the patient struggles to assert her autonomy.

Often, however, with bulimic patients, acting out and transferential/countertransferential interchanges may occur in an manner that is both insidious and not often addressed in the literature. It is when the treatment appears to be at its best that the patient may in fact be most defended, most guarded, most withdrawn in the room.

> About 2 years into treatment, Karen dreamt that she and an older woman were having tea at a fancy restaurant. She and the woman were very polite and gracious. Under the table, however, Karen brazenly sat in a pair of shorts and sneakers—dress that would be "outrageous" in this restaurant.

> Karen's associations to the dream followed. She noted that she always saw a cup of tea in my office. Shorts reminded her of bike riding, playing baseball with her boyfriend, letting go. She told me that she could never get angry when she wore a dress. She wondered if I had noticed that whenever she was upset with me, she dressed casually at later sessions, wearing jeans or shorts. (I hadn't noticed.) The session's material quickly turned to a discussion of what she perceived as our outwardly polite behavior; her more outrageous behavior was kept "under the table" to be seen if I wanted to look—but in the dream I obviously hadn't.

> Transferential issues regarding Karen's need to hide out and her wish to engage with me in a safe, formal manner were obvious. Her parents' wish not to see certain behaviors was now familiar information, included in the web of the treatment. However, the dream presented many countertransferential questions as well. What was it that *I* didn't want to see? Was "high tea" safer than the sweat and work that I associated with shorts and sneakers? Why didn't I look under the table?

The formal, gracious, polite interchange characterized in Karen's dream is a stance easy to assume with these patients. It is often familiar to them, and it is certainly seductive to the analyst who needs to contain the mess of the work within the confines of a 45-minute session. What may be perceived by the therapist as a treatment that is "going well"—with content flowing and associations produced—may very well be experienced by the ·patient as "polite" behavior. Has the patient unknowingly begun to speak your language, instead of finding her own? I believe that was partially the case with Karen.

"Politeness" hides impulsivity, fury, the hell of depression. It also keeps up a facade of a connection when the real experience in the room may often be one of being alone. Sprince (25) described the feeling in session as one of lack of involvement and "inner absence" (p. 77). Boris (23, p. 91) called it wishing he were someplace less lonely.

Often bulimic teenagers have a need *not* to let anything happen. Not only does this ensure the emotional stability of a polite interaction, but it avoids their fear that action implies control. In their overt or covert silence, they render the therapist helpless, avoiding the penetrating intrusion they fear from words and interpretations. For the analyst, the dread of loneliness at these times and the discomfort of being rendered helpless may be unintentionally avoided by attempts at exploration, interpretation, or otherwise "high tea" behavior. Therapists are not immune from unwittingly shaping the treatment to avoid the Sturm und Drang of the loneliness. Moreover, to do so *is* the transferential/countertransferential pattern that will emerge with these patients. "High tea" is inevitable. The work of the treatment is to notice when the therapy has lapsed into the "good life," to question how this has happened, and to take a good look under the table.

It is often only in retrospect that one is able to consider a period of disconnection between patient and therapist. As in Karen's case, dreams can provide clues, as can associative material in the sessions. A more direct and usually more reliable means of gaining access to the patient's experience is by noting the quality of interaction in the room. Bulimic patients have a remarkable capacity to talk about emotions and report information fluidly while at the same time remaining distanced from what they are saying. The only sign of their disconnection is a sense of "spaceyness" or distraction that pervades the session. Both therapist and patient wander off into their own private worlds. A therapist with a keen ear for his or her own distraction can use this time to question what's happening in the room. This may be a time to interrupt the patient's associations and ask what is really going on. Merely noting that the patient seems preoccupied with something else as she goes on talking (if the therapist believes this to be the case) can begin to bridge the gap.

Sometimes distancing from the therapist is a developmentally necessary part of treatment for the struggling adolescent.

Two and one-half years into treatment, Karen revealed that there were "things" she wasn't telling me.

> I feel private—like there are things about me that no one knows except me. I used to feel like the bulimia was the only thing I had that was a secret. Now the bulimia's not there as much but there are other things.

Karen reassured me that these were "okay things—not like the bulimia" but thoughts she wanted to keep to herself. The session was spent discussing what it meant for her not to tell me, and for me to know that she had "something I couldn't have" (and that I knew it).

On her way to our next session, Karen started to feel panicked, as though, as she put it, she were having a "nervous breakdown." Impulsively she rushed for food—two hot dogs, a muffin, a box of doughnuts, a big pretzel. A stop in a department store bathroom followed, where she vomited "violently." Twenty minutes late, Karen arrived pale, exhausted, crying, and we began the session.

Karen's panic was quickly understood by her as a reaction to having kept me out last session. Her autonomous move to assume a world separate and private from me threatened abandonment and rejection by me. She felt alone and feared retaliation. Discussion of Karen's rightful need for control over what I should and shouldn't know resulted in noticeable calm by the end of the session. Karen was binge-free for 2 weeks following the session and related the abatement in symptom to "permission to run my own life." Although the fears of separation and of leading her own life would continue over future sessions and would often directly result in a binge, our understanding of these needs gave Karen and me a mutually shared language with which to understand and discuss her bulimic behavior.

The need for the therapist to succeed at his or her work is often perceived by the patient as the very vehicle for control that impedes the adolescent's need to do what *she* wants. At times, it is in the leaving of treatment itself that the teenager feels she is ultimately taking control of her life. Ironically, some patients have reported that it was only when they left therapy that they were able to give up the binge behavior. When they are most desperate, they may even attempt suicide. "The only thing I have that's my own is the bulimia and my life," one 19-year-old told me. "Take away the bulimia, and the only thing *I'll* be able to take is my life."

In the face of such extreme and provocative behaviors on the part of the patient, countertransferential responses of the therapist are equally intense and ever-present. Collusion with "high tea" behavior is only one side of the coin. In an effort not to be shut out or controlled, the therapist may respond in many other ways that can further complicate treatment.

For example, as treatment progresses, the question remains as to when a direct focus on the eating behavior is a means of responding to the patient or one of abandoning her. As control issues permeate the room, a focus on the patient's bulimia may be a way to restructure the treatment or to renew one's presence with the patient.

The real difficulty in this work lies in the fact that the therapist cannot turn to the patient for validation. Responses from the patient that may normally indicate the treatment is going well, such as the continuation of associative material or the abatement of the symptom, may in these cases be the patient's attempt at pleasing the new authority figure in her life. Like the patient who was unable to turn to her parents for self-validation, so it is with the therapist who is unable to receive validation regarding his or her role and work with the patient. The therapist of the bulimic patient is left very much alone.

There is no easy solution. The therapist can only keep an awareness of these issues in mind and analyze material with a constant respect for the potential struggles that may lie just beneath the surface. The point is that bulimic teenagers, through their bizarre and provocative acts, are seeking an identity. In that regard, the goal of contract use and treatment in general is poignantly underlined. Taking away the bulimia is not the point; questioning who the patient is and what she is doing with the contract is the base of the analytic exchange.

As a final note, therapy with the adolescent should entail conjunctive treatment that is often not necessary with the adult patient. The families of these teenagers should not be neglected as individual treatment proceeds. Parents may unwittingly thwart the development that the patient strives for in treatment—or, at best, they are helpless bystanders who inevitably have many questions as to what their role should be regarding day-to-day issues about food and their daughter's well-being. What should they do when their daughter clears the house of food? Should they actively discourage binge behavior? If so, how? What issues other than those that are food-related hide behind the all-too-frequent battles at meals? Families need help disengaging from struggles with food and need to question how they are handling issues pertinent to normal adolescent development (for example, those regarding responsibilities, privacy, curfews, and so on [26]).

When approached according to their needs and motivation for change (27), work with the family—be it traditional family therapy or a more didactic approach—can facilitate the adolescent's strivings for autonomy and can provide an encouraging environment for the teenager's growth and independence.

CONCLUSION

The bulimic teenager has retreated from the world of people to a world of food where she has prematurely established a fragile attempt at an identity, replete with rules, structures, and inflexible laws as to how she should be.

An approach that attempts to minimize the focus on food and allows for a real relationship in which the patient has an effect on and is affected by another person is the goal of treatment. Contracting to abate binge-purge behavior is the vehicle not only to help the patient diminish impulsive acting out, but to understand who is doing what to whom. Only then is the patient free to experience various aspects of self that have previously gone under cover and to consider "what is my way of life" (2, p. 145).

In an arena where "how to be" is the dominant theme for the patient, the analyst must cautiously avoid his or her own predetermined decision as to "how to be." A flexible and real exchange with another person, in this case the adolescent, is needed in which the "high tea" of analysis is questioned, and the analyst and patient "play ball."

REFERENCES

1. Erikson EH: Childhood & Society. New York, WW Norton, 1963, pp 247–277
2. Blos P: On Adolescence: A Psychoanalytic Interpretation. New York, Free Press, 1962
3. Erikson E: Identity, Youth and Crisis. New York, WW Norton, 1968
4. Bruch H: Eating Disorders: Obesity, Anorexia and the Person Within. New York, Basic Books, 1973
5. Siegel M: Bulimia, object relations, and the therapeutic tie. Paper presented at meeting of the American Psychological Association, Washington, DC, August 1982
6. Bruch H: Perceptual and conceptual disturbances in Anorexia Nervosa. Psychosom Med 24:187–194, 1962
7. Johnson C, Connors M: The Etiology and Treatment of Bulimia Nervosa: A Biopsychosocial Perspective. New York, Basic Books, 1987, pp 88–126
8. Bromberg P: On the occurrence of the Isakower phenomenon. Contemporary Psychoanalysis 20(4):600–624, 1984
9. Fairburn CG: Cognitive-behavioral treatment for bulimia, in Handbook of Psychotherapy for Anorexia Nervosa and Bulimia. Edited by Garner DM, Garfinkel PE. New York, Guilford, 1985, pp 160–192
10. Johnson C, Connors M, Stuckey M: Short-term group treatment of bulimia. International Journal of Eating Disorders 2:199–208, 1983
11. Lacey JH: Bulimia nervosa, binge eating, and psychogenic vomiting: a controlled treatment study and long-term outcome. BMJ 286:1609–1613, 1983
12. Mitchell JE, Hatsukami D, Goff G, et al: Intensive outpatient group treatment for bulimia, in Handbook of Psychotherapy for Anorexia Nervosa and Bulimia. Edited by Garner DM, Garfinkel PE. New York, Guilford, 1985, pp 240–256
13. White WC, Boskind-White M: An experiential-behavioral approach to the treatment of bulimarexia. Psychotherapy: Theory, Research and Practice 18:501–507, 1981
14. Hogan C: Technical problems in psychoanalytic treatment, in Fear of Being Fat: The Treatment of Anorexia and Bulimia. Edited by Wilson CP, Hogan C, Mintz I. New York, Jason Aronson, 1983, pp 197–216
15. Mintz I: Psychoanalytic description: the clinical picture of anorexia and bulimia, in Fear of Being Fat: The Treatment of Anorexia and Bulimia. Edited by Wilson CP, Hogan C, Mintz I. New York, Jason Aronson, 1983, pp 83–113
16. Giovacchini PL: Developmental Disorders: The Transition Space in Mental Breakdown and Creative Integration. New York, Jason Aronson, 1986
17. Browning WN: Long-term dynamic group therapy with bulimic patients: a clinical discussion, in Theory and Treatment of Anorexia and Bulimia: Biomedical, Sociocultural, and Psychological Perspectives. Edited by Emmett SW. New York, Brunner/Mazel, 1985, pp 141–153

18. Brisman J: Treatment of the bulimic college student: considerations and complications, in The Bulimic College Student: Evaluation, Treatment, and Prevention. Edited by Whitaker LC, Davis WN. New York, Haworth Press, 1989, pp 191–204

19. Levenson E, Feiner A, Stockhamer N: The politics of adolescent psychiatry, in Adolescent Psychiatry, Vol IV. New York, Jason Aronson, 1975

20. Krystal H: Affect tolerance. The Annual of Psychoanalysis 179–219, 1974

21. Lewis O: The paranoid-schizoid position in pathologic regression in early adolescence. J Am Acad Psychoanal 15:503–520, 1987

22. Winnicott DW: Playing and Reality. London, Tavistock, 1986

23. Boris HN: Torment of the object: a contribution to the study of bulimia, in Bulimia: Psychoanalytic Treatment and Theory. Edited by Schwartz H. Madison, WI, International Universities Press, 1988, pp 89–110

24. Zunino N, Agoos E, Davis WN: The impact of therapist gender on the treatment of bulimic women. International Journal of Eating Disorders 10(3):253–263, 1991

25. Sprince MP: Experiencing and recovering space in the analytic treatment of anorexia and bulimia, in Bulimia: Psychoanalytic Treatment and Theory. Edited by Schwartz H. Madison, WI, International Universities Press, 1988, pp 73–88

26. Siegel M, Brisman J, Weinshel M: Surviving an Eating Disorder: New Perspectives and Strategies for Family and Friends. New York, Harper & Row, 1988

27. VanderEycken W: The constructive family approach to eating disorders: critical remarks on the use of family therapy in anorexia nervosa and bulimia. International Journal of Eating Disorders 6:455–468, 1987

10 The Anorexic Adolescent

William N. Davis, Ph.D.

The treatment of anorexia nervosa can be a daunting task. Frequently, the process is punctuated by draining, frustrating, even frightening moments. Far too often therapy is terminated prematurely, or grinds to a halt after a prolonged impasse. Many anorexic patients receive multiple courses of treatment and even then there may be little substantial improvement in their condition. Indeed, adolescents and in fact all people who have anorexia are among the most recalcitrant psychotherapy patients. The central dilemma for therapist and patient alike is the extent to which anorexic symptoms are first of all both highly adaptive and culturally valued and then (if sustained for a sufficient time) extraordinarily self-reinforcing. The result is a situation rather unique to psychotherapy. Instead of being regarded as a potentially helpful caregiver, the therapist is seen by the patient as an enemy. Instead of working with a person who wants help, the therapist is faced with a patient apparently so invested in retaining her symptoms, or so consumed by them, that she literally is willing to risk her life.

Fortunately, there is another side to the treatment coin. Successful psychotherapy with anorexic patients is possible and does happen. In the context of solid management and skillful caring, anorexic patients are willing to risk losing their symptoms and the self-protection their symptoms have provided. Less dramatic but equally important in the long term are the psychotherapies that enable an anorexic patient to move part of the way toward recovery. Treatment need not be complete in order to be a success.

The primary purpose of this chapter is to describe one therapist's experience with anorexia nervosa. As such, most of my discussion will be particularly relevant to individual psychotherapy conducted on an outpatient basis. If the reader has had little contact with patients with anorexia, then I am hopeful that this chapter will contribute to an increase in therapeutic confidence and skill. If the reader is experienced in the field of eating disorders, then perhaps this chapter will serve to strengthen existing convictions or to provoke thought about heretofore unchallenged assumptions and methods. The following sections will touch on the definition and history of anorexia nervosa, and then provide a brief overview of etiology and treatment. These areas will not be discussed in detail, but interested readers are referred to the excellent primary sources. Most of my effort here will be directed toward a discussion

189

of the significant issues that therapists must confront in the psychotherapy of anorexia nervosa.

DEFINITION AND HISTORY OF ANOREXIA NERVOSA

In recent years, anorexia has received a great deal of attention, both in the popular media and in professional publications. Indeed, eating disorders could be described as the emotional disturbances that currently most characterize and captivate us. Excellent reviews of the diagnostic criteria now utilized to identify anorexia nervosa are available in any of several major books on the disorder (1–3). For this chapter's purposes, it will be enough to echo the pioneering work of Bruch (4,5) and say that the defining characteristic of anorexia is a relentless pursuit of thinness and a concomitant dread of fatness. Consequently, the most obvious manifestations of anorexia include an overly thin or emaciated appearance; a history of rapid weight loss not induced by medical illness; a seriously distorted body image; and a pervasive preoccupation with food, eating, weight, and dieting.

There is nearly unanimous agreement among experts in the field that anorexia is a multidimensional disorder whose characterological underpinning, psychological etiology, and immediate onset may be relatively heterogeneous across individuals (1,3). Therefore, there is no simple correspondence between one particular type of adolescent, or one particular type of problem, and the development of anorexia.

One clinical implication is that the psychotherapist should not expect to find a known set of etiological circumstances or psychodynamic characteristics when he or she begins to treat an anorexic patient.

The multidimensional nature of anorexia is probably more pronounced today than it was when Bruch wrote about the classic anorexic patient (4,5). In part this is because in recent years our culture has embraced and thoroughly absorbed the idea that thinness represents a superior state of being. Consequently, more and more adolescents from increasingly different backgrounds and with increasingly different reasons to attain cultural "perfection" have set out down the yellow brick road of rigorous dieting. Most survive their trip to this land of Oz with few permanent scars. Others, however, keep looking for the wizard and are stranded with anorexia. In addition, anorexia may be serving as a kind of all-purpose emotional distress call in our time. Thus, regardless of antecedent conditions, some of today's teenagers may turn to anorexia instead of some other disorder to express their psychological turmoil because anorexic behavior is especially likely to capture the interest and attention of their peers and elders.

The foregoing paragraph suggests a bit of the very recent history of anorexia nervosa. Since the advent of Twiggy and our cultural infatuation with thinness, anorexia has left the realm of psychiatric obscurity to become a well-known, serious mental health problem. Indeed, the available evidence clearly suggests that the incidence of anorexic behavior has risen significantly in the last several decades (6). Gordon (7) has written a penetrating discussion of the relationship between the sociocultural milieu of the last 30 years and the increase of anorexia.

A brief glimpse into the past history of anorexic behavior raises important questions for the theoretician and has significant implications for the practicing clinician. Anorexia nervosa first gained some measure of medical recognition in 1873–1874. Working in Paris and London, respectively, Charles Lasegue (8) and Sir William Gull (9) published descriptions of patients who manifested behavior that closely resembles our modern notion of anorexia nervosa. Although Lasegue's commentary on "l'anorexie hysteriqué" was much more psychological in tone than Gull's primarily medical report of "anorexia nervosa," it is Gull who usually is credited with the first conceptualization of the anorexic syndrome.

However, the syndrome that we understand to be anorexia nervosa may have a history that extends far beyond its medicalization in the late 19th century. Bell (10) offers a fascinating account of medieval Italian saints who appear to have acted, thought, and felt very much like contemporary anorexic patients. Similarly, Brumberg (11) writes of young women who displayed anorexic characteristics from the medieval era to the late Victorian era, when anorexia nervosa began its tenure as a medical-emotional illness.

Intriguingly, it is females who appear to develop anorexia nervosa across the centuries. This is just as true today. A multitude of evidence suggests that about 90% of all people diagnosed with anorexia are female. Furthermore, although at present there may be some spread across chronological age, it is primarily female adolescents and young women who are most prone to develop anorexia nervosa. Theoretically, the question is why are women, usually young women, continually subject to psychological disturbances that are expressed through the medium of food, weight, and dieting, even in spite of vast cultural and social differences from one era to another? Clinically, there is an extremely important implication. Psychotherapists need to be aware of and understand feminine psychology in order to be as effective as possible in treating anorexia. Certain publications (12–15) are particularly instructive in this regard.

OVERVIEW OF ETIOLOGY AND TREATMENT

As I have mentioned, no one specific issue, conflict, or potentially predisposing factor will necessarily precipitate anorexia nervosa. Instead, the interaction of various biological, sociological, and psychological circumstances will foster the disorder in different kinds of people for different kinds of reasons. This is not to say that food, dieting, or eating has no psychological meaning, or that anorexia is not driven by emotional forces—only that the meanings and forces may not be common across individuals.

Most anorexic patients start their diets typically enough. It is the persistence of these diets that sets them apart and signifies their abnormality. This persistence, or relentlessness, happens because the diet "clicks," in the sense that it provides much needed psychological gratification and defensive capability. Sullivan's notion that psychiatric patients often hit upon a "happy solution" to some sort of internal dilemma they have been otherwise unable or unwilling to resolve is quite to the point (16). So, often without conscious awareness, the incipient anorexic woman is swept away into her diet. The course of anorexia is characterized by continual, sometimes rapid weight loss. Along the way the anorexic individual's eating habits tend to become more and more secretive, and often bizarre and ritualized. Frequently, her ability to maintain an extremely restrictive diet fails her, or temporarily lapses, leading her to turn to purging in a desperate attempt to avoid weight gain. Almost always her experience of her body becomes distorted. Although losing weight, she sees herself as fat and feels herself to be disgustingly flabby, thus strengthening the urgent need to diet. Her mood tends to alter in the direction of irritability and depression. Usually, she becomes increasingly isolated from friends and family. When those around her become concerned, it is invariably the case that power struggles will ensue over how much she should eat or when or what she should eat. Most if not all of the anorexic course is a function of the anorexic patient's relationship with her diet and her idealized goal of thinness.

The literature abounds with possible answers to the question of why someone would choose, relentlessly, to pursue self-starvation. The ideas advanced vary as to what aspect of the anorexic syndrome is considered to be especially meaningful, and they also differ as to the significance of the disorder itself. Some writers have attached particular meaning to food and the act of eating. Here, anorexia is seen as the symbolic representation of the vicissitudes of intrapsychic drives and conflicts (17–19). Others view food and eating as representing only a means to an intrapsychic end and focus on the anorexic patient's relationship with her body (20,21). Still others emphasize interpersonal dynamics and understand anorexia to be a by-product of either thwarted needs for autonomy and self-expression, or unspoken familial mandates (4,5,22). More recently, feminist writers have placed anorexia in a quasi-political context, asserting that the disorder signifies an anguished response to the debilitating effects of sexism (15).

In spite of the divergence of opinions, and regardless of the issue of multidimensionality, there are several aspects of anorexia's development that may be common to almost all cases. First of all, implied by most theoretical statements regarding etiology is the broad assumption that the disorder serves or functions as a kind of psychological holding pattern. In other words, whether the anorexic individual is in conflict about oral impregnation (18), or in dread of ingesting what is experienced unconsciously as an evil introject (20), or desperately proclaiming her right to be autonomous (5), her dieting indicates she is in the midst of psychological turmoil that she feels unable to resolve. Indeed, one effect of anorexia nervosa is to stop development—physically because of the impact of malnutrition, and psychologically because of the pervasive concern with food, weight, and dieting.

Second, if anorexia "happens" in order to preserve a tenuous psychological stalemate, then it is also generally self-protective and self-constructive in nature. By implication, therefore, it does not represent the manifestation of a self-destructive or suicidal urge. In fact, it is rare that an anorexic patient really wants to kill herself. Instead, from this point of view, she is trying very, very hard to retain a sense of psychological safety and security, albeit in a tragically misguided manner. This is not to deny that deaths occur. Anorexic patients do kill themselves, either passively through severely debilitating malnutrition or more actively as in a more typical suicide. However, the death that ensues from self-starvation is usually the unintended result of a "mistake" that follows from too frenetic dieting; and the death that comes from an overdose is most often the result of an overwhelming secondary depression that is produced by the depleted, tortured circumstances within which the anorexic patient finds herself trapped.

Third, the onset and course of anorexia almost always spawn their own self-reinforcing process. In part this happens because an anorexic diet rapidly loses (or, more often, really never has) any objective end point. The psychological function of the diet is not to reach a goal weight and then to go forward with life enhanced by a slimmer appearance. Instead, it is to seek security through continued avoidance. Therefore, no particular weight is safe enough. Only weight loss can signify that the horror of fatness is being overcome, and in turn that a state of psychological safety, however fragile, is being maintained. The self-reinforcing nature of anorexia is also generated by the psychological changes that accompany starvation. Most importantly, starvation causes an increasing preoccupation with food and eating. Because anorexic patients are consciously terrified of losing control of their diet, thoughts about food can cause them profound anxiety. This tends to lead to an even more determined and frantic avoidance of eating, which unfortunately further stimulates a preoccupation with dieting, and so on.

The point is that anorexia nervosa can produce what amounts to a secondary illness as it develops over time. This illness may become functionally autonomous (23)—that is, relatively disconnected from whatever were the specific internal and external events that precipitated the anorexic diet in the first place. This has an important clinical implication. The treatment of anorexia must often be two-tiered. Psychotherapy must address itself not only to the underlying etiology of the disorder, but also to the manifestations of the secondary illness. Furthermore, this means that the anorexic patient will be most successfully treated as closely as possible to onset of her illness. For it is usually the secondary illness that is primarily responsible for the enormous resistance and recalcitrance that is so common in anorexic patients.

Finally, there is one other feature of anorexia that seems common to most patients. As the disorder develops and the anorexic patient becomes more absorbed in her diet, she becomes less connected to people. They feel more distant from her and less significant or important to her. The anorexic patient begins to have her most intense, direct, and immediate relationship with food, dieting, and the goal of thinness. In short, within the anorexic patient's psychological world, her most significant objects, if you will, are not people but the evolving vicissitudes of her anorexia. Conceptualized in this manner, the entrenched anorexic patient is most connected to, in dialogue with, and in harmony or in conflict with food, weight, dieting, and thinness. By implication, therapists are not only experienced as threatening figures who would stop an anorexic patient from dieting, but also as relatively distant ones, with few distinguishing personal characteristics and traits.

Attempts to alter anorexic behavior patterns date back to at least the 14th century, when puzzled medieval confessors sought to convince some of their saintly charges that it was not healthy or reverent to severely restrict food intake (10). In recent years there has been a veritable renaissance regarding the treatment of anorexia. Because of increased public and professional interest in the disorder, the last decade has seen an explosion of information and conjecture concerning therapeutic modalities, techniques, and issues. As a result, certain general guidelines have begun to take shape that appear to improve the chances for a patient's full or partial recovery. For example, it is now clear that the best treatment is that which precludes its need (24). Thus, the primary *prevention* of eating disorders is gradually becoming an important focus for professionals in the field.

Regarding treatment itself, there is general agreement that psychotherapy must be accompanied by adequate medical monitoring of the patient's condition. Ideally, this means that the therapist who treats patients who have eating disorders will have a close working relationship with a physician who is familiar with the psychology and medical complications of anorexia. In this connection, it is an established fact that extremely poor nutrition can interfere with cognitive and emotional functioning. When patients are extremely cachectic, hospitalization to restore adequate nutrition is a necessary prerequisite to psychotherapy. Treatment effectiveness will be enhanced when therapists are knowledgeable about nutrition, the physiology of purging, and the psychobiology of starvation.

In addition to physicians and hospitals, there are other adjuncts to psychotherapy that appear to promote recovery. Especially in the case of adolescents, it is generally advised that the patients' parents receive some form of counseling or psychotherapy. Again, ideally, a patient's therapist will refer parents to a colleague with whom he or she can maintain a close working relationship. The possibility that the treatment will be undermined by ignorant, anxious, or unconsciously manipulative parents will be greatly reduced under these circumstances. Support groups for both the anorexic patient and her parents are another adjunct that is often recommended. These are particularly helpful in mitigating the sense of social isolation that tends to develop in people who are anorexic, and in quelling the angry and guilty feelings that can be overwhelming to their parents. Nutritional counseling can also be an effective adjunct, but only in the later stages of treatment when recovery is well on its way.

Apart from restoring adequate nutrition, hospitalization can also function as a therapeutic adjunct. This is particularly the case when the anorexic patient is placed into an inpatient eating disorders unit where she will be exposed to multiple therapeutic inputs such as movement groups, body image groups, sex information groups, and the like. There are several treatment issues that need thoughtful consideration in this regard. One is that adjunctive hospitalization works best when an outpatient therapist can follow his or her patient into the hospital. Another is that inpatient units should not be expected to produce complete psychological recovery. At best, they can function to provide the anorexic patient with the message that something is drastically wrong and that, in spite of her conviction to the contrary, it is possible to lead a more fulfilling and less frightened life. The benefits that hospitalization can afford— immersion in a well-structured program that may help the anorexic patient to curtail her dieting and begin to assess her psychological state—need to be weighed against the fact that inpatient placement will of necessity further disrupt her ongoing functioning in the real world. A final issue concerns the therapist. It is important that he or she not see an adjunctive hospitalization as an instance of therapeutic failure but instead as an additional opportunity to move the patient toward recovery.

The important point here is that a variety of carefully selected adjuncts are likely to advance the treatment. Accumulated experience suggests that patients with anorexia nervosa are treated most successfully when multiple therapeutic inputs are brought to bear on the clinical situation. Parenthetically, psychiatric medication has not proven to be an especially worthwhile adjunct, at least insofar as anorexic symptoms themselves are concerned. Antianxiety drugs as well as antidepressants may have a limited role in ameliorating some of the secondary responses patients develop as a result of their eating disorder, or in connection with the life conflicts that anorexia tends to generate. However, it is usually difficult to persuade anorexic patients who are deeply frightened of losing control to take any medication on a regular basis.

Anorexia nervosa probably has been treated by every known form of psychotherapy. At this point there is general agreement that on an outpatient basis the disorder is best approached with either individual and/or family therapy. Group psychotherapy appears to be relatively ineffective and in some cases may actually promote symptom exacerbation, as anorexic patients will tend to compare notes on how to lose weight or compete secretly with each other. This is in contrast to patients who are primarily bulimic. In this population, short-term psychoeducational groups have been impressively effective in reducing instances of bingeing and/or purging (25).

There is some controversy regarding the relative merits of individual and family treatment. Those who prefer the latter point to the importance that anorexia may have within the family system and argue that only an approach that addresses the entire family at once can undermine the meaning and function of anorexic symptomatology (22). Adherents of individual psychotherapy are far and away the majority of those therapists that work with anorexia. Unfortunately, this is not necessarily because individual therapy has proven to be especially effective, but more because it is what most therapists are trained to do. One common claim, however, is that anorexic patients are particularly prone to be overly responsive to the needs of others and so require treatment that will focus just on them and on their needs (26).

Within the realm of individual therapy there are also conflicting claims as to the orientation that will be most helpful. The major area of disagreement is between those therapists who focus their treatment on the cognitive-behavioral aspects of anorexia (27), and those who emphasize the importance of the psychodynamic underpinnings of the disorder. This is by no means a schism. Garner and Garfinkel (6) have pointed out there is a growing recognition among clinicians in the field that the most successful psychotherapy for anorexia will include both cognitive-behavioral and psychodynamic emphases and techniques.

Psychodynamically oriented therapists are further split among those who advocate traditional psychoanalytic methods (19), self psychological techniques (28), various more interpersonal approaches (some of which are influenced by feminist thinking), and a nurturant-authoritative model (26). One clear implication of the multiplicity of recommended approaches is that no one treatment method has been demonstrated to be singularly successful.

SIGNIFICANT THERAPEUTIC ISSUES

The treatment of anorexia nervosa has several equally important goals. Ideally, recovery is complete when a patient's weight and eating habits have been restored to a reasonably appropriate standard, when her anxiety about weight and eating falls within acceptable cultural norms, and when the fears, conflicts, or developmental lacunae that originally fueled the anorexic diet have been resolved sufficiently to allow her to adopt a reasonably normal life style. Generally speaking, some amount of symptom amelioration is the necessary ingredient for genuine recovery. Real movement in this direction makes it increasingly possible to actually deal with the patient's nonanorexic psychology. On the other hand, failing to effect any change in anorexic behavior patterns continually interferes with the ability to do any lasting psychotherapeutic work, because the patient is likely to remain enmeshed in her preoccupation with food, weight, and dieting.

As I mentioned at the outset, there is a profound dilemma that faces the therapist as work begins with almost any anorexic patient. Typically, the anorexic patient understands the therapist to be an enemy, someone who will attempt to prevent her from remaining thin or becoming thinner. Furthermore, because any change in her pursuit of dieting tends to feel like a loss of hard-won control (the consequence of which is to raise the specter of fatness), the therapist is seen not only as a diet stopper but also as a fat maker. Perhaps most important, because the anorexic patient has often developed an intense and complex "object relationship" with her diet and the ideal of being thin, the therapist is experienced as someone who threatens to leave the patient utterly bereft and alone.

Thus, most anorexic patients enter treatment in an extremely resistant frame of mind. This tends to be true regardless of the patient's underlying character structure and regardless of the specific problems or conflicts that were responsible for the eating disorder in the first place. Also, this is true in spite of the outward compliance and eagerness to please that sometimes characterizes the patient's response to the therapist.

Dealing with the profound resistance of anorexic patients is undoubtedly the most difficult and also the most important aspect of the treatment. Without any progress in this regard, little change can be expected in the anorexic patient's symptomatology, making it impossible to effect any genuine recovery. Furthermore, given the assumption of a multidimensional etiology, it follows that the resolution of anorexic resistance is the central common task in the psychotherapy of anorexia nervosa. In other words, beyond the resolution of resistance—a requirement in every case—the treatment of anorexic patients will differ as a function of their specific clinical characteristics and character formations.

The resistance of anorexic patients can be extremely upsetting to any therapist. For example, as a function of her resistance, the anorexic patient is unlikely to provide the therapist with very much gratification for his or her efforts. This is in marked contrast to most other psychotherapy patients. In general, psychotherapists view themselves and believe they are viewed as helpful, dedicated caregivers. Anorexic patients, on the other hand, are often silent, rejecting, or hostile about therapeutic interventions. Even when their patients appear interested or attentive, therapists are frequently left with the

feeling that they are not really getting through or connecting in any significant way. The result can be a growing sense of frustration, leading to a whole
host of nontherapeutic thoughts and feelings. Typically these include but certainly are not limited to an angry petulant demandingness, a needy pleading
manipulativeness, or a kind of lethargic hopeless resignation. Even worse, the
anorexic patient whose resistance successfully deprives the therapist can create
a creeping, gradual sense of inadequacy and ineffectiveness that threatens the
therapist's self-definition as a helpful caregiver.

Indeed, anorexia nervosa may produce more countertransferential responses in trained psychotherapists than any other psychiatric disorder. With
this in mind, it is important to mention the potential impact of the patient's
appearance and her health. Some anorexic patients enter therapy in an extremely emaciated state, looking and acting as if close to death. A skeletal
adolescent who sits painfully upon her bare bones and stares listlessly out of
sunken eyes can be very frightening or even disorganizing to the therapist.
Sometimes the case will be lost before it begins as the therapist consciously or
unconsciously "counterresists" and finds a reason to refer the patient elsewhere for her treatment. Just as unfortunately, the anorexic patient's appearance can intimidate the therapist, enabling her resistance to control the
direction and content of the sessions and consequently to disrupt the treatment process.

How, then, to prepare for the anorexic patient's resistance in a way that will
be helpful to the patient and protective of the therapist? First, the therapist
should always expect to meet resistance and to experience some degree of
countertransference. Accepting this strong probability helps to mitigate the
frustration that can so easily arise and so easily cause the therapist to feel out
of control of the treatment. Second, it is important to bear in mind that anorexic resistance is primarily a manifestation of the patient's constant and profound need to defend the predominant experience of her self—as a dieter
whose thoughts, feelings, and behaviors are focused on promoting thinness
and avoiding fatness. From her perspective, therefore, the resistance serves a
highly adaptive and self-constructive purpose. In short, it is necessary and
meaningful for her to frustrate, manipulate, and obfuscate the therapist's best
intentions. Relying on such a framework of understanding can be especially
helpful, because it tends to strengthen the therapist's capacity to maintain psychological independence and yet feel compassion and concern for the patient.

Furthermore, it is extremely important for the therapist to begin treatment
with a sense of the anorexic experience in all its vicissitudes. Frequently, anorexic patients come to believe that others do not understand them. By the
time treatment is initiated, many of their previous interpersonal relationships
have been lost or have become fraught with such tension and conflict that
little real communication is possible. Although the lack of understanding that
anorexic patients experience from others may serve the needs of their resis-

tance, it often becomes only a hollow victory. Anorexic symptoms can and do take a terrible toll as they entrench themselves over time. The initial triumphs and joys as weight is lost and the diet is manageable give way in time to a grueling ordeal as the specter of fatness grows increasingly more powerful. As a result, the anorexic patient is confronted with a desperate situation wherein she feels unable to give up pursuing thinness and yet simultaneously trapped in a gray, bleak landscape with little hope on the horizon. Levenkron (26) puts it well when he suggests that anorexic patients can reach a point in the course of the disorder when their symptomatic patterns are experienced as sadistic and tyrannizing.

Knowing all this can be invaluable to the therapist. It underscores the terrible struggle that lies beneath the anorexic patient's resistance, making it possible to look beyond the patient's depriving, disturbing behavior. Moreover, it suggests that one need not be scared of or intimidated by self-starvation, but instead one can understand the anorexic patient to be a frightened, desperate child who feels unable to control her life because she cannot separate herself from her symptoms.

Finally, it is crucial to bear in mind that traditional psychotherapeutic methods may be minimally effective when addressing anorexic resistance. By traditional methods I am referring to the time-honored model of the relatively neutral, passive psychotherapist who conducts the treatment by reacting to data provided by the patient through the techniques of inquiry, exploration, and interpretation. Particularly, at the outset of treatment, it is important to have a significant impact on the anorexic patient. At best, the therapist will interest and attract the patient in spite of her resistance; at the least, he or she should make an impression on the resistance. Remaining personally neutral or anonymous and relatively passive in regard to the content and direction of sessions is a poor way to generate impact.

Usually, an anorexic patient enters treatment feeling emotionally alone, consumed and being consumed by her concerns about food, weight, and dieting. People have become less distinct. The patient's relationships are not really as interpersonal as they once were but have become more an appendage to and a function of anorexia.

A neutral and primarily reactive therapist unwittingly reinforces this state of affairs, and in turn further entrenches the anorexic patient's resistance. In addition, not only does this therapist appear to ignore the patient, but also to leave her in control of the terms of the relationship. In some instances this will frighten the patient and in others it will relieve her, but rarely does it aid the treatment process. Regardless of her protestations to the contrary, the anorexic patient who is in control of her therapy rarely knows what to do with it, and rarely makes beneficial use of the interventions that are offered to her.

The specific techniques of inquiry, exploration, and interpretation also tend to have little impact on the patient's resistance. To be effective these procedures depend critically on the patient's ability to cooperate with the therapist. They also assume that the patient has some interest in clarifying, understanding, and altering the nature of her psychology. Given that anorexic patients usually feel that they do not need treatment, there is little reason to believe they will be willing to make use of procedures that require them to take an active role in understanding themselves. Inquiry essentially means that the therapist asks the patient to reflect openly and to explain herself as best she can. But people suffering from anorexia don't know much about themselves, because they have a vested interest in remaining ignorant. To assist an inquiry and to explore its implications is to risk unsettling the rigid assumptions that motivate the anorexic patient to maintain her disorder.

For example, a serious exploration of the patient's attitudes about body image would quickly pose a challenge to her staunchly held belief that her thighs are too fat to wear a bathing suit or that only thin people are happy. Moreover, taking part in the inquiry is to risk making cognitive or emotional connections between eating-disordered behavior and other aspects of living. Connections imply explanations that in turn suggest that the anorexic patient's beliefs are not necessarily simple truths or an end in themselves. In addition, such connections raise the possibility that there are other ways to be and other ways to express who one is and how one feels. To the anorexic patient, whose mind is focused on food, weight, and dieting, inquiry and exploration seldom suggest either new opportunities or even fearful curiosity. Instead these techniques frequently provoke extreme anxiety. Not only might they undermine the original defensive function of anorexia, but more immediately and more significantly in the patient's experience they stimulate the horror of impending fatness.

Interpretations, however accurate, depend on a patient's capacity to think analogously and on her ability to reframe her cognitive and emotional experience. In effect, psychological or behavioral change is implied, and so it is often too dangerous for the anorexic patient to make use of the therapist's efforts. In addition, complicated interpretations that involve transferential behavior or genetic reconstructions require a relatively uncluttered mind to be effective. Unfortunately, this is too frequently beyond the capabilities of the anorexic patient who is obsessively preoccupied with her symptoms.

Whenever a therapist relies heavily on traditional psychotherapeutic methods, he or she is likely to feel increasingly "starved" by the anorexic patient's ongoing resistance and thus become particularly vulnerable to countertransferential thought, feeling, and behavior. This may cause the treatment to terminate abruptly and prematurely or to die a long slow death in prolonged impasse. One rather common variation on the theme of impasse is the compliant, approval-seeking anorexic patient who appears to make great strides toward self-understanding and yet leaves a long course of treatment still agonized by anorexic symptomatology. Indeed, the treatment may have moved the patient somewhat along the path to recovery. However, the insight is likely to feel superficial and the behavior changes may prove temporary when the patient finally leaves her therapist. This type of treatment outcome can be the result of an unwitting collusion between patient and therapist. In effect, the patient indicates that she will listen to her therapist and work hard at being a good psychotherapy patient provided there is little attention paid to her anorexic behavior. The therapist, in turn, indicates that he or she will work diligently to help the patient gain insight into her life—as long as she does not mention much about the ups and downs of her anorexic experience.

As an alternative to a traditional therapeutic model, I have come to believe that the therapist is best advised to take a dynamic, authoritative, and actively caring approach to the anorexic patient right from the outset of treatment. Such an approach provides the most effective means to disarm anorexic resistance while at the same time offering a rejuvenating relationship to the anorexic person who may be struggling with her symptoms. My point of view has developed over the course of a decade of clinical experience, and also has been influenced by the writings of Levenkron (26), Surrey (14), and Steiner-Adair (13).

At the extremes of the continuum of symptomatology there is less of a distinction between a traditional model and the one recommended. That is, when a patient has only a mild eating disorder, with little evidence of a pervasive preoccupation with anorexic symptoms, it may be entirely appropriate for the therapist to utilize the techniques of inquiry, exploration, and interpretation as the main tools of the treatment. In such circumstances, the decision as to how to proceed is more a question of underlying character structure than anything else. On the other hand, where an anorexic patient is extremely emaciated and displays real impairment in either her physical or cognitive functioning, the therapist's treatment approach is irrelevant. In all such cases, immediate hospitalization to restore the patient's general health is the first and foremost therapeutic task.

Many anorexic patients fall in between these two extremes when they are referred for outpatient individual psychotherapy. Here it is important to address the resistance as soon as possible in a forthright, authoritative, and friendly manner. First of all, this means that the therapist must indicate to the patient that he or she knows a great deal about anorexia and can understand what the patient is going through. For example, during the initial sessions, the therapist might ask the patient what kinds of food rituals she has developed and what are her "safe" foods and her "taboo" foods. The therapist can mention that he or she imagines that the patient has a magic number beyond which she must never gain, or can discuss in detail her particular method of purging. In addition, the therapist may remark about the patient's secret pleasure when she loses another pound, or wonder if she, like many anorexic patients, hears "voices" warning her about what to eat or how to act around food. The crucial point is that the therapist acquaint the patient with the fact that he or she is quite conversant with the patient's private anorexic world. In doing so, and without asking for such a description from the patient, the therapist communicates that he or she already possesses expert knowledge about anorexia and about the complexities of anorexic resistance. As a result, the patient is going to feel that she is faced with either a formidable adversary, a potentially empathic ally, or perhaps some combination of the two. In any case, she is likely to feel she has met someone who really can understand.

Throughout the beginning stages of treatment, the therapist must continually reinforce his or her role as expert on anorexia. The goal here is simultaneously to confront and assure the patient by showing her repeatedly that the therapist knows about her experience and about how her behavior is influenced by anorexic concerns. Moreover, neither silent denial, nor apparent compliance, nor sullen defiance will be enough to upset the treatment process. Slowly the patient will come to learn that she is not going to be able to ignore her therapist while remaining secretly preoccupied with anorexia.

Anorexic resistance is also undermined when the therapist is direct and confident about the patient's need for psychotherapy and about the process and goals of psychotherapy. By the former I mean it is necessary for the therapist to take the time to explain to the patient how she became anorexic and why anorexia has come to pervade her life. In most cases, it is possible to do this because the general function and course of the disorder tends to be similar in spite of multiple specific etiologies. Such an explanation is important because most anorexic patients entering treatment simply "feel" anorexic and have little idea how or why they came to be this way. Teaching anorexic patients about themselves helps to weaken denial and to enhance psychological sophistication, and it also offers a coherent framework of understanding. In contrast to other aspects of her life, an anorexic patient is usually intensely—although often secretly—interested in learning about her symptomatology. Straightforward explanations about anorexia and about therapy also tend to lessen resistance, because they explicitly contradict the patient's deeply held suspicion that treatment is essentially an exploitative process, intended only to trick the patient into becoming fat.

Consequently, at the outset the therapist should make an opportunity to explain that almost all anorexia begins with a normal diet. The diet becomes increasingly important to the patient because it feels so good to become thinner and thinner. In addition, the dieter is often complimented for her efforts and envied for her steadfastness and determination. However, as time goes on, others begin to worry or complain about the dieter and then try to force her to eat more. The dieter who becomes anorexic resists what others try to do about her eating habits. Instead, she redoubles her efforts and becomes increasingly preoccupied with food, weight, and dieting. This is because the diet began and persists not only for the sake of thinness, but also because it helped the anorexic patient in other ways. By concentrating on her food, she was able to ignore other things in her life that were causing her to worry and to feel bad about herself.

Thus, anorexia is more than a strict diet; it is a way to solve problems that seem insurmountable. And it continues and gets more and more intense because the anorexic patient cannot risk losing what she has gained by concentrating on her weight: the pride that goes with thinness and the chance to ignore the "other things" that seem so hard to face. In addition, eating less and less makes the anorexic patient think more and more about food because everyone's brain starts to fantasize about eating when it has been starved. However, this is very threatening to the anorexic patient, because it seems as if she could suddenly lose control and eat so much that she'll become fat. Consequently, she tries even harder to diet but never is able to feel truly secure; on the contrary, she usually feels increasingly endangered and unsafe. Everything in her experience begins to revolve around her anorexic thoughts and habits. Her relationships with others fade in importance, and she may forget altogether about the "other things" that once made her feel so bad. Eventually, the anorexic patient can feel completely overwhelmed by her eating disorder—controlled and often tormented by the very diet that once brought her such satisfaction and contentment.

This explanation of the onset and course of anorexia leads naturally to a discussion of psychotherapy's pitfalls and benefits, as well as to an explanation of how psychotherapy will work. Again, it is important that the therapist be explicit in order to undermine as much as possible the suspicions and assumptions closely held by the patient. Thus, the therapist informs the patient that she needs psychological help because she can't stop herself from wanting to be skinny and because her concerns about food, weight, and dieting have slowly taken over her life, making it impossible for her to do anything else.

In spite of the patient's deepest fears, the goals of psychotherapy will include helping her to gain enough weight to resume a normal life. This does not mean a fat life, but an opportunity to feel like other people who are not obsessed by food, weight, and dieting. An equally important goal will be to show her how frightened she is of the "other things" she does not want to face, and to teach her how to feel more confident about them.

The mention of weight need not and indeed should not be of any particular moment. Both therapist and patient know in advance that treatment has been initiated primarily because the patient has lost too much weight. Therefore, the goals of therapy include weight gain. Furthermore, if the therapist believes it is warranted, the patient's weight and medical condition will be monitored regularly by a physician; and if the patient's condition becomes dangerous to her health, she will be hospitalized to protect herself. On the other hand, when the patient begins to feel as if she is ready to gain some weight, the therapist will help her to formulate a meal plan that will enable her to gain slowly and steadily. The point is to introduce the idea that weight is firmly a part of the treatment plan, but by no means the only issue to be addressed. The patient will have the opportunity to choose when she wants to risk increasing her food consumption providing she does not place herself in physical danger.

Regarding the goals of therapy, it is helpful for the therapist to assume full responsibility for its course and conduct. In other words, the patient should be told that it will be the therapist's job to make the treatment work, and therefore its success or failure will not be dependent on her. Where it is possible to maintain this position, despite of the inherent countertransferential dangers, the patient's anorexic resistance is eroded. This is because the issue of control is nullified. Resistance depends in part on provocation, either real or imagined. When the therapist announces that he or she will not need the patient to be any particular way, there is less likelihood that a battle of wills or a power struggle will develop. In turn, the patient's anorexic resistance has little to resist. Furthermore, when the therapist assumes responsibility for the treatment, the patient is typically more willing to behave in a nonanorexic manner. This happens frequently during the course of a hospitalization. When the onus of responsibility or blame is removed, the patient can more easily risk changing her behavior because she does not need to feel guilty about her intentions or the consequences of her actions. In effect, when in dialogue with her symptoms and their rigid demandingness, it will be the hospital's or the therapist's fault—not hers—that she ate a different food or increased her calorie consumption. Finally, for the therapist to be responsible is to imply his willingness to care for the patient. Many anorexic patients enter treatment feeling like caretakers, in the sense that they have felt compelled to assume the burden of others and to be more responsive to others' needs than to their own. An opportunity simply to be nurtured and cared for instead of struggling to meet or resist the expectations of others can be extremely appealing, stimulating the patient's interest and curiosity in spite of her resistance.

In this approach to anorexic resistance, therapy is described in a manner that gives it concrete meaning and distinctive value. The therapist tells the patient that he or she is going to try and become a very important person in her life, because she needs a great deal of expert care to disentangle herself from anorexia. In effect, she has become totally enmeshed with and dependent upon her symptomatic patterns, yet they have not helped her to feel happy or secure. Therapy offers her a safer haven. Over time she will learn that it is more comfortable and more rewarding to depend on her therapeutic relationship than on her diet. And therapy will work because her therapist is not only safer than her symptoms but also more effective. That is, she will be taught how to really feel better about herself and her life in the everyday world because she will learn how to face and overcome those "other things" that anorexia has only helped her to avoid.

The effect and intention of this explanation, as well as what is said about the development of anorexia, is to startle, impress, and attract the patient—to be distinctive, relevant, and intriguing enough to draw her away from her symptoms and toward the therapeutic relationship. The general point is to undermine anorexic resistance not by attacking it, or by interpreting it, but by offering the patient a more desirable and rewarding alternative.

Telling patients about themselves and about their treatment should not comprise a single lecture during an initial appointment. Although there needs to be an "explanation" session or sessions, what has been described about the workings of psychotherapy in particular is actually a therapeutic model, to be implemented throughout the course of the treatment. Obviously, anorexic resistance does not break down all at once. The therapist must continually take responsibility for the work, demonstrate his or her expertise, and actually provide a safe haven for the patient.

Thus, the therapist's demonstration of expertise will certainly go beyond knowledge about anorexia. It may include such things as providing accurate information about calories, or helping the patient to conceptualize a term paper for school, or assisting her with a plan that will avoid conflict at Thanksgiving dinner. The therapist may answer her questions about sexual anatomy and the various positions for intercourse, or recommend a college for her to attend. In short, where possible, the therapist will give the patient the concrete benefit of his or her accumulated wisdom and abilities.

In order to provide a safe haven, the therapist will have to be prepared to really be nurturant, kindly, and caring in contradistinction to the patient's often tyrannical symptomatic needs. This includes the obvious—as, for example, to listen supportively and respectfully during sessions and to offer appropriate consolation or empathy when the patient is in turmoil. But it can and (depending on clinical circumstance, should) include more than the obvious. At times the therapist might speak to the patient's medical doctor to soften or alter the physician's behavior, or invite the patient's friend to a session to try and resolve a dispute. The therapist might touch the patient comfortingly when she is desperately upset, or call her up unannounced after a particularly stressful event. He or she might compliment the patient when she wears a new outfit, or even take her out to lunch when she needs special reassurance to try a new food. In other words, given the appropriate opportunity, the point is that the therapist conveys a genuine, nonexploitative concern for the anorexic person.

The therapeutic stance that I have described in this chapter differs from the traditional one not only in content but also in terms of the overall attitude that the therapist takes toward the treatment. Traditionally, the therapist is a relatively vague, preferably transferential medium, a vehicle through which the patient comes to better view her experience and understand her behavior. But here, the therapist is an active force, more realistic in manner and more exposed as a person. Rather than acting as a transferential medium, the therapist attempts to both direct and manage the treatment so as to undermine the resistance and demonstrate to the patient the concrete value of the therapeutic relationship.

At first, this can be a difficult, anxious undertaking for the traditionally trained therapist. It is a radical departure to try and take charge of the course of the treatment and to assume full responsibility for the changes that may or may not take place. Perhaps just as unsettling, it is a major shift to reveal one's knowledge and abilities about nonpsychotherapy issues and to go about actively nurturing a patient. In my experience, however, the anxiety that may result from attempting this approach is well worth the effort. Simply put, when maintained patiently and consistently, it frequently helps resolve the patient's anorexic resistance.

However, just as a more traditional approach to the treatment of anorexia will have particular consequences, so will the therapeutic stance I have described. When the therapist takes active charge of the therapy and assumes a more direct responsibility for the patient, he or she is likely to be faced with any number of relatively unfamiliar, complicated situations. For example, it may be advisable for the therapist to have sporadic or ongoing contact with a wide variety of people in the patient's life, such as parents, siblings, lovers, friends, and teachers. At these times, given the role of expert caretaker, the therapist may need to act as the patient's advocate, to persuade others of the wisdom of a decision that will affect the patient's life dramatically, or to provide very specific advice about what should or shouldn't be done for the patient. These are not typical therapeutic activities, insofar as they require the therapist to take forceful, definitive positions that may impinge on the behavior of many people. They can and will have a significant impact not only on the patient but on those who are close to her. As a result, the therapist may attain a central position within the network of the patient's interpersonal relationships. This will expose the therapist and the treatment process to an unknown, relatively uncontrollable amount of emotional reactivity, all of which may support (or possibly seriously undermine) the therapy.

Another consequence of this approach involves the nature of the interpersonal relationship that may evolve between patient and therapist. As anorexic resistance diminishes, the patient is likely to form a deeply dependent attachment to the therapist. Often this attachment will have a quality that is similar to the relationship the anorexic patient has had to her symptoms. That is, the patient may develop an idealized vision of her therapist's virtues; she may become excessively preoccupied—sometimes secretly so—with her therapist and the therapy; she may feel unable to do much of anything without the benefit of a session; and she may be convinced that she can't face any new problems in her life until she has had more therapy. In a manner that reflects her previous fears about anorexia, the patient may become terrified at the thought of losing her therapist. At times, this may drive her back into the eating disorder in an effort to assure herself of some measure of control over the therapy. The worst-case scenario here is therapeutic impasse—an interminable treatment that goes on and on because the end of therapy is experienced as too much like the loss of self.

The development of this kind of relationship poses a challenge for the therapist that is both similar and dissimilar to that of anorexic resistance. It is similar insofar as the therapeutic task is to help the patient understand that there is a more desirable alternative than remaining locked in psychotherapy—in other words, to persuade her to believe that it will be more rewarding for her to relate to her therapist and to her world in a different way. Specifically, the therapist needs to establish the conviction that foregoing a dependent attachment is not equivalent to being lost or abandoned, but instead makes possible mutually respectful, truly intimate relationships; and risking the demands, expectations, and vicissitudes of life is not tantamount to panic or failure, but rather can teach confidence, build self-definition, and restore a feeling of excitement for the future.

This is markedly dissimilar in that now the anorexic patient's focal relationship is human and interpersonal, not a rigidly prescribed network of rules, rituals, and solitary fantasies. The enemy is now a withdrawal of relational support, protection, and guidance, not the sudden loss of illusory self-sufficiency and the imposition of imagined fatness. This gives the therapist a decided advantage. The psychotherapy is now a two-person interaction. Consequently, the therapist has the opportunity to make beneficial use of the ongoing real relationship, in the here and now, to discuss subtle and not-so-subtle shifts in the treatment situation. Moreover, the therapist can share and invite discussion of his or her thoughts, feelings, and behaviors as they affect and are affected by the patient. In contrast to the relationship the patient had with her symptoms, the therapist-patient relationship is not a closed, inflexible self-reinforcing system. The therapist's patience and skillful work can therefore provide the therapeutic relationship with a chance to evolve over time, enabling the patient to grow out of her dependent attachment and experience a new and more satisfying form of relatedness.

REFERENCES

1. Garfinkel PE, Garner DM: Anorexia Nervosa: A Multidimensional Perspective. New York, Brunner/Mazel, 1982
2. Emmett SW: Theory and Treatment of Anorexia Nervosa and Bulimia: Biomedical, Sociocultural and Psychological Perspectives. New York, Brunner/Mazel, 1985
3. Johnson CL, Connors ME: The Etiology and Treatment of Bulimia Nervosa. New York, Basic Books, 1987

4. Bruch H: Eating Disorders: Obesity, Anorexia Nervosa and the Person Within. New York, Basic Books, 1973
5. Bruch H: Golden Cage: The Enigma of Anorexia Nervosa. New York, Vintage, 1979
6. Garner DM, Garfinkel PE: Handbook of Psychotherapy for Anorexia Nervosa and Bulimia. New York, Guilford, 1984
7. Gordon RA: Anorexia and Bulimia: Anatomy of a Social Epidemic. Oxford, England, Blackwell, 1990
8. Lasegue C: "De l'anorexie hysteriqué." Archive Générales de Médecine 21:385–403, 1873
9. Gull WW: Apepsia hysterica, anorexia nervosa. Transactions of the Clinical Society of London 7:22–28, 1874
10. Bell R: Holy Anorexia. Chicago, IL, University of Chicago Press, 1985
11. Brumberg JJ: Fasting Girls. Cambridge, MA, Harvard University Press, 1988
12. Gilligan C: In a Different Voice. Cambridge, MA, Harvard University Press, 1982
13. Steiner-Adair C: The body politic: normal female adolescent development and the development of eating disorders. J Am Acad Psychoanal 1:95–114, 1986
14. Surrey J: The "Self in Relation": A Theory of Women's Development (Works in Progress, No 13). Wellesley, MA, Stone Center Working Paper Series, 1984
15. Orbach S: Fat is a Feminist Issue. New York, Paddington Press, 1978
16. Sullivan HS: The Interpersonal Theory of Psychiatry. New York, WW Norton, 1953
17. Waller JV, Kaufman MR, Deutsch F: Anorexia nervosa: a psychosomatic entity. Psychosom Med 2:3–16, 1940
18. Thoma H: Anorexia Nervosa. New York, International Universities Press, 1967
19. Wilson CP: Fear of Being Fat. New York, Jason Aronson, 1983
20. Palazzoli M: Self-Starvation. London, Chaucer, 1974
21. Crisp AH: Anorexia Nervosa: Let Me Be. London, Academic, 1980
22. Minuchin S, Rosman BL, Baker L: Psychosomatic Families: Anorexia Nervosa in Context. Cambridge, MA, Harvard University Press, 1978
23. Allport G: Pattern and Growth in Personality. New York, Holt, Rinehart & Winston, 1961
24. Levine MP: Student Eating Disorders: Anorexia Nervosa and Bulimia. Washington, DC, National Educational Association, 1987
25. Johnson CL, Connors ME, Stuckey M: Short term treatment for bulimia. International Journal of Eating Disorders 2:199–208, 1983
26. Levenkron S: Treating and Overcoming Anorexia Nervosa. New York, Scribners, 1982
27. Garner DM, Bemis KM: A cognitive-behavioral approach to anorexia nervosa. Cognitive Therapy and Research 6:123–150, 1982
28. Goodsitt A: Self psychology and the treatment of anorexia nervosa, in Handbook of Psychotherapy for Anorexia Nervosa and Bulimia. Edited by Garner DM, Garfinkel PE. New York, Guilford, 1984, pp 55–82

11 Depressed Adolescents

Stephen Zaslow, M.D.

The therapist who encounters a depressed adolescent is faced with many tasks. These include creating rapport, establishing a diagnosis of the type of depression, assessing self-protective versus self-destructive trends (1), determining the likelihood of suicide risk (2), formulating dynamic, interpersonal, and intrafamilial issues (3), evaluating personality structure and the possibilities for regression to psychosis (4), and explicating a plan of treatment (5).

In this chapter I outline a typology of depression in adolescence, elaborate upon two specific types—the anaclitic and the superego depressions—and consider some psychodynamic and familial factors that contribute to the genesis and perpetuation of depression. I then share what it is like to explore these issues with adolescents and conclude by focusing on the individual psychotherapy that is the outcome of these efforts.

The following framework is a useful conceptual tool for therapists, adolescent patients, and their parents as they consider what depressed adolescents may be up against. This orientation owes much to the work of Anthony (6,7) and its explication to the work of Blatt (8), both of whose articles merit careful study. Others whose concepts are closely allied and interwoven include Feinstein (9) and Malmquist (10).

TYPOLOGY OF DEPRESSION IN ADOLESCENCE

1. Normal depression of adolescence—moodiness.
2. Reactive to current loss—including family stress.
3. Depressive equivalents—boredom, restlessness, nostalgia, stimulus-chasing, acting out.
4. Depressions secondary to character pathology (6).
5. Anaclitic depression (parallels Anthony's Type-1 depression) (6).
6. Superego depression (parallels Anthony's Type-2 depression [6] and Blatt's introjective depression [8]).
7. Depressions of borderline patients and psychotic patients—especially in those at risk for (familial) manic-depressive and schizophrenic illness.

Some elaboration will clarify the different types and identify, if not resolve, some areas of controversy. Moodiness has been called the normal depression of adolescence. It refers to sulking and irritability or "touchiness" to painful issues, including disappointment, loss, criticism. It is not to be found in DSM-III-R (11) as a formal diagnosis. But it is first on the list because it is so common, normative, average, and expected in adolescence, and because it can be mistaken, especially by parents, for more serious clinical syndromes. Assessing its presence, with teen and parents alike, permits the therapist to establish a general and nonthreatening area to explore and to relate to age-appropriate (or better) "phase-specific" issues and ego-capacities (12–17).

Depression reactive to current loss is the well-known "reactive depression." Loss is the most prominent precipitant of depression (18), be it loss of a sustaining, supportive, or gratifying relationship (19), loss of an ideal figure (including the parents of childhood or the body image of childhood), and loss of body part in injury or of bodily function in sickness, to mention a few. Some authors, including myself, stress that the "in-betweenness" of adolescence, between the worlds of childhood and adulthood, inevitably and inextricably carries loss as an inherent aspect of the adolescent condition. Anthony put it best, describing the adolescent's predicament: "caught between two worlds, he feels imprisoned, as it were, within a developmental phase" (7, p. 841). These are internal, endogenous shifts that might explain, in part, why adolescents are prone to moodiness and to the next category of depression, that of depressive equivalents.

Adolescent boredom, restlessness, nostalgia, stimulus-chasing, and acting out have been regarded as depressive equivalents, a concept akin to that of masked depression (20). The heuristic question—whether or not depressive equivalents substitute for or deny an underlying depression—may be argued theoretically and researched experimentally. From the clinician's standpoint, the concept of depressive equivalent, or masked depression, is useful in several ways. It draws attention to the possible development of a serious depression—either spontaneously, as life unfolds for these teenagers who are bored, restless, seeking the nostalgic old days, recklessly chasing stimuli, or variously acting out; or as their therapy unfolds and they develop commitment, object constancy, and the capacity to experience ambivalence and concern for others. The latter progression to depression is frequent in successful psychotherapy with this group of people. It may be relevant that the adolescents who are severely acting out—the alcohol and drug abusers, the repetitively delinquent—have rates of suicidal behavior that rival those of patients who are clinically depressed. Thus the clinician is well advised to anticipate these developments and to prepare patient and family, when indicated.

Depressions may be secondary to character pathology in two major respects. Inherently, many character disorders by their very nature are anhedonic, and thereby limit the experience of pleasure in various ways and to varying degrees. For example, an individual who is workaholic and compulsive is unable to relax, much less to experience free release and spontaneous fun. Those hampered by restrictive personality problems, be they obsessional, compulsive, schizoid, or passive-aggressive, may well find themselves depressed because they alienated others. This can happen because these patients are argumentative (people with obsessive-compulsive disorders), or are more isolated than they desire because people find them too distant and detached (people with schizoid disorders), or because they lose jobs or cannot advance in work situations (people with passive-aggressive disorder). The more introspective and psychologically-minded may become depressed as a result of their introspection, insightfully assuming responsibility for their predicaments, the situations that occasioned their reactive depressions. Where depression is part and parcel of the personality pattern, and especially where there is the self-reflective recognition that one's personality is deficient or skewed in areas of functioning and relatedness, this category is clinically useful. The clinician must pursue personality issues when faced with a patient for whose depression no obvious cause, loss, or stress suggests itself.

Anaclitic and superego depressions, respectively, will be discussed at length later in this chapter. Briefly, anaclitic depressions refer to those formed depressions that occur in persons who yearn for contact, cannot bear being alone, lack substantial object constancy, and primarily are fixated at the pre-Oedipal phase. The superego-depressive patients are those for whom guilt and criticism are primary experiences. They have internalized parental disapproval and are more approval-seeking than need-seeking. Each requires distinctly structured psychotherapy, which I will propose and explicate.

The depressions of patients who are borderline or psychotic are linked with their major character pathology, as are those of patients with character disorders. Anaclitic or superego types may occur, or the depression can be mixed or alternating with other clinical syndromes. Three things seem of particular importance here. First is the recognition of the borderline or psychotic diathesis and the structuring of a comprehensive treatment plan, usually multimodal, in specific response to the individual and his or her family's strengths and weaknesses. Second is the need to prepare for sudden regressions and decompensations in advance as part of the treatment plan and orientation of the patient and family. Third is the delicate task of exploring possible familial transmission, tracking its interpersonal, historical, and genetic pathways, and putting these data into perspective.

Anaclitic Depression

The adolescent with an anaclitic depression presents with object hunger, clinging dependency, anxious helplessness, and feelings of weakness and incompetence. He or she feels a sense of depletion and a fear of being unloved and unlovable. Hypochondriacal symptoms frequently exist, and psychosomatic illness can coexist with the vegetative disturbances of depression: disorders of appetite, sleep, concentration, sexuality, or activity-passivity balance. Cigarette smoking is common among these patients, as are conflicts over eating. They also frequently use stimulants and depressants.

Blatt (8) cites the psychoanalytic literature to delineate the dynamics of anaclitic depressions. He mentions salient points that merit summarizing. The level of object relations, internalization, and object representations determine in large measure a patient's vulnerability to depression. The issue of maintaining contact with the need-gratifying object is of paramount importance in depression. The processes of internalization described by Freud in 1917 (22) are, in part, an attempt to preserve contact with the object and to retain its love and approval. Anaclitic depression is consistent with Freud's use of the term to describe a type of object choice in which the mother is sought to soothe and provide comfort and care. Spitz and Wolf (21) described anaclitic depression occurring with severe deprivation around 6 to 8 months of age, when the infant begins to consolidate a differentiation between the primary need-gratifying person and others, but before the development of object constancy. Older anaclitic individuals are depressed because of narcissistic regression to a state of archaic regulation of self-esteem, which does not have the benefit of an introjected superego structure.

When these young people feel too depleted and give up efforts to reach out—when their sense of being overwhelmed and despairing has led to motor retardation and compromised their thought processes—incipient psychosis or suicidal activity become real possibilities. Even if these worrisome developments have not yet taken place, the astute clinician knows to anticipate regression when he or she treats anyone with an anaclitic depression. The phenomenology of the depression and the combination of defenses used are in themselves regressive, along both libidinal and ego-coping lines (30). It is the form and structure of the depression that captures our concern and shapes our therapeutic strategy every bit as much as do mental content and psychodynamics. The defensive repertoire of the anaclitic-depressive patient includes somatization, ego-regression (preoccupation with physical experience and oral gratification, and interpersonal dependency at a need-satisfying level), and denial of aggressive impulses. Object loss is a major trigger of many depressions. It can precipitate either an anaclitic or a superego depression, as can failed ideals, stalemated transactions and transitions, and awareness of deficits in personality functioning and their interpersonal consequences.

Case History: Karen

Karen was nearly 12 when her parents conferred about her one late September. They had hoped that a summer of family togetherness and camping would cure her doldrums, but it hadn't. A year earlier, her mother had returned to work full-time, and Karen's schoolwork had fallen off, within 3 months, from Bs to near-failing levels. Karen's teacher reported she didn't pay careful attention, concentrate well, or participate as she once did. When her parents asked her about this, Karen was vague, but said she thought the work too hard for her. Psychological tests revealed that she had a high average IQ, no evidence of learning disorder, themes of helplessness and anger, more involvement with the mother than the father figure, defensive wish fulfillment, and regression.

Karen's parents became involved with her schoolwork. Karen became whiny with them. She clung to and forced herself on her older sister. She avoided and forgot chores. She quit the after-school gymnastics program, saying it wasn't fun any longer. She complained that her friends no longer called her. It emerged that she had tried to buy and bribe their interest. She spent a lot of time in her room.

Historical review revealed no major trauma. When Karen was 3 months old, her mother was hospitalized for pneumonia. Her father and grandmother pitched in, and Karen showed no distress. When Karen was 2, she was operated on to correct an eye problem. She did not regress or act upset for long. A placid, somewhat passive child, Karen had always seemed happy. She enjoyed sports, family camping, and helping her mother in the kitchen. Aside from sleepovers at her grandmother's or at the homes of friends, there were no separations from home.

Karen's parents had explained to their daughters that their mother was returning to work because of economic necessity. Changes in family routine were anticipated and outlined. The girls had seemed to understand. In retrospect, the parents suspected they had overlooked Karen's hesitancy and qualms. We pursued the matter in a meeting with Karen. She stoutly denied that her mother's return to work made a difference! She externalized all problems. Anger flashed briefly when she insisted she *did* put her dishes in the dishwasher.

A cute, regular-featured girl, Karen seemed relaxed and comfortable in individual session. She moved and spoke slowly, and her speech was factual and ordinary. Signs of puberty were not in evidence. She did not abstract well. I judged her to be intelligent from an adequate fund of knowledge. Denial, externalization, and evasion prevented exploration of family or social matters. She quickly grew bored with my pursuit of her interest in sports and music. Happily, she preferred only to draw.

I saw Karen as an early adolescent girl with a moderately severe depression and a passive-dependent personality. The depression was of several origins:

1. *Normal depression of adolescence*—Karen's sulkiness and easy boredom reflect this dimension.
2. *Reaction to current loss*—Karen's regression was clearly related to the

return of her mother to full-time work and the resulting changes in family roles and schedules.

3. *Character depression*—Karen's immaturity and passive-dependence prevented her from maintaining friendships. She could not face or learn from this because of denial, externalizations, and wish-fulfilling escapism.

4. *Anaclitic depression*—Karen showed clinging dependency and helplessness, ego-regression (disordered concentration, work inhibition), and denial of aggression.

I will discuss Karen's treatment later in this chapter.

Superego Depression

Superego depression is suggested by feelings of guilt and self-recrimination, shame and self-criticism, along with the classical signs of depression. Adolescents with superego depression not only internalize their criticism and retroflex rage, but being adolescent, often do not spare others their barbs, judgments, and contempt. Frequently these teenagers are hypermoralistic, obsessional, and perfectionistic. Their defensive repertoire leans heavily toward intellectualization and rationalization, suppression and isolation of tender affect, displacement, reversal, and reaction formation. Interpersonally, they may be provocatively demanding and critical, or aloof and withdrawn, or involved and related. Their rigid superego functioning is related to the pattern of defenses used and indicates strong resistance to possible regression.

Again, Blatt (8) explains why such depressions (which he calls "introjective" depressions) are more stable and less apt to disintegrate in primitive directions than are anaclitic depressions. Again, his discussion merits summarizing. The object relations of the superego-depressive patient are at a more advanced level than those of the anaclitic-depressive patient. The patient seeks objects more for approval and acceptance than for need-gratification. Because object relations are at the later stages of separation-individuation, the superego-depressive patient is capable of more internalization, particularly of parent-aggressors. Such identification with the aggressor maintains internal contact with the object through the proclivity to assume responsibility and blame and to be hard and critical toward the self.

Blatt (8) asserts that the Oedipus complex resolves through internalizations that promote full separation from primary love objects, and foster the capacity to seek new and enduring relationships, not hypercathected repetition-compulsions.

Case History: Brian

His mother brought 14-year-old Brian to a session because he talked of wishing to be dead and of lacking any pleasure or meaning in his life. In addition, he raged often, taunted and hurt his younger brother, was socially isolated, and stayed in his room, uninterested in anything except TV and his computer.

After a series of arguments, Brian's friends had all left him. He allowed that he had been unreasonable and unforgiving to them, aggressive in wanting things done his way, and unable to admit when he was wrong. He suffered headaches but no other physical distress. Brian was of high intelligence, but his long-standing fine academic work was sliding downhill.

His parents had divorced when Brian was 3 and his brother 1. Neither parent had explained what happened at the time nor discussed it since! The boys' father moved to another state and remarried, and their mother remained single.

On interview, Brian presented as a tall, sturdy ramrod of a lad—a clean-cut preppie who showed dignity and composure. He related with respect and was both spontaneous and responsive. His speech was clear, direct, and relevant, and his affect was contained but appropriate to content. He thought little of himself and was ashamed and apologetic. He admitted past misbehavior (arguments, putdowns, etc.) but saw no other way to be: that was the way he was. There was no overt indication of psychosis. His dreams revealed profound isolation: for instance, he was on another planet, cut off from Earth, which he could see from afar. His wishing to be dead reflected hopelessness without actual or planned self-harm.

I saw Brian as an adolescent with a severe depressive reaction and an obsessive-compulsive personality disorder. The depression was of multiple origins:

1. *Normal depression of adolescence*—Even at his best, Brian was sullen and moody.
2. *Reaction to current loss*—Brian had lost all his friends and was socially isolated. Family stress was intense as a result of arguments and lack of friendly communication. This reactivated the unresolved loss of his father and the family structure of early childhood.
3. *Character depression*—Brian's was more accurately depression inherent in and secondary to character pathology. His obsessive-compulsiveness prevented relaxation, ease, and enjoyment and necessitated anhedonia, competitiveness, and deadly perfectionism. These qualities, expressed in argumentativeness and an inability to give in and admit he was wrong, had cost him his friends. His painful awareness of personality limitations and destructive patterns of relating resulted in hopelessness and lowered self-esteem and led him to feel helpless about changing his life.
4. *Superego depression*—Brian was as hard on himself as he was on others and felt guilt and self-depreciation.
5. *Borderline depression*—I suspected a borderline personality organization

because of Brian's rigid and uncompromising attitudes, history of rages and relative absence of tenderness, and dreams of extreme isolation.

I will discuss Brian's treatment later in this chapter.

Factors Predisposing to Depression in Adolescence

There are a number of losses, inherent in adolescence, which must be experienced, grieved, and overcome in normal development. Internal losses include the loss of the internalized parent images of childhood, the loss of the body image of childhood, and the loss of the childish capacity for free, imaginative, "ludic"(14) play. External changes, which parallel these inner losses, involve the break from childhood dependency upon parents, the actual changes in body structure during puberty, and the shifts in social roles as the adolescent tries on new identifications (23).

The adolescent's sense of time can be dreamily abstract and universally perspectivistic when he or she is free of conflict. Amidst intense conflict, the adolescent's perspective may be limited to the near and immediate future. Together with heightened narcissism (a regressive response to conflict), this can precipitate impatience and intolerance and create a dichotomous cognition (either/or), which prohibits consideration of options and predisposes the person to impulsive action.

Various family constellations foster weakness and exacerbate conflict in the adolescent. The enmeshed "symbiotic" family breeds helpless dependency while punishing independent strivings with the implicit or explicit threat of expulsion from the family. Separating or divorcing parents deprive adolescents of a secure home base from which to venture forth and to return for "refueling," even if they are able to maintain healthy individual relationships with their adolescent children. Parents may be unavailable to adolescents as needed sources of strength and perspective and may prematurely thrust them onto their own resources. Narcissistic parents who viewed children as intrusions into their orbit may be death-demanding (24). Parents who cannot experience and mirror pleasure will stifle their children and adolescents (25).

Sociocultural factors are obviously important. Peer group norms and group and gang behavior and turf conflicts can be primary threats to life and health, and psychological threats to security needs and value systems. Familial pressure for academic achievement may overwhelm a marginal student. Medical illness may threaten to channel a person into a limited, if not deviant social role. Endocrinopathies may prevent the expression of age-appropriate aggression and sexuality.

Hereditary factors merit consideration, especially with a family history of bipolar illness, of major depression, or of completed suicide. There is research (26) that indicates that there are family links to suicidal behavior that are independent of the genetic links to bipolar disorder, schizophrenia, and alcoholism, which are the psychiatric conditions most often connected with suicide. The idea that there may be a heritable suicidal diathesis impels us to look at the behavioral family history as closely as we look at the family history of illness.

Abuse of alcohol and/or drugs will diminish coping skills, dissolve inhibitions, increase denial and grandiosity, alter motivation, and predispose to acting out, depression, and suicidal behavior, to varying degrees.

Assessment of Suicide Risk

Valid points often made regarding suicidal behavior include the fact that the incidence of suicidal behavior is on the rise, especially among 15- to 24-year-olds. Although it knows no geographic, economic, or social barriers, its greatest increase is in the cohort of angry, impulsive, adolescent males (27). A large majority of persons who kill themselves have given definite clues or warnings of suicidal intent. A suicidal person, though very unhappy, is not necessarily mentally ill. Yet suicidal behavior is more frequent in the life histories of those diagnosed as depressed, schizophrenic, or with an anxiety disorder. Suicides can occur during periods of seeming improvement from despairing states—periods when the individual has the energy to put morbid thoughts and feelings into self-destructive action.

General and nonspecific warning signs include decline in school attendance and level of achievement; withdrawal from people; insomnia or oversleeping; intensely felt helplessness, anxiety, or guilt; drug or alcohol abuse; violent, disruptive interactions; an event, often a loss, that causes feelings of depression, worthlessness or failure; irrational behaviors that suggest mental illness; and preoccupation with suicide.

The urgent warning signs that suggest a person is beyond the thinking stages and actually planning death are the giving away of possessions; inappropriate, sudden, inexplicable elation; the development of a specific plan of suicide; and the breaking off of important relationships. A previous suicide attempt is ominous, and the risk factor is heightened if a family member has attempted or committed suicide. Extensive hopelessness and pessimism are the most significant common denominators in the depressed mental states of those who kill themselves (27,28).

The risk factor of suicide is reduced when the adolescent has someone to turn to for help, who cares if he lives or dies, and who can relate to and empathize with him or her as a separate person. Such a person can be internalized as a loving parental figure who sanctions and supports separation, individuation, ego strengthening and growth, and the formation of a unique identity. This is a complex of roles that the therapist of a depressed adolescent is challenged to fill.

PSYCHOTHERAPY

Interview Data

The psychotherapy of depressed adolescents is carried out during the phase of assessment and evaluation, the phase of sharing feedback with adolescent and parents, and the formally designated phase of psychotherapeutic treatment. Beginning with the initial interview, the therapist measures the impact of effectiveness of his or her participation. In assessing the adolescent's responsiveness, one must judge whether the adolescent's communication is becoming more or less integrated, syntactic, and meaningful. The therapist relies in large measure on his or her own feelings. Is there a sense of developing connection? Is there felt empathic resonance? Or is the adolescent being regarded from a distance, from a fog within the therapist's thinking? If so, is the therapist reacting to factors within the adolescent and subtly communicated—bizarreness, dissociations, distortions? When the therapist thinks he or she can understand and share the patient's concerns, and the adolescent's communication becomes more integrated, then there is a good chance that individual therapy will be helpful.

The therapist should test, as Havens has suggested (1), for human connectedness and for self-protectiveness. Therapists will also find these concepts helpful in thinking about suicide potential. Testing for human connectedness, for Havens, is an exercise in empathy, of placing oneself close to the patient and judging how large an empathic effort is required in order to connect. In addition to connecting by contagion of affect, he also recommends weighing psychological closeness by seeing if the therapist inwardly completes what the patient has started to say. Self-protectiveness is a measure of differentiation and integration. It is the ability to be the author of one's own thoughts, to express one's own ideas. It is the opposite of obedience and of negativism, and is related to personal freedom and independence. Havens thinks that perhaps it is best recognized intuitively, but it is also tested out by making statements of fact or possibility that explore the patient's need to agree with the examiner. Such comments stimulate fresh information or fantasies whenever the patient has a degree of independence.

Self-defeating behavior should be differentiated from self-destructive behavior. The self-defeating behaviors of neurotic inhibitions, constrictions, symptoms, and certain self-punitive activities do not raise the same alarm signal as do truly self-destructive behaviors. Situations viewed with urgency include:

1. *Addiction to drugs or alcohol.* Addictions must be diagnosed and made the prime focus of treatment, often in an inpatient setting.
2. *Extensive signs of a thought disorder.* When grandiosity, paranoia, per-

severation, and poverty of thinking are present, family support should be enlisted and hospitalization considered for a thorough medical, neurological, psychodiagnostic work-up and a trial of medication, along with psychotherapy. Easson's discussion (4) of the early signs of a thought disorder spotlights those adolescents who "can't think straight," "aren't with it," "can't maintain attention," "aren't well put together" and "don't know" what they are thinking, and thereby merit most careful diagnostic scrutiny.

3. *Family entrapment.* When parents' tyrannical demands, symbiotic needs, inflexible binds, destructive blaming or shaming, and enforced helplessness entrap the adolescent, the therapist should recommend family therapy or conjoint therapy alongside the teenager's individual therapy. Hospitalization is considered for the most serious cases.

4. *Previous suicide attempts by the patient.* Here the therapist shares his or her awareness with teenager and parents that such could happen again. It is important to share the responsibility for assessing this risk with patient and family—whether or not therapist and patient/family will continue to work together, whether or not hospitalization is required. The therapist lets the adolescent and his or her parents know that they can call at any time, and at home, and of any limits upon his or her availability (e.g., calls during therapy hours are not answered, unless the therapist has been alerted to expect a particular call).

5. Other factors that loom ominously and require exploration and evaluation of their impact on current functioning include a long-standing history of use of maladaptive coping mechanisms (e.g., running away from home, truancy, stealing); a history of being accident-prone; social isolation; a suspicion of past or present child abuse or incest; or homosexuality that is ego-dystonic to the adolescent and/or rejected by his or her parents.

At this juncture, let us assume that the therapist will be able to work with the seriously depressed adolescent, that medications and hospitalization are not required, and that family therapy will not be the primary therapy. What are the priorities of treatment?

Tasks of Therapy

In this urgent situation, the therapist's priorities are:

1. *To assist or ensure recompensation for the anaclitically depressed adolescent,* to mobilize coping capacities, to preserve functioning, and to prevent regression and withdrawal that may foster psychosis. Here, *attachment-building* is of central importance within the therapy.

2. *To rebuild or build the self-esteem of the adolescent with superego depression,* to diminish suffering, and to ease the self-destructive cycle of severe

depression and attacks upon the self, with the potential risk of suicide. Here, *superego work,* in the form of analysis and easing of primitive, punitive patterns, is of central importance.

Although people are not as simple and clear as these categories, the therapist who thinks and works along these lines has guidelines for structuring the therapy and explaining depressions clearly to adolescents and their families. One of the goals of therapy is to provide the missing ingredients to assist the adolescent in the tasks of separating and individuating. The missing ingredients vary with each individual's gaps and lacks and are provided by the person of the therapist in the interaction. Therapy is conceptualized as a bridging experience. Arieti and Bemporad (18) conceive the role of the therapist to be that of a dominant partner who gradually shifts and weans himself or herself to become a "merely" significant partner of the depressed patient. This makes good sense.

General Considerations in Working With Adolescents

In supervisory sessions, Schimel stressed that patients must first "prehend" that the therapist cares for them. This facilitates their attention to the information conveyed. The following remarks are directed to enable the therapist to be experienced as caring—without the drawbacks of a deadly seriousness, for which Schimel prescribed a sense of humor as the best antidote (29).

The weaker the ego of the adolescent, the more the therapist should remember (not neglect) the healthy areas of his or her personality and his or her positive interests. The therapist will be alert to the interpersonal and manipulative uses of depression but will be loathe to interpret or intellectualize such dynamics early on. He or she keeps in mind the multiple functions of depression, as a plea for attention, understanding, concession; as avoidance of new challenges, as with learned helplessness; as punishment in self-righteous martyrdom; and as masked or retroflexed rage. The therapist will delineate affects, seek contexts of interaction, demonstrate patterns of behavior, and leave the explication of intentionality to the adolescent. Nothing stings a teenager more than to have his or her mind read, or, in street parlance, to be "mind-fucked." Adolescents are keenly sensitive to experiences of psychological intrusion and can experience almost any comment about intentionality as a shaming experience (before the establishment of a firm working alliance and the building of emotional awareness and stability). They are less sensitive to comments on their dress, posture, or even their mental mechanisms.

Although the therapist will use direct, everyday language, it is suggested that he or she not challenge, confront, or eyeball the patient—at least not frequently or harshly. The adolescent chooses where to sit—opposite the therapist, or at an angle. The therapist's efforts are geared to creating an intermediate space, which will serve as a screen, upon which ideas and images about minds and persons will take shape. The concept of mind includes cognition, affect, values, and will. It is essential to try to create a relatedness in which the therapist and the patient can both play as they think, feel, and communicate seriously, increasingly free to be observed, commented upon, and speculated about by each other. (See Schimel [30] for a masterly presentation of this art.) The therapeutic aim that becomes apparent to the adolescent over time is working together to develop an understanding of his or her emotional life as well as that of others.

Working With Depressed Adolescents

The therapist must listen very actively to depressed adolescents, and must pace interventions to their level of ego-strength—their apperception, concentration, ideation, and activity-passivity balance. He or she must be careful not to proceed too rapidly—not to overwhelm, overestimate, overimpress, nor in other ways take over. The goal is to seek to establish conditions that favor mutual exploration. The therapist can check observations by giving feedback piecemeal, progressing from parts to wholes. It is valuable to discuss a wide ranging hodgepodge of data, for integration and synthesis will emerge gradually; it is also best to usually avoid the pressure of a single focus or task assignment, except those involved in listening and attending together.

It is essential to preserve any functioning defense of the depressed adolescent. For instance, if the patient discusses matters from an intellectualized or rationalized approach, the therapist can usually join with him or her, hoping to confirm his or her thoughtfulness, perhaps letting loose an idea or two as trial balloons. This sets the stage for inquiry about missing elements (e.g., feelings, fantasy, action, contexts). With compulsive Don Juanism, the therapist may acknowledge the patient's attractiveness to the opposite sex and inquire about methods of introduction and seduction. With compulsive bodybuilders, gymnasts, or dancers, the therapist might applaud their concern with health, strength, grace, and self preservation, wonder if they pursue these concerns in other areas of living, and leave ideas about need for control, vulnerability to attack, narcissistic demands, and fears of passivity for a later discussion. With a compulsive reader, the therapist might approve the adolescent's efforts to improve the life of the mind, the ability to amuse and interest oneself and not succumb to loneliness, and so on.

Relationship and Attachment-Building
With Anaclitically Depressed Adolescents

In working with regressed adolescents, attention must be paid not only to areas of the self-system (regulation of security operations and self-esteem) but also to the patient's significant others and his or her physical objects. The latter, by their enduring structure and usefulness, give a sense of order and permanence to the patient's world.

Attending to these areas builds a relationship, provides shared and contrasting human experiences, and allows a breadth of communication in dialogue, in which prejudice and predilections, sensibilities and insensitivities, categories and confusions can be discussed without the oppressive focus being on the adolescent or on the shared immediate therapeutic interchange.

This sort of relationship-building is crucial in the treatment of the anaclitically depressed adolescent. The therapist seeks to convey closeness and connection through tones, posture, affects, and sympathies. In discussing such topics as politics, art, and sports, when asked, the therapist does not hesitate to state his or her opinions and values, even if they differ from the adolescent's. The aim is to establish close contact and to ride with it when possible. There are, of course, dangers in appearing to accept the patient totally and indiscriminately, without limits, and of seeming to encourage the idealization of the analyst. Initially it is preferable to sugarcoat the pill (31) to accentuate the positive, while acknowledging the negatives and using them to guide the search for the missing ingredients of self-esteem or personality, the missing experiences in interpersonal relationships, the failed idols or ideals, or the transitions that were not negotiated successfully. The therapist accepts the patient's dependency and hopes that he or she will prove reliable and dependable enough for the patient. Fears of engulfment and the dangers of magical symbiotic fusion may emerge later on with anaclitically depressed patients; but early on, they seem to take hope and heart from a giving relationship. They do not tolerate therapeutic distance or challenge well, both of which prematurely force them to differentiate themselves, thus intensifying the dreaded state of emotional isolation and the feeling of abandonment.

> Karen's therapy began with drawing. Over the first few months, her drawing progressed from idealized figures and themes (flowers, princesses) to sad and weak figures (Bambi, lost cats, and stray dogs). I offered that perhaps she had felt like a princess and was protected until her mother went to work full-time; then maybe she had felt more like a little puppy who had lost her mother. She responded with a flicker of recognition and drew some more. We discussed affects and situations within the metaphors of the drawing (31,32). She spoke of friends who had rebuffed her, and permitted me to verbalize her hurt and anger. She asked why friends didn't return her calls. I wondered if they had different interests. We talked about that possibility.

> After about 4 months of therapy, her parents reported that Karen was getting feisty and developing a sense of humor. She said she didn't care about what her friends did. Unasked, she made a meal for her parents. Her grades improved.

Karen then brought in matters to discuss with me. We spent sessions deciding on the pattern of her sneakerlaces and the colors of nail polish. She styled her hair and chose lipstick. She tried out for cheerleading and made a couple of new friends. The next summer's camping trip was enjoyed by the whole family. Her parents said that Karen had regained her old self and had grown. They credited her with new assertiveness and initiative. Karen was happy and ready to leave therapy.

Treating the Superego-Depressive Adolescent

The therapist's approach to the superego-depressive adolescent relies less upon affective and more upon cognitive connections. Although the therapist is trying to be in the patient's corner, the therapist is more matter-of-fact or dispassionate in tone. He or she often will grunt or otherwise mirror feelings of anger or offense but will not stop there. The therapist will seek out the nature of the insult or the offense and will dig out the extent of the rage and the nature of the fantasized retaliation. He or she will muse aloud about how hard the patient is on others and himself or herself. The therapist will notice and map out the patient's value system, in which a mistake, error, or failure deserves and demands condemnation, punishment, and suffering.

The superego analysis continues beyond demonstrating the primitive, punitive value system. What are the origins of these sharply critical values? How did the patient get to be so hard, puritanical, and inflexible? The therapist becomes actively curious about crime and punishment, error and guilt, blaming and shaming within the family. Are there put-down artists at home? Are there trials and assessed punishments, formally, as with deprivations and "grounding," or on an *ad hoc* basis of emotional withdrawal, spitefulness, character assassination? Are the parents charging, judging, sentencing, and executing upon the children, or is there an extended family system in which anyone and everyone is free—even obligated—to spot, highlight, and attack any wrong behavior?

When there are vicious cycles of blame and shame, I intervene, not unlike the way Bergman (33) deals with the issue in family therapy:

> One thing I do in treatment is forbid blaming and name calling. I explain to couples that hurt precedes anger, and anger precedes attack and blame. It thus becomes incumbent on both partners to practice verbalizing their hurt and anger before the anger sours into blame and attack. I continue to point out that once hurt has turned to anger and then to blame and attack, the receiving partner immediately shuts down and becomes deaf to the attack's complaints. (p. 37)

The therapist must also focus on the negative intrapsychic consequences of self-blame, self-criticism, and self-attack, which result in lowered self-esteem and the false notion that something positive results from extended self-flagellation. It is preferable that the patient spot the process of self-attack and seek to understand the issues and interactions that triggered it. Then he or she can consider his degree of responsibility or guilt, making amends, and/or trying to change a pattern of behavior.

Eyebrows are raised at the patient's critical, intolerant attitudes toward others. The therapist seeks to understand what they have done to deserve the patient's contempt and scorn. The patient's pride in his or her criticalness is noted, as is his or her pride in self-righteousness. The therapist underlines how being right seems to be the patient's ultimate goal. Or is it proving the other to be wrong? If the therapist goes about this superego analysis in a dispassionate way, not succumbing to the temptation to countercriticize and counterattack these punitive patterns, the adolescent is often extremely helpful in delineating aspects of the superego system and in agreement about how it operates and functions. The therapist appreciates the patient's agreement and cooperation. After a while, however, he or she may develop the nagging suspicion that patient compliance is at work. So the therapist may suggest, "Gosh, I seem to be right an awful lot of the time." Does the patient feel this to be at his or her expense? Does the patient feel the therapist is acting too smart or being a know-it-all? Putting him or her down? On a therapeutic high horse?

In response to such questions a surprising number of these moralistic adolescents reveal a high degree of tolerance and compassion for the therapist. They say that the therapist is doing the job and doing it well, that they know he or she means them no harm and is acting in their best interests. They spare the therapist any attack. The therapist then openly acknowledges and values their understanding and appreciation. He or she does not try to provoke criticism or anger—only to offer the possibility that it will be welcome and accepted, if presented, and that the therapist will respect it and seek to put it into perspective. He or she respects patients' opinions and reactions, offers opportunity for rebuttal or confirmation in any difference of opinion. In offering him- or herself as a potential target for criticism, the therapist is ready to endure, absorb, and bear it when it arises. Perhaps then some of the magical omnipotence patients attach to aggressive attacks and destructive fantasies will be neutralized. The therapist almost certainly will not overreact or fail to react, as might the parents. Thus therapy may become a corrective emotional experience.

> Brian's treatment proceeded in stages. In a joint meeting with Brian and his mother, I elicited information about his parents' separation and divorce. I interpreted that Brian was suffering not only from deprivation of relationships (lack of contact with friends and with his father) but also from deprivation of information (regarding family history and relationships). Brian's mother responded

positively and was able to share historical detail with Brian, including the parents' conspiracy of protective silence and her own long locked-in pain. This opened old wounds, and made possible a path of healing through newfound intimacy between mother and son. Family stress diminished.

In individual sessions, I explained various sources of depression. I sympathetically and systematically exposed and analyzed superego pathology (per the previous discussion). I talked of Brian's criticalness and punitiveness—especially how hard he was on himself, how he believed he deserved to suffer and to be punished for his toughness on others, how he no longer merited enjoyment or any pleasure, according to his impossible standards. He was his own judge, jury, and jailer! Gradual repetition of these themes in dialogue led to easing of his superego depression and to forging a collaborative exploration of his obsessive-compulsive personality structure. Borderline phenomena did not emerge. I provided, in this phase, emotional reactivity, support for positive striving, encouragement, commiseration and sympathy for his losses, and appreciation of his felt despair and of his gallows humor. I maintained an implicit attitude of hopefulness and expectation that better solutions to his dilemmas would emerge in time.

As Brian gradually relinquished vicious self-attacks, the sharpness of his attacks on his brother eased. He began to concentrate better upon schoolwork, and decided that success at school would be his first goal. If he could do well enough, perhaps he could transfer to a private school, where he could start afresh with a new crowd. His concentration, perceptiveness, and insight sharpened. Humor emerged, initially gallows humor amidst despair, later sarcastic and bitter humor as depression waned. He grew to enjoy reading, to enjoy *thinking!* He reached out to a few family members, and these relationships partly eased his loneliness and isolation. He began to train his body, for instance, biking for hours, in the hopes of being ready to join a team. He thought about his parent's personalities and tried out a number of possible confrontations, in imagination and in therapy. In fact, he did not confront his actual parents. Rather, he avoided them less and related more on terms that he found comfortable. He was well over depression and was much less rigid and tight when he applied to, was accepted by, and eventually left for private school away from his hometown.

SELECTED ISSUES IN PSYCHOTHERAPY

A consideration of the developmental progression from early to middle and then late adolescence will explain why anaclitic depressions are more frequent among early adolescents and superego ("introjective") depressions among older adolescents. This chapter also provides a framework for considering the therapist's use of self and his or her approaches to certain issues and polarities that are universal for adolescents, and that arise during the course of intensive psychotherapy with anaclitic- and superego-depressed adolescents, as with other teenagers.

Lewis (31) traced the maturation of structural-dynamic constellations from early to middle to late adolescence. Early adolescents are more immature, and use the more primitive defenses of splitting, projection, and omnipotent denial to ward off the experience of persecutory anxiety. In this paranoid-schizoid position, "the ego strives to introject the good and to project the bad" (32, p. 13) as a rule, although more complicated dynamic shifts can occur. "Splitting is linked with increasing idealization of the ideal object, in order to keep it far apart from the persecutory object and to make it impervious to harm" (32, p. 14). Thus, good and bad are widely split, and thinking tends to the dichotomous. The outlook is largely one of externalization, and early adolescents are highly distractible, impulsive, and action-oriented. It is with the passage of time and the presence of good-enough caregivers that they mature into more deliberate, thoughtful, and controlled late adolescents. The older adolescent is more apt to have attained the capacity for the depressive position, in which he or she can feel anxiety about the loss of good objects, to feel disappointment, guilt, and mourning after loss, and to make reparative efforts. Older adolescents relate to people more as whole objects, who contain both good and bad elements and who stir up ambivalent responses, which contain mixtures of love and hate, approval and disapproval, satisfaction and dissatisfaction. They are more capable of caring for others as full human beings, a capacity that underlies the development of intimacy in human relations.

A useful personal style of doing psychotherapy is as dialogue, as near to ordinary conversation as possible. It is give-and-take, nonregressive talk. As a therapist, one does not generally want the adolescent to experience therapy as needing the patient to adapt himself or herself to the therapist. Nor should the therapist lead the patient to expect that talk or performing is necessary in order for the therapist to be comfortable or effective. The therapist raises questions sparingly and makes few overt demands. This style is favorable for the treatment of the anaclitically depressed patient because it is responsive to the budding inclination of the patient and thereby affirms initiative and autonomy in an accepting and undemanding context. It is preferable to comment, guess, offer possibilities, and make statements that invite responses, particularly with more differentiated adolescents, including those who have superego depression. This style lessens the person's sense that his or her pathology, illness, or problem is being scrutinized microscopically, and heightens the sense that therapist and patient are working and exploring together.

Sullivan's dictum that we are all more simply human than otherwise gives rise to an attitude, perhaps an existential perspective, on listening to adolescents' Sturm und Drang: "That's the way people are. That's life." The therapist analyzes the significant others of the adolescent, in a way that suits the patient's level of comprehension. We needn't fall into the "good guys, bad guys" trap (which either anaclitic- or superego-depressive patients might set forth), nor imagine that we can reform the human race. A sense of humor within the analyst is a remarkable antidote for excessive seriousness.

As with other adolescent patients, the therapist of the depressive adolescent pursues core issues, conflicts, relationships, transitions, efforts made, and gains and losses. The therapist feels for the deeper shifts of transference-countertransference tides beneath the surface ripples. The therapist repeats, remembers, and works through with the patient in the middle phase, by using reassurance, judicious confrontation, and challenge.

The therapist notices and validates the adolescent's maturation during treatment, including his or her bodily, sexual, mental, social, and moral development. In the final phase of treatment, it is important to acknowledge that the patient has expanded his or her horizons and has honed many skills in the treatment room and the outside world. The therapist ends treatment without implying that this is the end of the patient's and therapist's shared world or of the patient's problems. Nor does the therapist become more perfectionistic during termination, seeking every last manifestation or this and that. He or she lets go . . . and remains available for a phone call, chat, or another round of therapy. The adolescent knows he or she needn't get sick or in trouble to be seen again.

The therapist's attitude toward his or her lapses and errors may have quite as much to do with the adolescent's gain in the capacity to accept himself or herself, as do the therapist's abilities to understand the adolescent. It is easy to be comfortable in this area when one has much experience in making mistakes! It is always easier to admit the mistakes we know we make than to be told about new ones. I have been impressed by the gratitude and trust that is built when errors are acknowledged, when the affects that attend them are borne (including the simple apology, "I'm sorry"), and when errors can be put into a meaningful perspective in the therapist's own psychology and in relation to the ongoing dyadic interplay. The therapist's comfort and tolerance in this area leads the patient, eventually, to become a more tolerant and comfortable participant in mutual discovery. With time, patience, and luck, this ability extends. Thus the patient can go easier when recognizing and confronting his or her own mistakes or those of others, and when being confronted by others.

Often the experience of self-acceptance and self-forgiveness, as modeled by the therapist, evokes a realization of and a contrast with parental and self-condemnation. The patient's response is almost immediately palpable. At other times, the therapist is perceived as being self-excusing or avoiding the deserved criticism and guilt. These negative transferences require attention and analysis. Obviously, the mixed and ambivalent response to self-disclosure is more common, and both currents will flow in time.

SUMMARY

Specific ways of adapting to the anaclitic-depressive patient's need for emotional connection and support and the superego-depressive patient's need for understanding and easing of punitive dynamisms are carried out within the wider framework of psychotherapeutic approaches with adolescents. When a therapist can be relatively free of anxiety, accepting and tolerant of his or her own lapses and errors, then he or she can maintain perspective and can accept and respect the adolescent. The therapist then offers the adolescent a new and corrective emotional experience: a relationship that is for him or her—but not symbiotic, exploitative, or idealizing; a relationship that is clear, direct, and real—but not shaming, blaming, evaluative, or conditional on performance.

The therapist's lack of anxiety permits patients 1) to reveal, test out, and differentiate themselves—by question, discussion, argument, dialogue, and various internal monologues and trials of action, and 2) to take in and make their own those aspects of the therapist's character they find to be of value. Gradually patients relinquish distancing and competitiveness. Compulsive blaming and shaming attacks give way to an appreciation of possibilities and options as either-or and all-or-nothing orientations recede. Independence and autonomy arise from the choice of valid goals and the capacity for self-assertion. In the process, relationships with parents often become more respectful and sympathetic and less defensive. Relaxation of family tensions can help to heal old wounds and lead to new family equilibrium.

REFERENCES

1. Havens LL: The need for tests of normal functioning in the psychiatric interview. Am J Psychiatry 141:1208–1211, 1964
2. Maltsberger JT: Suicidal Risk: The Formulation of Clinical Judgment. New York, New York University Press, 1986
3. Weltner J: Matchmaking: choosing the appropriate therapy for families at various levels of pathology, in Handbook of Adolescents and Family Therapy. Edited by Mirkin MP, Koman SL. New York, Gardner Press, 1985, pp 39–50
4. Easson WM: The early manifestations of adolescent thought disorder. J Clin Psychiatry 469–475, 1979
5. Frances A, Clarkin J, Perry S: Differential Therapeutics in Psychiatry: The Art and Science of Treatment Selection. New York, Brunner/Mazel, 1984
6. Anthony EJ: Depression in adolescence: a psychodynamic approach to nosology, in The Adolescent and Mood Disturbance. Edited by Golombek, H Garfinkel BD. New York, International Universities Press, 1983, pp 151–165
7. Anthony EJ: Two contrasting types of adolescent depression and their treatment. J Am Psychoanal Assoc 18:841–859, 1970

8. Blatt SJ: Levels of object representation in anaclitic and introjective depression, in The Psychoanalytic Study of the Child, Vol 29. Edited by Eissler RR, Freud A, Kris M, et al. New Haven, Yale University Press, 1974, pp 107–157

9. Feinstein S: Adolescent depression, in Depression and Human Existence. Edited by Anthony EJ, Benedek T. Boston, Little, Brown, 1975, pp 317–336

10. Malmquist C: Depression in childhood and adolescence. N Engl J Med 284:887–893, 955–961, 1971

11. American Psychiatric Association: Diagnostic and Statistical Manual of Mental Disorders, 3rd Edition, Revised. Washington, DC, American Psychiatric Association, 1987

12. Erikson E: Childhood and Society. New York, Norton, 1963

13. Flavell J: The Developmental Psychology of Jean Piaget. Princeton, NJ, Van Nostrand, 1963

14. Sarnoff C: Psychotherapeutic Strategies in Late Latency through Early Adolescence. Northvale, NJ, Jason Aronson, 1987

15. Sullivan HS: The Interpersonal Theory of Psychiatry. New York, Norton, 1953

16. Blos P: The second individuation process in adolescence. Psychoanal Study Child 22:162–186, 1967

17. Zaslow SL: The threat from below. Contemporary Psychoanalysis 6:361–366, 1970

18. Arieti S, Bemporad J: Severe and Mild Depression. New York, Basic Books, 1978

19. Semrad EV: Teaching communication. See Semrad EV: The Heart of a Therapist. Edited by Rako S, Mazer H. New York, Jason Aronson, 1980

20. Lesse S: Masked Depression. New York, Jason Aronson, 1974

21. Spitz RA, Wolf KM: Anaclitic depression. Psychoanal Study Child 2:313–342, 1946

22. Freud A: Normality and Pathology in Childhood. New York, International Universities Press, 1965

23. Blos P: On Adolescence. Glencoe, IL, Free Press, 1963

24. Sabbath JC: The suicidal adolescent: the expendable child. J Am Acad Child Psychiatry 8:272–289, 1969

25. Shapiro R: Separation-individuation and the compulsion to repeat. Contemporary Psychoanalysis 21:297–308, 1985

26. Roy A: Genetics and suicidal behavior, in Suicide Among Youth: Perspectives on Risk and Prevention. Edited by Pfeffer C. Washington, DC, American Psychiatric Press, 1989, pp 165–183

27. Shaffer D: Suicide in childhood and early adolescence. J Child Psychol Psychiatry 15:275–291, 1974

28. Beck AT, Steer RA, Kovacs M, et al: Hopelessness and eventual suicide: a 10-year study of patients hospitalized with suicidal ideation. Am J Psychiatry 142:559–563, 1985

29. Schimel JS: The function of wit and humor in psychoanalysis. J Am Acad Psychoanal 6:369–379, 1978

30. Schimel JS: Psychotherapy with adolescents: the art of interpretation. Annals of Adolescent Psychiatry 13:178–187, 1986

31. Lewis O: The depressive position and middle adolescence: developmental and therapeutic considerations. J Am Acad Psychoanal 17:377–395, 1989

32. Segal H: An Introduction to the Work of Melanie Klein. London, Heinemann, 1964
33. Bergman JS: Fishing for Barracuda: Pragmatics of Brief Systemic Therapy. New York, WW Norton, 1985

12 Older Adolescents With Academic Achievement Problems

Margaret Crastnopol, Ph.D.

In a particularly sensitive account of his work with a young underachieving female patient, Masud Khan wrote:

> The first task was to make the girl recognize and realize that her "madness," her "being crazy" . . . her being *empty-headed,* were all masks protecting something she valued deeply in herself, to which she herself had lost the clues. It is not difficult to interpret symptoms . . . but how does one interpret "something" to a person, of which that person has no memory, indeed, *can* have no memory. (1, p. 123)

These observations capture the complexity of treating the constellation of problems that are the subject of this chapter, the academic difficulties of the older adolescent. Scholastic achievement problems are actually quite prevalent—an estimated 25% of all school-age children do more poorly in school than their intellectual abilities would permit (2). Not surprisingly, academic underachievement is a prime presenting complaint leading adolescents to seek psychotherapeutic aid (3). Scholastic endeavors are, after all, one of the first major arenas where the child succeeds or fails largely "under his or her own steam." The youngster must function more independently than ever before, in a setting apart from the family. He or she must carve out a new niche in an environment that may be radically different from that of his or her family life. Often, the child may face this challenge under quite adverse circumstances: These factors include family and neighborhood value systems that minimize the importance or utility of formal education; policies and attitudes in the schools that are insensitive or unsympathetic to the needs of minority, disadvantaged, and first-generation American youth; and peer-group attitudes that stamp scholastic success as unmanly for the boys or unfeminine for the girls (2).

High school and college in particular are seen as rehearsals for the adult tasks of establishing a vocation or career and charting a meaningful life course for the future. Doing well in school therefore takes on enormous significance for the adolescent's efforts to construct a viable self-identity—both for the present and for the adult "self-to-be."

Scholastic achievement has been defined and operationalized in many different ways. In their remarkably comprehensive study, *The Psychology of Underachievement: Differential Diagnosis and Differential Treatment,* Mandel and Marcus (4) define achievement as "accomplishment at a level consistent with one's abilities and expected by reasonable and proper internal and external standards" (p. 4). Following this definition, "underachievement" is performance below one's expected aptitude level. Questions immediately arise as to how we determine an individual's aptitude, and which measures of performance are the most relevant to consider? In the past, social science researchers relied on the subjective impressions of teachers, parents, and other significant figures to make these judgments. Recent studies adopt more so-called "objective" criteria and formulas to operationalize these concepts. For example, standardized measures of intellectual capacity are deemed suitable to gauge a student's aptitude, and scores on achievement tests or grade point averages represent his or her performance level.

These approaches are useful for accumulating data relevant to general educational and psychological principles. They provide a shorthand useful for analyzing and interpreting trends in various student subgroups. However, they don't fully suit the needs of the practicing clinician, who must adapt his or her view to reflect the specific concerns of the troubled teenager referred for individualized help. The clinician must listen very closely to the personal lexicon of the patient in order to learn what constitutes "academic accomplishment" for him or her. How does the patient think about his or her capacities and performance to date? How do others in the teenager's interpersonal world view them? What is the impact of their attitudes on the adolescent's self-evaluation? What conflicts exist among the expectations held by the patient, his or her parents, teachers, peer group, etc.? The child of average intellect and a poor school record will have a qualitatively different type of problem if he or she comes from a long.line of college professors than if his family background is working class.

Also of great significance is the particular form of academic "bête noire" faced by a given youngster. What exactly *caused* the low grade point average? Does the student panic during exams? Is he or she phobic of attending school (2)? Some students have subjects that are particular sore spots such as English, mathematics, or the sciences; others have trouble with a specific learning task irrespective of subject matter (e.g., memorization, paper writing, studying for tests, etc.). Certain educational settings may pose a problem for the student's ability to perform—while one student excels in an individualized tutorial, another might feel too much "on the spot" in such a situation.

It seems valuable to view an academic problem as being a behavioral sign that reflects something meaningful about the adolescent's psyche. The same overt manifestation may have very different meanings and etiologies from one student to the next (4). It is important for the clinician to help the patient decipher the multiple meanings inherent in his or her own performance difficulties. By making these meanings accessible to the patient's "rational" mind—"making the unconscious, conscious," as it were—we enable the patient to choose more satisfying approaches to the self-educative process.

When we think of achievement problems, we automatically focus on the situation in which the youngster's accomplishments fail to meet his or her supposed potential. However, the so-called "overachiever" or the truly "gifted" adolescent may also have significant problems associated with his or her achievement level (5,6,7). The highly talented adolescent could become anxious about excessive academic expectations placed on him or her by virtue of his or her apparent potential.

For the purposes of this chapter, however, we will confine ourselves to the far more prevalent problem of underachievement. We will further restrict our focus to that type of underachievement for which there are no known or suspected organic causes. We are not, therefore, talking about the adolescent whose educational difficulties are caused by biological disease or deficit. Excluded from consideration here is the adolescent diagnosed as "learning disabled." Such youngsters, who comprise about 10% to 20% of the population (3) have a presumed perceptual/neurological deficit that can be diagnosed via neuropsychological assessment. Problems of this nature require highly specialized psychoeducational techniques, which are beyond the intended scope of the present chapter. (It should be mentioned that the underachievement associated with a learning disability, particularly when the disability has gone undiagnosed, is very likely to have profound psychological consequences for the individual. Intensive psychotherapy can be quite valuable—in conjunction with the appropriate remedial work—in addressing and working through the frustration and shame associated with the disability and its effects on learning.)

The variables that contribute to a student's inability to perform are multiple. One study cited by Sugar (3) found that social and emotional problems accounted for only 25% of underachievement. Retarded or borderline intelligence explained 38%, speech and hearing disorders accounted for 10%, and the remaining 25% were due to developmental and learning difficulties (i.e., those presumably involving neurological or other organic deficits). External aspects of the student's environment also have a sizable impact on scholastic achievement. The quality and stability of one's family life as well as the nature of the school system itself both color the student's capacity to function well academically (6).

From large-scale studies we get a descriptive overview of the general phenomenon of underachievement. According to Mandel and Marcus (4) children and adolescents who underachieve are a notably heterogeneous group. Many studies support the image of the underachiever as highly anxious, impulsive, dependent, hostile, and socially maladjusted. The underachiever has a less favorable and less mature self-concept and is more self-critical than other youngsters. He or she has a greater fear of failure and is likely to behave in a passive-aggressive manner vis-à-vis the parents (2). Interestingly, it appears that there are no consistent differences in overall intelligence level between "normal" adolescents who achieve versus those who do not achieve academically.

It seems that low achievement is related to certain childrearing practices (4). Specifically, authoritarian as opposed to democratic/participatory practices on the part of fathers have been associated with lower achievement in children. Greater permissiveness and uncertainty on the part of mothers were linked with lower-achieving offspring. Some studies indicated that underachievers came from families where the parents had a lower occupational status; however, such findings are inconsistently reported (4). Also equivocal are the results with respect to ethnic and racial variables (4).

Overall, the following factors are considered salient in contributing to underachievement (4): low motivation or interest; an overweening wish for peer acceptance; a school's authoritarianism; the student's poor study habits; and parental overprotectiveness, authoritarianism, or overpermissiveness. Factors related to the student's own personality include obsessive-compulsive characteristics, impulsivity, hypercompetitiveness, an inability to persevere, and unfavorable temperamental traits (4).

In general, one is impressed with the variety and complexity of the phenomenon of underachievement. Each student is affected by a different set of factors, and each one interprets his or her inner and outer realities in a unique way.

PSYCHODYNAMIC FORMULATIONS CONCERNING ACADEMIC UNDERACHIEVEMENT

Attempts to conceptualize the psychological underpinnings of scholastic underachievement are much influenced by the theoretical bent of the writer. A skilled and sensitive clinician, however, will have much to offer in helping to articulate the emotional life of the patient, regardless of the metapsychological language used for the purpose.

In an early paper on the subject, Klein (8) takes a classically psychoanalytic perspective on what he terms "school problems." He notes that the ego may become restricted due to the child's wish to avoid a task at which he or she might possibly fail. The goal is to forestall a narcissistic hurt or humiliation. This injury is, in his view, linked to an earlier sense of inferiority whose genesis is Oedipal-phase envy of the father's penis. Especially bright students might avoid applying themselves to studying because of the narcissistic need to succeed without expending effort. Equally disturbing may be an ego inhibition due to "superego harshness." The student develops excessive expectations for acceptable performance, and feels ever dissatisfied with his or her accomplishments. This leads, of course, to a profound sense of worthlessness and despair. Klein notes that the inability to tolerate relative failure can be further aggravated during adolescence as such failure becomes "sexualized." A specific precipitating event (such as a homosexual experience) can trigger the intrapsychic conflict between id and superego that results in school avoidance and failure.

Klein's clinical observations are as astute now as they were in 1949. Obviously, his theoretical formulations center on psychosexual issues and his treatment stance and techniques appear to be quite classically interpretive and "neutral." Although the psychosexual orientation certainly appears to be on target in some of his examples, it is evident that many of the psychoemotional situations described revolve more around issues of identity, self-esteem, and autonomy than on the vicissitudes of libidinal and aggressive energies.

A very different perspective is presented in a collection of more recent psychoanalytic studies on late adolescence edited by Brockman (9). The editor refers to the problem of underachievement as a "learning inhibition" rather than "school failure," the term used by Klein. This choice in itself suggests a more optimistic, health-oriented attitude on the clinician's part. In the view of Brockman and his contributors Sklansky and Hoit, underachievement is the result of a normative learning process that has gone astray. Through appropriate psychotherapeutic intervention, the psychological factors that interfere with that learning process can be understood and resolved.

Sklansky (10) feels that learning inhibitions reflect a "maladaptive striving for autonomy" (p. 213). This is a major difficulty for the children of high-achieving parents, who pressure their children to excel academically. The teenager consciously wishes to gratify the parent's wishes, but unconsciously perceives a vital threat to his or her newly emerging autonomy. The result is an unconscious rebellion against the very goal the youngster is consciously pursuing. Sklansky also points out that a child's love of learning can sometimes be compromised by a parent's overzealous and misguided efforts to steer the child toward the parent's own intellectual interests.

Hoit (11) deals with the particular difficulty of being unable to bring academic work to completion. In this case, the teenager may deny defensively that there is any difficulty in functioning. He or she may rationalize dilatory, lax behavior as being the product of an attempt to experiment or "find oneself." In actuality, the paralysis stems from a breakdown in the "work-ego," which in turn may reflect a developmental arrest at a pre-Oedipal level. The cohesiveness of the self may be threatened, with the patient desperately in need of a selfobject relationship that could help provide the missing internal structures. Adequate academic performance is heavily reliant upon the sense of security and vitality that accompanies a cohesive self.

A more finely honed analysis of adolescent underachievement is provided by Baker (12). Writing about failure among college students, Baker notes that academic performance is greatly influenced by the student's ability to tolerate small blows to one's self-esteem. These blows naturally occur in the course of making the errors that go along with teaching oneself something new. She or he must also be able to set realistic goals and have the inner resourcefulness needed to carry them out. If a student possesses an "unmodified grandiose self" (p. 450), she or he may make such perfectionistic demands on the self that his or her self-esteem plummets, leading to further weakening or fragmentation of the self.

Another possible difficulty occurs when the individual lacks the ability to soothe him- or herself due to the failure of appropriately idealizing selfobject relationships in childhood. As a result, tension may mount uncontrollably during the studying process, making it impossible for the student to concentrate and absorb new information. When the adolescent has failed to internalize necessary strengths from early selfobject relationships, he or she may remain overly reliant on direct guidance from teachers and advisers.

The explanations for adolescent underachievement offered by Sklansky, Hoit, and Baker (10–12) are certainly quite cogent. However, they presuppose that the clinician is familiar with and receptive to ego psychology, self psychology, and their tenets. Such formulations are useful to the practicing therapist in that they attempt to capture the flavor of the adolescent's inner emotional experience as he or she struggles with achievement issues. Inherent in these explanations (and perhaps not explicit enough) are implications for how the clinician can go about treating the troubled adolescent. For instance, if the difficulty is a failure to internalize the self-soothing capacity necessary for arduous study, presumably good therapeutic results will follow if the clinician focuses on temporarily providing that selfobject function as a means of enabling the patient to acquire this capability internally.

In their own extensive research efforts, Mandel and Marcus (4) have developed a differential diagnostic scheme for distinguishing among five personality types of underachievers. The first type, the Overanxious Disorder underachiever, is marked by a chronic state of excessive anxiety and apprehensiveness. Such a person is desperately in need of approval, but may be unconsciously ambivalent about achieving. For example, achievement may intrapsychically represent submission to an admired authority figure who is unconsciously resented.

The Conduct Disorder underachiever (4) engages in persistent unacceptable or antisocial behavior. He or she is impulsive, unable to tolerate frustration, and eager for immediate gratification. Such an adolescent may overtly "act out" by flouting school rules and regulations. Of primary importance is the individual's need to acquire and maintain power over others. Cheating in class, lying to school authorities, and/or drug abuse are to be expected.

The third type described by Mandel and Marcus (4) is the Academic Problem underachiever. This individual is someone whose intellectual abilities seem quite adequate. Nevertheless, he or she consistently (and seemingly inexplicably) obtains failing grades. There is no apparent mental, emotional, or developmental disorder (i.e., organic, neurological) to explain the poor performance. This diagnostic group comprises 40% to 50% of all nonachieving adolescents, a very high proportion of the total group. These individuals appear to be lazy or unmotivated though they express the intention to do better when confronted with their failure. Apart from the underachievement symptom, they seem quite well-adjusted. Other aspects of their poor performance are procrastination, difficulty completing school work, and a tendency to give up easily when challenged. The Academic Problem underachiever is said to be strongly (though unconsciously) driven by a wish to avoid achievement at all costs. Fundamentally, this individual is afraid of encouraging the expectations of others to do well, for fear that he or she will incur onerous responsibility for future success.

The Identity Disorder underachiever (4) is caught up in the throes of trying to integrate disparate aspects of the self. All his or her emotional energy is invested in this search. As a result, conventional scholastic endeavors fall by the wayside. The adolescent become confused, anxious, and depressed as a function of this overarching personal quest.

The fifth and final type described by these authors (4) is the Oppositional Defiant Disorder underachiever. The hallmark of this type is an ongoing overt rebellion against the "establishment." Such a student is similar in some ways to the Conduct Disorder underachiever, except that his or her defiance is directed specifically against older authority figures. Students in this group behave in a "counterdependent" fashion. Through their contrariness and obstinacy, they are misguidedly trying to establish their sense of independence.

The diagnostic scheme offered by Mandel and Marcus (4) highlights some highly relevant and diverse personality patterns associated with underachievement in school. It is of unquestionable importance for the clinician to be able to place the adolescent's symptomatic underachievement in the context of an overall personality structure that supports that symptom. The danger is that the patient may become stereotyped instead of being seen as the complex, unique, multifaceted individual she or he is. To their credit, Mandel and Marcus note the existence of overlap in their diagnostic entities, with one individual potentially possessing traits of more than one underachievement group. Other factors impinging on a student's life—discord in the parental relationship, for example—are given their due. Nonetheless, the clinician must be careful to remain attuned to the sometimes contradictory nuances of the patient's intrapsychic life, to comprehend fully his or her psychological state.

THERAPEUTIC APPROACHES TO
ADOLESCENTS WHO UNDERACHIEVE

In the past, psychodynamically oriented therapists have tended to treat their underachieving adolescent patients according to the same overall principles that would be applicable to any patient at a given psychological level (neurotic, borderline, or what have you). Writers in recent decades have shown a greater appreciation for the specific therapeutic needs of the adolescent as opposed to the child or adult patient. In his well-known book *The Fragile Alliance* (13), Meeks maintains that the main function of the therapeutic alliance with the teenager is to foster an understanding of his or her *current* behavior and its relationship to his or her ongoing inner life. The rational, conscious aspects of the relationship should be stressed rather than focusing on genetic determinants of a symptom or on unconscious, irrational, or deeply primitive aspects of the personality. The therapist must move to limit acting out behavior that interferes with the therapy. Otherwise, she or he must maintain a "neutral, sympathetic, but inquiring attitude" (p. 87). The therapist must beware of being judgmental or overcontrolling toward the teenager. He or she must be alert to the adolescent's tendency to criticize and demean him- or herself.

Meeks's views (13) have much to offer in working with the underachieving adolescent. Especially sound are his observations about the potential value of the therapeutic relationship itself as a tool for promoting the patient's ability to explore his or her achievement difficulties. It seems questionable, however, to suggest that it is beyond the capacity of most teenage patients to benefit from a deeper look at their more primitive unconscious life. It is important to consider in this regard that the particular phase of adolescence in which we find the patient will influence how readily he or she can delve into the complexities of his or her inner life. It seems quite likely that with proper tact and timing, active interpretation of unconscious currents *can* be both enlightening and tolerable for many teenage patients.

Psychoanalytic clinicians such as Sklansky, Hoit, and Baker (10–12) seem to agree with much of Meeks's (13) general approach toward treating adolescents. Of course, their interpretations emanate from their particular frames of reference—ego psychology, self psychology, separation-individuation theory, or whatever. It is unclear from their accounts how "deeply" they pitch their interpretations or how much primitive or genetic material they cover.

What *is* evident is the emphasis on a careful and close exploration of the patient's current life circumstances. Often used as a vehicle for this work is an analysis of the patient-therapist relationship itself, including both "transferential" and "realistic" components. I will discuss this aspect of treatment further in a later section.

To round off the discussion of treatment approaches, we turn to Mandel and Marcus's work (4). Reviewing the relevant research literature, they report that a wide range of techniques have been tried over the years. These included group counseling, one-to-one behavioral therapy sessions (using such methods as individual goal setting and reinforcement procedures), rational-emotive counseling, group therapy combined with a didactic presentation about underachievement itself, and so on. In general, the results were quite inconclusive, with some studies showing positive outcomes and others not.

Based on their own theorizing and research, Mandel and Marcus (4) have developed one-to-one treatment approaches for individuals in each of their five diagnostic categories. For the Overanxious Disorder underachiever, the authors suggest any one of the panoply of anxiety-reduction methods—including behavioral relaxation, study skills training, cognitive restructuring, or psychodynamically oriented supportive counseling. The goal is to reduce the student's anxiety level to make it more conducive for academic performance. It is essential in treating the Conduct Disorder underachiever that the therapist recognize a characteristic "bind" created by the patient. As part of this bind, the therapist will experience a subtle pressure to go along with the student's antisocial ways in order to preserve the therapeutic alliance. The alternative is to confront the patient actively about the consequences of his or her comportment—but this would certainly jeopardize the therapist's rapport with the patient. The clinician should explain and demonstrate to the patient that this bind is unproductive for them both. The student must be helped to find more acceptable means of meeting his or her needs and managing his or her impulses.

The Identity Disorder student in treatment must be helped to develop and shore up his or her self-concept, rather than be pushed prematurely to choose a personal direction. A client-centered, nondirective approach is considered most effective toward achieving this aim. Curiously, no specific treatment suggestions are offered for the Oppositional Disorder student. Presumably, the patient's ongoing rebelliousness and anger would be the focus of an intensive treatment effort.

Treatment of the Academic Problem underachiever receives the most methodical attention from Mandel and Marcus (4). The hallmark of their approach is the use of different kinds of "constructive confrontation." It may be recalled that this student constantly rationalizes and externalizes his or her academic failure in order to avoid acknowledging the underlying wish *not* to succeed. The therapeutic strategy recommended is 1) to help the patient select a goal for academic improvement, 2) to isolate and explicate particular problem areas and then refute any excuses offered by the student, and 3) to link up each excuse with its likely consequences. Finally the patient is asked to find a solution to the problem and to act on it. The methods described by Mandel and Marcus are eclectic ones, drawing their principles and techniques from psychodynamic as well as cognitive social learning theory perspectives. Their ecumenical framework for dealing with underachievement is wise, given the multifaceted nature of the problem itself. Moreover, they do draw on well-established and justly revered psychotherapeutic techniques in developing their own methods. For instance, it is striking how much similarity there is between their treatment of the Academic Disorder student and the psychotherapeutic procedures described by members of the interpersonal school (compare Sullivan [14]). As in interpersonal psychoanalysis, the patient's difficulties are conceptualized as "problems in living," and careful attention is paid to the student's conscious explanations for his or her seeming contradictory behavior. The unconscious forces at play are thereby "demystified," and emphasis is placed on analyzing the maladaptive defenses that operate to protect the student's self-esteem. Denied and dissociated information about the patient's "student self" is gathered and mutually acknowledged by patient and therapist.

Mandel and Marcus's treatment approaches (4) seem quite apropos for a patient whose academic difficulty is the primary problem. However, often an adolescent is referred for treatment when underachievement is part of a constellation of intrapsychic, interpersonal, and social problems. In this case, a focal approach on academic behavior per se may miss the mark. The therapist must be prepared for a longer, more thoroughgoing exploration of the patient's character structure as well as his or her inner world. Ideally, the therapist should be capable of applying specific techniques for dealing with underachievement (such as those described by Mandel and Marcus) while doing so in the context of an ongoing, intensive psychotherapeutic effort. In this way clinicians can optimally address the changing emotional needs of the adolescents under their care.

THE EDUCATIONAL ENVIRONMENT AND ADJUNCTIVE TREATMENT STRATEGIES

A teenager's efforts to function well academically are obviously much influenced by the sociocultural milieu. In the opinion of some professionals (3,6), our society is relatively apathetic regarding the importance of establishing and maintaining high standards of intellectual accomplishment. Many aspects of the educational system itself militate against a student's performing optimally. These include the tendency to pass children on from grade to grade irrespective of true readiness; the presence of teachers who are insensitive, unsympathetic, or untrained in dealing with psychoeducational difficulties; and poor communication between teachers and parents regarding the child's growth and development in school. Scarce resources also can prevent educational institutions from providing each individual with the particular type of educational experience most in harmony with his or her learning style.

Nonetheless, the school setting has considerable potential for being a valuable adjunct to the psychotherapy of a troubled adolescent. Some clinicians even suggest that the right teacher or classroom climate could ameliorate the effects of maladaptive parental influences on the growing child. With a junior high or high school underachiever, it is often beneficial for the therapist to act as a liaison between the student and school personnel. As an example, Berkovitz (15) cites the situation where an anxious, impulsive student could be inadvertently provoked into an aggressive outburst by an overworked or harassed teacher. The teacher might then overreact to the teenager's hostility, resulting in punitive action taken toward the student by school authorities (e.g., expulsion from school). If the clinician working with that student foresaw the potential for such a vicious cycle, he or she could contact school personnel in advance to advise them of the student's psychological state of mind. The unfortunate outcome could be short-circuited by engaging the teacher's understanding and cooperation in helping the student control his or her temper.

Berkovitz outlines guidelines for collaborative effort between therapist and teacher (15). The therapist is encouraged to get the parents' perspective on the school's role in the student's difficulties (though this view must be interpreted cautiously, considering the likelihood of some bias in the parents' report). A face-to-face conference between therapist and school authorities is recommended, on condition of the adolescent's acceptance and approval of such a meeting. The therapist should be discreet in choosing what information to impart to the school, out of concern for the patient's privacy. He or she should listen closely to the teachers' impressions, in order to gain a clear, well-rounded picture of the student's social as well as scholastic functioning.

Berkovitz advocates involving the school more than most clinicians apparently would (15). Perhaps other therapists fear seeming overly mistrustful or intrusive if they were to seek the school's report instead of relying on that of the student alone.

Perhaps the wisest course of action is to encourage and educate the student to report on the school experience as accurately as possible. She or he could be urged to have individual conferences with significant teachers or advisers, in order to clarify any confusion or misconceptions about the ways in which she or he exacerbates the achievement problems. Only if the therapist—or the teenager—felt that the intervention of a third party was necessary would the clinician take on the role of liaison. The impact of such an intervention on the patient-therapist relationship would also have to be open for scrutiny in the course of the psychotherapeutic work.

Furthermore, the therapist should be alert to the potential benefits of arranging for the troubled teenager to obtain academic tutoring. One example of using tutoring in tandem with psychotherapy is found in Khan's discussion

(1) (as I mentioned previously) in which the therapist explicitly prescribed and insisted upon his patient's compliance with a regimen of individual home tutoring. In this instance the therapist's action was part and parcel of his efforts to shore up the boundaries of a very fragile self; however, tutoring can be of just as much or more value with the higher functioning patient.

The therapist might recommend a tutor at the outset of treatment, or wait until a point where the intrapsychic blocks have presumably eased sufficiently to permit new, uninhibited learning to occur. The tutoring should ideally be begun in one of the problem areas which, though difficult for the student, is more accessible to him or her, in the hope that the student will be able to make some visible, rapid gains. This would provide an early sense of accomplishment that would reward his or her efforts and break the vicious cycle of failure and shame. The clinician would have to be alert to the significance of the recommendation for tutoring from the student's perspective. Is it likely to deepen his or her anxiety and intensify the sense of inadequacy? Or could it enable the student to understand that the problem—as a psychoeducational difficulty and not an inborn "defect"—is eminently open to change? The clinician should foster the latter viewpoint to enhance the optimism and motivation of the troubled teenager (as well as encouraging frustrated teachers and parents).

When a tutor *is* used adjunctively, the therapist can better concentrate his or her efforts on the psychodynamic aspects of the academic problem. The clinician should try to include the teenager in the decision as to whether or not there will be direct contact between therapist and tutor. Often the student has a strong preference in this regard. The therapist does well to take this view under consideration, whether or not it can be directly heeded. For a more extended discussion of the complexities of using tutoring as an adjunct to therapy, the reader is referred to an earlier paper by Opperman (16).

Similar questions arise as to the level of participation the parents should have in the treatment of the adolescent underachiever. The college-age teenager may live away from home and have much less contact with the parents than during high school. The teenager may have sought and entered treatment on his or her own. Thus motivated to resolve the academic problem, she or he may be able to do so with a minimum of parental involvement. The treatment itself can become part of the overall thrust toward separation-individuation that often occurs at this time. For the high school student it may be more appropriate and more desirable to encourage the participation of the parents.

As I mentioned previously, parents are far from impartial in their efforts to help their underachieving adolescent. Their input into the situation will be highly colored by whatever parent-child dynamics already contributed to their offspring's achievement-related conflicts. It is therefore necessary for the clinician to exercise the utmost care in determining whether and in what way the parents could be brought into the treatment efforts. This tack might be taken, for example, when the clinician feels that the parents are unresponsive to efforts on the teenager's part to change maladaptive aspects of their interpersonal relationships. When improvement in the symptom is itself gradual, it may be especially valuable to meet with the parents in order to enhance their trust in the overall direction the therapy is taking. It is best if parents can be made to feel that they are partners in the treatment process. To this end a conference between parents and therapist may be arranged. As always, a meeting of this nature must be planned with the involvement (if not necessarily the approval) of the adolescent. If the teenager is not to be present at the meeting, all the salient features of the conversation should be conveyed to him or her by the therapist.

A CURRENT PSYCHOANALYTIC PERSPECTIVE ON INTENSIVE PSYCHOTHERAPY WITH THE UNDERACHIEVING ADOLESCENT

The psychotherapist doing long-term, intensive work usually does not have the luxury of focusing solely on the patient's academic performance. The work with a given teenager should endeavor to simultaneously cover all aspects of the patient's world—from failing grades, to fights with peers or parents, to job-hunting for part-time work—not to mention the inevitable task of exploring his or her burgeoning sexuality. It is valuable, therefore, to keep in mind that the aim is to treat the whole person, whose strengths and weaknesses form a coherent (if complex) unit. The therapist must demonstrate a respect for the patient's defensive structure and for the symptoms themselves, which may well be fulfilling a self-protective function. It is helpful if one can (wholeheartedly) take the stance that academic success is not the one and only benchmark of someone's personal worth, and that underachievement is not in itself heinous or shameful. In fact, the patient may need to forego (if necessary) any concrete improvements in achievement for a while in order to do the self-exploration so vital to the therapeutic endeavor. By helping the adolescent adopt an attitude of self-tolerance and patience, the therapist can create a "holding environment" (17) that places "on hold" self-defeating attitudes and behaviors to which the troubled adolescent is prone.

The purpose of this approach is to reframe the visible phenomenon of academic underachievement by uncovering its significance as an expression of unrecognized aspects of the patient's self. As the therapy unfolds, the therapist ponders what the learning inhibition is telling him or her about the patient's intrapsychic, interpersonal, and sociocultural worlds. How much of this is the patient capable of understanding? How can this self-knowledge be put into practice in order to obviate the necessity for the learning block itself?

The daily "manifest content" of the treatment sessions will come from the patient's articulation of his or her life experiences. Special attention will be paid to achievement-related phenomena, especially during the periods in treatment when this issue is on the proverbial "tip of the patient's tongue." The teenager will recount his or her efforts to study and learn, reactions to the parents' perceived attitudes toward academic endeavors, and responses to the educational environment. The therapist will try to discover the patient's own specific attitudes, behaviors, and inner emotional states during the various stages of the learning process. What goes on *internally* as the teenager reads, memorizes, takes notes, writes papers, and so on?

In the meantime, the therapist must keep a sharp eye out for manifestations of thinking difficulties. Because we are not dealing here with a situation of diagnosable learning disability, we are looking for cognitive signs of anxiety or defenses against it. Memory lapses, problems in logical thinking or coherence, loss of concentration, distractibility, tendencies toward concrete as opposed to abstract conceptualization—all are potential indicators of the very kind of cognitive interference that might be impeding the educational process. When these signs crop up in therapy there is an unparalleled opportunity for the therapist to recreate the unconscious scenario that contributes to the learning inhibition.

In following up the conscious manifestations of cognitive difficulties, we are attempting to help the patient conceptualize and explicate his or her inner world and its painful affective components. This involves building a comprehensive picture of how the patient's parents, siblings, and influential "others" were internalized to form both gratifying and hostile inner images or "introjects" (17). The therapist may ask the adolescent to describe moods, fantasies, or interior dialogues that accompany the various stages of academic striving. It may then be possible, for instance, to trace back who it actually was who "always said" that the only worthy achievement was one that was accomplished without working too hard.

Behind a superficially supportive and warm relationship with the parents may be an implicit demand to produce academically (on pain of ostracism, if not death). This is particularly true of families imbued with the "humanistic, accepting" values of the 1960s and 1970s. The parents may have *intellectually* grasped the importance of allowing a child to realize his or her own inner bent, academically oriented or not; however, they may not have sufficiently "worked through" their own deeply ingrained narcissistic need to have a son or daughter who will scale the academic heights.

As the therapy progresses, the therapist and patient gradually develop a scheme of the individual's internal object relational world. Particular attention is paid to exploring the hostile introjects that attack, deprecate, or shame the patient. What fantasied internal dangers does the patient face if he or she should achieve too little, or too much—humiliation? abandonment? impersonal or unloving adulation? narcissistic engulfment? It may become evident that the teenager is provoking attacks from these inner objects; or the patient may be avoiding scholastic responsibilities in order to quash possible attack. It is often necessary to spell out concretely the implications of this work for the patient's life. The teenager is likely to respond to the developing interpretive perspective with, "Well great, so what do I do with this? How is it supposed to help me?" Here the therapist may wish to put aside an interpretive stance to answer directly that the important thing is to catch oneself while one is in the midst of the object relational conflict. When one notices any of the characteristic signs of an inner struggle—edginess, confusion, feeling "bummed out" or whatever—one must pause and consider what inner situation might have become stimulated by some external occurrence. It may come as a novel idea to the adolescent that he or she can directly influence his or her own emotional equilibrium by consciously trying to make contact with (and work on) his or her ongoing inner life.

A consideration of the patient's actual interpersonal world is also part and parcel of a sound treatment approach. How are the figures in the patient's world jibing with—or contradicting his or her internal objects or images? Here it is important to facilitate the articulation of *how*, for instance, one's teacher is being unfair, or how one's parents might be giving conflicting messages about the significance of school grades. It is also critical to help the teenager recognize how he or she is projecting intrapsychic reality onto external situations. Does the teacher who assigns "too much" material for a given exam really "want" the student to fail, as he or she may believe? Or is this notion a reflection of the patient's unconscious sense that the internalized maternal object demands perfection but is eager to find fault? If it is the latter, then the patient can be helped to reconstruct the probable genesis of her mother's (and now the maternal object's) harshness. Perhaps the mother viewed her daughter as a narcissistic extension of herself (expecting her to redo and rectify the mother's own imperfect academic career), but at the same time she unconsciously might not want to be outshone. This would provide the kind of explanation that may help a teenager rethink her own inner ambivalence regarding success. Here also, a careful and explicit working through is extremely important. (The clinician might ask, "Is it really necessary to disparage oneself simply because one was inadvertently taught to do so by a frustrated, depressed mother?")

A central component of this mode of treatment approach is a careful exploration of the therapeutic relationship itself. Psychotherapy is, after all, similar to school in that it is an institution whose goal is ultimately to develop oneself further, to enhance one's understanding, and to better one's life. Often the teenager experiences therapy as one more test of his or her ability to perform and achieve—but here the prized outcome is the nebulous achievement of psychological "health." The adolescent may feel as if his or her "performance" in treatment is being monitored and graded—as indeed it often is by overeager or cost-conscious parents. This feeling may then be projected onto the therapist, as if the therapist were also evaluating his or her "progress" in therapy and reacting to the patient with either approval and appreciation or disapproval and rejection. (Unfortunately, there may be more than a grain of truth in this, at times.)

The therapist can make use of this analogy between therapy and schoolwork by being attuned to the patient's immediate, ongoing experience of being in therapy (18,19). Patient and therapist are sharing in a process that each can directly experience. The therapist should feel free and even be bold in asking the patient how he or she felt on hearing a particular interpretation from the therapist. Perhaps it seemed "too smart," making the patient feel inferior to the therapist and reducing his or her faith in the patient's own contributions to the therapeutic endeavor. The clinician should watch closely for patterns in the patient's reactions to interventions. These patterns provide a strong, immediate basis on which to build an understanding of the patient's intrapsychic world. With the aid of self-understanding and self-analysis, the therapist can help the patient determine to what extent he or she may be projecting troublesome internal objects onto the therapist. The clinician should also use careful judgment in deciding when to bring reality to bear in the interpretation. It is beneficial at times to concur with the patient's accurate perceptions of the therapist's attitudes. For instance, it is not unusual for the troubled teenager to become preoccupied with the therapist's own level of achievement (e.g., as attested to by the diplomas on the office wall) and then to become convinced that the therapist could not possibly respect or like someone as unsuccessful as the patient. The therapist can acknowledge the importance of academic accomplishment in his or her own life while simultaneously conveying an acceptance of the patient for who he or she is, "with or without credentials."

Initially, the therapist may expect the patient to relate to him or her transferentially according to whatever ways authorities are customarily dealt with by the patient. This is clearly of value in helping develop a sense of the patient's inner expectations or images of others. There will also, however, be the unique aspects of one's "real" relation to the patient. The therapist strives to be the "good enough parent," both idealizable and fallible, who is needed for this particular patient at this juncture in time. It is crucial to maintain an appreciation of the unconscious obstructive forces within the patient without absolving him or her of responsibility for any conscious or intentionally self-defeating behavior.

The psychotherapy as an analogue for other learning/performance situations will provide ample opportunity for the patient to demonstrate characteristic "resistances to achievement." Deterrents to progress in therapy can be carefully analyzed both to facilitate the treatment process and as an example of defenses against achievement-related anxieties. If, for example, the patient comes in one day with "nothing to say," the therapist can gently probe the meaning of that statement—is the patient afraid that what is on his or her mind will not be the "right" thing? Or perhaps he or she is concerned that using too much initiative will allow the therapist to be lazy and unforthcoming (i.e., it would let the therapist forfeit his or her role as nurturer and guide). These beliefs would be significant clues to the patient's experience of his or her parents, and in turn they would reflect importantly on his or her intrapsychic reality. There is a special impact in talking about "me and you" for the adolescent—it makes the inner life feel more consequential and worthy of attention if the therapist can become involved in this intimate way.

In the early stages of treatment the therapist may wish to develop and capitalize on the good overt rapport that comes with a positively toned transference. The patient may be briefly allowed to idealize the therapist and model him- or herself after the clinician with respect to certain attitudes essential to the work (e.g., patience, introspection, nonjudgmental exploration, etc.). This is especially true if the patient needs to offset the demoralizing influence of angry, frustrated, antagonistic parents or internalized parental images. In this case, inner self-regard and vitality must be strengthened before the more painful and arduous work of psychotherapy can be done.

The countertransference experienced by the therapist at times when the positive transference holds sway may be a pleasurable one of feeling valued, special, and even complicitous with the patient. Eventually, however, intensive long-term work with the adolescent will evoke a wider range of countertransferential feelings: anger, pity, pride, dismay, envy, frustration, and so on. These feelings must be examined (most often, in private) for their ability to provide clues as to the internal object relations that promote the patient's nonachievement. Over time, the therapist and patient are likely to become more involved with each other and their mutual task, in the controlled and admittedly asymmetric way unique to psychotherapy.

ILLUSTRATIVE CASES

Case History: Jane

A 17-year-old girl named Jane applied to a psychoanalytically oriented clinic for help with her difficulty functioning in high school. She found it hard to complete assignments, and was failing many of her subjects. She had always been praised for her apparent intelligence, which was evidenced by her excellent ability to attune herself to interpersonal situations and to handle them with great maturity. Her discourse, particularly on social and political matters, demonstrated her capacity for understanding complex and thorny issues. It was a surprise and disappointment to all—herself included—when her report cards consistently were returned with comments like "Could try harder," or "Is achieving below her potential."

Jane was the third of three children born to an upper-middle-class midwestern couple. Her father was a modestly successful businessman, and her mother worked as an administrator at a local hospital. Both parents were extremely invested in the academic successes of their children. Jane had an older brother and older sister, both of whom met (with flying colors) parental expectations along these lines. Her sister, three years her senior, was unusually attractive and quite popular with her peers. She was admitted to a prestigious college and had a steady boyfriend. By comparison, Jane herself felt scrawny and unattractive. She shied away from social gatherings and tended to deny obvious overtures from boys who might have been interested in dating her. She could not believe that they could actually be interested in *her*—there must be "darker motives" for their attempts to approach her.

Relationships with her parents were superficially warm and close. Jane described her mother as her most devoted friend and confidant; she cared more about Jane and knew her better than anyone else (perhaps including herself, she felt). The father was seen as somewhat more distant and preoccupied with his financial concerns, but as basically caring and responsive to his children.

As the treatment unfolded, a definite interpersonal dynamic was revealed in relation to the problems doing schoolwork. Jane would discuss her workload with her parents, who would make suggestions as to where study materials could be found, how she could approach the topic under study, or whatever. Jane would then make plans to carry out her assignments in a serious and methodical way, only to realize with great chagrin that she had left the necessary texts at school, or lost some notes that were vital to the work at hand. She would spend hours castigating herself for her "laziness and unreliability," until—depressed, anxious, and exhausted—she would fall into a deep sleep. Invariably she would oversleep and miss her first few classes of the following day. More self-recriminations would follow, until Jane became numb with despair. The family would make tense inquiries as to how the work was going. When the course of events became clear, her father would sit silently while the mother would rant and rave about Jane's thoughtlessness and immaturity. Jane's shame and despair would deepen, as she agreed with her mother and vowed to try harder. This scene was repeated time and again with countless variations.

Much time was spent during therapy sessions discussing Jane's complicated feelings about her mother. Respect and admiration for the mother made it hard to defend herself against the latter's attacks. The enmeshment between the two was obviously extreme; their relationship not only heavily colored her inner object world, but seemed to overrun it. Jane heard her mother's voice so clearly in imaginary reactions to her academic "misdeeds" that she was unable to distinguish it from her own self-evaluation. She was enslaved by her need to please both the external mother and the internal maternal object. She was caught between continuing to court her mother's potential favor and deciding to give up once and for all. Suicidal ideation occurred when the intrapsychic balance tilted toward accepting her "inevitable" inferiority.

As might be expected, Jane's relationship with the therapist was rife with symbiotic and sadomasochistic themes. The patient would come for a session after another episode of academic failure with the conviction that the therapist would be angry, frustrated, and disdainful of her. Mournfully, Jane would wonder how the therapist "put up" with her. These transferential feelings were translated into a powerful reenactment of the mother-daughter dynamics when Jane began to "simply forget" to come for a scheduled session, or repeatedly failed to bring in the therapist's payment. Harnessing countertransferential frustration, the therapist probed beneath Jane's overtly respectful, fond attitude toward her. Gradually she unearthed Jane's anger at "having to take one more class" (the therapy itself) and "having to do well" in it. She was furious at the therapist for sitting (as she imagined) in constant, self-satisfied judgment of her.

The therapist acknowledged that it was disappointing to have Jane violate their working arrangements repeatedly. However, this did not make the therapist see Jane in the negative, debased light she imagined. Instead, said the therapist, she saw it as a misguided but significant attempt to vent suppressed anger and to begin establishing a measure of autonomy in their relationship. Jane's natural intelligence and psychological sophistication enabled her to recognize the reflection of her relationship with her mother in her behavior with the therapist. It gradually became her *wish*—rather than her obligation—to attend therapy and make payments regularly. Her studying began improving slowly but steadily.

A further "working through" occurred several years later. The patient, now in college, began to experience a resurgence of her self-defeating academic behavior as she faced the task of selecting a major that would lead to a career. Her parents were quite eager that she "set her sights high enough" and were pressuring her to take prelaw courses. She was struggling with whether or not she truly wanted to go into law. After doing poorly on an economics midterm, she came in to a session filled with self-disdain and indignation. Her mother's interpretation was that she hadn't tried hard enough. She turned her anger onto the therapist, saying "My mother is right and always has been, and you are wrong. How can you possibly believe I have the strength of character to do well? I'm obviously worthless. You must have some personal investment in leading me on and making me think I'm anything more than that. What's wrong—you can't admit having failed with me?"

The therapist took a deep breath and noted aloud that Jane seemed to be feeling quite strong and self-assured in saying this. It must be terribly reassuring to lapse into agreement with her mother. To do so would solidify their bond (self-punishing though it might be) and would absolve her of the need to define and test her own true capacities. It also allowed her to borrow from the source of her mother's "strength," by adopting the same tactic of criticizing and tearing down the other.

Jane was deeply affected by this interpretation. She was able to see that her true inner alliance had remained with the attacking, scornful, demanding mother. It had been gratifying to attack and dismiss the therapist as "not really knowing [Jane's] true awfulness." What she took for being "too easygoing" in the therapist's manner was actually tolerance and respect for the patient and her difficulties. It soon became more satisfying to recognize her own real strengths and accomplishments and to strive for new ones, rather than to take refuge in the truly "familiar" habit of flagellating herself as an "incorrigible sinner."

In this case the patient's resistance to treatment and the powerful dynamics between her and the therapist were used in the therapy to help articulate the patient's inner object relations as they related to her academic inhibitions. It is possible that only a strong patient/therapist bond—and its careful explication could have offset the deeply entrenched conflicts in the patient's internal and external worlds. Jane eventually completed her senior year of college with As and Bs in her major and went on to pursue a career in publishing.

Further insight into the use of interpreting the transference in working with adolescent underachievement is provided by Baker (12). He describes the long-term treatment of a male college undergraduate named Tom who was enrolled in a high-powered university. Tom was the oldest of three children whose parents divorced when Tom was 14. The mother was both interfering and seductive toward her son, while the father was an inveterate gambler who was unable to fulfill either his financial or emotional responsibilities to his children. Tom apparently did extremely well on standardized tests but was nonetheless failing his courses. He had trouble studying and was unhappy with his school performance.

Evidently the therapist tried making Oedipal interpretations concerning the ambivalent relationship between the son and his inadequate father. Though these seemed apt at the time and were accepted by the patient, his schoolwork as well as his inner object relational situation remained unchanged. Improvement began only after the therapist shifted his focus to Tom's "untamed grandiose self" and his intense disappointment with his parents' failure as idealizable selfobjects. Adds Baker (12), "Most important, we tried to understand the ways he felt I failed him and how he reacted to disruptions in the selfobject relationship between us. He began to tolerate minor failures and felt that they taught him how to work more effectively" (p.

455). The outcome was quite favorable, with gradual improvement leading to the completion of graduate school and a happy marriage.

Here it is clear how the therapist's adherence to a particular theoretical school—in this case, a classically Freudian one led to the patient's having to reexperience an early failure in empathy between himself and his parents. The patient had a need to merge with an idealizable therapist, so he accepted the Oedipal interpretations on an intellectual level despite their apparent hollowness on an emotional level. This was probably a repetition of a childhood pattern of making himself conform to his parents' selfobject needs at the expense of pursuing his own. The failure to improve academically here acts as a profound manifestation that the heart of the object relational "truth" had not yet been reached. His nonachievement needed to be understood on one level as a cry for a different kind of help, and on another level as a response to a selfobject relationship disruption in his bond with the psychotherapist.

In conclusion, it seems fair to say that the clinician has cause to be optimistic in undertaking the task of aiding the underachieving adolescent. The transition to adulthood is surely a complicated one, fraught with potential obstacles. However, it is also a time when the individual is geared toward expecting and welcoming new experiences. The psychotherapist may find that his or her patient is quite receptive to the help—and the relationship—she or he has to offer. Although the effort may not be easy, it can be highly rewarding for therapist and patient alike.

REFERENCES

1. Khan MMR: Hidden Selves: Between Theory and Practice in Psychoanalysis. New York, International Universities Press, 1983
2. Weiner IB: Psychopathology in adolescence, in Handbook of Adolescent Psychology. Edited by Adelson J. New York, John Wiley, 1980, pp 447–471
3. Sugar M: Diagnostic aspects of underachievement in adolescents. Adolesc Psychiatry 14:427–440, 1987
4. Mandel HP, Marcus SI: The Psychology of Underachievement. New York, John Wiley, 1988
5. Hogan R: The gifted adolescent, in Handbook of Adolescent Psychology. Edited by Adelson J. New York, John Wiley, 1980, pp 536–559
6. Miller D: The Age Between: Adolescence and Therapy. New York, Jason Aronson, 1983
7. Miller A: The Drama of the Gifted Child. New York, Basic Books, 1981
8. Klein E: Psychoanalytic aspects of school problems. Psychoanal Study Child 3(4):369–390, 1949
9. Brockman DD: Late Adolescence: Psychoanalytic Studies. New York, International Universities Press, 1984

10. Sklansky MA: Some observations on learning inhibition in college students: a developmental failure in the sense of autonomy, in Late Adolescence: Psychoanalytic Studies. Edited by Brockman DD. New York, International Universities Press, 1984, pp 213–225

11. Hoit M: Diagnostic implications of the collapse of the work ego in adolescence, in Late Adolescence: Psychoanalytic Studies. Edited by Brockman DD. New York, International Universities Press, 1984, pp 227–240

12. Baker HS: Underachievement and failure in college: the interaction between intrapsychic and interpersonal factors from the perspective of self psychology. Adolesc Psychiatry 14:441–460, 1987

13. Meeks JE: The Fragile Alliance: An Orientation to the Outpatient Psychotherapy of the Adolescent, 2nd Edition. New York, Robert E Krieger, 1980

14. Sullivan HS: The Psychiatric Interview. New York, WW Norton, 1954

15. Berkovitz IH: The adolescent, schools, and schooling. Adolesc Psychiatry 12:162–176, 1987

16. Opperman J: Tutoring: The remediation of cognitive and academic deficits by individual instruction, in Child Analysis and Therapy. Edited by Glenn J. New York, Jason Aronson, 1978, pp 495–528

17. Winnicott DW: The Maturational Processes and the Facilitating Environment. New York, International Universities Press, 1965

18. Gill M: The Analysis of the Transference, Vol 1: Theory and Technique. New York, International Universities Press, 1982

19. Hoffman IZ: The patient as interpreter of the analyst's experience. Contemporary Psychoanalysis 19(3):389–422, 1983

SECTION III:

THE PSYCHOTHERAPEUTIC PROCESS WITH BOTH CHILDREN AND ADOLESCENTS IN SPECIAL CIRCUMSTANCES

◆ ◆ ◆ ◆ ◆ ◆ ◆

13 Psychotherapy With Children of Divorce

Hector R. Bird, M.D.

THE NATURE OF THE PROBLEM

Marital dissolution can be counted as one of the most severe of life stressors. It has a marked potential for negative psychological effects on all the individuals involved in the crisis. In general, personal and psychological characteristics, as well as environmental factors, have been noted to mediate the process of adaptation to stress (1). However, unlike other stressful life events in which there is a time-limited response to a specific event, such as the loss of a job, the death of a loved one, or the loss of personal property after a disaster, the reaction to marital dissolution is protracted and can extend over a prolonged period of time during which other stressors are engendered (2).

The epidemiologic considerations are significant. Bane (3) estimates that during the decade of the 1970s approximately 30% of American children under age 18 experienced parental divorce. Kalter and colleagues (4) reviewed the records of 400 children referred in 1974–1975 for outpatient evaluation in the Department of Psychiatry at the University of Michigan. About one-third of the children came from divorced families, whereas at that time such families constituted only 16% of the general population from which these children were referred.

Notwithstanding the deleterious effects that divorce may potentially engender, divorce is a fact of life—and often an unavoidable one. The children of broken homes seem to react more adversely when there is a great deal of marital discord, hostility, or outright violence surrounding the separation. Rutter (5) has suggested that it is the discord, rather than the breakup itself that has the main adverse influence on the children. This corroborates previous research that has shown that broken homes in which harmony has been restored result in significantly less juvenile delinquency than do unbroken but quarrelsome and neglecting homes (6).

Although it is evident that the children of divorcing parents frequently reflect the deleterious effects of their parents' conflicts, there is compelling evidence that divorce exerts a harmful effect on children, above and beyond the psychological damage that may have been caused by parental conflict and discord leading to the separation. Children of divorce have been reported to suffer increased rates of cognitive, affective, behavioral, and psychophysiological problems (7,8). They may experience self-blame and feeling different from peers, as well as a heightened sensitivity to interpersonal slights or rejections. Quite frequently there is a diminution in prosocial behaviors with a high frequency of acting out and overt aggression. Academic performance is often affected by anxiety, preoccupations leading to inattention, and by attention-seeking behaviors that interfere with schoolwork. Almost all children are upset by the breakup of their home and exhibit reactions of sadness, anger, regression, or outright depression, feelings of deprivation and insecurity, and emotional conflicts whose outward manifestations may include behavioral problems, psychophysiologic symptomatology, or special symptoms such as enuresis.

During the period of uncontrolled hostility that generally accompanies the process of a marital breakup, the parents are intent on defending themselves and on attacking one another. In the midst of the turmoil of separation, even the most caring parents can overlook their child's needs, thus leaving them unattended. When the parents have sought professional help, a similar reaction may be observed in their therapist, who stays with the material brought up by his or her patients and often fails to inquire sufficiently about how the children are doing. The parents frequently provide very different versions of how the children are faring; usually the abandoning spouse reporting that the children are coping well, whereas the spouse who feels abandoned reporting that the children are terribly affected. The role of the child therapist is to arrive at a more objective assessment of how the child is functioning and to clarify the child's particular reactions to the stress. In many ways, the children are more vulnerable than the adults and may be less likely than their parents to recover from the stress of separation.

RISK FACTORS ASSOCIATED TO OUTCOME

Several variables have been found to predict the child's postdivorce adjustment. These include demographic, personal, situational, and parental factors.

The child's age at the time of parental separation gives a clue to the normative developmental tasks that may have been affected by the breakup in the family ties (9). The literature on the impact of age at the time of divorce is equivocal. Landis (10) reports that children who were younger at the time of the event subsequently rated themselves as happier and more secure than older children. Hetherington (11) reports that adolescent girls whose parents separated in their early childhood experienced greater difficulties in their relations with males than those girls whose parents had divorced later. Wallerstein and Kelly (12) observed that adolescents ranging in age from 13 to 19 found the transition as extremely painful, displaying increased anxiety and concerns about their future adequacy as marital partners.

Although beset by the limitations imposed by small subsamples and the inherent attrition of longitudinal follow-up, the data provided by Wallerstein are useful in delineating the long-range psychological effects of divorce and their association to age. Her report of the children who were in their early latency years at the time of the divorce and who were followed up 10 years later during their adolescence (13) shows that a majority continued to express feelings of sadness, neediness, and a sense of their own vulnerability. There was a high level of anxiety related to relationships with the opposite sex, marriage, and personal commitments, with serious concerns about betrayal in relationships and about being hurt and abandoned. Girls were more likely to become involved in dating and sexual relationships, whereas boys were more likely to be lonely and to hold back in their relationships with girls. One-half of the boys and one-fourth of the girls were considered to be poorly adjusted and at high risk at follow-up.

For those who were followed up in early adulthood and whose parents had divorced during their adolescent years (14,15) the findings were somewhat more striking. A high proportion (two-thirds) of the group had engaged in mild to serious illegal activities during their adolescence or young adulthood, although for one-half of this subgroup, the delinquency consisted exclusively of underage alcohol consumption or of drug use. One-third of the women had been pregnant outside of marriage. The predominant mood in looking back at the period of the divorce was one of regret, sadness, and yearning, and about one-half of the subjects still retained some degree of anger at one or both parents. Most were eager for a lasting marriage, but two-thirds of the subjects expressed conscious fear of marriage despite their wish to marry, and a similar proportion expressed moderate to intense worries that they would be repeating the mistakes of their parents in their own relationships. A subgroup (one-third) of young women had left home at high school graduation or before graduation to live with a man. They seemed to be drifting from job to job and from man to man. Several had taken on older men as lovers. The solidarity among siblings was impressive, and it appears that love, intimacy, and loyalty among brothers and sisters became a strong protective influence.

Outcome also seems to be related to the child's sex. Research has consistently shown that divorce has more adverse long-term effects on boys than on girls (16–19). Nevertheless, females have been noted to report being more anxious and depressed than their male counterparts (20).

A number of premorbid personal characteristics also predict adjustment. Children who tend to be critical of themselves and those who tend to minimize or deny the impact of events end up being more anxious, depressed, and hostile (20).

Parental variables also exert an effect. The extent of predivorce marital hostility has been found to be related to the child's self-esteem (21). The quality of parenting skills pre- and postdivorce, and the custodial parent's adjustment to the separation, as well as the availability of the noncustodial parent to the child (22) also seem to affect outcome.

Caplan (23) has outlined a number of psychosocial hazards that can be expectably associated to the crisis. These include the loss of one or both parents, the feeling of abandonment, a real reduction of psychosocial support, the involvement of the child in the parents' battles, economic hardship, and the practical necessity of moving that often accompanies the marital breakup.

Greater vulnerability to the impact of divorce and poorer adjustment has been associated to such situational factors. Children fare much worse when there is a high level of parental conflict surrounding the divorce and when they are extensively drawn into the conflict (12,24). The availability to the child of other social support systems can mitigate the adverse effects of divorce (25). Those children who were farther from home during the process of separation and divorce have been noted to be more anxious, depressed, and hostile than those living closer to home or at home (20).

These authors note that whereas it may seem logical that distance from home may afford older adolescents a way to disengage from the stressful situation, in fact the adolescents living farther from home had higher levels of depression, anxiety, and hostility. Thus distance does not seem to act as a buffer, but rather may serve to increase uncertainty and confusion about what is happening at home and may make the task of obtaining social support from other family members more difficult. Parental remarriage and the stress of adapting to a new family system can also have a negative outcome (26). Rickel and Langner (27) report that the incidence of pathology in boys, mainly of an antisocial type, is highest in homes with surrogate fathers. Their longitudinal follow-up revealed that there was an attenuation of this effect over time, suggesting that the effect is a proximal disrupting influence to which the majority of children eventually adapt. At a 6-year postdivorce follow-up, Hetherington and colleagues (19) noted that remarriage of a custodial mother is associated with an increase in behavior problems in girls and some decrease in problems in boys. Although stepsons are not as well adjusted as sons in nondivorced families, they are better adjusted in the long run than those who remain in households headed by divorced mothers.

THERAPEUTIC CONSIDERATIONS

Given the high potential for divorce to adversely affect emotional life and developmental course, a number of school-based intervention programs have been developed in recent years for children of divorce (4,28–30). These programs take the stressful event as a warning sign to implement a preventive intervention in order to forestall negative psychological sequelae.

This chapter focuses on the child whose family is in a process of marital dissolution and divorce, who is referred to the mental health practitioner and who may be already manifesting some signs of maladaptation. We are concerned with the intervention with children in such families and specifically with the intervention revolving around an individual child. The data generated by systematic research as well as by clinical observation suggest that this is a population at high risk and that some form of intervention by mental health practitioners is warranted. The task of the clinician involves at least a thorough diagnostic assessment of the child and both parents. When there appears to be a fair balance of the forces at work and of the coping resources and mental state of all involved, an "open-door" approach may be all that is necessary over the ensuing months after the evaluation. This is, however, an unusual situation. More often than not forces within the system are off balance, and short-term or long-term professional help may be necessary. By necessity such an intervention is bound to be interpersonal and systemic in its orientation because what is affected is the family, one of the fundamental systems of human ecology.

Regardless of whether or not the professional chooses to focus the intervention on the child, the child's treatment needs to include the parents. The goal is to improve the child's capacity to adapt to the situation, not only by helping him or her to deal with conflicts and strengthen his or her ego, but by preserving an optimal relationship with each parent, and by counseling the important others (his or her parents) about practical measures that can serve to mitigate the effects of adverse environmental circumstances. For families in which the adaptive task of family reorganization is adequately mastered, divorce may actually be a positive event, promoting a new equilibrium that involves lower levels of conflict and greater cohesion (20).

Although it is impossible to undo marital hostility that has already taken place or to reverse the environmental changes that come as sequelae of the marital dissolution, the treatment of the child by necessity involves a modification of the child's response to these influences. This is done by increasing the child's awareness and understanding of parental interactions, and helping to modify his or her perception of the events that led to the parental breakup and to develop behavioral skills necessary to deal with the new situation. Understanding the confusing world around him or her should serve to reduce the child's anger, frustration, and guilt (31).

One of the primary treatment goals is to have both parents continue to be responsible for their children and to continue to develop in their role as parents, notwithstanding the fact that they have decided to terminate their role as spouses. Unavoidably, divorcing parents, regardless of their sense of moral justification or of being "right," react to a divorce with a sense of having failed in one of life's major roles. The parental adjustment may be enhanced if they are able to develop a sense of competency in managing their child's situation with sensitivity.

Psychotherapy of a child of divorce is the psychotherapy of an individual undergoing a severely stressful situation. The two major stressors in this situation are the heightened conflict existing between the child's two parents and the feelings of abandonment and rejection that the child experiences. Therefore, it is imperative that both parents be included as integral elements of the treatment. Other aspects of the child's pathology must be attended to as well, because the stress of the situation may result in affective symptomatology as well as in the surfacing of other problems—neurotic, psychotic, or characterological—that might have been kept in abeyance until that time. We must keep in mind, however, that not every problem that the child has is necessarily attributable to the divorce.

In general, child psychotherapy requires a complex therapeutic alliance involving not only therapist and child but the therapist and the parents as well. With the dissolution of the family unit, the alliance becomes three-way: an alliance with the child as well as with each parent. Achieving this is a complicated task because the parents are more often than not in an oppositional stance with one another. Often it is sufficient to have one parent take a position to make the other parent be at odds and disagree.

INVOLVEMENT OF THE PARENTS

Consultation is generally sought by one of the parents, usually the parent who feels abandoned in the separation. The more common presentation is that of a mother who on the surface considers that the child is extremely affected by the separation and needs professional help. There may be other underlying reasons for this perception, which are not always at the level of the parent's awareness. Women are twice as likely to have made the final decision about the divorce as men. Nevertheless, this decision usually attributes the cause for the divorce to the husband (infidelity, emotional or physical maltreatment, etc.), so that the woman, more often than not, sees herself as the "abandoned" spouse and the one who has been treated unfairly. Although mothers generally have custody over the child, generally the court has dictated that the father is financially responsible for the child's medical care. In seeking consultation for the child, the abandoned spouse is often also seeking confirmation that the other spouse's wrongdoing has seriously affected the child's emotional health. Another hidden and generally unconscious agenda may be to create an added financial hardship for the father—to make him pay for his rejection or abandonment of the mother.

As a result of these dynamics there may be a tendency to exaggerate the degree of emotional turmoil in the child, or even to inadvertently create incidents and situations in which the child becomes greatly affected. This does not necessarily obviate the fact that the child may be in need of professional help, but the therapist needs to make an objective assessment of the child's psychiatric status and emotional state. It makes it imperative that both parents become involved in the intervention. From a practical standpoint this is also useful, because children do not pay for their treatment and the issue of financial responsibility, which is part of the therapeutic contract, needs to be clear at the onset of treatment.

There may be a great deal of resistance from one of the child's parents to participate in the process. This may require a great deal of outreach from the clinician in order to get both parents to participate, even if only by telephone. Ideally there should be at least one joint session with the two parents. Although this is likely to degenerate into a fighting match, it can be extremely informative to the clinician in witnessing the interpersonal dynamics that operate in the parents and to which the child is subjected. Often, however, the parents are adamantly opposed to being seen by the therapist together in session, in which case separate appointments should be given. Generally more than one appointment is necessary. Separate appointments need to be made during the course of the evaluation as part of the information gathering process, as well as at the end of the evaluation to communicate the results of the evaluation and to discuss the recommendations and the therapeutic plan.

It is important to have both parents conclude at the end of the diagnostic process that they are in agreement about the intervention with their child. The therapist has to convey to both parents that they are his cotherapists in the effort to help their child. The therapist needs to convey empathy about the fact that they are both going through a difficult situation in which their own sense of anger and frustration and all of the feelings associated with the separation often prevent them from being aware of what their child is going through.

Contact with the parents needs to be an ongoing process. The child should be made aware that the therapist will not share with the parents any confidential material that comes up in the therapy, but that periodically he or she will communicate with the parents when there is something that they are doing that makes it difficult for the child to deal with the situation. Parents often use their child as a go-between or inadvertently try to obtain from the child the support that they feel is lacking, by getting the child to side with them. Negatively influencing the child with the other parent is also common, and the child is caught up in a raging battle that often extends for many years after the divorce has been finalized. The extent to which the therapist can interpret these events and put a stop to these maneuvers helps cement the therapeutic alliance with the child and results in the facilitation of his or her development.

Relatively simple issues that are generally not a problem can acquire conflictual proportions in this situation.

> Fourteen-year-old Lisa was graduating from the eighth grade. Because of the heightened level of hostility surrounding the divorce that had occurred 3 years before, the parents were no longer on speaking terms with one another. They wanted to celebrate their daughter's graduation, but they refused to have a single graduation party to bring together both their families and friends, which would have been what Lisa wanted. Instead, each parent decided to have a separate graduation celebration for their side of the family and were of course involved in outdoing one another. Lisa wanted to be able to invite her friends to a single party, and each parent wanted their party to be the biggest treat and to have the friends included in their celebration. Lisa refused to have her friends invited to two separate parties, because this would require explaining what was going on between her parents and exposing her personal difficulties to her peers. The parents thus decided to have two parties for their respective families and friends and a third party for Lisa's friends.

> By this time Lisa was wondering whether there should be any party at all and questioning whether she should have studied so hard in school in order to graduate. The therapist had to intervene to put an end to this absurdity by persuading the parents to set aside their hostilities for a few hours and provide their daughter with a single, true celebration of her accomplishment. The young child was subsequently able to give her parents feedback in those instances in which she felt "used" by them to get at each other.

INTERVENTION WITH THE CHILD

The child is caught in a world of conflicting loyalties. He or she may find himself tied up in a knot and withholding because any anger expressed at either parent is seen as an act of treason and as taking sides in a conflict that the child wished did not exist in the first place. The therapist provides a neutral person who can be the child's ally and with whom the child can feel comfortable exposing anxieties and feelings. The child may see the therapist as the ally of the parent who brings him or her for consultation, and it is crucial to get the child to realize that the therapist is the child's ally and no one else's.

Individual psychotherapy with the child includes the major components of psychotherapy that are present in any psychotherapeutic intervention: a corrective emotional experience provided by the relationship with the therapist, a forum for the emotional release and rechanneling of feelings, insight gained by acquiring an awareness of conscious and unconscious processes, cognitive restructuring through reeducation and suggestion, and emotional support (32). Generally the maxim that a competent therapist is what is essential, holds true. However in the case of divorce, there may be an abandoning parent, and thus the necessity for a reparative emotional experience becomes paramount. In some instances it is advisable that the therapist be of the same sex as the absent parent. This will more immediately stabilize the child and allow the transferences to the absent parent to be more quickly addressed.

The central areas of psychological exploration relate to what has been found in research to be the long-range effects of parental separation on children: feelings of anxiety and anger, anxiety about dependency, abreaction, feelings of guilt, diminished self-esteem, cognitions about the divorce, being placed by either one or both parents in the position of an informer, or having to take sides.

A number of common themes have been noted to emerge in the therapy of children of divorce. Toomin (33) notes that a predominant theme is the issue of "loss," and that the process of dealing with loss is similar when the loss is due to death, divorce, or a widening of social or actual physical distance between the child and a parent. It is necessary that the mourning process be facilitated in the psychotherapeutic process. Toomin's approach involves dealing with the child's mourning and helping the child to work through feelings of sadness and anger. In actuality the mourning process at the death of a parent is less conflicted because of its finality. The loss of a parent through divorce is more difficult and fraught with greater ambivalence, because the loss is generally partial and the lost object, while totally or partially absent, is still alive and in and out of the picture. The therapist must make an objective assessment of the degree of abandonment, deal with the parents in an attempt to mitigate the abandonment, and deal with the child to find ways through which the child can learn how to ask for more support and to develop new relationships.

Fostering a child's relationship with another relative or with a particular friend of the family often allows the child to disengage from the loyalty conflict. Quite often this is the role that the therapist plays, and the real, nontransferential aspects of the therapeutic relationship cannot be underestimated. Children of divorce frequently tend to develop an idealization of the absent parent and a quest for that parent that can manifest itself as a wish to be like that idealization (34). This overidealization and this quest often serve the purpose of impeding the mourning process and the development of new attachments (35). This can become complicated when the parent starts attributing personality traits of the estranged spouse—mostly defects—to their child.

Fifteen-year-old Dianne's parents had divorced after the father discovered that his wife had been involved in an extramarital affair. The father's concern, expressed to the therapist, was that Dianne would end up being "sexually promiscuous and a whore, like her mother." Although this concern was never so explicitly presented to Dianne, in one of her therapy sessions she was extremely upset because on the previous evening her father had phoned to tell her that he had driven through the city's red-light district on his way from work and thought that he had seen her walking in the crowd. Dianne tearfully expressed to the therapist that she had never been in that section of town and that her father must think she was a prostitute. A few weeks later she was unusually late for an appointment and the explanation for her lateness was quite revealing. She had missed three subway stops, had gotten off in the middle of the red-light district, and given that she only had the exact amount of money necessary to get back home after the session, had walked back 25 blocks to the therapist's office. This meant walking through the exact area where her father had claimed to have seen her and obviated the fact that at the particular station where she got off, she could have switched to an uptown subway train without paying an additional fare.

It was not difficult to make Dianne aware of the fact that her behavior related to her father's accusation. This in turn led her to talk about her mother's infidelity and the conflicts surrounding the divorce, issues about which both parents had assured the therapist that Dianne was unaware. The therapy in this instance required more interpretation and exploration and truly served as a maturational experience. Being able to express the shameful "secret" enabled Dianne to increase her awareness of her parents' conflicts and to arrive at her own delineation of the parental problematic, seeing the extent of her father's exaggerated posture and accepting her mother's behavior as symptomatic of deeper problems that existed in the marriage.

Associated with the sense of rejection, abandonment, and loss of parental divorce comes a lowering of the child's self-esteem. If the feelings of rejection are not addressed, a diminished sense of self-worth can become internalized and lead to future problems.

Gardner (37) has observed the tendency of children of divorce to use a great deal of denial with regard to their feelings about the divorce process. The child may present with a pseudo-mature stance whereby he or she seems to be dealing with the whole process rationally and does not seem to be in touch with unavoidable feelings of sadness and anger. The ongoing therapeutic process may be painstaking, but as is generally true with children, the underlying affect breaks through sporadically and the process of dealing with the child's denial can be achieved through interpretations of the child's behavior and his or her dreams or fantasies.

Other themes that are common among children of divorce include feelings of responsibility and guilt about the parental separation. Many children, particularly those in the younger age groups, feel that somehow they are to blame for the conflicts between their parents that led to the breakup. Older children and adolescents are better equipped cognitively to extricate themselves from the process. With the younger child guilt can be an extremely complicated issue given that, in the preseparation period, many of the mutual hostilities between the parents are often displaced on the child, or on issues related to the child's management. This can lead to the child's perception that he or she was the source of the parental difficulties. No amount of reassurance can modify this perception, and it is at this point that more in-depth exploration with the child, and frequently with the parents, is needed in order to modify the child's cognition. A therapeutic interaction with a 6-year-old boy illustrates this point.

> Therapist: Many kids whose parents break up tell me that they felt they had something to do with it. Have you ever felt that way?
>
> Child: (Eyes fixed on the floor, nods)
>
> Therapist: Well, tell me what made you feel that way.
>
> Child: I didn't want to eat my string beans.

The anecdote would be humorous if there was not so much pathos attached to it. Given the child's concrete interpretation of the situation, the issue had to be dealt with concretely. In reviewing the situation with the child's parents, it was evident that the child would become the focus of many of their mutual hostilities in arguments over what to eat, what to wear, when to take a bath, and so forth. Their clarification of these issues in the presence of the child resulted in an amelioration of the child's sense of guilt by increasing the child's awareness of the parents' interactions and by modifying his cognition. Occasionally such joint sessions with the child and each parent can be extremely useful.

The therapist must inquire frequently about either or both parents' attempts at pumping information from the child about the other parent or about the tendency to devalue the other parent in the child's presence or directly to the child. This process, which may be in many instances inadvertent, is oriented at collecting ammunition with which to further the attacks on the spouse and to enhance the parent's own sense of moral rectitude.

> In his attempt to maintain an alliance with both of his parents, 11-year-old Johnny would echo each of his parents' perceptions of the other. He confirmed to his mother that he thought his father was irresponsible, erratic, inconsistent, and untrustworthy. He agreed with his father that his mother was inflexible, excessively strict, self-righteous, and unfeeling. Both parents felt quite secure in Johnny's alliance with each one of them. It took some doing on the therapist's part to get Johnny to look at the other side of the coin—to increase the parents' awareness of the process that was taking place and to make them realize that they were making their child's inner life the arena of their own conflicts. A series of family sessions with both parents and Johnny served to relieve him of the burden.

To summarize, the psychotherapy of children whose parents are divorcing or divorced involves three major aspects. The therapist's intervention needs to focus initially on how the child manages the divorce crisis. Children need assistance with their own overwhelming affects, as well as in dealing with extreme affects and reactions in their parents. The parents have to be counseled in their management of the child, and the clinician has to offer practical advice to the parents to create the most facilitating environment possible for the child. This may involve interpretation of their behavior as well as mediation to secure a reasonable schedule of visitation. The child also needs help in constructing a personal story of the divorce and in reconciling him- or herself to the breakup of the home, dealing with loss, and redefining his or her relationship with both parents. Ongoing work with both parents may be necessary in order to help them redefine the relationship as well. Finally, ongoing psychotherapy is, more often than not, necessary to deal with the child's characterological problems or other pathology that may exist. At least periodic follow-up is useful to assess how the child is faring and to intervene more intensively when necessary.

REFERENCES

1. Dohrenwend BS: Social stress and community psychology. Am J Community Psychol 6:1–14, 1978
2. Felner RD, Farber SS, Primavera J: Children of divorce, stressful life events and transitions: a model for primary prevention, in Prevention in Mental Health: Research, Policy and Practice. Edited by Price RH, Ketterer RF, Bader BC, et al. Beverly Hills, CA, Sage, 1980, pp 16–25
3. Bane MJ: Marital disruption and the lives of children, in Divorce and Separation: Content, Causes and Consequences. Edited by Levinger G, Moles OC. New York, Basic Books, 1979, pp 276–286
4. Kalter N, Pickar J, Lesowitz M: School based developmental facilitation groups for children of divorce: a preventive intervention. Am J Orthopsychiatry 54:613–623, 1984
5. Rutter M: Parent-child separation: psychological effects on the children. J Child Psychol Psychiatry 12:233–260, 1971
6. McCord W, McCord J: Origins of Crime: A New Evaluation of the Cambridge-Somerville Youth Study. New York, Columbia University Press, 1959
7. Hetherington EM: Divorce: a child's perspective. Am Psychol 34:851–858, 1979
8. Kurdek LA: An integrative perspective on children's divorce adjustment. Am Psychol 35:856–866, 1981
9. Wallerstein JS: Children of divorce: the psychological tasks of the child. Am J Orthopsychiatry 53:530–543, 1983
10. Landis JT: The trauma of children when parents divorce. Marriage and Family Living 22:7–13, 1960

11. Hetherington EM: Effects of paternal absence on personality development in adolescent daughters. Developmental Psychology 7:313–326, 1972

12. Wallerstein JS, Kelly JB: The effects of parental divorce: the adolescent experience, in The Child in his Family: Children at Psychiatric Risk, Vol 3. Edited by Anthony EJ, Koupernik C. New York, John Wiley, 1974, pp 479–506

13. Wallerstein J: Children of divorce: report of a ten-year follow-up of early latency-age children. Am J Orthopsychiatry 57(2):199–211, 1987

14. Wallerstein J: Children of divorce: preliminary report of a ten-year follow up of older children and adolescents. J Am Acad Child Adolesc Psychiatry 24(5):545–553, 1985

15. Wallerstein J, Blakeslee S: Second Chances: Men, Women, and Children a Decade After Divorce. New York, Ticknor & Fields, 1989

16. Hetherington EM, Camara KA, Cox M, et al: Effects of divorce on parents and children, in Nontraditional Families: Parenting and Child Development. Edited by Lamb ME. Hillsdale, NJ, Erlbaum, 1982, pp 233–288

17. Guidubaldi J, Cleminshaw HK, Perry JD, et al: The impact of parental divorce on children: report of the nationwide NASP study. School Psychology Review 12:300–323, 1983

18. Guidubaldi J, Cleminshaw HK, Perry JD, et al: Impact of family support systems on children's academic and social functioning after divorce, in Family Strengths 5: Continuity and Diversity. Edited by Rowe G, DeFrain J, Lingrin H, et al. Newton, MA, Education Development Center, 1984, pp 208–215

19. Hetherington EM, Cox MC, Cox R: Long-term effects of divorce and remarriage on the adjustment of children. J Am Acad Child Adolesc Psychiatry 24(5):518–530, 1985

20. Farber SS, Felner RD, Primavera J: Parental separation/divorce and adolescents: an examination of factors mediating adaptation. Am J Community Psychol 13:171–185, 1985

21. Emery RE: Interpersonal conflict and the children of discord and divorce. Psychol Bull 92:310–330, 1982

22. Stolberg AL, Kiluk DJ, Garrison KM: A temporal model of divorce adjustment with implications for primary prevention, in Crisis Intervention With Children and Families. Edited by Auerach SM, Stolberg AL. New York, Hemisphere, 1985, pp 260–276

23. Caplan G: Preventing psychological problems in children of divorce: general practitioner's role. BMJ 292:1431–1434, 1986

24. Raschke HJ: Family structure, family happiness and their effects on college students' personal and social adjustment. Conciliation Courts Review 15:30–33, 1977

25. Cauce AM, Felner RD, Primavera J: Social support in high risk adolescents: structural components and adaptive impact. Am J Community Psychol 10:417–428, 1982

26. Young ER, Parish TS: Impact of father absence during childhood on the psychological adjustment of college females. Sex Roles 3:217–227, 1977

27. Rickel AU, Langner TS: Short- and long-term effects of marital disruption on children. Am J Community Psychol 13:599–611, 1985

28. Stolberg AL, Cullen PM, Garrison KM: The divorce adjustment project: preventive programming for children of divorce. Journal of Preventive Psychiatry 1:365–368, 1982
29. Pedro-Carroll J, Cowen EL: The children of divorce intervention project: an investigation of the efficacy of a school based prevention program. J Consult Clin Psychol 53:603–611, 1985
30. Pedro-Carroll J, Cowen EL, Hightower A, et al: Preventive intervention with latency-aged children of divorce: a replication study. Am J Community Psychol 14(3):277–290, 1986
31. Stolberg AL, Garrison KM: Evaluating a primary prevention program for children of divorce. Am J Community Psychol 13(2):111–124, 1985
32. Bird HR: Individual psychotherapy with young children, in The Clinical Guide to Child Psychiatry. Edited by Shaffer D, Ehrhardt AA, Greenhill LL. New York, Macmillan-Free Press, 1985, pp 554–565
33. Toomin MK: The child of divorce, in Therapeutic Needs of the Family. Edited by Hardy RE, Cull JG. Springfield, IL, Charles C Thomas, 1974, pp 130–149
34. Tessman L: Children of Parting Parents. New York, Jason Aronson, 1978
35. Hodges WF: Interventions for Children of Divorce: Custody, Access, and Psychotherapy. New York, John Wiley, 1986
36. Kalter N: Children of divorce in an outpatient psychiatric population. Am J Orthopsychiatry 47:40–51, 1977
37. Gardner RA: Psychotherapy With Children of Divorce. New York, Jason Aronson, 1976

14 Children of Affluent Parents
Robin B. Shafran, Ph.D.

In thinking about the issues involved in treating children of parents who are affluent, extremely affluent, or unquestionably very rich, the question comes up whether working with this group of children differs from working with other children. Children are, essentially, children, with the same needs, facing the same developmental challenges, and running into the same roadblocks and difficulties. As Pittman (1) noted, most things that happen in "normal" families happen in rich ones. The wealthy are not exempt from random violence, emotional neglect, family disruption, or even despair. The rich, he points out, "may be as ignorant in the rules of the world as the poor" (p. 468). Wealth is not an illness, however, and children born to wealthy parents are not, by virtue of their finances, in psychological distress. Wealth may prove to be a complicating factor, though, in treating those children who do develop symptoms requiring professional intervention.

Without challenging the assumption that children are more simply alike than otherwise, it must also be noted that children with extremely wealthy parents are in some ways different from their less affluent counterparts, and that therapeutic intervention presents some different issues and problems. This chapter will address some factors specific to the lives, and therefore to the treatment, of children raised in homes with great material abundance. Some comments about why this is a distinct population or subgroup will be followed by a discussion of some special issues in the lives of extremely wealthy children. Possible complications in establishing and maintaining treatment, and other selected issues in the treatment process, particularly those related to transference and countertransference, will be explored in this chapter, and I will present a clinical illustration.

SPECIAL ISSUES IN THE LIVES OF WEALTHY CHILDREN

There is a small, but consistent, literature regarding the variables that make the rich a distinct group, and which lead to different conditions in which children are raised. Pittman (1), referring to the lessons F. Scott Fitzgerald learned from Zelda, notes that money "is only the starting point for a quite different functional relationship with the world, making the rich, like the poor, different from those of us who are driven by hope and go through life striving to improve our selves and our lot" (p. 461). Wealth, according to Pittman, is simply not good for children. It can belittle their achievements, distort their relationships with peers, and increase their sense of what is enough. He points out that rich children growing up with ordinary people may be seen as different, subjected to envy, or sought after for the wrong reasons.

Grinker (2) called the children of the "super rich" a "grossly neglected minority group" (p. 913). Although he was referring to the adult children of the rich, his comments about the factors underlying the development of wealth-related pathology speak to the environments in which these adults were raised. Among the factors he and others (1,3,4) have pointed to are inconsistently available parents, servants serving as parental substitutes, few and unclear role models, great freedom, and little consistent discipline.

Parental deprivation among some children of the rich has been considered a fundamental difference between these children and their middle-class counterparts. It is one of the similarities in the upbringing of the very wealthy and the very poor (2,3). As Stone points out, however, such deprivation is more easily masked among the rich. Isolation within the family, and particularly from the parents, often takes the form of children being raised by servants. They may not see their parents for more than small amounts of time daily, if that, are fed, dressed, and bathed by nannies, and entertained by governesses or housekeepers. Stone speaks of the "poor little rich girl," rich in material possessions, but impoverished in parental love, attention, and consistent guidance.

Relying on housekeepers, nannies, and other employees to serve as parental surrogates may be the clearest hardship faced by children of the wealthy. The degree to which parents delegate their responsibility, authority, and involvement to others, and the frequency with which child care providers change, will, of course affect the degree of hardship experienced by the children involved. Fluctuations in the presence and attentiveness of the "mothering one," whether that person is the biological mother or father or is an employed nanny, will interfere with the development of a secure sense of self, with the confidence that one's needs will be respected and met and that the world is populated with people who can be counted upon. The child's self-esteem may well be impaired. In such a setting, the child may grow up with the sense of being a nuisance, albeit a special, privileged, and entitled one, whose demands for toys and treats are met without frustration. His or her real needs for consistent love, attention, and interested involvement may be met only sporadically, and in a manner which the child can neither predict nor control. Children raised under these circumstances may then be in the peculiar situation of having to explain to themselves how it is that they can be both very important and privileged, and—to the people with whom it counts, their parents—insignificant and of little consistent, intimate regard.

The lack of consistent parental presence and involvement, then, presents significant difficulties for the affected children. Without the security and reassurance provided by their parents' clear interest in them as developing individuals, these children may feel unloved and undervalued. The development of a stable self-image may be impaired as well (2,4). The absence of clear role models with whom to identify is another complication for these children (2,3,4). Particularly in those situations where children are surrounded by their parents' employees, rather than by their parents and parents' friends, they may have difficulty developing clear ideas about how adults of their own economic group function in the world. Instead, the adult world to which they have access as children is one from which they will be excluded as adults.

The importance of appropriate role models, and their not infrequent absence for the children of the very wealthy, is also emphasized by Wixen (5). He describes a condition he called "dysgradia," which refers to the failure to have and to identify with a series of important role models and images during childhood and adolescence. Without such role models, children may miss the opportunity to internalize various values, attributes, goals, and styles of thinking, feeling, and behavior. The consequences are impairments in the development of character, and in interpersonal and intrapersonal traits. For Wixen, this is a clear result of the absence of important individuals during development, or the absence of meaningful interactions with them.

The absence of clear parental expectations goes hand in hand with the absence of appropriate role models, and further complicates the difficulties children of the rich may have in figuring out who they are, how they should behave, and what is reasonable in the way of identifications and aspirations. Stone (3) discusses the lack of clearly communicated parental expectations, which, he believes, "if communicated in reasonably healthy way form the backbone of a child's ambition and sense of direction" (p. 30).

Related to the issue of parental expectations, or to their absence, is the lack of clarity regarding the child's place and function within the family. Pittman (1) discusses the need for children of the wealthy to deal with the reality that they are not needed by their families for their concrete contributions. Chores are done by servants. There is no need to provide real services; "Rich kids don't do useful work—they take lessons—music, dance, tennis, even charm, whatever will make them more decorative and socially acceptable" (p. 464). Education, then, may lose its function of informing or training or stimulating. Its value may seem to lie solely in grades that parents can brag about.

Despite high self-regard and perhaps the conviction that they have status or are in some ways important or entitled to special consideration, children of the rich tend to have low self-confidence. These children have not grown up feeling as if they know anything useful or have anything useful to contribute. They lack, in Pittman's (1) view, a give-and-take relationship with the world. He further points out that awe for successful and/or distant parents may replace the more personal kinds of interactions through which self-esteem develops.

Children of the very wealthy may not be able to use teachers or other adults outside of their homes to compensate for the deprivation within their homes, as do children from other economic and social groups. Rather than seeing them as people to look up to, teachers, health care professionals, and other individuals who look after the educational and physical development of wealthy children may be seen as an extension of the caretaker group—one step above the housekeeper. Pittman wryly comments: "Rich kids may have a hard time respecting underpaid, polyester-clad teachers who don't go to Aspen for Christmas" (p. 464).

In a study of 50 wealthy families, Pittman (1) found two obvious differences between the rich and others. The first was that there were many more graduate degrees and high achievers among children of the rich. He pointed out that wealth provides opportunities for cultural experiences, education, social and professional contacts, medical and psychotherapeutic treatment, style and social ease, mobility, and a sense of being someone. However, he also found a significant level of functional incompetence, this because the need to function is simply not so pressing. Rewards are independent of functioning. Survival and comfort are assured whether the child functions or not.

Pittman (1) observed that rich children seem to grow up to become doctors, lawyers, or other professionals, or bums living on trust funds. There were few in the middle (i.e., working as carpenters, shoe salesmen, or in other such ordinary occupations). He further observed that most rich children seem to take advantage of their opportunities and achieve success in their education and their careers. However, he believes that they do not get as much pleasure from their successes as do middle-class children: "By the standards of the society in which they have been raised, most rich kids turn out just as expected. The failures are particularly visible and seemingly inexplicable" (p. 463).

Pittman elaborates that children of the wealthy run into difficulties for a number of reasons (1). He suggests that performance expectations that derive from success-oriented forebears may be quite intimidating. If the child cannot see his or her way clear to being spectacularly successful, he or she may feel damaged and give up any effort toward productivity. This is particularly so if there is no need for the growing child to learn any means of supporting him- or herself through independent efforts.

In addition to facing special difficulties in relationships with parents and other adults, which may invariably interfere with the growing child's sense of self and his or her deserved place in the world, wealthy children may run into difficulties in establishing solid relations with their peers, thereby losing out on vital interactions and perhaps their last opportunities to get what they have missed all the way through. Here, various factors come into play. Stone (3) refers to the social isolation of the wealthy, which may deprive these youngsters of opportunities to meet and mingle with other children. Social skills developed primarily with adults may not help as they try to cope with interactions with their peers. This is further complicated if the wealthy child is operating in an economically mixed group, by a sense that he or she has so much more than many others, and by fears and doubts about the motivations of other children in seeking friendship. One doesn't know whether one is liked, genuinely, for oneself, or for the access to a privileged world that the friendship brings. Often, children who are growing up without a sense of their own real skills, strengths, and positive attributes do not feel adequate to compete in the world of other children, and so choose, instead, to withdraw.

The difficulties that bring children of the wealthy into treatment are, for the most part, similar to those around which we see other children. However, the antecedents of the presenting school or behavior problem, anxiety or depression, or disorder in sleeping or eating may be somewhat different. Often these children present around one or more of the issues just discussed. Prolonged parental noninvolvement, frequent and unpredictable shifts in nannies and housekeepers, and the consequent impairments in sense of self and self-esteem, lead to the symptomatic displays that lead to referral.

These are often children who simply do not have any idea how to get around in the world, how to deal with their teachers or classmates, or how to deal with their own reactions when they are frustrated or deprived or do not do as well as they believe they should (or fear their parents believe they should). Further, exposure to other children, and the witnessing of the relationships which they have, and to which they feel entitled, may exacerbate the rich child's sense of inadequacy, inferiority, and deprivation. Despite every material advantage, children growing up in such circumstances may well come to us impoverished. The therapeutic relationship may be the first in which the child learns about him- or herself in interaction with another. It may be the first opportunity for consistent, predictable attention, and response. In addition to the addressing of the symptoms articulated by the parent, teacher, or other referral source, the therapy may well have to address underlying deficits that accompany a life-style of material abundance and emotional scarcity.

Although my focus in this chapter is on the difficulties that arise in growing up rich, it must be emphasized that these are scenarios where things go awry—where parents are too involved with themselves to attend to their children and have the financial means to delegate those responsibilities to their staffs. This is not necessarily descriptive of the situation faced by all, or even most rich children. As Pittman (1) states:

Being a rich kid has both advantages and disadvantages. The point should be underlined that most rich families are made up of sane, sensible, caring people, who put a major share of their considerable energy and resources into raising their children and are cognizant of the disadvantage under which they are growing up. Most rich parents guide their kids successfully through these dangers. Some don't. (p. 468)

ESTABLISHING AND MAINTAINING TREATMENT

Many of the considerations in establishing and maintaining treatment with children of the wealthy are similar to those in working with children from any other group. This section will address some possible differences that are the result of dealing with wealthy parents and their troubled children.

From the outset of treatment, initial conversations with either the referral source or the parent, there may be indications that the family's wealth, success, or influence in the community may play a role in the therapy of the child involved. Often, when the referral is made by the school, it may become clear that the family is treated differently, often with circumspection or deference. For example, in a situation in which the 6-year-old son of an extremely wealthy and well-known father was referred for evaluation, the school psychologist from his prestigious private school made it clear that if the results were not to the liking of the family, they would simply not permit treatment. The referring psychologist further cautioned that the impression the parents had of the therapist might influence whether other referrals would be made. Before the therapist had even spoken to the parents or met with the child, she was on notice.

A situation such as that described above emphasizes a crucial point in the treatment of the rich and powerful: the importance that the therapist not yield to pressure and deviate from standard procedures and not allow the consequences of his or her judgment to interfere with evaluating and treating the situation as seems appropriate. The wealthy may well attempt to use their money and their position to have things go their own way (3). Despite the status of the parents of these young patients, it is extremely important that the therapist establish him- or herself as the expert in the room and the person in charge of the treatment. This is important both because it ultimately increases the likelihood that treatment will "take" and will be successful, and because it may be the first time that the patient, the child, sees that someone is willing to set limits with his parents for his benefit.

Conflict with the parents around scheduling, vacations, missed appointments, and so on will be minimized, as well, if the therapist assumes control from the outset. Establishing oneself as the authority, in a clear, nondefensive manner may be difficult in situations with people used to having things go their own way, who are used to giving directions rather than following another's lead (6,7). As Stone (3) has commented: "The wealthy are not alone in trying to control the therapist and thwart his attempts to organize treatment as he sees fit; they are merely better at it" (p. 22).

Despite the therapist's best efforts to set up treatment with the child of wealthy parents along guidelines similar to those with any other family beginning treatment, these parents may well present certain difficulties having to do simply with the logistics of the therapy. It may be more difficult than usual, for example, to find a time to have both parents in for an initial consultation. Parents who have delegated childrearing responsibility all along may not immediately see the need for their actual presence in the consulting room. Once they have been convinced of this necessity, scheduling may prove to be the next hurdle. This may be further complicated by what Stone (3) refers to as "geographic elusiveness"—the frequency with which these parents may be out of town. Again, these are frequently busy and powerful people who are accustomed to having the rest of the world accommodate them. We all have busy lives; this particular group often sees their brand of busyness as more important.

Just as it may be difficult, initially, to have the parents in, it may be difficult to schedule regular sessions with the child, and to establish therapy as a priority among the many activities in the child's week. The therapy situation must be highlighted as "special," not just another lesson or after-school activity. This is complicated by the busy after-school schedules of many children, but appears to be more of an issue in situations where the number of "classes" one can enroll in is not limited by money, and in situations where there isn't an adult setting consistent limits on how busy a child should be after a day in school, or in helping the child set priorities about those activities that are clearly more important than others.

Setting a fee may be more complicated as well, despite the reality that the amount of money involved may not be significant for people with high incomes, who routinely spend more than a therapist's fee for their own pleasure and enjoyment. The straightforward stating of one's standard fee, accompanied by a brief explanation of policies regarding cancellations and payments for missed sessions, leaves the field clear of countertransferential issues. Stone (3) stresses the importance of resisting the temptation to set a fee somewhat higher than would usually be charged because of the ease with which payment could be met, warning that once this occurs, a situation is set up in which this patient becomes more important or "special" than others, deserving special consideration and differential treatment. For similar reasons, he cautions against recommending greater frequency of sessions because paying for them would be no hardship.

Stone (3) also comments on the occasional pressure to charge a higher fee than one would typically charge. Families who can afford the "best" may insist on seeing someone who, by virtue of his higher fee, might appear more expert or better qualified: "In such a way, it sometimes happens that a therapist would be passed up unless he charged substantially more than he is accustomed to receiving. Otherwise he would be regarded as a 'nobody'" (p. 25).

Yielding to such pressure would once again set up a situation in which the therapy was "different." The child again would be at risk for differential treatment, not necessarily to his benefit.

On the other end of the spectrum, and to Stone a more irritating group, are those parents who resent having to pay the therapist's fee (3). These are largely wealthy men who have made their own fortunes, who, he points out, may well continue to view life in the way they did when they were poor. Both the fee charged by the therapist and the intangible nature of the service provided may lead to resistance on the part of these parents to paying for treatment.

As with any other therapeutic relationship, it is important that from the start, the therapist establish him- or herself as the expert in the room, who initially structures the treatment and sets the ground rules. With many people seeking treatment, this is not a significant issue; the therapist is seen this way from the start. However, with such a successful group, respect cannot be assumed on the basis of education and training. Often, these parents are as well educated and at least as accomplished in their own fields. Parents born into wealth and who have grown up in an extremely wealthy environment may see the therapist, no matter how well trained and highly regarded in the field, as someone of lesser breeding and lower status. As Stone (3) puts it, the therapist may be viewed, though more rarely, as just another of "the irksome innominate rabble of butchers, bakers, and candlestick-makers with whom they must, when unavoidable, have dealings" (p. 33). Without the aid of the trappings of the profession and the respect assumed to be generated by virtue of degree, title, and generally acknowledged expertise, the therapist must rely on his or her own resources, sense of self-worth, and confidence in his or her competence to set the tone and the conditions for treatment.

Initial contact between the therapist and child, will be, as with a child from any other group, affected by the child's presenting difficulties, feelings about entering into a psychotherapy, and prior experiences with significant adults. Children who have been exposed to, and disappointed by, a succession of caregivers hired by their parents to "love" them and tend their needs, may approach yet another situation orchestrated by their parents, presumably for the benefit of the child, with understandable hesitation. Once again, the child may feel that responsibility for his or her well being is being shifted from parent to paid "other." As one child complained, early in treatment, "my mother tells me now to go tell you if something bothers me; she says she pays you to listen to me." In this situation, the therapist must make clear just where his or her loyalties lie and the nature of the therapeutic agenda, which does not happen to include relieving parents of their obligation to attend to the needs of their children.

Children growing up in very wealthy environments may have found themselves surrounded by adults from early on, and may well have learned to conduct themselves with a facade of maturity and sophistication that belies their age and developmental levels. These children may present in treatment as older than their ages, able to conduct themselves and converse in a way suggestive of an older child. In this situation, in which the child appears overly at ease and comfortable with the task of therapy, it may be the primary initial task for the therapist to make contact with the child underneath the mask, and create a situation in which a kid can simply act, talk, and feel like a kid. Again, these are the tasks that child therapists face with all new patients.

Once treatment is under way, the potential complications and interferences are quite similar whether working with children of the wealthy or children from other economic and social groups. There are, however, situations in which parental wealth, influence, and power may further complicate things. This is a group that often has children brought to therapy by child care workers and other household staff; one young child seen by me was delivered by his father's chauffeur, who then waited in the car for the child to be finished. Although children are often brought reliably for their sessions in this manner, the extent of parental noninvolvement may contribute to their disinterest in the course of treatment. Often the therapist ends up working in a vacuum, receiving little information, except that provided by the child, about what is going on in life outside of the consulting room. Having parents in on a regular basis may prove difficult because of their travel plans or business schedules, particularly if therapy is seen as one more after-school activity for the child. One parent commented that in agreeing for treatment, the emotional well-being of his son was in the hands of the therapist. He no longer felt responsible, he was not willing to become involved in the particulars, and he had no inclination or intention to come in for meetings with the therapist. Again, although this eventuality could occur with any parents, it seems that the more money one has, the easier it is to delegate one's responsibility.

Despite the difficulties in maintaining regular contact with parents who are used to delegating their responsibilities for childcare to nannies, housekeepers, tutors, and others, it is crucial that should this situation arise, the therapist take a clear stand. It is at this point that our professional stature and expertise differentiate us from other personnel engaged in caring for other people's children. From the outset of treatment, the expectations for parental involvement (i.e., frequency of sessions with them and how such sessions will be scheduled and including some accommodation to travel and business needs) must be articulated and agreed upon. Making clear what is required and that it is a nonnegotiable condition for the child in treatment is an essential prerequisite for successful work.

The example referred to above, in which the father attempted to distance himself from the treatment and from his child, was such a situation. My refusal to yield, however, resulted in this parent's becoming a more active participant in his son's life. This occurred at first reluctantly and with considerable resentment but over time with greater willingness and interest. This was accomplished, I believe, by my conveying clearly to the father that his participation was not optional, and in fact, was crucial for his child's improvement. It was a new thought to him that he could play so vital a role in his child's development.

Receiving regular payment may be another source of frustration when dealing with wealthy parents, and for reasons other than ability to pay in a timely fashion. Stone (3) has observed that "both the rich and the poor tend to be unsympathetic to the monetary needs of the doctor" (p. 42). People with little income tend to see the therapist as earning vast amounts, certainly more than he or she needs. The rich, in Stone's assessment, may regard the therapist's concerns about payment as undignified. Careless and casual attitudes about money on the part of those born with it may lead to a sporadic pattern of payments, unacceptable to anyone who works for a living. The "self-made" man, despite accumulated fortunes, still feels poor and has difficulty paying what he considers to be a huge bill for a vague product on a regular basis. Maintaining an open, nondefensive channel of communication with parents who the therapist may see only infrequently may be pivotal in dealing with this situation should it arise.

In addition to establishing comfortable working relations with parents of the child patient and the child himself, the therapist in this situation may need to work with other adults involved in the child's daily life. Good rapport with the housekeeper or caregiver in the home may be important, as communication between therapist and home may be with that person rather than the parents. Tutors may be a more integral aspect of the child's interpersonal life, as is the situation in the case to be discussed in this chapter. Relations with school personnel may take a different cast, particularly if the school is awed or intimidated by the family's status. The therapist may find herself in the role of child advocate, repeatedly emphasizing the feelings and needs of the child in conversations with other involved adults. Again, the therapist's ability to keep his or her function and competence in that function clear to him- or herself will be crucial in successfully negotiating in the world the child occupies.

SELECTED ISSUES IN TREATMENT

Children find their ways into therapists' offices for many reasons. Difficulties in school or at home, obvious signs of excessive anxiety, fear, anger or sadness—all may precipitate an initial consultation. The children of the very wealthy are as vulnerable as any others and may have the same stated presenting problems. In addition, they face a particular set of circumstances which can be qualitatively different from their more middle-class counterparts. As I mentioned previously, these are children who may have trouble negotiating the ordinary world of school, including developing working and nurturing relationships with teachers, and satisfying friendships with peers. The demands to perform and conform may be new to them, and they may experience difficulties fitting into a heterogeneous class group. Feelings of inadequacy and unpreparedness may be exacerbated in circumstances where their own privileged entitlement is not taken as a given.

In his discussion of interpersonal therapy with children, Green (8) delineates two major purposes to treatment. The first is the facilitation of intimacy. The second is the restoration or improvement of competence wherever it is "restricted or handicapped by interpersonal problems" (p. 556). The special circumstances, expectations, and demands faced by many of the wealthy youngsters who ultimately find their ways into therapists' offices lead to difficulties along both of Green's dimensions.

Warm, supportive, intimate relationships, originating with that between the child and the mothering one, and expanding to include relations with other family members and then with friends, often have not been prominent in the lives of those who are simultaneously privileged and deprived. The lack of such intimate experiences is, in fact, an underlying determinant in the development of symptomatology. It is for this reason that the therapeutic relationship assumes such importance, as the crucial mutative factor in treatment. As I have emphasized, the interaction between therapist and child may be the child's first experience with a consistently reliable, available adult whose interest is genuine, whose attention is directed solely to the child, and who demonstrates through this consistent attentiveness and interest a respect for the child's feelings, thoughts, and needs. Through the give and take of this new and nurturing relationship focused on the child's concerns and reactions, new patterns of interacting may be opened for him. As this occurs, the child's sense of himself will be more clearly articulated and feelings of self-worth will develop and be enhanced.

Concerns about competence, the second of Green's general areas (8), are certainly relevant to the children of the wealthy. Here, the therapist must work along at least two dimensions: feelings of individual competence and personal self-worth at home, and the development of competence in regard to skills in the child's interactional world of school and peers.

How competence is defined and measured may be distorted in homes where the extremes of success have been achieved. The goal of treatment, in this situation, is to modulate the child's and parents' expectations to the point that they are realistic and reasonably attainable. Not limited to school performance, grades, or increasing facility in extracurricular events, social ease and agility are at issue here as well. Expectations about how the child presents himself, behaves during long, formal dinners in exclusive restaurants, and handles conversations with adults must all be addressed. Here, there are two goals. The first involves increasing the child's feelings of competence, and correspondingly of self-worth, as the standards by which the child judges him-self and is judged by others are adjusted. The second goal is an increase in actual competence. The latter will occur as a by-product. No longer feeling hopeless and certain to disappoint and fail, the child can begin to perform at higher levels.

Doubt about their abilities, as well as actual deficits, are issues for many wealthy children learning about themselves in their larger interpersonal worlds. Having to function without adequate experience in the areas of devel-oping friendships, cooperating and collaborating in a peer group, delaying or foregoing one's own satisfactions for the sake of another, puts the sheltered, pampered, and socially awkward child at a disadvantage. The work of the ther-apy, in this regard, is directed toward improving the child's ability to live in his interpersonal world, working on skills that so many other children start to develop in nursery school.

As the work proceeds simultaneously along the lines described here, in-creasing the child's capacity for intimacy and facilitating the growth of inter-personal and functional competence, the particular dilemmas and complications arising from the family's financial or social status may be ad-dressed as well. Feelings of loneliness and isolation resulting from the amount of time one or both parents may be absent from the child's daily life need to be heard and validated, while coping strategies are developed. As such chil-dren become more aware of the nature of their parents' wealth, its impact on them and the symbolic significance of money to them must be explored. The differences between their own life-styles and those of their schoolmates, if that is the case, is also an issue requiring reconciliation. One child, for example, was surprised and troubled upon a visit to a friend's home, to view what she considered a dearth of toys and games, two children sharing one room, and a dining table in the kitchen rather than in a proper dining room. Children who are raised in luxury often need help fitting into a less luxurious world, for to remain on its outskirts may well mean remaining with few friends.

Burlingham (9), who wrote what Rubenstein and Levitt (10) called the "definitive treatise on the role of parents in the analysis of children" (p. 16), concluded that the child analyst must handle a transference situation that is really double, between him- or herself and the mother, as well as between him- or herself and the child. As active fathering has gained increasing societal acceptance, the numbers of players in transferential-countertransferential in-teractions has further increased. Although relations between therapists and the children of the rich and their parents are subject to many of the same possible relational issues as are treatments with patients from other social and economic groups, the focus in this chapter will remain on delineating some of the more common transferential and countertransferential dilemmas that are particular to this group.

The duality of the transferential-countertransferential dyad (therapist and child, therapist and parents) is clearly an issue in the treatment of the children of the rich, where issues of parental finances, status, and influence threaten to assume exaggerated importance in the treatment of the child. Stone (3), in a discussion of qualities important in treating the wealthy, observes:

> The child is at the mercy of the parents, and the parents are at the mercy of the therapist . . . who is dependent financially on the parents, whose relationship with the therapist is rendered the more tenuous by virtue of their not being the designated patient. To keep the fragile symbiosis alive, the therapist must be a person of unimpeachable integrity. It doesn't hurt, however, if he makes his integrity a little more noticeable than usual. (p. 45)

Parents bring a variety of expectations and reactions to their children's treatment, and assume many different stances regarding their degree of interest and involvement, ranging from the virtual disinterest mentioned in the examples above, of parents delegating as much of their responsibility as is possible, to attempting intrusive control of both the structure and content of the treatment. Again, in this way wealthy parents do not necessarily distinguish themselves from their economically less well-off counterparts. However, to the extent that extremely successful or wealthy parents are used to controlling what goes on around them, they may bring similar expectations to their children's treatment (3,6).

The previously discussed potential difficulties in initiating treatment contain the beginnings of several transferential difficulties. Parents who tend to view their child's therapist as just another worker—as someone to assume responsibility, or as someone to follow their directives in shaping the child in a particular way, accomplishing the goal of making the child more to the parents' liking—will have difficulty both yielding to the therapist's expertise and authority and in working collaboratively with the therapist for the benefit of the child patient.

As McKamy (6) has pointed out, the wealthy are used to controlling their own environments, and rarely experience situations where their own resources are not sufficient to solve their problems. This is the situation with which they are confronted in bringing their children to a therapist, a situation that may trigger the rather unusual feeling, for them, of being out of control or helpless. This may lead to a parental transference reaction of anxiety-generating dependence, or of hostility to the therapist, who will be blamed for putting them in that situation. Either way, the therapist is faced with assessing the needs of the parents as well as those of the child, and shaping his or her interactions with the parents to ensure the continuation of the child's treatment.

Stone (3) also speaks to this issue, noting the tendency among those who are responsible for paying for treatment to behave in an obstructionist manner, and to attempt to control the therapist and the course of treatment. All of the issues about wealth and status come into play as well, if the parents find it difficult to view someone who is clearly less well off as the expert in the situation. He notes the importance of such superficialities as maintaining an office with a degree of elegance and size in an appropriate location.

The presence of parents in the treatment situation, regardless of their degree of involvement and visibility, leads to reactions on the part of the therapist, too. Kohrman and colleagues (11), in discussing problems of countertransference, comment that the range of problems with parents is extensive, ranging from the regulating of the routinized activities of the treatment (i.e., ensuring that the child arrives regularly and promptly and that bills are paid, to premature termination). They point out that parents may overcomply or constantly test the limits of the analyst's power and authority. Countertransference reactions arise in response to whatever styles, concerns, and modes of interactions are presented by the parents of young patients, and are not limited to situations in which there is appreciable wealth or status. I will limit the following discussion to certain specific reactions often triggered by the rich or influential.

Envy and contempt are often cited as common countertransference reactions when working with very wealthy populations. Grinker (2) notes that one factor in assessing treatment prognosis is the capacity of the therapist to tolerate and understand his or her countertransference reactions. He cautions that countertransference may overwhelm the therapist, the patient, and the treatment. Grinker points to the ease with which the therapist may become contemptuous of the patient's values or lack of them, feel disinterested, convey envy or anger, or feel the treatment time is being wasted. The therapist may envy the wealth, time, and freedom of the patient. The middle-class values of the therapist, including the work ethic, may impair understanding of this parent group. The therapist may feel depreciated and bored.

Stone (3) also raises the problems of envy and contempt. He notes that money is not the only source of envy for therapists; it is possible to envy our patients' youth, beauty, vitality, and so on. However, he believes that envy of wealth "can exert the most corrupting influence on our professional character" (p. 37). Contempt, to Stone, is a potential result of a struggle with envy, in which the envy experienced is converted into feelings of contempt.

Stone discusses the need to work as a spur to excellence, but warns that it is often accompanied by feelings of bitterness and entrapment (3). The patient whose life-style represents freedom from such mundane concerns may be regarded as special and treated as such. Pollak and Schaffer (7) discuss a related reaction, that of idealization, which they view as another defense against envy. The potential danger in this mode of reaction is that underdiagnosis may occur (7), or that the patient and his or her parents may be treated as special (3), neither of which is in the best interests of a child who may easily have spent his lifetime feeling different.

It is hard for the therapist not to compare his or her own family's economic and social status with that of an especially successful patient family. Listening to someone else's child tell of extravagant living circumstances, vacations, and gifts, it may be hard to not wish for the same for one's own family, or to defend against such wishes by viewing the child with pity for the circumstances that bring him into treatment. Acknowledging and accepting such reactions, as a first step in dealing with them, is the therapist's best insurance that such countertransference responses will not get in the way of the treatment. Stone (3) speaks of the need felt by some patients to seek out therapists with whom they have a good deal in common, based on the assumption that such a person will understand them more easily. He maintains that wealth is one such parameter, commenting that "if the gap in socioeconomic background is too wide between patient and therapist, it will prove unspannable as well" (p. 38).

The child's reaction to a new and developing relationship with his therapist will reflect more than issues of wealth and a history of being treated as special. Just as with any other child patient, the transference relationship will include a variety of feelings, impressions, and wishes, and will reflect the particular style of interaction that characterizes the child. However, to the extent that the child is accustomed to adults being engaged by his parents to relieve them of the need to parent, the therapist may be viewed skeptically as yet one more person in that category. Whatever disdain, arrogance, contempt, or frustration is generally directed toward such an individual is likely to be present in the initial stages of therapy as well.

Whatever factors influence or interfere with adequate communications between therapist and parents are likely to have an impact on the child's ability to settle into a treatment relationship. Children of the wealthy, like any other children, can be acutely sensitive to the interactions among significant adults. To the extent that the child patient is aware of the presence of the reaction patterns previously discussed, his or her ability to fully enter and be engaged in treatment will be compromised. No child needs to have loyalties torn between parents and therapist. For children who have never been certain of their parents' commitment to them, the situation is untenable.

CASE ILLUSTRATION

Like many children of wealthy parents, and like many children in general, the child whom I shall call Elizabeth was taken to see me because she was, in certain very fundamental ways, a disappointment to her parents. Elizabeth—8 years old, in the third grade, and an only child—was neither pretty enough, thin enough, smart enough, or sufficiently at ease with adults and popular with her peers to meet their expectations. In fact, her schoolwork was merely average. Elizabeth was alternately withdrawn and inappropriately aggressive with other children and had few social skills and fewer friends. Her lack of self-control and her attitude of defiant indifference was disruptive to the point that her continuation at her very exclusive girls' school was tenuous. She was verbally abusive to her parents and their housekeeper. Additionally, Elizabeth could not be relied upon to behave appropriately on the numerous occasions when she was taken to dinner or to various events with her parents, their friends, and the always impeccably behaved offspring of the other couples present. She was annoying and irritating, and an embarrassment to her parents.

What distinguished these parents, at least the mother, from those wealthy parents who lack concern and interest for their children, as discussed previously was that she was genuinely distressed about her daughter's clear unhappiness. The child's father was primarily concerned that his daughter shape up and cease being an embarrassment. He acknowledged Elizabeth's obvious distress and admitted to his own feelings of frustration and sadness about it only after many meetings with the therapist.

Elizabeth grew up in very privileged circumstances, cared for by both her mother and a nanny. In addition, the family housekeeper was often given responsibility for her, but this woman's role was, for the most part, limited to either babysitting or escorting her from one activity or appointment to another. Elizabeth's father, who was a self-employed, self-made millionaire, was rarely home, and when he was, he spent his time in his study. Her mother was busy with charity work or involved in various political causes.

In preliminary discussion with the parents, it quickly emerged that Elizabeth's mother was in a constant state of anxiety regarding her daughter, always fearful about the next blowup, and tearful about her daughter's lack of invitations to other children's homes. She was furious with her husband who tended to deny that there was much of a problem, except insofar as their daughter lacked appropriate table manners and was frequently rude to her parents and sullen with their friends. He did confirm that few children seemed interested in playing with her. He saw his wife as overinvolved, overanxious, and somewhat hysterical, initially insinuating but as time went on directly stating his belief that she was responsible for their daughter's difficulties.

I was surprised to find, upon meeting Elizabeth, that she was neither fat nor ugly, but a rather pretty youngster, tall for an 8-year-old, with striking brown eyes and long dark hair. She entered treatment casually, commenting that seeing a psychologist was no big deal; many of her friends did so. I was impressed with the lack of significance attributed to treatment. I was indeed one more activity, one more adult. It was not until we reached the end of the first year of treatment that it was clear to me that I had earned a significant place in her life—that our relationship was important and useful, and that I was becoming someone in whom she could begin to confide, and upon whom she could depend. This transition was gradual, and I believe was facilitated, initially, by my willingness to accept her versions of events, to try to see the world through her eyes. She also began to experiment with the possibility of expressing an array of feelings. This was begun through a drawing we worked on together for months, adding sheets of paper as the work expanded. Verbal expression was secondary and came significantly later. What occurred through this first year was her growing feelings of security in relation to me.

Elizabeth presented with many of the underlying difficulties typical of children growing up with material abundance—more toys, activities, and lessons than she knew what to do with, many dinner hours spent alone or in the company of nanny or babysitter, and in some very fundamental ways, ignorance of the rules of the world of children. No amount of money spent by her parents was sufficient to provide access to the after-school play shared by the children in her class. Although they were only too willing to attend the rather extravagant birthday parties arranged by her parents, her invitations were not reciprocated. Teachers and tutors alike were intimidated by parental stature and reluctant to speak with her parents in a straightforward manner. From the start, I became the conduit, the one who was not afraid to deal directly with these somewhat formidable people.

Although much of the work with this child has been like that with any other—time spent in a combination of play and conversation—there have been some differences as well. From the start, the playroom had no appeal. There was nothing I could offer that she didn't have at home, including a paid companion. I felt as if I were simply one more stop in a busy schedule, nothing special. There was also no resistance to coming for sessions—again, one more stop. The passivity with which Elizabeth reacted to her circumstances for so long was reflected in the treatment as well. However, once she began to make use of the therapy to work through this passivity, her anger was directed toward everyone but her therapist, who became the one individual spared her temper. This may have been a result of a degree of idealization in the transferential relationship (i.e., that no one else was as understanding or interested or accepting of her as was I). Therefore, everyone else was, to some extent, a disappointment. Alternately, there may have been an underlying concern that were she to experience anger toward me, she would lose me, as well. I would become yet another disappointment. This might have been an unbearable possibility.

Elizabeth was a child who simultaneously took everything and nothing for granted. She expected and received much in the way of material acquisitions, tickets to special events, and luxurious vacation trips. She did not know what it was like, however, to receive regular phone calls from the girls in her class whose attention she craved, to be certain that someone reached out to her because they liked her, rather than because they were paid to do so. Thus, when I asked for her address at summer camp so that I might send her a card, she commented that she hadn't realized that "I had to do that, too." Upon hearing that I didn't "have to," that my interest in hearing how camp was going and keeping in touch that way was genuine and not orchestrated by her parents, she was surprised and touched. This interaction was pivotal in Elizabeth's developing a sense that people could like her for who she was, that she might be a person who was, indeed, likable.

Despite her genuine desire for friendship, Elizabeth was a child with few real friends. She cried easily in school and so was a target for teasing, and lashed out when she was frustrated. Much of what transpired in the therapy concerned relating in a more constructive and appealing manner, which she developed in interaction with me during treatment. Although this child still lacks a "chum" and has not yet experienced the kind of intimate relationship Sullivan (12) considered vital to the course of development, she is acknowledging the wish and the need for one, and is exploring those factors that get in her way.

Ongoing interaction with Elizabeth's parents, although also similar in most respects to that with other parents of children in treatment, had some of the transferential-countertransferential elements I have described in this chapter. I was seen, particularly at the outset, as someone who had been engaged to "fix" their child in the manner they deemed appropriate. My repeated attempts to engage the parents, particularly the father, more directly in the day-to-day events in their daughter's life were met with faint interest and little action. For example, rather than finding a regular time to work with Elizabeth on her homework, help her with her reading, and so on, they engaged a tutor. Thus, they solved the problem, which they defined as "Elizabeth needs help with her homework." It took 2 years for them to hear and respond to the problem restated as "Elizabeth needs her parents to be interested and involved in her homework, and to provide the help."

Although Elizabeth's parents were consistently pleasant and polite in their interactions with me, it was clear that it was I who would have to accommodate them. From the beginning, our appointments had to be scheduled around business meetings, social commitments, and the like. They were casual about paying for treatment and often gave little notice about missing appointments. Paying for a missed session was clearly not a deterrent.

My reactions were also of a mixed nature. Although to some extent I was impressed with their concern for their daughter, I was struck by their unwillingness, which later was clearly seen as inability, to involve themselves usefully in her life. I was aware of the disparity between the attention they arranged for her and what they provided themselves. Initially, I was intimidated by their wealth and found myself actively working to keep that feeling out of my interactions with them and to not treat them in any deferential or special way. Treating Elizabeth and her parents like any other family may have been one of the more useful things I did for her.

In many other families, Elizabeth's appearance, performance, social skills, and so on would not have been a cause of concern. She would have been an acceptable child in average surroundings. Instead, she is an average child in exceptional surroundings. This is the issue Pittman (1) speaks to in his discussion of the often exceptional expectations that accompany growing up as the child of exceptionally successful parents. One of the goals of the treatment, therefore, had to be the adjusting of expectations to more realistic levels, without that being viewed as failure, thereby increasing Elizabeth's sense of her own competence and self-worth. For example, the possibility that this child does not have to go to the "best" prep school and then on to Princeton, does not have to garner the most party invitations or be in constant demand for after-school and weekend play, and can still be seen as "okay" is an important part of the work.

These factors were explored from a number of perspectives. Elizabeth's parents' own background, including their parents' expectations of them and their childhood experiences around these issues were discussed, as were the more personal meanings for them of what it symbolized to have a child who was not a "star." I believe that as the treatment progressed and Elizabeth became an easier child to live with, happier, less verbally abusive of her parents, and more popular with her peers, her parents became more realistic in their expectations and pleased with her actual accomplishments. Although they were clearly better able to see her for who she was and adjusted their demands accordingly, I think they were still a bit disappointed that she did not meet the image they had created.

SUMMARY AND CONCLUSIONS

In this chapter, I have focused on those factors that relate to child patients who come from wealthy families. These children can be seen to face certain difficult issues while growing up, despite what is often a luxurious and enriched life-style. Highlighted in this chapter have been problems arising from parental absence or lack of involvement, and a lack of preparedness for engaging in the social world of school and peers. These two major areas were discussed as fundamental in the course of treatment, the goals of which were conceptualized, generally, as increased capacity for intimacy, and greater competence (8).

Throughout this discussion of the special problems faced by children of the rich, and consequently the special problems faced by those of us who see them in psychotherapy, it was emphasized both that not all wealthy children live under these conditions of emotional neglect, unrealistic expectations, and social isolation, and that in most ways, children are children. The children of the wealthy come to us with similar needs and worries as do children of other social and economic groups, and for the most part, therapy runs a similar course. Wealthy young patients need to be listened to and accepted for who they are, not for who their parents are. To the extent that therapists can do that for them, get to know them for themselves, their strengths as well as weaknesses, wishes and dreams along with fears and anxieties, we may facilitate their better knowing and accepting themselves. Although working with children with wealthy parents may involve several technical issues, once they are resolved the treatment can be effective, focusing on the psychological needs of the child rather than the financial status or social influence of the family.

REFERENCES

1. Pittman FS: Children of the rich. Fam Process 24:461–472, 1985
2. Grinker RR: The poor rich: the children of the super-rich. Am J Psychiatry 135:913–916, 1978
3. Stone MH: Treating the wealthy and their children. International Journal of Child Psychotherapy 1:15–46, 1972
4. Stone MH, Kestenbaum C: Maternal deprivation in the children of the wealthy. History of Childhood Quarterly 2:79–106, 1975
5. Wixen BN: Children of the Rich. New York, Crown Publishers, 1973
6. McKamy EH: Social work with the wealthy. Social Casework 57:254–258, 1976
7. Pollak JM, Schaffer S: The mental health clinician in the affluent public school setting. Clinical Social Work Journal 13:341–354, 1985
8. Green MR: The interpersonal approach to child therapy, in Handbook of Child Psychoanalysis. Edited by Wolman B. New York, Van Nostrand Reinhold, 1972, pp 514–566
9. Burlingham DT: Child analysis and the mother. Psychoanal Q 4:69–92, 1935
10. Rubenstein BO, Levitt M: Some observations regarding the role of fathers in child psychotherapy. Bull Menninger Clin 21:16–27, 1957
11. Kohrman R, Fineberg HH, Gelman RL, et al: Techniques of child analysis: problems of countertransference. Int J Psychoanal 52:487–497, 1971
12. Sullivan HS: The Interpersonal Theory of Psychiatry. New York, WW Norton, 1953

SECTION IV:

THE PSYCHOTHERAPEUTIC PROCESS IN SPECIAL CIRCUMSTANCES

◆ ◆ ◆ ◆ ◆ ◆ ◆

15 Short-Term Psychotherapy With Children in Foster Care

Daniel J. Pilowsky, M.D.

The psychodynamic issues underlying the symptoms and problems with which children in foster care present are multiple and complex. Among the issues to be considered, the following are paramount: the child's background prior to placement in foster care (usually a background that includes neglect and/or abuse); reactions to separation from the biological parents; adaptation to a new environment, with its own expectations; and, last but not least, the child welfare agencies and the foster-care system, with their own problems and deficiencies.

The number of children in foster care has grown rapidly (1). Foster care is often defined as temporary. The child is placed while the agency works with the child's biological parents to help them create the conditions that would allow the child to return home. However, it has been repeatedly shown that a high percentage of children remain in foster care for 2 years or longer (2). Due to agency inertia and legal obstacles, these children are not released for adoption. Even when they are released, adoptive parents for troubled older children are often unavailable. Despite the assumption that it is a transitory arrangement, a significant number of children remain in foster care indefinitely. This is a feature of the foster-care system that has profound psychodynamic implications for children in placement and has often been criticized. Several experts have suggested changes that would allow for a more permanent disposition of these children (3,4). I will discuss these implications later in this chapter.

This chapter includes a detailed discussion of the short-term psychotherapeutic treatment of these children and a cursory review of the treatment of their biological and foster parents. It should be understood that it is important to help all three parties; but the focus here, in keeping with the theme of this book, will be on the child and short-term treatment. Short-term treatment is the preferred modality in this population, because the therapist cannot control the child's environment. The life of the child in foster care is often unstable; multiple caretakers and social agencies are involved, resulting in frequent relocations.

Children in foster care are likely to be poor, from chaotic households, and

291

neglected or abused, resulting in their foster-care placement. Abuse and neglect are believed to negatively affect the development of children (5–8). The empirical studies in the area have been reviewed (9), and their results will be briefly mentioned here.

It has been shown that young abused children will assault friendly caretakers who have not abused them, thus displacing their aggression from the abusive parent to nonabusive caretakers, such as day-care teachers or foster parents. In addition to aggression, which is the most frequent finding, a greater number and frequency of behavior problems both at home and in school occur in physically abused children as compared to nonabused children. These problems include noncompliance, tantrums, poor school adjustment and academic performance (10–18), poor peer relationships (10,14,17), social skill deficits (15,19,20), decreased social involvement (20), and decreased empathy (21).

Neglected children have been found to display more behavior problems (22), be more aggressive, and have greater school and academic difficulties than children who have not been neglected (10). The attachment behavior of maltreated children has also been studied extensively, and it will be discussed later in this chapter. To summarize, the abused child who has been placed in foster care is likely to display aggressive behavior toward peers and caretakers, to present academic and behavior problems in school, and to suffer from deficiencies in social skills and other areas. Such a child may be a shock to a foster parent who expects a child to appreciate his or her love and respond accordingly.

PSYCHOLOGICAL ASPECTS

The Parental Child

When a child lives in a household where neglect is the predominant parental behavior, the child may become a caretaker for younger siblings and parents as well as for him- or herself. It is common in all families that children may help their mother to care for younger siblings under her guidance. However, in this situation the child assumes a parental role as a result of the caretaker's abdication of her or his parental responsibilities. The child fills in for the parent without guidance or support, as the only way to survive in the neglectful household (23). I have worked with children of neglectful parents who at age five fed themselves and at age seven took care of younger siblings, sometimes for an entire day. In assuming such a role, these children deny their dependency needs. The renunciation of their dependency needs is an expensive price for these children. It renders them unavailable to the nurturing and care that their foster parents would expect them to need.

As a result of their experience with their neglectful-abusive biological parents, these children have learned that "authority figures are unreliable and unable to meet their needs. It is therefore adaptive when living with incompetent biological parents for these children to attempt to take care of their own needs. It would be surprising if any child did not apply this rationale to new situations" (23, p. 15). Therefore many foster parents have to deal with children who not only take care of many of their own needs, but who also mistrust the availability or willingness of adults to care for them effectively and consistently.

The Relationship to the Biological Parent: Attachment and Idealization

Rejecting mothers display aversion of physical contact with their infants and/or active rejection of their infants' bids for contact. Main and Goldwyn (24) suggest that maternal rejecting behavior correlates with the infant's avoidance of the mother in the "Ainsworth strange situation". Furthermore, they write, "infants who are avoidant of their mothers in the strange situation are particularly avoidant of other adults at the moment when they attempt friendly overtures" (24, p. 209). Nor is this a transitory phenomenon: Infants who are found to be avoidant of their mothers in the strange situation were found to be hostile, isolated, and/or disconnected in relationship to others in the preschool setting (26). Thus, maternal rejecting behavior will lead infants and children to be disconnected from caretakers. The same behavior occurs when the child is confronted with friendly overtures from the foster parents.

Therapists who work with abused children placed in foster care have repeatedly seen how these children express an intense desire to return to their abusive caretakers, in most cases the biological mother. Steele (8) reports that when such a child was asked why he wanted to go back to a bad situation, the child said very simply, "I know they are shitty but they are mine" (p. 289). In this context, Steele reminds us that "what many people often conceive of as a lack of attachment is really only the lack of a good attachment, while a very bad attachment exists" (8, p. 289). The "bad attachment" observed with these children seems to correspond to the two types of anxious attachment described by Ainsworth, the avoidant type and the ambivalent type (25). In the first type, the child rarely cries when separated from the mother and avoids her when reunited; in the second type, intense distress is observed on separation, yet it is followed by ambivalence on reunion.

A second common observation of therapists who treat these children while they are in foster care is that the children often do not seem to be angry at their abusive mothers, and, furthermore, often idealize them. Main and Goldwyn (24) suggest that abused children show a similar denial of anger toward their mother's abuse and a compensatory idealization. It has also been suggested that the child represses this anger for fear of destroying the parent (27). It is difficult for the child in foster care to express anger in the absence of his or her parents' reassuring physical presence, lest his hostile, destructive wishes destroy his loved and hated parents (27,28). Clinical experience suggests that the more intense the denied anger, the more rigid the idealization of the abusive mother or caretaker. Such a rigid idealization is bound to interfere with the child's relationship with his or her foster parents. First, the foster parents, when compared with idealized parental figures, will appear inadequate. Second, to view the foster parents as adequate would require these children to confront the incompetence of the biological parent, and to face their anger toward that parent (23). These children display a tendency to place a wall between themselves and their foster parents. They do not trust their foster parents to be consistent, reliable figures—that is, "good parents." Therefore, the only good parents left to them are the idealized images of their abusive parents. The effects of this rigid idealization on the treatment process will be discussed later in this chapter.

Ingratiating and Manipulative Behavior

The fact that these children do not trust their foster parents to be reliable does not imply that they have no expectations from their foster parents. On the contrary, they often expect that the foster parents will satisfy their every wish, and they will ingratiate themselves as long as they do so. This ingratiating behavior has a clearly manipulative quality—it turns into angry behavior when the foster parents either place demands on the child or fail to gratify the child's wishes. Sometimes foster parents are bewildered to see that, if frustrated, an "adorably cute child" becomes a "monster" in a few minutes. It has been suggested that this behavior may be related to the child's view of the foster parents as need-satisfying objects or part-objects (29). The manipulative behavior also appears in psychotherapy, as seen in this clinical vignette.

> Mary, a 6-year-old, was placed in foster care because of parental neglect. She was disobedient and defiant in the foster home. The foster parents tolerated her behavior, because "sometimes she can be so cute." Their tolerance ended when Mary set a fire in their home. During treatment Mary was a delightful and seemingly cooperative girl. She often praised the therapist but became rapidly hostile toward her if frustrated. In a session Mary said to her therapist "It is so nice to play with you, I love it." A few minutes later, she wanted to play with the therapist's phone. She was prevented from such play. Mary reacted by saying: "I hate you. There is a much nicer doctor here. . . . I want another doctor."

If foster care is successful, the child will eventually wish to be loved by the foster parents and will cease to treat them as need-satisfying objects. At that point, "as he begins to accept his foster parents, he transfers to them some of the feelings he bears his parents, especially the anger at them for abandoning and neglecting him" (28, p. 297).

The Foster Child's Anger

I have already mentioned that many of these children do not express anger toward the biological parents for abusing or neglecting them, or for allowing the disruption of their life brought about by their placement in foster care, or, if the biological parents fail to visit them after placement, for abandoning them. This anger is repressed, or selectively unattended to, and is bound to be displaced or acted out while the child is in foster care. One of the most common and at times dramatic forms of acting anger out is behaving in a provocative manner toward the foster parents to see if they too will abandon the child. It is suggested here that the management of the children's anger is one of the major issues in the therapeutic work with foster children, and it will be discussed in some detail later.

Low Self-Esteem and Depression

Children whose placement with a foster-care agency was necessitated because of parental maltreatment must explain to themselves why they were mistreated. Often the explanation they come up with is that they were unworthy of their parents' love. This egocentric type of explanation is not only prevalent among young children, but also among older ones. Therefore a cognitive explanation, in terms of the Piagetian stages of development, will not suffice. Psychodynamically, it can be understood as the result of the need to keep the idealization of the biological parents intact. It is as if the children said to themselves "my parents are good, I am bad; therefore, I am not worthy of their love." Were the children to accept that their situations were the result of their parents' personal problems, as opposed to the children's own, they would feel insignificant and lacking any control of the situation. "To most children, the omnipotent fantasy that they are responsible for everything is more comfortable, even though it leaves them feeling unlovable" (28, p. 297). Such children carry with them a persistent sense of worthlessness and low self-esteem. The resulting guilt, combined with the loss of the parents, may result in chronic depression, with a pervasive sense of hopelessness and passivity.

Some children can tolerate neither blaming their parents nor blaming themselves. In such cases they may go a step further and blame the agency (28). It is as if these children said to themselves: "My parents are good, and I am good; the evil social welfare agency took my parents away from me and is keeping me separated from them." The "evil social welfare agency" may easily be replaced by the "evil judge," "the evil therapist," and the "evil foster parent" who are forcibly separating child and parent. Such displacements are not uncommon and may ultimately include all those who work with the children, thus leading to a pseudo-paranoid view of the world, in which the children and their parents are "good" and the rest of the world is maliciously keeping them apart.

When such a situation develops, a child may oppose or attack the foster parents to test their love and commitment. The child unconsciously hopes that the foster parents will not prove to be "evil" after all; yet at the same time he or she consciously hopes to be removed from foster care and to return to his or her biological parents. Such a development may lead to multiple foster-care placements and a vicious cycle of mistrust, aggression, and negative omnipotence. The negative omnipotence refers to the child's ability to alienate any and all foster parents, even the most determined ones.

The child's reluctance to accept his or her foster parents as parents and the attempts to alienate them have been described. However, at the same time the child wishes the opposite—that is, he or she wishes to find a place in the new family and to have a stable, permanent family. The daily care and nurturing provided by the foster parents is the foundation upon which the wish for permanency is built.

The Permanency Principle and the Child in Foster Care

"I don't have to worry about being moved around. I'd have one place to live and I know I would stay there. Most places I go to, I don't want to get involved because I know I will have to leave" (child in foster care explaining why he would like to be adopted, cited by Bush and Goldman [30], p. 232).

"So far as the foster child is concerned, he will, at least after infancy has passed, feel the impermanence and the insecurity of the arrangement which clashed with his need for emotional constancy" (31, p. 25).

The theory of psychological parenting, expounded in the work of Goldstein and colleagues (3,31,32), suggests that the psychological parent-child tie is more important than the biological tie. The correlate of this theory is the permanency principle: The parent-child relationship has to be permanent and exclusive in order to count as psychological parenting. Therefore these authors opposed placement of children in foster care, except for short periods of time. They suggest that the insecurity of the arrangement is incompatible with the child's need for emotional constancy.

The permanency principle was a response to the conditions that prevailed, and unfortunately continue to prevail, in the child welfare system. Children stay for long periods of time, even years, in "temporary options," such as foster care. They are frequently moved from one home to another, and they often become anxious and concerned about the instability of their lives (30). Foster children, such as the one quoted above, are often reluctant to become emotionally involved with their foster parents, because they know they can be removed from their new homes unexpectedly. They may fear, or hope, for such a removal. Be that as it may, the child's therapist needs to empathize with this painful uncertainty and help the child cope with it. This uncertainty may also affect the therapist. He or she may develop feelings of impotence and rage when the child cries for an answer that may not be available for a long period of time. The court may surprise the therapist with a decision that he or she deems inappropriate, thus increasing the sense of impotence and frustration. Another potential source of surprises is the biological parents. Sometimes they are absent for a long period of time, and after the child accepts their absence and accepts the foster parents as psychological parents, the biological parents unexpectedly reappear, precipitating a crisis of loyalty in the child's mind (23).

On the other hand the foster parents are also aware of the unstable nature of the relationship. They erect their own defenses against involvement with the child so that they can be psychologically prepared for the child's removal. Such defenses may be rigid or exaggerated, leading to a cold, distant approach to the foster child. The unstable nature of the parent–foster child relationship thus often negatively affects both parties.

PSYCHOTHERAPY WITH THE FOSTER CHILD

So far in this chapter, the psychodynamics that affect the foster care child have been presented. This section consists of treatment approaches based on the psychodynamics discussed previously. Before these approaches are reviewed, the overall goals for psychotherapy with this particular group of children will be reviewed. I have discussed the child's idealization of the biological parents and identification with them. The first major goal is to help the child to partially give up his or her idealization of and identification with the biological parents, so that the child can tolerate having ambivalent feelings toward them. If the child is to be permanently separated from the biological parents, a second major goal is to help the child work through this loss.

In cases where the child is likely to return to his or her biological parents, the deidealization of the biological parents and the tolerance of ambivalent feelings toward them will help the child to see them in a more realistic fashion. Such a view of his or her parents prepares the child for the return to their care. On the other hand, it also helps the child's relationship to the foster parents, as the conflict of loyalties and the need to disparage them diminishes. The psychotherapeutic management of these children will be discussed in the next section.

Defining the Child's Situation

As the child begins to deal with the new environment (i.e., the foster home), he or she may ponder a series of questions (35): Why am I living with strangers rather than with my own family? How long is this situation going to last, and what is going to happen to me? Children are supposedly prepared for their removal from the parental home. However, some children are removed with little preparation, if any.

The first task of the psychotherapist is to raise the issue and find out how the child has answered these questions for him- or herself. Discussing these questions may help the child deal with his or her own confusion, and also conveys the message that the therapist will not avoid these thorny issues. If the child is unable to deal with these issues, it is necessary for the therapist to explain why the child was removed. The issues regarding the removal of the child must be directly handled by the therapist. He or she should describe the parental neglect or abuse in a factual rather than an evaluative manner. For example, a neglected child could be told: "You were taken away from home because your mother (or parents) was not preparing breakfast for you and was not making sure that you go to school. Now you are in a home where you will get your meals and you will be sent to school every day. We think this is important for you. . . . " An abused child could be told, "You were taken away from home because your mother (or father) was hitting you with a stick, and the agency wanted to protect you from that."

Referring to the abusive parent in evaluative terms is unnecessary. The therapist should also avoid telling the child that he or she "must be angry" at the biological parents, because the child often is not conscious of such anger. When the child is told this, the affect is uncovered prematurely, thus increasing the defensiveness of the patient. In those cases where the child *is* conscious of it, he or she will tell the therapist without much prompting. Making the patient defensive early in the therapeutic process leads to distancing from the therapist. There is already a distance created by the child; adding to that will only make the therapist's work much harder.

The next question in the child's mind is, "how long?" The child often sees the therapist or the agency as omnipotent or evil and may believe that the therapist can determine the length of his or her stay in foster care. Therefore the child may try to be ingratiating, so that his or her wishes will be granted. Sometimes there is some truth to the child's assumptions; therapists at times make recommendations to courts, which the judge may or may not follow. However, in most cases the therapist does not know what the outcome of the case might be. This should be acknowledged to the child, with a commitment to keep him or her informed. This is especially true in the case of adolescents and older children. An empathic acknowledgement of how painful this uncertainty can be is helpful: "I am in the same boat as you are. I don't know how long we have together, but I want to work with you and accomplish as much as we can in the time we have." If it is known that the child is not to be returned to the biological parents, there are other uncertainties to be dealt with: "Where will I go from here? Will somebody adopt me? Would my foster parents adopt me?" Uncertainty is a permanent part of the world of the child in foster care.

Working Through the Defenses Against Affects

Children in foster care often display little affect when reporting the traumatic circumstances that led to their placement. They may report instances of abandonment and abuse factually and without affect. Fraiberg (27) has suggested that, early in the work with children in placement, the therapist needs to deal with the defenses against affects. She suggests that the therapist give the child permission to feel and that he or she show the child omissions of justifiable feelings of anger and displacements of affects. The recognition of affects opens the door for deeper work and is an essential first step in treatment.

The Child's Anger and Oppositional-Disruptive Behavior in the Foster Home

Oppositional-disruptive behavior is perhaps the most common reason for referral of children in foster care. The child's repressed anger toward the biological parents, the conflict of loyalties between the foster family and the biological parents, and the aggressive and unempathic behavior often seen in abused young children have been discussed. I have also mentioned the child's need to test the commitment of the foster parents to him or her. I will now focus on the therapist's approach to the management of the child's anger—one of the major problems in the treatment of these children.

If the anger is indeed displaced from the biological parents to the foster parents, the approach that logically suggests itself is "to put the anger where it belongs." Such an approach would threaten the child's need to idealize the image of the biological parents; therefore, the child will often resist it, increasing his or her defensiveness. I chose this approach in the case history presented here.

Deborah was the 9-year-old daughter of a neglectful addicted mother. (The case has been described in some detail elsewhere [23].) She was removed from her mother's home due to lack of supervision and placed in foster care. Her foster parents were unable to tolerate her oppositional and defiant behavior, which resulted in multiple foster-home placements. She also ran away from foster care several times. A year after the initial placement, Deborah threatened to kill herself. Her treatment started after she made these threats. While in treatment, she often spoke of her desire to live with her mother and denied her mother's inability to care for her. However, occasionally Deborah referred to her mother's neglect. In a session Deborah reported an incident in which her home was burglarized. Her mother was intoxicated and "mom couldn't get up . . . and he [the burglar] locked me in the bathroom. . . ." In another session, she reported her mother "fell over the stove" while trying to cook "after she was taking drugs."

Deborah's therapist confronted the child's denial of her mother's neglect, saying, "Sometimes your mom was not able to take care of you. You told me she fell over the stove because she was high. . . ." Deborah replied, "You are causing trouble; you are lying." Later, Deborah stated that she had lied; her mother had never been high.

It is clear that Deborah's defenses became more rigid when confronted with her mother's limitations. She vehemently denied her own descriptions of neglect. She was in pain as a result of the separation from her biological mother, and her idealized internal images of her were Deborah's only consolation.

In such cases it is often helpful to encourage the child to talk about her life with her biological parents. The therapist initially focuses on expressions of affect. As the child relates tales of neglect and abuse, angry and depressed affects may emerge. The therapist can gently point out to the child the presence of such affects as they emerge—for example, "When you told me how you used to prepare dinner for yourself when your mom was not home, you seemed sad." Rather than confronting the child with parental neglect, which only increases her defensiveness, it is more therapeutic to first address the child's affects. This puts the child in touch with her feelings without making her feel that she must defend her mother.

As such work continues, the child will intermittently connect his or her sadness and anger with experiences in the relationship with the biological parents, only to deny it again shortly thereafter. Through recognition and denial, the child will eventually acknowledge his or her anger at the biological parents and mourn the loss of the idealized parental images. If the biological parents can tolerate this anger, the child will feel more comfortable expressing it. This expression of ambivalence—the child's hate and love toward his or her parents—is safer in such a situation. A significant number of biological parents cannot tolerate the child's anger. They convey the message that anger is unacceptable to them, and that the child's return to the parental home is contingent upon denial of the anger. In such cases, the child's need to repress his or her anger may predominate for a long period of time.

If the biological parents abandon the child permanently, then the child faces the task of mourning the actual loss of the parents as well as the loss of the idealized parental images. In such cases, the idealized parental images are often only partially abandoned, if ever. It is important for the therapist to understand that some of these children need to maintain such idealized images for a long time, perhaps indefinitely.

Another dynamic that in some cases underlies these children's oppositional attitudes toward the foster parents is that they were "parental children" before their placement in foster care. As parental children, they fed themselves, set their own schedules, and so forth. They may wish to continue parenting themselves in the foster home, thus clashing with the foster parents' attempts to impose discipline and to set limits. For these children, denial of their dependency needs is an entrenched defense that can only slowly be given up. It may be helpful to empathize with the child's wish to take care of him- or herself, while encouraging the child to accept the ministrations of the foster parents. An example of such an intervention would be: "It makes a little girl feel like a grown-up when she can take care of herself. That's a great feeling! But it is too much work for a little girl to take care of all the things she needs all the time." If the relationship with the foster parents is such that the child feels secure, he or she will slowly accept these dependency needs.

If the child's denial of anger and pain seems impenetrable, it may be helpful to use therapeutic stories as a treatment technique. It has been suggested that a child's identification with a character is facilitated when that character is sufficiently distant from the child's reality so as to not represent a threat to the child's defenses (33). The "Suitcase Story" (34) is a therapeutic story designed specifically to help children in out-of-home placement. It was developed as a vehicle for the expression of many of the feelings experienced by these children. The suitcase was selected as a protagonist because it symbolizes the lack of permanence in the child's life. As an inanimate object, it does not represent a threat to the child. This story has enabled children in therapy to express their anger, fears of abandonment, and longing for permanence. The mutual storytelling technique, as described by Gardner (33), is also useful in working with these children.

Anger Inhibition

As has been mentioned, some children in foster care repress their anger toward their biological parents, displace it toward their foster parents, and act it out in the form of oppositional-disruptive behavior. There is also a group of children who repress their anger without displacing it. They are fearful of expressing their anger and their aggression. They let other children victimize them rather than defend themselves, and they are often helpless in dealing with their peers' aggression. Instead they are constantly requesting the protection of adults, and they become whiny and regress if such protection is not provided immediately. This behavior can be seen as a pattern in itself, or it can alternate with periods of aggressive behavior toward peers.

These children show exaggerated fears of consequences of aggression.

These exaggerated fears emanate from several sources. First, the child expects that aggression, no matter how restrained, would result in being sent away, as the biological parents sent the child away. Second, the child expects an exaggerated punishment that is equal to the strength of the undischarged aggression—that is, the child is afraid of the destructive power of his or her rage (27). Third, some of these children have been subjected to arbitrary and exaggerated forms of punishments by their caretakers in the past, and feel confused as to what a caretaker's reasonable response to their aggression might be. The therapist's work with these children will consist of helping them identify the sources of their fears so that they feel free to display age-appropriate aggression. As such work proceeds, an inhibited child may temporarily become excessively aggressive. Should such a situation emerge, the cooperation of the foster parents and the school become essential. An explanation of the process that the child is going through is helpful in eliciting their cooperation. The therapist may also help the child to exercise judgment in fights with peers and other forms of aggressive behavior. A great deal of aggression and hostility can be expressed during this period in therapy, where it can be used for the advancement of the therapeutic process.

Depression and Low Self-Esteem

"Being foster is like being a piece of garbage. You are just something somebody tossed out. . . ." (an adolescent girl in foster care, quoted by Lee [36]). Foster children often feel that they were discarded by their biological parents, and, like other things that people discard, are useless or garbage. On the other hand, they feel envious of children who live with their biological parents. They often pity themselves, feeling that they not only lost the love of the mother, but they also were left with a scar that will make them inadequate or inferior for the rest of their lives. Being foster becomes equated with being a second-class citizen, surrounded by a large majority of first-class citizens— children who live with their "real parents." The connection between parental loss and their feelings of worthlessness is often the first step in the treatment of these children.

The child who is in foster care will often attribute his or her sense of worthlessness and hopelessness to a real or imagined deficiency in the self. Viewing him- or herself as deficient allows the child to keep a measure of control over a confusing and bewildering situation. Such a view is also compatible with the need to keep the idealization of the parents intact. The therapist needs to gently point out the source of the child's feelings: "You told me that your mom put you in foster care because she doesn't love you. You probably figured out that if your own mother didn't want to bother with you, then nobody else will. No wonder you feel so lousy about yourself." If the child believes that his or her mother or father loves him and that he or she is the victim of an evil agency, then a less ambitious intervention is indicated. An empathic comment connecting the depression with missing the parents and feeling mistreated by everybody would be appropriate in such cases.

As has been discussed here, the child represses anger toward the biological parents, displacing it to the foster parents, the agency, the social worker, and so on. It is important to add that as the child blames him- or herself for the placement ("I was put in foster care because I'm bad, not because of my parents"), he or she also turns the anger inward, contributing to depression. Therefore, the deidealization of the biological parents and the recognition of the child's hate and love toward them are also helpful in dealing with the depression. As the child deals with anger and depression, his or her coping abilities improve, and thus he or she has more energy available to deal with the outside world.

The low self-esteem of these children is also related to actual deficiencies in their abilities and in their social repertoire. A significant subgroup of these children have missed school and have not participated in sports and other age-appropriate activities. Remedial education and other therapeutic activities are often necessary in conjunction with the psychotherapeutic intervention to help these children improve their self-image. It is also important for the therapist to keep in mind that the demands of the new placement may well be above the demands of the old, because of differences in school quality, social class, and parental expectations. The cooperation of the school, the foster parents, and the agency are necessary if the therapist is to intervene effectively in this complex but important aspect of the child's life.

A rather extreme case, where the relationship between the child and the foster parents was grossly disturbed, will be described here. Several of the dynamics described previously will be briefly illustrated.

Case History: Ronda

Ronda, an 11-year-old girl, was the oldest of four siblings. The other siblings were nine, seven, and one. Ronda was originally placed in foster care at age nine. Her parents were chronic drug addicts who neglected their children, thus prompting the children's involuntary placement in foster care by the child welfare authorities. Originally the two oldest children were placed together in one foster home, and the two youngest were placed together in another. Later the two older children were separated. Ronda was changed from one foster home to another because of her running away and impulsivity. After 19 months in placement, Ronda threatened to kill herself with a knife and was hospitalized. This episode took place 3 days after she was made to appear in family court. The court was dealing with a petition for termination of parental rights.

Whenever Ronda ran away from placement, she did so in order to find and care for her biological mother. Ronda knew the street corner where her homeless mother was likely to "hang out," and she would go there in a desperate attempt to find her. Ronda firmly stated that she wanted to return to live with her mother, insisting that her mother could care for her. At the same time, she described with little affect how she often prepared meals for herself and her younger siblings when her mother was in the streets, sometimes for the entire day. No anger was expressed by Ronda toward her mother, but Ronda freely expressed her anger toward her foster parents and the foster-care agency. She saw the agency as an evil institution that separated children from their parents. She maintained an idealized image of her mother using a great deal of denial: "My mom took care of me. The stupid social worker took me out of my home. I want to be with my mom." The therapist recognized that the denial could not be confronted directly, so he replied: "It would be so nice if you could be with your mom. You miss her so much." Such an intervention is empathic, and it respects the patient's defenses.

Ronda's transference can be described as alternating between ingratiating-seductive behavior toward the therapist and anger and contempt toward him. The ingratiating behavior was invariably related to her desire to obtain a concrete benefit from the therapist, such as getting passes to go outside the hospital or going to the coffee shop. The anger and contempt followed any refusal on the part of the therapist to fulfill her numerous requests. In such situations, Ronda refused to talk to the therapist or showed open contempt for him, but she would soon attempt to ingratiate herself with him again, and so the cycle continued.

Ronda's relationship to the milieu consisted of displaying her independence, her ability to care for herself, and a stubborn refusal to accept directions from adult caretakers. Her dependency needs and the need for nurturing seemed absent. On one occasion, a maternally inclined nurse offered Ronda help in caring for her braids. This offer was promptly rebuffed: "You think I can't take care of my own hair. I always do it by myself. I know how to do it. . . ."

The therapist attempted, with limited success, to help Ronda express affect when it seemed appropriate: "When you told me how your mom stayed out late hanging out on the corner, you seemed a little sad." Ronda listened to such remarks without a reply. Later the therapist attempted to help her tolerate her ambivalent feelings toward her mother by pointing out to her that even when a girl loves her mother, she might still feel some anger toward her for disappointing her. "Sometimes kids love their mom and are angry at her at the same time, because she can't be at home to take care of them." Here the therapist met major resistance: Ronda's need to idealize the mother remained so strong that even the suggestion that she might feel some anger toward her mother, yet still love her, was unacceptable. Her desire to run away and find her mother was very persistent.

In view of this situation, the therapist felt it necessary to empathize again with Ronda's pain at being separated from her biological mother before attempting again to help her tolerate her ambivalent feeling toward her mother. Ronda was more open to this type of intervention. As she became more acquainted with the staff, she was able to tolerate some nurturing and some limit-setting. However, she did not develop the ability to tolerate ambivalent feelings toward her mother and was not able to deidealize her to any significant extent. At the same time, her compulsion to run away and to find and save her mother remained unchanged. Because of this, it was recommended that Ronda be placed in a Residential Treatment Center, where long-term psychotherapeutic work would have to take place before an attempt to place her in a foster home is made.

This case illustrates the following dynamics: idealization of the biological parents, denial of dependency needs, displacement of the anger toward the parents, inability to tolerate ambivalent feelings toward the biological parents, and a negative omnipotence demonstrated by Ronda's ability to defeat the efforts of several sets of foster parents.

In more mild cases, the child slowly manages to express affects, moves toward some degree of tolerance of ambivalent feelings toward the biological parents, and becomes more emotionally available to the foster parents. If the child is not returned to the care of the biological parents, dealing with this permanent loss becomes a lifelong task.

WORKING WITH THE FOSTER PARENTS

There are multiple reasons for an adult to decide to become a foster parent. They can be found singly or in various combinations and include the need for financial compensation, a desire to save children and rescue them from "bad parents," a sense of emptiness after biological children leave the household, and the hope that being a parent will give the foster children a sense of fulfillment and worth. This hope "can be a heavy burden to place upon an already psychologically handicapped child who is more interested in receiving than in giving" (29, p. 58).

Foster parents are told that they are temporary caretakers. They may accept the role, only to change their expectations as they become more attached to—or more hopelessly frustrated with—the child. In the first case they may wish to adopt the child, and in the latter they may want, as they often do, to return the child to the care of the agency. Some foster parents may have never accepted the role; they may have secretly wished to become permanent parents from the very beginning. The financial rewards they receive for their care may or may not be a major factor in their decision to become foster parents. Regardless of their own wishes and feelings, they find themselves in a social role that is not nearly as clearly defined as the role of a biological parent. They are referred to as "parents," but they cannot make decisions regarding the foster child's education, religion, and medical care, to cite just a few areas where their decision-making power is limited or altogether absent. Their ambivalence about their role, and the ambiguity of that role, are bound to be transmitted to the foster child. It is important for the child's therapist to learn about the overt and covert expectations of the foster parents and their views of the foster child and his or her biological parents. Psychotherapy with the child in foster care always requires work with the foster parents, separately or jointly. Often it is necessary to work with the child's biological parents as well.

A great deal of preventive work can be done with foster parents, educating them about the psychodynamics underlying the behavior that these children are likely to display and about child development and management. Nevertheless, I will refer only to therapeutic work with foster parents whose child is undergoing psychotherapy.

The foster parents will feel relief if they come to understand that the child's unhappiness and acting out are not directed against them but are displacements of feelings toward the child's biological parents. It is especially important to explain to them that these children will often test the patience of their foster parents to see if the foster parents will return them to the agency or will "stick with them," even when they misbehave. The foster parents can be told that this is a "test of love"—the child feels compelled to test them, and so forth.

The foster parents are often confused about their own feelings toward the child. They may be distant because they fear that they may become too attached. If the child is to return home or to be adopted by another set of parents, they may need help working through the loss of the child. On the other hand, some foster parents become disappointed with a difficult child and find it hard to discuss openly their wish to have the child placed elsewhere. Such foster parents need help in acknowledging their feelings and in discussing the possibility of giving the child an opportunity to improve. The therapeutic alliance between foster parents and therapist is essential if the child is to be given a chance. Where foster parents are totally unwilling to form such an alliance and only want to stop fostering, the reality of the situation needs to be identified so that the child can be removed from the foster home. The therapist's wish to spare the child from another painful separation can interfere with acknowledgement of the situation.

It is also helpful to explain to the foster parents the nature of the foster child's loyalty conflict. Specifically, they may be less resentful of the child's tendency to disparage them if they understand that were the child to acknowledge his or her attachment to them, the child would feel this as a betrayal of the biological parents. Visits to the biological parents are often distressing. The child's acting out at the foster parents' home is likely to increase after such visits. The foster parents may feel that the visits are not worth the trouble. They are less likely to react negatively if they are told in advance to expect disruptive behavior after such visits and if the importance of the visits for the child is stressed. They may also need to have the therapist available to them after such visits for counseling and support.

The foster parents may become very attached to the child and wish to adopt him or her or make arrangements for long-term foster care. The policy of many agencies is against allowing the adoption of these children by their foster parents, but there is no unanimity in the field regarding such adoptions (37). However, it is helpful to the foster parents if the therapist can empathize with their wishes and emphasize their love for the child, rather than immediately remind them of the agency policy. Other foster parents have a very different approach: They see themselves as "professionals" and are very careful not to become overinvolved with the child. They may need help in dealing with these children in a more affectionate manner, because they often erect defenses so that their feelings toward the child are kept under tight control. A tactful approach to such parents would include appreciating their professionalism and their wish to learn about child management and child development.

WORKING WITH THE BIOLOGICAL PARENTS

The biological parents may be seen by the child's therapist or by their own therapist, depending on agency policy and the clinician's preference. This controversial area will not be dealt with here. I will focus instead on the kinds of interventions that might be helpful in working with the biological parents. The biological parents often display a deep sense of shame about the label "bad parents" that is attached to them. They feel very defensive about it and often spend most of their psychological energy in defensive maneuvers (i.e., denying their neglect or abuse or claiming that it was "not as bad as the social worker says"). Other parents may argue that they have the right to treat their children however they wish. These parents often see their child as their property and the agency as an intruder with evil intentions. Focusing on the feelings of shame and humiliation is the most likely way the therapist can help diminish the parents' defensiveness. Focusing on the future is also helpful. Discussing with biological parents how they would treat their child differently if and when the child is returned to their care shifts the focus from blaming them about their deficiencies to forming a therapeutic alliance with a concrete goal: the return of the child to their care.

The discussion of visitations is a concrete way of looking at the biological parents' interaction with the child and their use of projection in this relationship. Visitation is the single most powerful predictor of a child's return to his or her biological family (2). It is therefore crucial to encourage visitation whenever the child's return to the biological family is tentatively or definitely planned. Visitation is also a testing ground that allows the biological parents to demonstrate in a constructive way their interest in caring for their child. It also allows the therapist to gauge the situation—that is, to become aware of the nature of the biological parents' interaction with the child and the degree of their commitment to him or her.

There are a host of other issues in dealing with abusive or neglectful parents with children in placement. These include the pathological identification they have unwittingly given the child, their use of projection and projective identification in their relationship with the child, their relationship with their own parents, and the compulsion to repeat the abuse through several generations. The description of these issues is beyond the scope of this chapter, and the reader is referred to the literature on child abuse (5,38). Interventions other than psychotherapy are very important in dealing with these parents: crisis nurseries, casework by social workers, support groups, homemakers, and other social services.

THE SOCIAL SERVICE AGENCY

Theoretically, both therapist and agency have the best interest of the child in mind. But in practical terms, the situation is more complex: Social agencies have to follow their own policies and are often reluctant to be flexible when special clinical needs arise. The primary role of the therapist is thus to advocate for the child rather than the agency.

The reality of the agency's power, coupled with the fantasies and projections of the child, often determine his or her view of the agency as the evil force that separated the child from the parents. The therapist may help the child see the agency in a more realistic fashion. The child often sees the agency as the enemy of his or her parents, and therefore as a personal enemy as well. As the child sees that the agency helps him or her and the biological parents, he or she may, with the help of the therapist, come to see the agency as an ally in this desperate fight for stability and parental love.

LONG-TERM GOALS

The long-term goals of treatment vary according to the particular situation of each child. When the child is totally abandoned by the biological parents, the child will need help in mourning the lost parents. The issues that face the child who returns home to his or her biological parents are different: this child may need help in dealing with anger toward the biological parents. This anger has multiple determinants: the abuse, neglect, disease, or other event that lead to the placement; anger at the parents' inability to prevent the separation and the placement; and, in some cases, anger resulting from the child's resentment at the biological parents for having him or her return to their care. There are children who are neither totally abandoned by their biological parents nor returned to their care. These children stay in long-term placement and have irregular contact with their biological parents, and they may need help in adapting to a situation of chronic uncertainty.

In spite of the variability described here, there are some common issues to consider. Children in foster care are left with scars that need to be addressed (39). One of the most pervasive long-term issues is fear of emotional closeness, which results from the unconscious expectation of repeated rejections following the model of the original one (i.e., the rejection by the biological parents). The child's expectation of rejection is coupled with the unconscious need to be rejected. This complex web of expectations and self-fulfilling prophecies needs to be worked through in long-term therapy. Such a process would include repeated illustrations of the pattern, both in the transference and in the patients' other interpersonal relationships.

The child's reaction to separations and his or her increased sensitivity to later separation experiences is also a dynamic that will be part of the child's life for many years (38).

The low self-esteem and depression often seen in these children are additional scars that result from the placement experience. The possibility of helping the child in dealing with these issues is contingent on the satisfactory resolution of the child's life situation. If the life situation remains unstable— that is, if the child is subject to multiple placements and multiple rejections— these scars may become permanent. After multiple placements, this last group of children may develop a defensive emotional unavailability, with lack of empathy. Such children may display a psychopathic personality, which renders them partially or totally unavailable to psychodynamically oriented therapy.

Finally, the long-term psychological cost of repression is significant; "It freezes psychological energy that would otherwise be available for meeting and mastering new life situations" (39, p. 24). The child, as it has been pointed out, represses anger toward his or her biological parents, and also represses dependency needs. Such repression may have a negative impact on future relationships and may consume the child's energy. The lifting of these repressions becomes a major long-term goal in therapy and may indeed become a lifelong task for these children.

REFERENCES

1. Shyne A, Schroeder A: A National Study of Social Services to Children and Their Families. Washington, DC, U.S. Children's Bureau, 1978
2. Lawder EA, Poulin JE, Andrews RG: A study of 185 foster children 5 years after placement. Child Welfare 65:241–251, 1986
3. Goldstein J: Why foster care—for whom, for how long? Psychoanal Study Child 30:647–662, 1975

4. Derdeyn AP: A case for permanent foster placement of dependent, neglected, and abused children. Am J Orthopsychiatry 47:604–614, 1977
5. Cicchetti D, Rizley R: Developmental perspectives on the etiology, intergenerational transmission, and sequelae of child maltreatment, in New Directions for Child Development: Developmental Perspectives in Child Maltreatment. Edited by Rizley R, Cicchetti D. San Francisco, CA, Jossey-Bass, 1981, pp 31–55
6. Martinez-Roig A, Domingo-Salvany F, Llorens-Terol J, et al: Psychological implications of the maltreated child syndrome. Child Abuse Negl 7:261–263, 1983
7. Egeland B, Soupre LA, Erickson M: The developmental consequences of different patterns of maltreatment. Child Abuse Negl 7:459–469, 1983
8. Steele BF: Notes on the lasting effects of early child abuse throughout the life cycle. Child Abuse Negl 10:283–291, 1986
9. Lamphear VS: The impact of maltreatment on children's psychosocial adjustment: a review of the research. Child Abuse Negl 9:251–263, 1985
10. Reidy TJ: The aggressive characteristics of abused and neglected children. J Clin Psychol 33:1140–1145, 1977
11. George C, Main M: Social interactions of young abused children: approach avoidance and aggression. Child Dev 50:306–318, 1979
12. Reid JB, Taplin PS, Lorber RA: A social interactional approach to the treatment of abusive families, in Violent Behavior: A Social Learning Approach to Prediction, Management and Treatment. Edited by Stuart R. New York, Brunner/Mazel, 1981, pp 83–101
13. Egeland B, Sroufe LA: Attachment and early maltreatment. Child Dev 52:44–52, 1981
14. Kinard EM: Emotional development in physically abused children. Am J Orthopsychiatry 50:686–696, 1980
15. Perry MA, Doran LD, Wells EA: Developmental and behavioral characteristics of the physically abused child. Journal of Clinical Child Psychology 12:320–324, 1983
16. Martin HP, Beezley P: Behavioral observations of abused children. Dev Med Child Neurol 19:373–387, 1977
17. Kent J: A follow up study of abused children. J Pediatr Psychol 1:25–31, 1976
18. Calam RM: The long term effects of child abuse on school adjustment. Paper presented at the 91st annual meeting of the American Psychological Association, Anaheim, CA, August 1983
19. Wolfe DA, Mosk MD: Behavioral comparisons of children from abusive and distressed families. J Consult Clin Psychol 12:337–346, 1983
20. Mash EJ, Johnston C, Kovitz KA: A comparison of the mother child interactions of physically abused and non-abused children during play and task situations. J Clin Psychol 12:337–346, 1983
21. Barahal R, Waterman J, Martin H: The social-cognitive development of abused children. J Consult Clin Psychol 49:508–516, 1981
22. Aragona JA, Eyberg SM: Neglected children: mother's report of child's behavior problems and observed verbal behavior. Child Dev 52:596–602, 1981
23. Green B, Pilowsky D: Absent parents revisiting: its contribution to intrapsychic conflict in emotionally vulnerable foster children. Unpublished manuscript, 1985 (Copies can be obtained from Daniel J. Pilowsky, M.D., 260 West 72nd Street, Suite 1-B, New York, NY 10023)

24. Main M, Goldwyn R: Predicting rejection from mother's representation of her own experience: implications for the abused-abusing intergenerational cycle. Child Abuse Negl 8:203–217, 1984

25. Ainsworth MDS, Blehar MC, Waters E, et al: Patterns of Attachment: A Psychological Study of the Strange Situation. Hillsdale, NJ, Erlbaum, 1978

26. Sroufe LA: Infant-caregiver attachment and patterns of adaptation in preschool: the roots of maladaptation and competence, in Minnesota Symposium in Child Psychology, Vol 16. Edited by Perlmutter M. Hillsdale, NJ, Erlbaum, 1983, pp 41–83

27. Fraiberg S: A therapeutic approach to reactive ego disturbances in children in placement. Am J Orthopsychiatry 32:18–32, 1962

28. Katz P: Dynamics and treatment of foster children. Can J Psychiatry 13:295–299, 1968

29. Burland JA: A psychoanalytic psychiatrist in the world of foster care. Clinical Social Work Journal 8:50–61, 1980

30. Bush M, Goldman H: The psychological parenting and the permanency principle in child welfare: a reappraisal and critique. Am J Orthopsychiatry 52:223–235, 1982

31. Goldstein J, Freud A, Solnit A: Beyond the Best Interest of the Child. New York, Free Press, 1979, pp 3–133

32. Goldstein J, Freud A, Solnit A: Beyond the Best Interest of the Child. New York, Free Press, 1979, pp 3–138

33. Gardner R: Therapeutic Communication With Children: The Mutual Storytelling Technique. New York, Jason Aronson, 1971

34. Wenger C: The suitcase story: a therapeutic technique for children in out-of-home placement. Am J Orthopsychiatry 52:353–355, 1982

35. Sprey WT, Portz P: Some aspects of identity problems in foster families. Journal of Comparative Family Studies 13:231–235, 1982

36. Lee JA, Park DN: A group approach to the depressed adolescent girl in foster care. Am J Orthopsychiatry 48:516–527, 1978

37. Meezan W, Shireman JF: Foster parent adoption: a literature review. Child Welfare 61:525–535, 1982

38. Kempe RS, Kempe CH: Child Abuse. Cambridge, MA, Harvard University Press, 1978

39. Littner N: Some Traumatic Affects of Separation and Placement. New York, Child Welfare League of America, 1956

16 Group Psychotherapy With Children in Psychiatric Hospitals

Jill Bellinson, Ph.D.

Children who are psychiatrically hospitalized are almost always seen in groups—recreational, community meeting, health and grooming groups, as well as therapy groups—and yet group treatment techniques for them are rarely discussed in the literature. Yalom's (1) work on inpatient group therapy does not address children's or adolescents' groups. Most texts on child therapy (cf., e.g., 2–14) focus on individual treatment with outpatient children. Alterations in techniques to be used for psychotic and otherwise severely disturbed children (15–23) are sometimes discussed, but these are for treatment of individual children, not groups. Group treatment for children and adolescents is presented (24–41), but researchers explicitly state that they believe such groups are not appropriate for severely disturbed children and children with poor reality testing, inadequate impulse control, or history of severe emotional deprivation beginning in early infancy—the population of a psychiatric inpatient service.

In this chapter, I propose techniques to adapt children's group treatment to these populations so that relationship-oriented psychoanalytic groups can succeed with a psychiatric inpatient population. The goals for groups described in this chapter are to provide activities that are interesting and enjoyable and that will help children identify and express thoughts and feelings and reveal conflictual material. Expression is aided by these activities because they allow discharge of nervous energy, symbolic portrayal of unconscious issues, and a more comfortable atmosphere for verbal communication. The therapist can clarify or interpret material that arises in group and can raise issues for children to take up with their individual therapists. Usual group therapy goals (24,26,27,34,35,37,41–45) of forming trusting relations with therapist and peers, consensual validation, and so on can also be met, although to a limited extent due to the limitations imposed by the population and the milieu. In interacting with a therapist and each other, observing the way an accepting therapist reacts with group members, and attempting to communicate with the help of the group leader, children also acquire social skills as a by-product of this method of expressive, relationship- and analytically-oriented psychotherapy. In addition, the inpatient unit benefits because ward tension is reduced and patient-to-patient and staff-to-patient relations are often improved.

GROUP THERAPY LITERATURE

Activity Group Therapy

Classic group psychotherapy for children follows techniques for Activity Group Therapy defined by Slavson (35,37) in the 1930s and 1940s. His method involves providing latency-age children with a large indestructible room filled with a variety of constructive materials and a group leader who observes and provides snack, a permissive environment, unconditional acceptance, and an occasional extra hand for work or play. Children form attachments to the group leader as a parent substitute and to the other group members as peers, and gradually, over 2 years of weekly group meetings, develop less anxiety and solitary self-interest, and more social interest, impulse control, appropriate superego restraint, and self- and group-esteem. Crucial to Slavson's method is selection of group members (35–37). Appropriate group members are children who are uncommunicative, infantilized, rivalrous or symbiotic with siblings, emotionally exploited or rejected, or economically deprived. His groups are also useful as a transition into psychotherapy for children who are inaccessible (Slavson's groups were called "clubs" and were seen as interesting and fun to join), or for diagnostic evaluation or gradual termination of individual treatment.

Children should be formed into groups with balanced numbers of active, passive, aggressive, or shy children, as well as "instigators, neutralizers, and neuters" (37, p. 113). "*The effectiveness of AGT* [Activity Group Therapy] *is in direct relation to the care taken in selecting and grouping children correctly*"(37, p. 111 [italics in the original]). Some children—those who are narcissistic, sadistic, punishment-seeking, homosexual, extremely aggressive, acting out by theft or homicidal behavior, psychotic or otherwise severely disturbed, psychopathic, mentally deficient, or lacking a minimum level of ego function, superego function, or object-relating capacity—are inaccessible to Activity Group Therapy. Thus, it is clear that Slavson's Activity Group Therapy is inappropriate for children in a psychiatric hospital, because they virtually always possess at least one of these contraindicated characteristics.

Variations in Activity Group Therapy

Variations in Activity Group Therapy have been developed for populations that do not respond well to standard treatment as defined by Slavson. Play Group Therapy (24,31,37,38,41,46) allows children, usually preschool-age children, to use symbolic play to express fears, anxieties, conflicts, angers, and other emotions, while the therapist proposes interpretations of underlying themes and motives. Researchers have found that children with histories of sexual overstimulation, exposure to severe traumata, extreme sibling rivalry, or physical or emotional abuse are not suitable for play group therapy except in special circumstances.

Activity-interview therapy sessions (26,30,37,47–52) are split between activity group-type projects and a "talking part," when the therapist and children sit for therapist-directed discussion. Group materials are designed for less elaborate constructions and more symbolic play than in Activity Group Therapy, and the group leader explores children's problems and makes interpretations. Activity-interview therapy was designed for children who are too seriously disturbed, fearful, anxious, hyperactive, or aggressive to respond to Activity Group Therapy. Nevertheless, Slavson says, children should be excluded if they have "uncontrollable aggression, autism, psychosis, brain damage; children with severe sibling rivalry, affect hunger, psychopathic trends, and [who are] devoid of impulse control" (37, p. 298). Again, most hospitalized children would have to be excluded from even these specially adapted groups.

Beginning a Group

According to the group therapy literature, usual methods for starting a group involve interviewing prospective patients, selecting for appropriateness (27,35–37,42,45,53), deciding group size (27,38,41,42), balancing membership (28,35–37,42,45,50,53–56), and setting up appointment times and contracts for attendance, confidentiality, treatment goals, and so on. The nature of an inpatient service is such that most of these preliminaries are impossible. As in outpatient groups, it is important that the age range be limited to one of 2 or 3 years (35,36,41,42). The size of the group can be restricted to five to seven members (37,38,41,42), although this is sometimes unnecessary; groups of older children and adolescents can often be offered to an entire unit. Beyond this, however, prospective membership is usually defined merely by presence on the unit; it is rare that an inpatient children's facility has a population large enough to afford a group leader the luxury of selectivity beyond eliminating the most disturbed children or selecting for age groupings.

Balancing membership according to level of activity or passivity, aggressivity, and so forth is generally not possible, because the pool of prospective members is not large enough and the population of the pool tends toward the more disturbed, more aggressive children. Eliminating the children who are aggressive, impulse-disordered, mentally retarded, psychotic, psychopathic, ego-deficient, superego-deficient, and object-relating-deficient would eliminate the group altogether. Hence, one cannot design the population to fit the group; one must design a group to fit the population.

Because short hospitalization is expected in most child inpatient settings, the process of beginning a group must be facilitated. If, as outpatient group therapists suggest, each prospective member were interviewed and contracted with individually before the group was formed, a large percent of the group would be discharged before the first group meeting, and the interviews would have to begin all over again! The inpatient group therapist will be more successful if decisions regarding whom to include or exclude, when and where to meet, and what theme, if any, the group will have, and so on are made and implemented quickly and changed over time as needed. Therapists of inpatient groups must be comfortable deciding such issues and changing decisions frequently, sometimes in mid-session. A medication group can become a community meeting, a separation group can turn into a discussion of suicide, and patients and staff may be sought to attend or asked to leave, as situations dictate.

SPECIAL ISSUES FOR INPATIENT GROUPS

Confidentiality

Confidentiality is a particularly sticky issue on an inpatient service. The patients spend time together and discuss their treatment with each other and with other staff on the unit. The therapist's successes and foibles are exposed to everyone. In addition, the group leader is generally a member of the treatment team on the unit and is often expected to contribute to treatment plan decisions and to write chart notes on group progress; thus, the group leader, far from requesting or promising confidentiality, must realize that a good deal of group process will indeed be shared with a number of people outside the group. This makes the development of trust and full disclosure a bit slower, but it need not hamper it altogether if the therapist is sufficiently open and flexible to accommodate some degree of secrecy along the way.

> The therapist of a group of girls, aged 11 to 14, entered the ward one morning to be accosted by all the girls at once. They were shouting about the terrible unfairness of the punishments that had befallen them at the hands of a very angry night nursing staff. It seemed that the night before, well after lights out, some of the girls had entered the room of the ward scapegoat and frightened her; others of the girls had cheered on the instigators, while still others had known nothing of the incident until it was almost over. All of them, however, had been awake and storming the halls when the nursing staff discovered the incident, and none of them would tattle on the instigators. The nurses had therefore placed all girls on restriction and canceled all weekend passes. The

girls felt this was unfair and requested a group session to help them discuss the problem.

In group, the girls asked for promises of confidentiality, but these were refused. The therapist insisted that if anything was divulged that should rightfully be disclosed to the rest of the treating staff, it would be. The girls therefore began the discussion on a cautious note, with a great deal of complaining about the unfairness of the punishments, the ward, the night staff, and the world in general. The therapist listened, then raised questions about what the group felt would have been fair punishment, hypothetically.

There was rapid agreement on three categories of restriction for the three categories of participation in the event. Two of the girls—including the instigator, it later turned out—were not in attendance, and the group disbanded temporarily while delegations were sent to fetch the absent members. When the entire unit was present, the girls explained their discussion to the new members and reached an agreement, now unanimous, as to meting of punishments. The group leader agreed to present the plan to the night staff, who were the decision-makers in this case, and to argue in its favor. Only after the plan had been presented and endorsed did the girls confess to their crimes, each to her own level of participation.

In this example, it is clear that confidentiality was not essential to group process and progress; even the sensitive issue of rule-breaking could be discussed constructively as long as the therapist was willing to handle cases "hypothetically" and to be nonjudgmental, accepting, and facilitating of the group interaction. This can weigh heavily on a therapist who also holds a position of authority on the unit and takes that responsibility seriously. During group time, the therapist must try to be solely a group leader, placing group issues above all others and making that clear to the children, even while acknowledging that other roles and other rules exist outside the group.

Multiple Roles

Another issue pertinent to inpatient work is that of role definition. In outpatient groups, it is common for group members to be forbidden to meet covertly outside of group meetings (35,37,45,54) and for the therapist to have no other interaction with group members, or at least an identical relation with all group members (either as no one's individual therapist or as everyone's). This allows group process to unfold and for everything that happens in group to be understood as part of group process. With inpatient work, however, this is rare. Group members, of course, live together outside group meetings, and thus spend more time together and share more experiences outside group than in it. The therapist is thus an outsider rather than the center and determinant of the group's existence. The therapist knows each child differently, functioning as individual therapist to some of the group members, handling medication or psychological testing or parent therapy or discharge planning for some others, being the first person on the unit others met, and so on. Exclusivity of relationship is the exception rather than the rule. Again, as with the question of confidentiality, this creates an unusual situation that alters the understanding of group process, but is not necessarily a problem as long as the therapist is comfortable with the differences in roles with patients and is open to hearing about the differences.

> One group of girls who were in early adolescence was discussing fantasies about the cotherapists (one male and one female). Most of the girls imagined—and demanded confirmation—that the therapists were married to each other or at least in love and planning to marry. The one exception was a young girl who was also the individual patient of the female therapist. She was angrily certain that the two therapists were not related; the female, her therapist, was already married, she was sure, to someone much more important than the other therapist—a policeman, perhaps, or a judge.

> During another group, the patients were discussing therapy and therapists in general when they decided to role-play therapists. Several of them acted out their own therapists, and several portrayed the group therapist. Discussion then centered on what was the same about all of them and what made each different, and what group members' feelings and wishes about their therapists were.

In each of these cases, it was impossible for the therapist to be unknown to the patients outside the therapy room, but she was cognizant of the fact that she was known, and that knowledge was a part of what she and each group member brought to the group that could be discussed within the group. In addition, the role the therapist plays in the group is somewhat different from the role he or she would play elsewhere, but the therapist remains the same person; this is a valuable lesson in object constancy.

Occasionally, children will bring up the question of which therapist "belongs" to which child, often talking about a group therapist perceived as better—or worse—than other therapists. Here, as with most transference issues, the therapist should be as neutral as possible in helping children explore feelings of pride or resentment as well as discover what makes a good or bad therapist. Of course, it is easier for a therapist who is cited for excellence to help her or his group examine these issues. But it can be a beneficial investigation for both therapist and patients in either case if the therapist can help group members explore their feelings and judgments and at the same time learn something about how people perceive her or him.

Cotherapists can be helpful with this kind of exploration. The roles and personalities of the two therapists outside the group will never be identical, so each can add a different perspective. Cotherapists can also make inpatient groups easier, because two can share the work and the therapeutic roles—one can structure the meeting, for instance, while the other listens for dynamic themes. They can also make the therapy experience richer, because they can discuss the group afterwards and share insights. However, cotherapists are not necessary; one therapist can certainly lead inpatient groups alone.

One-Session Life

Outpatient groups function over the course of many weeks or even years (27,35,37,42,45,48,57–60)—building relationships, observing patterns, waiting for reticent members, expanding to include all patients over time, working through, and terminating. Because the population of most inpatient facilities changes from day to day, group membership in such a facility will also change; the composition of the group is rarely the same in any two consecutive sessions (1). Although the ward census occasionally remains stable and allows continuity in group therapy, this consistency cannot be counted upon, and the group leader must behave as if each group lasts only one session.

This means that all the relationship-building, observation, and encouragement of nonparticipating children must be accomplished rapidly. The leader cannot wait for group process to move but must actively structure the group to establish a trusting relationship, encourage each member to participate, and provide some gain for each patient in each group meeting. Each member at each session must be enticed into attending, engaged into participating, and satisfied for remaining, and issues that arise must be dealt with effectively and immediately. There can be no waiting for the next session, for the issue will be dealt with on the ward outside the group if it is not resolved within the session.

This aspect of inpatient groups can be the most frustrating for the therapist. Group process is forever starting over from scratch; just when patients are beginning to improve, they leave the group and the unit. The therapist must do much of the therapeutic work done by group members in outpatient groups, including helping reticent members to participate, stopping resistant members from obstructing, and keeping members on speaking terms with each other. These therapists often work harder than outpatient therapists and see less overall progress.

The multiple roles of the therapist mentioned as a difficulty in the previous section can be useful in easing the frustrations of short-term work. Because the leader generally knows members outside the group—from individual therapy, other professional interactions, or even just hearing about patients in team meetings or from other patients—she or he enters each session with information about presenting problems, history, and interactive patterns that can help in formulating a treatment approach and in understanding group interactions. Thus, group meetings need not feel like first sessions even if they are usually the only sessions.

Group Issues

Outpatient groups deal with relationships among group members, group dynamics, conflicts, and common patterns of interacting that members bring to the group. Patients are encouraged to deal with issues that occur within the group, and discouraged from discussing incidents that occur outside and cannot be related to other group members (33,35,37,45,54). Within-group issues are also appropriate in inpatient group work; however, because the members know each other, relate to each other outside group sessions, and share common environmental problems, extra-group incidents can also serve as appropriate topics for group discussion. Conflicts among and between patients and ward authorities, such as the nighttime incident discussed previously, can serve as material for group intervention, because all members share knowledge of and some degree of at least passive participation in the incident. Children who are hospitalized experience similar questions about separation from their families (61), hospital procedures, discharge planning, what to tell friends at home about where they spent their absence, and so on. These topics, although not directly occurring within the group session, can be discussed as shared experiences.

Many authors who discuss groups for residential, deprived, or severely disturbed patients recommend behavior modification groups (62–68), social skills training (69–72), or problem solving (54,62,65). These techniques may be useful as far as they go; but analytically-oriented work should not be abandoned, as some have suggested (27), merely because it is difficult and requires some adaptation.

Special Rules

Some special rules for inpatient groups are indeed required if the group is to function at all. Attendance at all group sessions is generally a contract discussed and agreed to by individuals interested in joining an outpatient group that is forming (28,35–37,45,73). As I mentioned previously, pregroup screening of individuals is rare for inpatient groups; contracts are not possible. In addition, most of the daily activities on the ward—from meals to bedmaking, from school to sitting in the day room for "recreation" therapy—are required of inpatient children. Many of these children, particularly children with conduct disorders and most adolescents, refuse to cooperate with requirements imposed on them by authorities. This means they may find ways to refuse to attend a compulsory group or agree to attend but remain resistant, oppositional, and obstructive. Thus, the therapist's time and energy must be

devoted to getting children to attend and cooperate rather than to conduct-
ing a therapeutic group. These groups are therefore more effective as optional
activities (1,28,74).

Children will test whether group is indeed optional; they all have experience with caretakers who tell them that activities are not required, only to
state later that there are punishments for refusing to participate. Each child
who is invited to attend will probably refuse once, either the first or second
session of the hospitalization, depending on how cooperative or oppositional
he or she is. If the group is truly optional, there are no consequences of the
child's inattendance at all, except that there is generally little else to do during
group time and—if the group is well run—other children are interested in and
excited about the session. The absent child will often be the first seated at the
next group meeting.

Another rule of many groups (1,42,45,54) is that members must come on
time and stay for the duration of the session, but this often complicates inpatient work with children unnecessarily. First, as was just stated, the optional
status of the group leads most children to test limits by refusing to join. How
much easier it can be for children and group leaders if children can refuse to
attend and then change their minds in 5 or 10 minutes, rather than having to
wait several days because the door is locked when the session begins! Second,
severely disturbed and aggressive children often need time out to control
themselves, and they should not be punished for these needs. This lesson was
quickly learned during one group meeting.

One girl was rapidly becoming agitated as the group's envy of the sheltered
position of a young, attractive nurses' pet was discussed. She rose in fury, shouting at the two group leaders. When it was suggested that she might leave before
she lost control and threw the chair she was holding somewhat threateningly,
the girl—no stranger to normal group rules—screamed that she did not want to
be excluded from the rest of the session. The leaders, who had discussed this
question inconclusively up to that point, made the rule on the spot, and allowed
the child to leave the room and later return. She did in fact return rather
quickly; and this marked the first time this disruptive, assaultive child was able
to calm herself without medication or restraint.

Limit-Setting

A question always arises when working with children, in or out of hospitals,
regarding limit-setting and restraint. Slavson (35,37) strongly recommends
that the only limits imposed be "situational restraints"; that is, the environment should contain only those items that can be used without limits, and
children then acquire their own restraint through participation in the group.
Slavson also firmly suggests that the kind of children in psychiatric hospitals
are not appropriate for such groups, and that group controls only evolve in

properly constituted, balanced groups. Groups for more aggressive or more disturbed patients (37,39,40,49,50,54–56,75–78) often set up more restrictions than Slavson described.

It could be argued that the success of Slavson's groups or modified Slavson-type groups over the last 45 years suggests that his philosophy should be modified as little as possible even with inpatient children. As few rules as possible, and only those that the therapist can and will physically enforce, should be imposed. Inpatient children cannot sit still and discuss their problems, wait patiently for everyone to listen at once, or play freely in a large, fully-equipped playroom; they do not have the ego controls, and they tend to fidget, dance, yell, and get overexcited. When engaging in group discussion, they may sit on their chairs for a moment, then stand on, crawl under, run around, or pick up their own chairs, then move to another position in the room and begin again—all while fully involved with the group activity. Each therapist will have to determine what degree of loud, chaotic, or sometimes aggressive play is tolerable and act accordingly. However, it cannot be stressed enough that the group will function best with the fewest rules (28,31,37), and the therapist must be prepared to stand physically behind any rules that are applied.

It will probably be important to most therapists—although not to Slavson, who has a surprising success rate—to restrict bodily harm inflicted on group members. The therapist must be prepared, then, to stand between the threatening child and the threatened one. Announcing this rule from across the room will be ineffective and lead only to ridicule of this and all other rules made by an impotent therapist. A child who is repeatedly aggressive may be required to leave the room; here again, the therapist must physically remove the child and lock the door or be subject to ridicule and even further flaunting of unenforced rules. In this instance, permission to return as soon as the child is calm or after some fairly short interval of 1 or 2 minutes is useful to both punished child and group. With inpatient children, any rule made will be tested; a group leader who imposes many rules will spend much of the group time enforcing the rules rather than structuring a therapeutic experience for the members. Groups run best when there are as few rules as can be tolerated by the group leader and any rule made is enforced physically. Otherwise, the whole group can be chaotically out of hand.

Special Requirements of the Therapist

A therapist who leads groups in a child or adolescent inpatient setting must have special qualifications. Groups of severely disturbed children and children with low ego controls tend to be noisy and chaotic. Many children will be talking or shouting at once, no one will be able to sit still through a full session, children will threaten and strike each other, passive members will lie draped on the furniture or the floor, and there will be limited verbal interaction and powerful but primitive defenses often aimed at the group leader. The therapist of such a group must have tolerance for noise, chaos, anger, aggressivity, and regression. He or she must be more active and energetic than with outpatient groups, and often will end sessions feeling more frazzled. Through all this, it is important for the therapist to have a sense of humor and a sense of fun; the leader must enjoy these groups if the children are ever to be able to do so. The therapist, as in all groups, must listen carefully to group issues. Here, they are hard to hear and often buried under layers of defenses, resistances, and disturbed behavior and respond to individuals' and the group's needs. This is a demanding task.

Most important, the therapist must be strong, approaching each session with an active plan and the flexibility to alter the plan if necessary. The Christmas group described in a later section is an example of the importance of flexibility, as is this example.

The plan for group one day was the usual morning hour and a discussion of some photographs of children interacting, but the unit was engaged with the departing night staff until school time. Group was postponed until after lunch, and then, again due to ward activities, until after dinner. That evening, however, the children wanted to watch a favorite television program and wanted group, important to both children and therapist, to meet afterwards. The therapist was not willing to stay later, so the children suggested that she let them watch their show and "you can talk to us during the commercials." Group met, then, in front of the television set. The show was a situation comedy that happened to present a dilemma for a teenager who gambled away money saved for his mother's birthday present, then stole to replace the lost money and buy a present. No therapist could ask for a better subject for a group of preadolescent patients to discuss! During the commercials, the sound was turned off, and the moral dilemma was considered in detail.

Because the therapist was determined to hold a group meeting and could be flexible about the time, place, and content, a rewarding experience was provided for all.

To summarize what has been said thus far: groups of hospitalized children are subject to similar principles as ongoing outpatient groups with some alterations in method required. Inpatient groups tend to begin and function quickly, usually without prescreening. They also tend to operate with whatever patients are available on the unit at any given time, to lack confidentiality and specific role definition, to deal with shared experiences as well as group dynamics, to require leeway in terms of allowing children to roam around the room and talk simultaneously rather than insisting that they sit still and listen, to demand as few rules as possible and only those that can and will be physically enforced. In addition, these groups require that therapists and patients work within each session rather than over time to develop relationships, identify patterns of interacting, entice participation, and enhance progress of each member. How does the therapist go about doing all this?

THE THERAPIST'S ROLE

In any relation-oriented group psychotherapy, the group leader's job is to open communication, encourage group process, listen, observe, hypothesize, and formulate a treatment plan (27,42,45). In analytically-oriented treatment, the leader also identifies conflictual material that he or she then clarifies and interprets (4,5,7,19,20,27,28,34,45,48). In child psychotherapy, the leader encourages and attempts to understand symbolic play (3–7,12,14,37,41,61,79).

These functions are important with inpatient group psychotherapy, too, but they are not sufficient. Children who are hospitalized are generally too severely disturbed and/or lack ego strength to function in an unstructured group. This, coupled with the fact that the therapist must work quickly within each group session, points to a requirement that the leader be more active and do more structuring than in ongoing outpatient groups (1,27,28, 30,31,37,39,40,57,73,77,78). The therapist should approach members individually to invite them to attend the group, actively speak up to begin the session, control who speaks when and for how long, structure interactions between members, encourage reticent members to participate, and generally organize the experience for the group. There is no room for a leader to wait silently for the members to speak or for the group to approach a member who is uninvolved or annoying. The leader must be a strong force who assures that each member who wishes does speak in each session, that members who are uninvolved are encouraged but not coerced to participate, and that annoying behavior is gently controlled.

GAMES

The best therapy in the world would be useless if no patients were present, of course, and in an optional group on a coercive unit, patients must be enticed to attend. Snacks and interesting toys make the group appealing but are not always enough to sustain attendance and participation. The best way to do this is to make the group itself fun, through games and activities that are enjoyable for the children (13,23,25,80,81). The activities that are appropriate to a particular group will vary according to the age range and the average level of functioning of the group; adolescents and higher-functioning groups can sustain more verbal interaction and require less play, less frequent changes of subject, and less therapist direction than younger and lower-functioning groups.

Almost anything can serve as interesting stimulation for discussion. Photographs, movies, television shows, or popular songs raise issues that can be used as beginning of discourse. Themes of anger, death, or "Three Wishes" can be presented by the therapist for group conversation.

Construction materials are usually of interest to latency-age children. These can include crayons, clay, collage materials, tongue depressors and glue, Lincoln Logs, and so on. These can serve as group activities if there is only one type of material provided per session, if there is a group table or floor area provided for all children to congregate around if they wish, if the therapist listens for and structures group discussion while construction occurs, and if children are encouraged to work together if they wish. For instance, paper for drawing can be a large long roll rather than individual pieces; that way, children can stretch out on the floor, each contributing to a group mural. The therapist can suggest a theme, such as "Scary Monsters" or "What's Wrong With This Hospital" or "What I Wish I Could Have For Christmas." Children then have the choice of participating in the group drawing or not, drawing something consistent with the theme or not, or discussing the theme or not—all while the therapist gently engages each child in the interaction.

One interesting material to use for construction projects is food. Children can be nurtured with oral supplies and engaged in an interesting activity if they make their own peanut butter sandwiches or even bake their own cookies where facilities permit.

A group of 5- to 7-year-old boys met on a unit where a small kitchen was available. The group leaders provided packaged refrigerator cookie dough and a collection of sprinkles, chips, silver drops, and frosting tubes; the children received slices of dough and decorated them as they wished. The cookies then were baked for less than 10 minutes while the boys decorated the next batch, then each ate the one he had decorated. The activity held their interest beyond their appetite for cookies, and they faced the dilemma of what to do with the uneaten treats. Together, they decided to offer them to the nursing staff and the other children on the unit, and there was an animated dispute over who could decorate cookies for which guest.

Physical activity is an important component of games for hospitalized children. All children, but especially those with weak ego controls, hyperkinesis, powerful anxieties, and overwhelming fantasy lives, have a great deal of anxious energy to discharge (13,31,80). They can do this if permitted to jump and dance while participating in group, or if allowed to engage in some motor task such as drawing or playing while participating in a verbal group interaction, as described above. Their energy can also be harnessed in discharge that is a part of the group interaction itself. Sometimes this energy release is vital, as in this example.

One holiday time, the staff from the entire floor held their Christmas party in the day room of one unit, the group's usual meeting room, while the children on the unit were required to sit quietly in another day hall for most of the afternoon. They watched staff pass them to go to the party, smelled holiday food, and listened to sounds of laughter and music escape each time the door opened to let someone in or out. When the party at last broke up, the children reclaimed their hall and filed in for a group meeting. They were, however, too angry to meet. They stormed into the room criticizing the unit and the staff and the whole world, and announced that they were not willing to cooperate with anything.

The group leaders quickly abandoned the plan of discussing a movie the children had seen the evening before and retrieved the record player, which had been removed after the party. Music was played, louder even than at the party, and everybody danced. When the initial angry energy had been discharged, the leaders structured the dancing—high, low, sitting, jumping, stomping, loud, soft, on one foot, holding hands, and so on. Next, children danced together in a line dance, allowing each a moment of exhibitionism and appreciation. Finally, they sat and agreed that it was hard to watch a party going on, that they all wished they could have been there and that nobody would be there, and mentioned parties they had and had not been invited to on the outside.

At other times, energy release is not so vital to group functioning but is simply useful to contain children who otherwise may be too anxious to remain in an exclusively verbal therapeutic setting (13,80).

Games That Elicit Emotionally Relevant Material

Some very useful games are those that generate material for discussion as part of the activity itself (3,4,7,80). Storytelling, for instance, particularly when one member of the group begins the story and others finish in turn, not only is an entertaining game for children but also symbolically expresses issues in the children's conscious and unconscious minds. Children may have fun while telling each other and their therapist about their wishes, fears, anxieties, and conflicts.

Games With Both Active and Emotional Components

The most all-inclusive activity for a therapeutic group is one that is fun and allows discharge of energy and at the same time provides expression of emotional and symbolic material. One such game is role-playing. Children can enjoy dramatizing interactions, decrease anxiety by discharge of physical energy, and express conflicts, fears, wishes, and unconscious content. Roles can be assigned to one child or to two or more, can be played with puppets or without, can be emotionally neutral or full of conflictual content, and can ideally be tailored to the issues germane to the child and/or the group. They can be played for a moment or a whole session, once or with dozens of revisions, and can lead to discussion of the content of the roles and a myriad of associated topics.

To begin and end a group gently, first and last role assignments should be emotionally neutral or pleasant. These can include such portrayals as winning the lottery, walking a dog, reading a funny book, meeting an old friend on the street, scoring in soccer or basketball, or passing a test in school. Midgroup roles can involve more anxiety-arousing issues as reading a pornographic book, missing a score in soccer or basketball, failing a test, dealing with a bully, or thinking about shoplifting. Roles specific to hospitalized children include many authority issues—negotiating with night nurses for extra time before bed, asking therapists for passes home, regaining privileges after a restriction period—as well as topics such as meeting friends on the first day back in regular school, moving into a group home or foster home, or expressing anger toward a parent who rarely visits.

Once a role is assigned and children have played for a time, the therapist should intervene to structure discussion of the role-playing. Players can be asked what it felt like to play the various parts, observers what it felt like to watch. All group members can evaluate the probability of the event really happening as it was played and share their own similar experiences, and the therapist can clarify and interpret group responses. The discussion often leads to other topics for discussion or role-playing, and the group session progresses.

A group of youngsters were dealing with authority issues, and two were assigned a school scene: a teacher accused a student of cheating on a test. A third patient asked to play the student whose paper was cheated from (or not; this was never clarified by either therapist or group). The student denied the teacher's accusation, and both became angry at each other and unable to back down from their positions. The group was a particularly active one, and several other patients jumped in or were called in to act what became a long, complicated scene. First, the teacher, feeling impotent, called in the principal, who also got nowhere with the angry, insistent student, so she called in a police officer—the largest (although not at all the strongest) patient on the unit. The police took the student to court, where a severely regressed, psychotic patient eagerly and quite effectively played the judge.

After all had joined the play—and this certainly was play, for group and observing leaders—they sat to discuss the action. The frustration that authorities have with unmanageable children—children such as many of the group—became clear to them for the first time. The children discussed their feelings in each of the roles and explored what alternative behaviors might have been possible, and the feelings of and about the large but weak patient serving as law enforcer and the regressed patient serving as judge were expressed.

Sometimes, as in this example, a group session revolves around a single role-playing scene, with discussion centering on all the many issues arising from a series of related roles. At other times a leader will feel that a role-playing scene has elicited all the material possible and can begin a new one, either on a somewhat related topic or on a completely new one. Younger and lower-functioning children tend to need shorter roles; older and higher-functioning children can play longer and more complicated roles, often revising and re-playing related roles for as much as a full session or more.

A therapist leading role-playing games should actively assign roles and structure the conversation about them so that all group members have a chance to participate on their own level and so the discussion yields as much dynamic material as possible.

Other games that serve well in inpatient groups to structure group process, discharge energy physically, and interest children in enjoyable activities include variations of Gardner's (82–84) approaches to resistant children. These encompass mutual storytelling and several games in which children pick a card, word, or object from an array and make up a story about the chosen subject or respond to an assigned talking, doing, or feeling task. Words and objects, like role-playing, should include neutral items—bicycle, pizza, watching television, cup, comb, toothbrush—and more highly charged ones—hospital, medication, sex, baby bottle, Band-aid box, weapon—related to the children's environment in and out of the hospital. For group work, it is better not to use dice and playing boards, because these tend to take up time unnecessarily and to focus the game on competition, rules, and winning (81,84,85) rather than on the expressive task. The therapist should structure these activities and discussions as all others in inpatient groups—by choosing which child should play when, organizing discussion of the assignment and the child's response to the assignment, and determining when each topic is played out and the group should move on.

Use of Games in Psychoanalytically-Oriented Treatment

Many groups of inpatients are cognitive restructuring or skills training groups (54,62–72) using behavior modification techniques to teach children to interact properly or learn appropriate social behaviors. The groups described here are different from behavior modification groups in that no overt rewards or punishments are specifically given for acceptable or unacceptable behaviors. The goal in these groups is expression of whatever each child is thinking and feeling so that these thoughts and feelings can be shared with the group and clarified or interpreted by the therapist.

Some researchers (54,86–88) have described games designed by Schachter as catalyst for expression of emotions for children with low verbal abilities. Schachter's techniques, however, use the games to elicit expression only; once a child's characteristic pathological way of responding is demonstrated, the therapist (86–88) and/or the children (54) call "Stop the action." The game stops, the targeted child is required to stop the objectionable behavior, the group discusses how the unacceptable behavior affects others, and the game continues. In the groups described here, the goal is not to train behavior but to understand it. If children object to a group member's behavior, all are encouraged to discuss the objections and the feelings that arise from both exhibiting and observing the behavior.

Some authors (1,25) have described games as catalysts to begin therapy and get patients started talking to each other. Because of the unique nature of these groups that work with children, severely impaired patients, and a rapidly changing population, I recommend use of the games as the therapy itself rather than as a prelude to therapy. Some groups of these patients—especially adolescent, higher-functioning, and longer-term groups—can work on more traditional verbal or symbolic play levels, but the therapist who waits for this to happen is bound to be frustrated and ineffective.

Gardner's (82–84) games, while developed for individual therapy, are useful when adapted for group work. Again, the psychoanalytically oriented groups described here would use the games differently than in Gardner's examples. The therapist may indeed play along with the children in the group, as Gardner recommends. However, the therapist's contribution can be to continue to clarify and interpret the conflicts raised by the children's play rather than to demonstrate more adaptive ways of handling them, as Gardner seems to do.

Examples of Analytic Use of Group Games

Throughout these group games, the group leader should be structuring interaction among group members, making sure that all children have an opportunity to speak or play, calming and quieting children when they get overstimulated and overly loud, determining game play, and creating a supporting, explorative environment. The analytic task is to attend to emotionally important themes, conflicts, anxieties, transferences, and defense mechanisms. This is done in the usual ways of listening when the group task is one incidental to dynamic content, as when children build with Legos while discussing their wishes for the Thanksgiving holiday. When the group task itself elicits emotional material, as when children put on a puppet show or draw Halloween monsters or role-play a parent catching a child stealing a piece of cake, the listening is done as in play therapy. Dynamic themes are expressed symbolically in the play, and the therapist can identify them explicitly and/or metaphorically.

The therapist can listen for both individual and group issues that arise in the activities. Groups of children who live together are particularly liable to experience issues that affect the group as a whole and to express these themes through the comments of individual children.

> One group near the end of a therapist's time on the unit was playing the "Bag of Things" (84) game, with each child choosing an object from a grab bag and telling a story about the object, followed by group discussion and/or other stories. This session was a quiet one; there was very little of the raucous play usually characteristic of this ward. One child picked a baby bottle, often the source of giggling tales of gratification, and told of a mother with no milk, uncertain whether to let the baby go hungry or leave the baby alone while she went out to the grocery store. A second child picked a Band-aid box, which had been the source of many stories of the unit staff healing wounds, and told of watching through a window as a peer fell, needed a Band-aid, and received none. These children were experiencing the loss of a therapist, both individually and as a group.

> Another group of children was plagued by problems with a provocative abused child who provoked fights almost hourly during her stay. She was absent from group during this session, and the therapists thought it would be a fine opportunity to allow the rest of the unit to be free of the overwhelming presence of this child. Pictures of children laughing and playing cooperatively together were shown to begin discussion. What was noticed by all of the children immediately—but not previously by the therapists—was one small child buried under a pile of larger children and looking miserable. This was focused on and easily identified as the provocative child on the unit, the target for the group's rage.

In these examples, individual children spoke or told stories that expressed their own conflictual themes, but the themes were also related to issues pertinent to the group as a whole; both aspects of these issues can be addressed by the therapist.

CONCLUSION

In this chapter, I have described techniques of group therapy for inpatient children and adolescents. The usual group therapy techniques have not proved adequate for this population because of the children's severe pathology and aggressivity, inability to sit still and focus, and weak impulse control, as well as the rapidly changing census that precludes waiting for ongoing group process to take its course. Accordingly, the therapist must begin the group without prescreening and with whomever is available on the inpatient unit, controlling only for age range and sometimes for group size. Children must be permitted to discharge physical energy by fidgeting, jumping, dancing, roaming around the room, and talking out of turn where necessary, and by playing therapist-directed activities wherever possible.

Therapists should actively structure the group meeting, determining who will speak when, enticing all children to participate, and gently controlling behavior that makes continuation of group impossible but imposing as few rules as can be tolerated by the therapist. Games, which are enjoyable and interesting and allow discharge of nervous energy in adaptive ways, are useful tools to facilitate group process. If these games can also elicit psychodynamically relevant material—as can, for example, puppet shows, role-playing, and storytelling—all the better. The therapist then can listen for emotional themes and clarify and interpret them, thereby helping the group members to deal with their conflicts as well as to raise issues to bring up in their individual treatment. As a side benefit of this group process, through watching a nonjudgmental, permissive, supportive, constructively active therapist and through interacting with peers, children also acquire social skills and more appropriate behaviors. Tension on the inpatient unit can decrease, and relations among patients and between staff and patients can improve as well.

REFERENCES

1. Yalom ID: Inpatient Group Psychotherapy. New York, Basic Books, 1983
2. Adams PL: A Primer of Child Psychotherapy. New York, Little, Brown, 1974
3. Axline V: Play Therapy. New York, Ballantine Books, 1969
4. Freud A: The Psychoanalytical Treatment of Children. London, Imago Publishing, 1946
5. Glenn J (ed): Child Analysis and Therapy. New York, Jason Aronson, 1978
6. Hayworth MR (ed): Child Psychotherapy. New York, Basic Books, 1964
7. Klein M: The Psycho-Analysis of Children. London, Hogarth Press, 1932
8. Maclay D: Treatment for Children. New York, Science House, 1970
9. McDermott JF, Harrison SI (eds): Psychiatric Treatment of the Child. New York, Jason Aronson, 1977
10. Moustakas C: Psychotherapy With Children: The Living Relationship. New York, Ballantine Books, 1970
11. Moustakas C (ed): The Child's Discovery of Himself. New York, Basic Books, 1972
12. Schaefer CE, O'Connor KJ (eds): Handbook of Play Therapy. New York, John Wiley, 1983
13. Schaefer CE, Reid SE (eds): Game Play: Therapeutic Uses of Childhood Games. New York, John Wiley, 1986
14. Wolman BB (ed): Handbook of Child Psychoanalysis. New York, Van Nostrand Reinhold, 1972
15. Axline V: Dibs: In Search of Self. New York, Ballantine Books, 1964
16. Bettleheim B: Love is Not Enough. New York, Free Press, 1950
17. Bettleheim B: Truants From Life. New York, Free Press, 1955

18. Bettleheim B: A Home for the Heart. New York, Alfred A. Knopf, 1974
19. Ekstein R: Play therapy for borderline children, in Handbook of Play Therapy. Edited by Schaefer CE, O'Connor KJ. New York, John Wiley, 1983, pp 412–418
20. Ekstein R, Caruth E, Cooper B, et al: Psychoanalytically oriented psychotherapy of psychotic children, in Child Analysis and Therapy. Edited by Glenn J. New York, Jason Aronson, 1978, pp 649–707
21. Escalona S: Some considerations regarding psychotherapy with psychotic children, in Child Psychotherapy. Edited by Hayworth MR. New York, Science House, 1970, pp 50–58
22. Fraiberg S: Technical aspects of the analysis of a child with a severe behavior disorder, in Child Psychotherapy. Edited by Hayworth MR. New York, Science House, 1970, pp 207–228
23. Willock B: Play therapy with the aggressive, acting-out child, in Handbook of Play Therapy. Edited by Schaefer CE, O'Connor KJ. New York, John Wiley, 1983, pp 387–411
24. Anthony EJ: Group-analytic psychotherapy with children and adolescents, in Group Psychotherapy: The Psychoanalytic Approach. Edited by Foulkes SH, Anthony EJ. Baltimore, MD, Penguin Books, 1973, pp 186–232, as cited in Group Therapy with Children and Adolescents. Edited by Siepker BB, Kandaras CS. New York, Human Sciences Press, 1985
25. Corder BF: Therapeutic games in group therapy with adolescents, in Game Play: Therapeutic Uses of Childhood Games. Edited by Schaefer CE, Reid SE. New York, John Wiley, 1986, pp 279–289
26. Foulkes SH, Anthony EJ: Group Psychotherapy: The Psychoanalytic Approach. Baltimore, MD, Penguin Books, 1973, as cited in Group Therapy with Children and Adolescents. Edited by Siepker BB, Kandaras CS. New York, Human Sciences Press, 1985
27. Lampel AK: Stage II: exploration, in Group Therapy with Children and Adolescents. Edited by Siepker BB, Kandaras CS. New York, Human Sciences Press, 1985, pp 86–109
28. Meeks JE: Structuring the early phase of group psychotherapy with adolescents, in Psychiatric Treatment of the Child. Edited by McDermott JF, Harrison SI. New York, Jason Aronson, 1977, pp 487–503
29. Rachman AW: Encounter techniques in analytic group psychotherapy with adolescents, in Psychiatric Treatment of the Child. Edited by McDermott JF, Harrison SI. New York, Jason Aronson, 1977, pp 471–478
30. Sands RM, Golub S: Breaking the bonds of tradition: a reassessment of group treatment of latency-age children, in Psychiatric Treatment of the Child. Edited by McDermott JF, Harrison SI. New York, Jason Aronson, 1977, pp 479–486
31. Scheidlinger S, Rauch E: Psychoanalytic group psychotherapy with children and adolescents, in Handbook of Child Psychoanalysis. Edited by Wolman BB. New York, Van Nostrand Reinhold, 1972, pp 364–398
32. Siepker BB: Children's and adolescents' group therapy literature, in Group Therapy with Children and Adolescents. Edited by Siepker BB, Kandaras CS. New York, Human Sciences Press, 1985, pp 35–53
33. Siepker BB, Kandaras CS (eds): Group Therapy with Children and Adolescents: A Treatment Manual. New York, Human Sciences Press, 1985

34. Siepker BB, Lewis LH, Kandaras CS: Relationship-oriented group psychotherapy with children and adolescents, in Group Therapy with Children and Adolescents. Edited by Siepker BB, Kandaras CS. New York, Human Sciences Press, 1985, pp 11–34
35. Slavson SR: An Introduction to Group Therapy. New York, International Universities Press, 1943
36. Slavson SR: Criteria for selection and rejection of patients for various types of group psychotherapy. Int J Group Psychother 5:3–30, 1955
37. Slavson SR, Schiffer M: Group Psychotherapies for Children. New York, International Universities Press, 1975
38. Sugar M: Interpretive group psychotherapy with latency children. J Am Acad Child Psychiatry 13:648–666, 1974
39. Van Scoy H: An activity group approach to severely disturbed latency boys. Child Welfare 50:413–419, 1971
40. Van Scoy H: Activity group therapy: a bridge between play and work, in Psychiatric Treatment of the Child. Edited by McDermott JF, Harrison SI. New York, Jason Aronson, 1977, pp 461–469
41. Ginott HG: Group Psychotherapy With Children. New York, McGraw-Hill, 1961
42. de Neuhaus MS: Stage I: preparation, in Group Therapy with Children and Adolescents. Edited by Siepker BB, Kandaras CS. New York, Human Sciences Press, 1985, pp 54–85
43. Trafimow E, Pattak SI: Group psychotherapy and objectal development in children. Int J Group Psychother 31:193–204, 1981
44. Trafimow E, Pattak SI: Group treatment of primitively fixated children. Int J Group Psychother 32:445–452, 1982
45. Yalom ID: The Theory and Practice of Group Psychotherapy, 2nd Edition. New York, Basic Books, 1975
46. Speers RW, Lansing C: Group Therapy in Childhood Psychosis. Chapel Hill, NC, University of North Carolina Press, 1965
47. Blotcky MJ, Scheinbein M, Wiggins KM, et al: A verbal group technique for ego-disturbed children: action to words. International Journal of Psychoanalytic Psychotherapy 8:203–232, 1980
48. Charach R: Brief interpretive group psychotherapy with early latency-age children. Int J Group Psychother 33:349–364, 1983
49. Epstein N, Altman S: Experiences in converting an activity therapy group into verbal group therapy with latency-age boys. Int J Group Psychother 22:93–100, 1972
50. Frank MG: Modifications of activity group therapy: responses to ego impoverished children. Clinical Social Work Journal 4:102–109, 1976
51. MacLennan BW: Modifications of activity group therapy for children. Int J Group Psychother 27:85–96, 1977
52. Schiffer M: Activity-interview group psychotherapy: theory, principles, and practice. Int J Group Psychother 27:377–388
53. Peck ML, Stewart RH: Current practices in selection criteria for group play therapy. J Clin Psychol 20:146, 1964
54. Clifford M, Cross T: Group therapy for seriously disturbed boys in residential treatment. Child Welfare 59:560–565, 1980

55. Redl F: The phenomenon of contagion and "shock effect," in Searchlights in Delinquency. Edited by Eissler KR. New York, International Universities Press, 1949, pp 315–328
56. Redl F, Wineman D: The Aggressive Child. New York, Free Press, 1957
57. Ganter G, Yeakel M, Polansky NA: Retrieval from Limbo: The Intermediary Group Treatment of Inaccessible Children. New York, Child Welfare League of America, 1967, as cited in Lampel AK: Stage II: exploration, in Group Therapy with Children and Adolescents. Edited by Siepker BB, Kandaras CS. New York, Human Sciences Press, 1985, pp 86–109
58. Herndon CH: Stage V: Termination, in Group Therapy with Children and Adolescents. Edited by Siepker BB, Kandaras CS. New York, Human Sciences Press, 1985, pp 157–175
59. Kandaras CS: Stage IV: Cohesion, in Group Therapy with Children and Adolescents. Edited by Siepker BB, Kandaras CS. New York, Human Sciences Press, 1985, pp 137–156
60. Lewis LH: Stage III: anxiety, in Group Therapy with Children and Adolescents. Edited by Siepker BB, Kandaras CS. New York, Human Sciences Press, 1985, pp 110–136
61. Golden DB: Play therapy for hospitalized children, in Handbook of Play Therapy. Edited by Schaefer CE, O'Connor KJ. New York, John Wiley, 1983, pp 213–233
62. Fairweather GW (ed): Social Psychology in Treating Mental Illness: An Experimental Approach. New York, John Wiley, 1964
63. Hauserman N, Zweback S, Plotkin A: Use of concrete reinforcement to facilitate verbal initiation in adolescent group therapy. J Consult Clin Psychol 38:90–96, 1972
64. Heckel RB, Wiggens SL, Salzberg HC: Conditioning against silences in group therapy. J Clin Psychol 8:216–217, 1962
65. Olson RP, Greenbergh DJ: Effects of contingency-contracting and decision making groups with chronic mental patients. J Consult Clin Psychol 38:376–383, 1972
66. Rose SD: Group Therapy: A Behavioral Approach. Englewood Cliffs, NJ, Prentice-Hall, 1977
67. Wagner M: Reinforcement of verbal productivity in group therapy. Psychol Rep 19:1217–1218, 1966
68. Williams RI, Blanton RL: Verbal conditioning in a psychotherapeutic situation. Behav Res Ther 6:97–103, 1968
69. Frank PW: Behavioral Approach to the Treatment of Social Skills of Chronic Mental Patients in a Group Setting. Unpublished manuscript, Madison, WI, University of Wisconsin, 1974, as cited in Rose SD: Group Therapy: A Behavioral Approach. Englewood Cliffs, NJ, Prentice-Hall, 1977
70. Gutride MA, Goldstein AP, Hunter GF: The Use of Modeling and Role Playing to Increase Social Interaction Among Schizophrenia Patients. Unpublished manuscript, Syracuse, NY, Syracuse University, 1972, as cited in Rose SD: Group Therapy: A Behavioral Approach. Englewood Cliffs, NJ, Prentice-Hall, 1977
71. Pierce RM, Drasgow J: Teaching facilitative interpersonal functioning to neuropsychiatric inpatients. Journal of Counseling Psychology 16:295–298, 1969

72. Rose SD, Flanagan J, Brierton D: Counseling in a correctional institution: a social learning approach. Paper presented at the National Conference on Social Welfare, Dallas, 1971, as cited in Rose SD: Group Therapy: A Behavioral Approach. Englewood Cliffs, NJ, Prentice-Hall, 1977

73. Rinsley DB: Treatment of the Severely Disturbed Adolescent. New York, Jason Aronson, 1980

74. Mayer MP: The group in residential treatment of adolescents, in Psychiatric Treatment of the Child. Edited by McDermott JF, Harrison SI. New York, Jason Aronson, 1977, pp 445–460

75. Gratton L, Rizzo AE: Group therapy with young psychotic children. Int J Group Psychother 19:63–71, 1969

76. Lifton N, Smolen EM: Group psychotherapy with schizophrenic children. Int J Group Psychother 16:131–141, 1966

77. Scheidlinger S: Experimental group treatment of severely deprived latency age children. Am J Orthopsychiatry 30:356–368, 1960

78. Scheidlinger S: Three approaches with socially deprived latency age children. Int J Group Psychother 15:434–445, 1965

79. Ekstein R, Caruth E: Interpretation within the metaphor: further considerations, in Children of Time and Space, of Action and Impulse. Edited by Ekstein R. New York, Appleton-Century-Crofts, 1966, pp 158–165

80. Nickerson ET, O'Laughlin KS: The therapeutic use of games, in Handbook of Play Therapy. Edited by Schaefer CE, O'Connor KJ. New York, John Wiley, 1983, pp 174–187

81. Beiser HR: Formal games in diagnosis and therapy. Journal of Child Psychiatry 18:480–490, 1979

82. Gardner RA: Therapeutic Communication With Children: The Mutual Storytelling Technique. New York, Jason Aronson, 1971

83. Gardner RA: The Talking, Feeling, and Doing Game (therapeutic board game for children). Cresskill, NJ, Creative Therapeutics, 1973

84. Gardner RA: Psychotherapeutic Approaches to the Resistant Child. New York, Jason Aronson, 1975

85. Meeks J: Children who cheat at games. Journal of Child Psychiatry 9:157–174, 1970

86. Schachter RS: Kinetic psychotherapy in the treatment of children. Am J Group Psychother 28:430–437, 1974

87. Schachter RS: Kinetic psychotherapy in the treatment of depression in latency age children. Int J Group Psychother 34:83–91, 1984

88. Schachter RS: Techniques of kinetic psychotherapy, in Game Play: Therapeutic Uses of Childhood Games. Edited by Schaefer CE, Reid SE. New York, John Wiley, 1986, pp 95–107

Index